*Always an Adventure*

With best wishes

# THE WEST SERIES

Aritha van Herk, Series Editor

**ISSN 1922-6519 (Print) ISSN 1925-587X (Online)**

This series focuses on creative non-fiction that explores our sense of place in the West – how we define ourselves as Westerners and what impact we have on the world around us. Essays, biographies, memoirs, and insights into Western Canadian life and experience are highlighted.

# Always an Adventure

AN AUTOBIOGRAPHY

UNIVERSITY OF
CALGARY
PRESS

# HUGH A. DEMPSEY

**The West Series**
ISSN 1922-6519 (Print) ISSN 1925-587X (Online)

University of Calgary Press
2500 University Drive NW
Calgary, Alberta
Canada T2N 1N4
www.uofcpress.com

Library and Archives Canada Cataloguing in Publication

Dempsey, Hugh A., 1929-
         Always an adventure : an autobiography / by Hugh A. Dempsey.

(The West, 1922-6519 ; 3)
Includes bibliographical references and index.
Also issued in electronic formats.
ISBN 978-1-55238-522-7

         1. Dempsey, Hugh A., 1929-. 2. Historians—Alberta—Biography. 3. Archivists—
Alberta—Biography. 4. Museum directors—Alberta—Biography. I. Title. II. Series: West series
(Calgary, Alta.)

FC151.D44A3 2011          971.23'007202          C2011-902247-8

The University of Calgary Press acknowledges the support of the Alberta Foundation for the
Arts for our publications. We acknowledge the financial support of the Government of Canada
through the Canada Book Fund for our publishing activities. We acknowledge the financial
support of the Canada Council for the Arts for our publishing program.

Printed and bound in Canada by Houghton Boston
∞ This book is printed on Enviro 100 Antique - FSC Certified paper

Cover design, page design, and typesetting by Melina Cusano

# TABLE OF CONTENTS

# Acknowledgments

How many people can contribute to a person's life story? There obviously is overwhelming gratitude on my part for the large number of people who have helped me on life's path and to achieve a relatively successful career. Outstanding among these is Eric Harvie, who gave me a chance to contribute to his organization and at the same time fulfill my fondest dreams. He did not help me to write this book, but without him this book would not have been possible. Similarly, Pauline, my wife of fifty-seven years, introduced me to her wonderful family and to a distinctive culture that was so different from anything I had ever experienced in my boyhood. In addition, her support of her writer-husband called for years of patience and forbearance. Then there is my mother, who taught me to be independent and encouraged me to be creative.

My father-in-law, Senator James Gladstone, was my mentor and friend. He was so well respected in the Native community that his very name opened doors for me. Through him I came to know and admire such people as Sinew Feet, Jack Low Horn, Bobtail Chief, Percy Plain Woman, Jennie Duck Chief, and many other elders of the past. In the political field there was Ralph Steinhauer (later lieutenant-governor), John Samson Jr., Howard Beebe, John Laurie, Dave and Daisy Crowchild, and Albert Lightning, while at the personal level, lifetime friendships were forged with Irene and Gerald Tailfeathers, Everett Soop, Muriel and Peter Many Wounds, and Jack and Marge Ewers.

I don't know if I ever really contemplated writing an autobiography, but as I've always been an inveterate diary keeper and packrat such an end might have been inevitable. When the decision was made I turned to the Glenbow Library and Archives to provide the necessary documentation for such a project. Doug Cass and Lindsay Moir were unceasing in their support, as were their staff. In some instances I went farther afield, but it was amazing how much information was in filing cabinets right in my own basement.

In the end, this book turned out to be a labour of love, or perhaps ego, for I have never ceased to be amazed that the words I feed into the computer would willingly be read by other people.

Calgary, January 23, 2010

#  Beginnings

Truckloads of men were coming to our farm with guns. They looked big, sombre, and threatening as they turned off the main trail from Edgerton and followed the road past our flowing well. I grabbed The Old Cat (that was her name), ran upstairs, and hid under the bed. My mother tried to explain that these were simply a few neighbours and friends who had come to our place for a turkey shoot. That didn't help, for I could envision dozens of turkeys being slaughtered by a bunch of gun-happy farmers. Only later did I learn that in a turkey shoot, one used ordinary targets and won turkeys as prizes.

The year was 1933, and I was four years old. My father Otto had been a World War I veteran and now he was trying to make a go of it in the midst of the Depression. Not only was he running a farm, but he was secretary-treasurer of the municipal district and had a small shack that he used for an office.

When World War I broke out in 1914, my father enlisted the day after war was declared. He was posted to the 11th Battalion and spent most of the war in England and France as an armourer in the 3rd Canadian Railway Regiment. There he met my mother, Lily Louise Sharp, in Folkestone, Kent, where she was a servant for a wealthy family, and they were married in 1916.

At the end of the war, my mother was repatriated first and it proved to be an excruciating experience. She was a lively twenty-two-year-old girl from a close-knit seafaring family and was sent to the bleak Canadian prairies just before the onset of the winter of 1918–19. Her mother-in-law, Mary Jane, had married a farmer named Nelson McBride, so my mother went to their farm near Edgerton, 200 kilometres east of Edmonton. Just one look at old photographs of Mary Jane and one can sense what a cold, humourless person she was. "Black Irish," somebody called her. Mother says that anytime during that winter, if someone had given her the fare home, the marriage would have been over.

My father was demobilized in the spring of 1919, and as soon as he arrived at his mother's place, he announced that he had been given land under the Soldiers Resettlement Act. It was only a few miles away, close to Wainwright Buffalo Park. When they got there, Mother cried. It was a sandy, godforsaken place where someone had tried to farm and had given up. The "nice house" which the government people had said they could have was a log shack with newspapers plastering the walls, a dirt floor with straw spread over it, and a sod roof infested with weeds. To make matters worse, they arrived there on her birthday.

"How can we live here?" she cried to her husband.

"I'll put on a new roof and fix up the place," he promised.[1]

And he was true to his word. As soon as the first promised $100 a month came from Soldiers Resettlement, he replaced the roof, papered the walls, put linoleum on the floor, and bought a new stove. But the soil was marginal at best, and the promised help from the government was cut off at the end of the year. There was no way they could make a living on that miserable piece of land, so they rented a place a few miles closer to town, and in 1927 they moved again to a farm in the McCafferty district, ten miles south of Edgerton, where I was born on November 7, 1929.

I was the fourth boy in the family. There were no girls, a fact my mother always regretted. The oldest was Harry (actually Henry Varner), born in 1918 while mother was still in England. The second was Bill (William Samuel), born in 1920, followed by Glen Allen in 1924. Glen and I were close but because of age differences I didn't get to know my two older brothers until they were grown up.

In later years, my mother told me more about the turkey shoot that had struck such fear into my heart. "We used to hold them on Remembrance Day, November 11th," she said. "We had a big copper boiler that we filled with sandwiches, and had cakes and pots of coffee for the men. People came from Edgerton, Wainwright, and even as far away as Edmonton, and were charged so much a shot. This was your father's own doing. We raised the turkeys and they were given alive to the winners."[2]

This was the middle of the Depression, when my father was doing everything he could to feed and clothe our family of four boys. He organized a beef ring in which each farmer in turn slaughtered a cow a week and distributed equal parts to other members. Thus they could have fresh meat all year round and in the fall he pooled his money with a couple of friends so they could go moose hunting near Edson. They shared their kills so that there was a good supply of wild meat for the winter. But the crops were poor, grasshoppers plentiful, and prices low as he struggled to make a living from the land. As mother said, "We were hailed out, dried out, and frozen out for three years."[3] Then in 1934 further disaster struck when my father's little office for the municipality burned down and he was out of a job.

That's when he decided to move to the Peace River district. Father had heard that homestead land was still available and that the crops had been a lot better than in the arid south. We were renting our farm, so all he had to do was to hold an auction sale in the fall of 1934 and prepare for the trip. He got a pittance for his machinery as everybody else was broke, but there was enough money for him to hire a trucker to take our furniture and personal things to Edmonton. We brought along The Old Cat and three mink that my father wanted to use for breeding stock once we got to our new farm. His idea was to let the family stay in the city over the winter while he went north with his former hired man, Murdo Fraser, to scout out a piece of land for us.

Once in Edmonton, my father and Murdo left immediately for the north, but they ran into an early fall blizzard and had to turn back. Meanwhile, the rest of us stayed at the Hub Hotel and when father got back he rented a small house on 91st Street. We must have looked like a bunch of hillbillies when we arrived. I usually went barefoot and in winter I wore moccasins with rubbers pulled over them and sealer rings to keep them from falling off. My clothes were clean but ragged and I didn't have more than one or two changes of clothing. I'm told that even the patches on my trousers had patches on them.

Within the first week, our rustic behaviour was demonstrated to all our neighbours when the three mink escaped from their cage. We had them in an old barn at the end of our lot and almost tore the place apart before we could capture them. Once they were back in the cages, we got rid of them.

The only cash we had was from the paltry proceeds of the auction sale, so we had no recourse but to go on relief. My father was a very proud man and I think it was only the thought of moving north in the spring that kept him going. We got $40 a month relief money, with $15 of that going for rent. We also got food coupons, clothes, and shoes. However, the clothes were all the same, so as soon as we put them on, everybody knew we were on relief.

We survived the winter of 1934–35 as poor but proud country folk thrust into the alien world of the big city. Of course, my mother loved it. She had electricity, running water, and, most of all, close neighbours and St. Andrew's Presbyterian Church. She loved being with people and had suffered enormously because of the isolated life on the farm. We boys went to Sunday

School regularly, and during the church services, my brother Glen pumped the organ that provided the music.

In the spring, father's dream of moving to the Peace River area was shattered when he broke his ankle. He had been able to get a temporary job at Hayward Lumber Company but on his first day a pile of lumber fell on him. He was in the hospital for a while and then on crutches for several months. This meant we were taken off relief and placed on workmen's compensation; this immediately proved to be a greater hardship, for they provided the same amount of monthly aid but did not give food coupons or clothes. So instead of our traditional Sunday roast, Mother had to buy ends and scraps of meat for a stew. It also meant a strict rationing of money for milk and groceries. Even then, we had no new clothes for the rest of the year. But my only recollection of any food shortage occurred one day when Mother served a dessert made from leftover breakfast porridge with a few raisins added. I turned up my nose in disgust, but as I think back, Mother must have been desperate to serve something like that.

When my father was back on his feet again, our situation began to improve. When we went back on relief it was almost a bonanza to get a clothing allowance and food coupons. I started in Grade I at Parkdale School in 1935, and once a day all those on relief were given a glass of milk to drink at recess time. But the money was still scarce and my father had no luck in finding a permanent job. He did some bookkeeping, helped build houses and garages at 20 cents an hour, dug gardens, and even made some ironing boards which he sold from door to door. Each time he came home with a bit of money, it went right into groceries.

We moved in 1935 to a bigger house on 89th Street, two blocks away. It cost $5 more a month but it had both a dirt cellar and a front porch, which the other place had lacked. On the south side was a vacant lot and next to it were the tracks of the 114th Avenue streetcar line. Beyond them was a tiny flat-roofed shack on the back half of the corner lot. I never knew who lived there, but they had a windup phonograph player and only one record, "You Are My Sunshine." In the summer, with the windows wide open, the song blared out endlessly until I knew it by heart.

There were quite a few vacant lots in the neighbourhood. Over on 90th Street between 114th and 115th Avenues there was only one house on the west side about halfway down the block. From there to the streetcar tracks was an open field where we played such games as "Duck on the Rock," "Run Sheep Run," and "Guns." For the latter game, we had L-shaped pieces of wood with nails serving as pretend triggers. We were all impressed when a kid from the other side of the tracks (literally) showed up with a real toy gun. However, we found him to be a very strange fellow, for we all shouted "bang! bang!" during the game, while he yelled "pow! pow!" My fascination with the game ended when somebody got mad and threw their gun at me. It struck me in the face and I received my first black eye.

The north end of 90th Street at 116th Avenue consisted of a dense growth of willows which, to our active imaginations, was a deep forest. We made trails, built little shelters, and played all sorts of games far away from the prying eyes of our parents. The area was only half a block long and a block wide but it seemed as though it went on forever, and we felt we were indeed in the wilderness as we played hide-and-seek and other games.

If times were tough, I wasn't aware of it. Years later when I spoke to my mother about it, she agreed with me. "We lived a hand to mouth existence and were run down at the heels," she said, "but we didn't think anything of it at the time. Just about everyone else we knew seemed to be in the same situation."[4] Two of our best treats were fresh homemade bread with brown sugar on top and – especially as a birthday treat – wieners. One year when Mother apparently couldn't afford wieners for my birthday, she got bologna instead. She tried to tell me that the only difference between bologna and wieners was that one was rolled up tight and the other was flat. I wasn't convinced.

I enjoyed school and passed with honours the first few years. I had some good friends and was never at a loss for something to do. My parents were not strict about staying near the house or accounting for our time, so we wandered far and wide in our freedom. This gave me a sense of independence that never left me. Our favourite haunts were a deserted brick factory near the railroad tracks and the city dump alongside the North Saskatchewan River. At the first place, we could explore the deserted rooms, climb over abandoned machinery, and play games like "Cops and Robbers." At the city dump, we looked for things to sell, like rags and beer bottles. But we had to be careful, for two or three hoboes lived in tar paper shacks on the edge of the dump and they resented anyone encroaching on their territory.

Among my best friends were the Slobidnyk kids, who lived half a block away. Their father was a carpenter who had built them a fine two-storey house. Behind it was a small shack where the old grandfather lived. He could speak no English. He had a rickety old wagon with wobbly wheels which he dragged down alleys, looking in garbage cans for rags, bottles, or other saleable scraps. Sometimes we used to follow him, yelling out phrases in Ukrainian that we didn't understand, but were sure to make him furious. He would throw rocks at us and we would run away laughing. It's sad, when I think about it now, that sometimes the instigator of this "fun" was his own grandson.

In 1936 we moved again, this time to a house just off 118th Avenue (which was still being called Alberta Avenue by the local residents). This was another two-storey house where my brother and I shared an unheated upstairs room. It wasn't entirely unheated; there was an open hole in the floor originally made for a stovepipe and enough heat drifted through it to keep us warm. I had no complaints.

---

The following summer was a memorable one for me. The government had organized a Better Health Camp at Lac Ste. Anne for children on relief. My father applied for both my brother and me; I was a year too young, but as my brother was along, they let me go. It lasted a month and was the most joyous, agonizing, and unhappy time of my life. I cried when my mother left me at the bus, and in later years she told me she had cried all the way home. At the camp, my brother Glen, being four years older (I was seven and he was eleven), didn't have much time for me, as there were plenty of boys his own age to play with. I was painfully homesick for several days, crying myself to sleep every night.

We lived in dormitories in a rustic camp along the side of the lake. There wasn't much of a beach, if any, as the bulrushes choked the shores, and a rickety wharf extended out into the lake to a point where it was possible to swim. I had a few friends at the camp, but as the youngest I was often ignored and left alone. That was all right with me. I wandered along the shore, catching frogs and looking for birds' nests; sometimes I went to the ice house, where huge blocks of ice were buried in sawdust and sparrows fluttered around the rafters. Sometimes I went into the treed area near the camp (we weren't allowed to leave the compound) and pretended I was in the forest.

I always had a great imagination, even before that time, so it was easy for me to slip into my own dream world and see myself in a primeval forest, hunting one of the deer or ruffed grouse that sometimes ventured into our camp. Reality returned as soon as I went for lunch. We ate in a screened veranda and then we had an hour's rest period when we all lay quietly on cots. On reflection, I suspect that some of the boys may have been tubercular, so fresh air, rest, and sunshine were priority items. Then, at the end of the rest period, each of us had to drink a glass of warm water; supposedly it was good for our digestion.

Like the others, I hated the stuff, but the counsellors stood over us and saw that we drank every drop.

One day after the warm water dietetic, our supervisor announced that we were going to have a poster contest. The subject was good health. There was a groan from the boys, who wanted to be out on the lake, but they all dutifully took their paper, pencils, and crayons, and began their works of art. I had an idea, but when I tried to put it down on paper I was so unhappy with the result that I folded it and tucked it under my chair. When the counsellor came to collect the papers, she saw mine, made me sign it, and put it with the others.

That evening, at supper, I was astounded when I won first prize. The supervisor said my poster showed the most originality of all those submitted. As far as I can recall, I had carrots and other vegetables with arms, legs, and faces, saying that "We're good to eat." If I was surprised by my win, my brother wasn't. Two years earlier, he had heard me announce that I was going to be an artist when I grew up. I was fond of scribbling and even in the junior grades art was my best subject.

One day, the dining room program became an excruciating experience for me. Somehow, the supervisor discovered that I had memorized "Who Killed Cock Robin" – all umpteen verses – so on this particular evening I was called upon to perform the recitation. I was painfully shy, and although I stumbled through the verse, I was just about ready to run away to hide with embarrassment after my first public performance. However, the experience was soon forgotten when my father showed up for a visit. He was doing some carpentry work at one of the beaches and had walked several miles to our camp. Afterwards, as I saw him going down the road and out of sight among the trees, my homesickness welled up in me again and I cried as only a seven-year-old can cry when they're lonely.

The month at the Better Health Camp seemed like an eternity. When we finally got off the bus in Edmonton and I saw my mother waiting for us, my joy knew no bounds. Later that day I looked up my school friends, particularly a pal named Art, and pretty soon it was as though I had never left.

———— ⨯⨯⨯ ————

One of our favourite events of the summer was the Edmonton Exhibition. We had no money for the gate fee so it was necessary for us to sneak inside. Our best place was a stretch of fence on the east side of the grounds, close to where an old railway locomotive was eroding into dust. It had been the first train into Edmonton in 1905, but by the time I saw the relic, it was a piece of rusty junk.

Once over the fence, Art and I would go to see my mother, who was working at the St. Andrew's Presbyterian Church booth just north of the Administration Building. If we visited her at the back of the booth, she could slip us a corn on the cob or hot dog. Sometimes we even earned some food by peeling potatoes or doing other odd jobs.

Our afternoon at the fairgrounds was a study in enjoying one's self without spending a dime. We saw all the free exhibits in the Manufacturers Building and Women's Building, taking any samples that were being offered. We then wandered down past the original log *Edmonton Bulletin* building, which had a bust of its founder, Frank Oliver, in front. The only trouble was that Frank's marble nose was broken so it was hard to take him seriously. Then it was down the midway, checking the sawdust around the rides to see if anyone had lost any money. Surprisingly, we did find a few coins from time to time. After that, it was over to the sideshows to enjoy the free previews on the stages in front. On one occasion, a magician called me up to be his "victim." He filled a large metal cup with water, then asked me to pour it out. When I had done so, he asked me if I had poured all of it. I said yes. Then he tipped it and poured out another stream of water, and laughingly bawled me out for not doing it right. "Are you sure it's all out now?" he asked me in front of the crowd. "Yes," I said. So he handed it to me and said, "Try it again." I did, and more water came out. This time, I could see that the cup had false sides and small holes where the water was seeping in. By this time the show was over and I was given a free ticket to go inside.

If we really got hungry, we could always wander behind the booths, either looking for a free handout or finding food that was being thrown out. One time we came across a bunch of overripe bananas which were like manna from heaven; another time we found a couple of wieners which had been inadvertently left in a box that was being discarded. By the time we left the grounds and headed home along Alberta Avenue, we were as contented as anyone who had spent a week's earnings at the fair.

———— ∞∞∞ ————

Although I have a faint recollection of Christmases soon after we arrived in Edmonton, my detailed memories begin during the four years we lived near 118th Avenue. My brother and I were told that Santa Claus wouldn't come if we stayed awake, but who could sleep at a time like this? Our parents had been skilful in hiding our few presents, so to our knowledge everything depended upon Santa's visit. Finally, by some miracle, Christmas morning arrived and about five o'clock my brother and I crept downstairs and into the living room. There, under the tree, were what seemed to be piles and piles of presents. We excitedly shook a few, tried to read the name tags, and finally slipped back to our bedroom with our Christmas stockings. As soon as we heard our parents or older brothers stirring, we hurried downstairs and impatiently waited for permission to open our gifts.

On reflection, the presents themselves were less important than actually getting them. We were not a demonstrative family as far as hugging and kissing were concerned – something I always regretted – perhaps because I had no sister. In their own way, the presents, the stockings, and the tree were symbols of love and family. If I try to think back about the toys I had before I was ten years old, I'm more likely to recall the little trucks I made from wood ends or the lead soldiers I stole from Kresge's department store.

Christmas was a big day for us; mother said that the first year in Edmonton was the only time we went without turkey. Usually, she managed to save enough money for a bird and once she even won one at a bingo game. Quite a few other farmers had been dried out in the Edgerton district and, like us, they had come to Edmonton. My father used to meet people like Ernie Trotter, Knutt Tangen, and Jack Cram in the downtown Hudson's Bay store where they would stand around and talk. They all were on relief and they had nothing else to do. But often they came around at Christmas, particularly the bachelors like Murdo Fraser, who lived at the Salvation Army. As well, my Uncle Stuart and his family sometimes joined us. They still lived on their farm and Christmas holidays were a perfect time to get together.

When she could afford it, my mother made a fruitcake in the fall and stored it in the cellar where it could age until Christmas. Then, as the holiday approached, she made Old English plum pudding and always managed to get some small silver nickels which were scattered through the batter. The holiday took some careful planning on my mother's part, for she had to depend upon the little money she had been able to save in the fall to buy the important little extras. Some of the food was bought, but a lot came from home canning and from our cold room in the basement where we had the potatoes, onions, beets, and other vegetables from the garden.

Our guests usually arrived in the afternoon and we kids went out to play with our cousins or friends. Meanwhile, the women congregated around the coal stove in the kitchen while the men sat in the front room, smoking and talking about the farm, politics, and their army days. There was a lot of laughter and storytelling.

We did not have skates or toboggans, but we did have some rough sleds that my father had made, and if the weather was mild we took them to the hills of the North Saskatchewan River where we had a lot of fun. Otherwise, we played around the house, sharing the excitement of the holiday, smelling the aroma of food cooking in the kitchen, and looking over our presents again and again.

One special gift always arrived for me just before Christmas and was opened immediately. It was from my Grandma Sharp in Folkestone, England, and contained a bundle of English children's magazines all rolled up tight and wrapped with brown paper. I had heard of American comic books, but these were entirely different. Tabloid in size, they were a fascinating mixture of comics, stories, and puzzles. Hours were spent poring over the adventure tales and the continuing sagas of English actors like Harold Lloyd and George Formby in comic book form. And, just as important, they were exclusive to me; no other kid on the block had ever seen them. I never met my grandmother, but I loved her for thinking of me at Christmas.

Sometimes we would haul down the copies of Harmsworth's Encyclopaedia for a guessing game. At the beginning of each new letter of the alphabet was a third of a page containing a scene filled with objects beginning with that letter. It if was "C," one was sure to find a cat, clock, church, or chimpanzee, but might have more trouble identifying a clarinet or a condor. Even with our familiarity with the Encyclopaedia, I don't think any of us ever identified every item at a single sitting.

Finally, mother and her visitors set the dining room table, digging out her best dishes and silver. We could not afford soft drinks, so in the fall we went to the city dump to find wine bottles that still had the corks in them. Then my parents made a mild ginger beer out of wheat that friends brought from the farm, and the bottles were placed upside down to ferment until Christmas day. One of these was placed beside every plate.

What great fun we had opening the bottles! They were wired down to keep them from exploding and whenever anyone took the wire off, they never knew when the cork might suddenly go bang! and spray the wheat beer all over the place. An empty glass was kept handy so the bottle could be upended into it as soon as the liquid began to bubble out.

Soon, what seemed to my youthful eyes to be piles and piles of steaming food was brought in from the kitchen. This was the time when the potatoes were put through the ricer to produce a fluffy white mound that seemed to collapse under the weight of the gravy. Also, a mixture of peas and carrots was always present – something we called "Presbyterian mix" for some reason or other. And with the turkey came sage dressing and giblet gravy, all done with the professional touch which my mother had learned while working in the kitchens of people in England.

The dessert at the best of times was plum pudding, fruitcake, and perhaps hot mince pie. In lean years, it was plum pudding alone, and somehow my mother always managed the servings so that there was at least one nickel inside every serving, to be rescued before the sauce was poured over it.

The measure of the meal's success was the degree of immobility it produced afterwards. Usually I stretched out on the floor to groan happily in my overstuffed and satiated condition. Others were equally relaxed, except for the women, who seemed anxious to clear the tables and wash the dishes. Unless they were staying overnight, our guests left soon after the dishes were done, and we all settled down in the happiness and security of family life.

⊶⊷

In the summer of 1938, when I was eight years old, I got my first job as a delivery boy on a milk wagon. It may not have been much, but from that time on, there was never a year when I was not working for wages, even if only part-time. In later years, when I asked my mother about my working, she said, "You were always a go-getter. Glen and Bill weren't. Glen was the quiet one and Bill talked to himself and to his imaginary friend. Harry knew what he was doing, but he wasn't aggressive. You were highly aggressive and a leader, like me."

The deliveryman, Charles Hickey, and I had a routine. He got up at 5 a.m. and walked about two miles to the Edmonton City Dairy, on 109th Street across from the CPR station. He harnessed his horse, hitched her to a wagon, and waited in line for his milk. Once loaded, he set out for home, arriving in time for breakfast. I got up about seven and walked five blocks to his house, arriving just as he was getting ready to leave.

His route was in the Woodland and Delton districts, which included our house and was the reason I got the job. Our routine was simple. The milk wagon had covered storage bins on each side and an aisle down the middle. By opening the lids, we could take out the bottles we needed, put them into a wire basket, and make the delivery. Mr. Hickey would do one side of the street and I would do the other. I went up to the door (usually the back door), where I found empty bottles and tickets. I left the required milk, took away the empties, and put them into a special compartment. Almost invariably, the bottles were as clean as a whistle; seldom did we ever encounter one encrusted with dried milk.

One of the interesting features of the work was the delivery horse. She knew the route better than we did. When a delivery had been made and Mr. Hickey said "Giddyap" she plodded along and stopped at the next customer's house without being told. There was one place on the route where we had to shift over to the next street. After I had made my delivery, I crossed the road and followed Mr. Hickey, who delivered his milk, went through a backyard, across the alley to his next customer, and when he emerged on the other street, the horse and wagon were waiting for us. The only time Mr. Hickey had to take over was when a customer quit or a new one was added. After a few days, however, the horse adjusted to the change in the routine.

We finished deliveries at the northeast corner of the Delton district about noon. Mr. Hickey then swung over to 118th Avenue and we clip-clopped down that main thoroughfare, the empty bottles rattling in the bins, until we got to my street. There I was given my daily pay – five cents – and if I was lucky, a bottle of milk. I never understood how Mr. Hickey was able to give me milk one day and not another. Perhaps it had something to do with breakage or a miscount. However, I'd prefer to think that as a wage earner, he felt some sympathy for the skinny kid on welfare and every once in a while he would take a dime out of his pocket to make sure we had milk in the house.

That job lasted only for the summer but I felt as though I was rich. I had never received an allowance, and the money I had earned selling rags and bottles could be counted in pennies. A favourite use for my nickel was to buy something called a brazil nut slab. It was a chocolate bar containing whole brazil nuts and came in a cellophane bag. It was a feast in itself.

During the Depression, people on relief could apply to the City to take over a vacant lot as a vegetable garden. My father got one about a block away which he planted in addition to the one beside our house. Potatoes took up a lot of space but there also were carrots, peas, beets, cucumbers, onions, and other vegetables that could be dried, canned, or pickled. We boys pitched in (we had to) to weed, hill potatoes, thin the rows, and do the other chores necessary in a big garden. In early summer, we went down to the river to cut willows to use as pea sticks. These were shoved into the ground to provide supports for the pea vines. In the fall, we followed behind my father as he dug into the earthen hills and exposed stacks of white potatoes. We picked them up and put them into gunny sacks which, when filled, were tied with binder twine and carried home in a wheelbarrow. We had a cold room in the cellar next to the coal bin where the potatoes were kept.

The fall was the time when my mother did so much canning that there always seemed to be steam in the kitchen. She had a huge boiler for the jars, a table littered with sealer rings and metal caps, and pots for cooking. I'm sure she canned vegetables but all I remember were the peaches and pears which became standard fare throughout the winter. Pickled beets and cucumbers were other favourites of mine. Those, added to the bread she made every week and the moose meat my father got from hunting, made us pretty self-sufficient. On $40 a month for relief, with half going for rent, we had to be.

Besides the milk wagon, a few other horse-drawn vehicles passed our house every day. We had an ice box, a forerunner of the refrigerator, so once a week in summer the ice wagon stopped in front of our place. A few of us watched in fascination as the iceman chipped a block to the exact size needed, grabbed it with his metal tongs, and carried it on his back, which was protected by a rubber sheet. While he was inside the house, especially on hot days, we took the opportunity to grab some of the larger chips of ice and suck on them as though they were candy. They were a real treat.

We never could afford store-bought bread, so the McGavin's Bakery wagon just kept on going past our house. Another vehicle that passed us by was the honey wagon. Quite a few homes still had outside toilets, so periodically the honey wagon came down the alley, where the men opened the trap door at the back of the outhouse and shovelled out the mess. The honey wagons were solid vehicles with trap doors on the bottom so the load could be dumped without any further shovelling. When not in use, these wagons were stored on an open lot just west of Clarke Stadium. Needless to say, no one ever played on them.

After the summer season, it was back to school and no more milk deliveries. But that didn't mean I gave up earning money. In the winter there were sidewalks to be shovelled and in the spring I sometimes asked people for sprigs of blue or white lilacs, then made them into bouquets to sell to householders who had no flowers. Another way of making money was an adventure in itself. On a Saturday, I would get up at six o'clock and go to my friend Art's place two blocks away. From there we walked a mile and a half to a point called Lover's Leap at the end of Viewpoint Road. This is where couples liked to park, drink beer, and make love. Art and I tried to be the first ones there in the morning. We searched the parking area and along the slopes into the trees, looking for beer bottles. We wanted at least three each, but got more if we were lucky.

With our treasures, we walked along Jasper Avenue about three miles to the Alberta Liquor Vendors on 103rd Street. There we sold the empties for three for a nickel. If we had made more than a dime between us, we went to

Eaton's to buy broken cookies. Any broken or damaged ones went into a special bin, and for a nickel one could get a paper bag full. Sometimes, if we were lucky, we got specialty treats which were chocolate covered or had marshmallow centres. Usually, however, the bag contained a mixture of plain varieties, like oatmeal and ginger snaps.

Armed with these we walked a half mile to the Gem Theatre on Jasper Avenue, just east of 97th Street. Every Saturday it had a special five-cent program consisting of two full-length movies, cartoons, previews, and a thrilling serial which continued from week to week. All this lasted until late afternoon. When we came out into the bright sunshine, we were rested, happy, and ready for the three-mile walk home. I usually arrived just in time for supper.

"What did you do today?" my mother would ask.

"Aw, nothin'."

---

I got my second job during the winter of 1938–39 as a result of cleaning sidewalks. A regular customer was Mrs. Elgie Latta, who lived half a block north of us. From shovelling snow, I graduated to carrying out the ashes from her coal stove and furnace and dumping them in the alley. One thing led to another and pretty soon I was doing so many odd jobs that she hired me for 35 cents a week to be her nine-year-old handyman. And what started off as a simple task of keeping her sidewalk clear and carrying out her ashes soon turned into a year-round after-school occupation.

There wasn't much to do in winter except clean the sidewalk, bring in wood and coal, shake down the stoves, and clean out the ashes. As soon as spring arrived, I had the task of keeping her dugout cellar dry. She had a hand pump which consisted of a vertical pipe which extended from the floor to an outside drain. My task was to grasp a pump handle, and work it up and down until the water which had collected from the spring runoff was siphoned off. Later, when the snow had melted, I dug her vegetable garden and helped her plant. Fortunately it wasn't a large garden, as she also had flowers and raspberry bushes. During the summer I did the weeding and thinning, then cleaned up the yard in the fall.

If I worked well outside and in the cellar, Mrs. Latta assumed I could be of help around the house as well. So once a week I washed, waxed and polished her floors and did the dusting. This didn't take all my time, but as I was a skinny kid, I sometimes had trouble with heavy snows in winter, and the interminable pumping. Finally, Mrs. Latta suggested that I get some help, so my brother Glen joined me and our salary was set at 50 cents a week between the two of us.

Mrs. Latta was a nice lady. Being young and uninquisitive, I never knew if she was a widow, why she was alone, or where she worked. All I knew was that she treated me very kindly. I stayed with her for over a year, in fact until we moved away in the summer of 1940.

—∞∞∞—

Our lives slowly improved during the latter part of the Depression. On the farm, my father had been an active Conservative and had been asked to run for the Alberta legislature. On arriving in Edmonton, he had switched to the Social Credit party, which was just being organized by William Aberhart. He threw his support behind our local candidate, David B. Mullen, and worked hard on his behalf. Even Glen and I were pressed into service, delivering leaflets from door to door. When Mullen was elected, my father continued to be one of his active campaigners in the Alberta Avenue Constituency Association. I recall on one occasion, Premier Aberhart came to speak at the community hall and my father took me along. After the program, I was taken up to the stage to meet the premier. As we walked forward, I felt as though I was being ushered into the presence of God himself, and when I shook the Great Man's pudgy hand, people acted as though this was the greatest honour that could ever be bestowed upon a mere mortal.

In the fall of 1938, my father's work with the party paid off when he was given the position of elevator operator at the downtown Provincial Building. This was pure patronage, but it was the first time my father had held a regular job since we came to Edmonton. It made a world of difference, not only in his standard of income, but in the fact that he could now provide for the family without welfare handouts. As my mother said, "He hated charity, but what could he do?" His life insurance policy had been cancelled during the Depression and he was constantly worried about what would happen to the family in the event of his death.

As soon as he got the job, he was determined to be the best elevator operator the building had ever seen. Many times I visited him at work and saw how people respected him. Not only did he do his job well but he was constantly going out of his way to help others. He was very solicitous of his clients, sometimes checking on a person who was staying late to see if they were all right, or helping with deliveries. There wasn't much a person could do wrong as an elevator operator, but my father brought a pride and efficiency to the work that reflected his feeling about at last finding employment.

The work convinced my father that the only security in the world lay in the civil service. He emphasized to the rest of us how important it was to have a secure job; after his Depression experience, his attitude was not surprising.

When my oldest brother, Harry, came back from a two-year stint with a northern fur trading company, my father used his political influence with Mullen, who was now Minister of Agriculture, to get him a job with the Department of Fish and Game. Harry was born in 1918 so I hardly knew him as a child. During the war he enlisted in the Royal Canadian Air Force and served overseas. I greatly admired him and looked up to him as my hero. He was a handsome, dashing man with a lot of flair, and both of us seemed to have similar aggressive personalities.

After the war, Harry joined the federal Fisheries Department in Winnipeg and I stayed with him during one hitchhiking adventure. Then he was promoted to Ottawa and became Director of Consumer Services for the department. That's when I really got to know him, for I used to make frequent business trips to Ottawa and Harry often visited Calgary. It was funny, but we seemed to run along parallel lines. He had been a stamp collector, so I became a stamp collector. I started building a library of Canadian books, and he started a similar library. It was almost like a competition, but it wasn't. Rather, I think we were both so fond of each other that each naturally pursued the other's interests. He was the oldest so it seemed so unfair that he should be the first of the brothers to die. He was a heavy smoker, contracted lung cancer, and died in 1969 at the age of fifty-one.

Getting back to my dad, soon after the war broke out in 1939, he tried to enlist, but he was too old at forty-seven, and his eardrums had been damaged while testing guns in the earlier war. Then one day in the summer of 1940, my mother sat on my bed and told me we were going to move. It was a nice place, she said, closer to downtown so my father could walk to work. We didn't need a big house. The place turned out to be the upstairs of a box-like old house on 105A Avenue. There was no garden, no lawn, and for the first time, we had neighbours with only a floor separating us. But I didn't mind. I moved from Parkdale to Alex Taylor School, found new friends, and soon was comfortable in our new surroundings.

I was out of work again, but it took only a few weeks to find a new job. As in my previous employment, I became a gardener and handyman, this time for the lady who lived across the street. Her name was Miss Emma Holmes, and she was general secretary for the Alberta Wool Growers Association. She was a very businesslike person, not warm and friendly like Mrs. Latta but still a good and fair boss. And my work was very similar to what I had done before. She had natural gas or electricity so I didn't have any ashes to dump, but I did clean her house, tended the garden, and undertook any other odd jobs. My pay was 50 cents a week.

---

Alex Taylor was quite a different school from Parkdale. I was now in Grade VI and perhaps I was becoming more observant about things around me. There seemed to be a lot of "tough" kids at the school, and fights were not uncommon. During a football game, I was deliberately kicked in the kneecap by one of these punks, and my knee was never the same after that.

My best pals were a small group of four boys and three girls who liked to hang out on 105th Avenue, along a tree-lined street where a couple of them lived. At eleven, I was one of the oldest, the youngest being a girl of nine. We used to call ourselves the Fifth Street Gang, inspired no doubt by the movies. However, we were anything but a gang in the real sense of the word. We played skipping, marbles, hide and seek, and a couple of the bunch even had roller skates. We made a soapbox racing car using old wagon wheels and had scooters from apple boxes and roller skate wheels. When we weren't on 105th Avenue, we were two blocks away at Bissell Park, playing softball or soccer.

By the time the Japanese attacked Pearl Harbour in 1941 and the Americans joined the war, I had graduated from Alex Taylor and was now a Grade VII student at McCauley Intermediate. In that same year, my father finally settled into his lifetime career. All during the 1930s, he had listed his occupation as bookkeeper, but in Edmonton he had had few opportunities to practise it. Then, when the war broke out and men were enlisting by the hundreds, new jobs began to open up. With his military experience giving him preference, he was able to win a competition as Customs Officer for the federal government. It was a job he loved. He memorized its "Blue Book" by heart and soon became the resident expert on customs and excise duties.

Edmonton underwent a massive change in 1942 when we were invaded by the Americans. The Alaska Highway, Canol Project, and Northwest Staging Route brought thousands of military and civilian workers to the city. New buildings popped up overnight on Jasper Avenue and near the airport, and American troops became a common sight on the streets. This soon had an impact upon many of my fellow students as a whole new social hierarchy was created. American comic books, forbidden since the war, began to appear; boys sported USAF shoulder flashes on their jackets; and rationed items such as chocolate bars found their way into the classrooms. I was denied all these luxuries, for I lacked the essential ingredient for success: an older sister. Boys my own age regaled us with stories of rich American soldiers who dated their sisters and always came bearing gifts. While the girls traipsed off to the Trocadero Ballroom or Lover's Leap, the boys reaped the spoils of war. Sometimes they were willing to trade their treasures, but I had little or nothing of value to them. Money wasn't as important as prestige.

Like others, I was captivated by the romantic image of American soldiers, and the few I met were open, friendly, and generous. Even the civilians working for such construction outfits as Bechtel Price Callaghan of California left a good impression. Black soldiers were something of a curiosity on Edmonton streets, as was a black zoot suiter I saw one day near the post office. He had the whole outfit – yellow shoes, drapes, purple jacket with no lapels, wide brimmed hat, and a long keychain. As he stood on the street corner, people avoided him like the plague, myself included. Also during the war, I could never get used to seeing airplanes flying overhead bearing Russian markings. They were mostly Air Cobras, part of the lend-lease program to Russia. The planes flew to Alaska, where they were turned over to Russian pilots who ferried them across Siberia to the battlefields of Europe.

Aircraft identification became a fetish with some students. Cards slightly smaller than playing cards bearing silhouettes of aircraft were available, and we used them as flash cards. A boy would hold up a card and instantly someone would shout the name. Similarly, if we were out in the playground and aircraft flew over (as they often did) we accurately picked out the Air Cobras, Mustangs, Dakotas, Lightnings, and such Canadian training planes as Fairey Battles, Avro Ansons, and Harvards. Even though I had two brothers (later three) in the Air Force, to me the war was far away. The real excitement was right in Edmonton where we had American soldiers, Russian planes, food rationing, British Commonwealth Air Training Plan activities, and our own recruiting depots and armouries.

Life at McCauley Intermediate proved very difficult for me. I had managed to slide through all the elementary grades without studying and still passed with honours. As a result, I never picked up the habit of studying and tried to coast along on what I picked up in the classroom. By Grade VII I had slipped to a B grade and for the rest of my school years I was an indifferent student. This was partly due to boredom with the school system. Much of my time in classes was spent doodling and daydreaming. Only in English, art, and social studies did I maintain any level of interest. The rest I found tiresome.

Added to this was the fact that I was always working so that I seldom, if ever, participated in intramural activities. I was too skinny to be active in sports and too shy for the theatre. I always had lots of friends like Howie Carey and Cam MacLean but I also enjoyed my own company.

One of my best friends was a collie named Rex. I never had a dog of my own and half a block from us was a family with no children. I started playing with their dog and they had no objection to my taking him out for a run. Our favourite activity occurred in the winter. A half block from our house was the beginning of the Chinese market gardens. This was an area more than two blocks square which had once been the Edmonton Penitentiary grounds. In winter it was entirely barren and covered with snow. Rex and I would dash across the open fields, he barking and me laughing as we enjoyed each other's company. Quite often Rex would raise a rabbit and take off like a shot while I struggled to follow. "Here Rex! Here Rex!" I would shout into the darkness but the dog would return only when he was good and ready, tired and happy. At other times I looked into the night sky and searched for the North Star, the Big Dipper, and the few other constellations that I could recognize. It was a thoroughly joyful experience for me, and I suspect for Rex too.

My job with Miss Holmes lasted for about a year, but came to a crashing halt in the spring of 1942. Although there was no set routine, the usual proce-dure was to put in an hour or so after school, taking out the garbage, and doing odd chores. On Saturday I usually worked half a day in the garden, cleaning house, dusting, etc. One Saturday, Miss Holmes told me without warning that I would have to work all day. She had some guests coming that evening and had extra duties for me. I explained that I already had a date to meet some friends downtown and there was no way I could contact them. She told me in no uncertain terms that I had to decide which was more important, my job or my friends. I chose my friends and joined the ranks of the unemployed.

But not for long. Within a couple of weeks, I had presented myself to the circulation manager at the *Edmonton Bulletin* and became a paper boy. I had the two necessary prerequisites: a bike with a strap-iron carrier and a willingness to work. I was given a route flanking each side of 96th Street in one of the crummiest parts of town — although I didn't realize it at the time. Actually, I knew the area well as it was directly on my way to and from downtown. I delivered to homes, stores, and a couple of apartment buildings. In later years, I learned that one place on my route was a brothel, but I never saw anything or heard anything to make me suspicious. I simply went down the hall and slipped the newspaper under all the doors of the subscribers. And when I think back, they must have been a pretty literate bunch, as most of them took the paper.

Like other boys, I went to the *Bulletin* every day after school and waited at the back door until my turn came to get my list of new subscribers, cancellations, and complaints. The manager then counted off my papers, I stuck them in my bag, mounted my bike, and headed off for my route. At least it happened that way if I was lucky. Sometimes, if the papers were late on a Saturday afternoon, a few bullies in the crowd might decide to have some fun by terrorizing some of the younger lads. I was one of the youngest – a skinny shy kid who was a perfect target for their harassment. I was never actually beaten up, but I was threatened, chased, and ridiculed. One time, I was forced to flee down the steep slope behind the *Bulletin* to get away from the bullies, and then I got in trouble with the boss because I was late picking up my papers.

Once in a while, I crept through the doors into the pressroom to avoid trouble, and was awestruck by the roaring presses, the newspapers cascading down the racks in orderly rows, and the huge rolls of paper waiting to be fed into the hungry machines. The presses seemed to go all the way to the ceiling – which they did – and the smell of printers' ink and newsprint permeated the air and captured my imagination.

I had no wish to deliver papers during an Edmonton winter so I quit the *Bulletin* in the fall. And it did get cold in Edmonton. One morning, the air was perfectly still when I left the house for school. As I walked along, my breath left a vapour trail and the snow under my feet was as granular as sand. When a train whistle sounded in the distance, it echoed through the hollow air as though it was just across the street. It was less than half a mile to school but during the walk I saw no one. At first I thought I was early but even then I should have met others heading in the same direction. When I finally entered McCauley, a teacher waiting in the hall said that classes had been cancelled as it was −62°F. Together with a few other hardy souls who had wandered into the building, I was kept inside until we had warmed up, and then we were sent home.

I always bundled up warm for Edmonton winters – long underwear, thick flannel trousers, heavy socks, boots (or if it was *really* cold, moccasins), flannel shirt, sweater, windbreaker, scarf, toque, and mittens. One of my early acquisitions from the military was a Canadian khaki-coloured balaclava which I could wear rolled up as a toque but pull it down so only my eyes were showing when the weather turned cold.

McCauley was a typical city school, but one event sticks out in my mind, probably because it was so unique at the time. It concerned our drama teacher. He was a young man in his twenties who made me appreciate Shakespeare. Until that time, I had enjoyed poetry and had memorized such verses as "The Shooting of Dan McGrew" and "Frankie and Johnnie" – real classical stuff. I had appreciated poems like "The Song My Paddle Sings" and "The Highwayman," but The Bard had left me cold. Then came our drama teacher. He didn't teach Shakespeare, he acted it. He actually stood on top of his desk one day when he recited Hamlet's soliloquy, after which he explained it to us in terms we could understand.

Then one day in mid-term he was gone. No explanation, just replacement with another of those humdrum teachers whose monotonous drones were guaranteed to bring on utter boredom, if not sleep. Then the whispering began. Our drama teacher had been fired. Why? He was one of those, a faggot! (We didn't have such neutral terms as "gay" or "homosexual"; in fact, "faggot" was perhaps one of the kinder words bandied about.) I was as shocked as the rest of the class, but even then I wondered how such a wonderful teacher could have been such an "evil" man. There had never been a hint of scandal involving any of the students and, in fact, rumour had it that he was living with a man a few blocks west of the school. Perhaps someone with his sexual proclivities shouldn't have been teaching young boys, but I know he was the finest drama teacher I ever had.

My first brush with sex during this time scared the wits out of me. One Saturday afternoon when I was fourteen, I had pedalled down into the river valley and across the Dawson Bridge to the Riverside Golf Course. During World War I, part of this area had been a shooting range, and there was a cut-bank where one could dig out rifle bullets. After a successful foray, I was on my way home, pushing my bike up the hill below Alex Taylor School when a boy I knew slightly called to me from some bushes. When I went over, I found two boys and three girls settling down to the serious business of necking. They obviously were a boy short, so I was elected. A rather nice-looking girl of my own age nestled up beside me while the others paired off, one going into passionate kissing and the other talking in low murmurs.

I was at a loss as to what to do. My experience with girls was absolutely nil and, coupled with my natural shyness and my unfamiliarity with girls my age, I didn't know what to do next. The girl, sweetheart that she was, set me at ease by saying she didn't care what the others did, all she wanted to do was chat. It seemed doubtful but I never found out if she really meant it, for after a few minutes the caretaker from the school came down the hill and told us to get out. As we scampered away, the girl told me that they were going directly to a little place in Rat Creek ravine where they could *really* be alone. I had my bike to contend with, so I promised to meet them later. But I never did. I went home, grateful that I had escaped a situation that seemed to be beyond my emotional capabilities, yet cursing myself for not going. It was tough being a teenager.

---

In the fall of 1942, after I had made up my mind that I was not going to deliver newspapers, I had to decide what to do next. Up to this time, most of my winter work experience had been indoors, except for shovelling sidewalks. I had never received an allowance from my parents and I wasn't about ready to start; neither was I prepared to be unemployed. So when I learned that Graydon's Drug Store needed a "boy" with a "wheel" I hurried down and got the job. At first I was puzzled about the required "wheel," as all I had was a bicycle, but I soon learned that this was its English term.

Graydon's was located on Jasper Avenue, just east of 99th Street, and in later years was demolished for the extension of the Macdonald Hotel. It prided itself on being the oldest drug store in Edmonton, having been established by George Graydon in 1890. He was dead by the time I was hired, and his two assistants had taken over the business. They were as opposite as night and day. One was Nels Ferris, a small owlish man who was a good druggist and businessman but was somewhat cold and aloof. He was a family man and lived in the West End. The other was Charles Miller, an older man with flowing white hair, a florid face from too much drinking, and with a warm and friendly personality. He was a bachelor who lived at the Queen's Hotel but spent most of his free time at the Elks Club farther east on Jasper Avenue.

I got along with both men, but Mr. Miller was my favourite. He used to chat about the early years of his pharmacy work when he was with George Graydon. One day he described how opium had been shipped direct from China when the drug was still legal. It arrived, he said, looking like "a big elephant turd" and they had to refine it themselves, using the drug in their own elixirs and medicines. He also told me that during the prohibition era the only way a person could get liquor was with a doctor's prescription and the drug store did a roaring business.

My job stretched into a five-year association with Graydon's during which time I was clerk, handyman, and delivery boy. I worked for two hours every day after school, all day Saturdays, and part time for the summer. I got 30 cents an hour, which was the minimum wage, and I loved it. My routine during the week was to make any needed deliveries, then go to the National Drug Company warehouse to pick up anything the store needed. When I got back, I took out the garbage, filled the shelves, and helped with the clerking if they got too busy. On Saturdays I swept out the store and usually spent the morning dusting.

Being an old store, Graydon's was very traditional. In the windows were two huge glass jars, one filled with red liquid and one with green; these were pharmaceutical symbols. When you entered the door, you came into a huge room with rows and rows of bottles down both walls. These contained strange liquids and powders with Latin names, and a few recognizable things like cinnamon sticks and powdered liquorice. The floor was wood and the display cases ancient. Halfway down each side was a counter for serving customers, and at the back of the room was a massive beaded curtain that extended from the ceiling to the tops of display cases and down to the floor. It had a peacock design and I was told it had come from China with one of the opium shipments.

My weekend chore was to start at one end of the room and begin dusting the bottles. This meant that all the bottles on a length of shelf had to be removed, wiped with a damp cloth, and then returned to a shelf that had been dusted clean. Between clerking, delivering, and other tasks, I could do about a quarter of one side of the room in a day, but by the time I had done the entire room, the first ones were dusty again. It was a job that I hated.

During the summer, I did everything except fill prescriptions, and even there I sometimes helped by assembling the necessary medicines on the table, or scraping the brand names off bottles so the prescription labels could be glued on. Graydon's was one of the few drug stores at the time that commonly mixed its own prescriptions rather than just taking something from a bottle. Many times I saw Mr. Miller or Mr. Ferris carefully weighing powders or herbs on a delicate scale, dumping them into a mortar, and grinding them with a pestle, or measuring a mixture of several liquids into a beaker.

Although I didn't handle prescription drugs, I did mix herbal remedies. The store had a tattered old book which contained the formulas for making such items as Chinese Herbal Tea, Graydon's Balsam Mix, and Graydon's Blood Tonic. The herbs came to the store in small bales. I dumped these into well-marked barrels, and when we ran short of an item I took the recipe book, a bunch of small boxes, a weigh scale, and set to work. With a scoop I shovelled the required amounts of several herbs into a container which I stirred thoroughly. Then, using a smaller scoop, I filled each box with the mixture, sealed it, and stuck on the label.

The drugstore also had its own brand name items which, like cough medicine, were mixed by the druggists while I bottled and labelled them. Some, such as Graydon's Zinc Ointment, were simply taken from large containers and bottled in small jars.

While they did handle the usual patent medicines, shaving cream, toothpaste, candy, and other items found in "modern" drugstores, they still emphasized the medical side of pharmacy. Besides the prescriptions, they did a good business in trusses, body belts, and other medical appliances.

When I joined Graydon's, we were in the middle of a war and rationing was a visible part of the business. For example, anyone wishing to buy a tube of toothpaste had to return their old tube so that the lead could be salvaged. The allotment of chocolate bars was so limited that they were kept behind the counter and sold only to regular customers, and the sale of some of the store's herbal mixtures was suspended because it was impossible to import the necessary ingredients.

My work as a clerk was fairly routine, although when I started I was pretty green. For example, a man came in one day and placed three fingers on the counter in front of me. I asked him what he wanted, but he didn't say a word. He just looked angry and repeated the three-finger motion. Then Mr. Miller stepped in. He reached under the counter and produced a package of three condoms and handed them to the customer. That sign language was standard during the five years I worked there. Many men were either embarrassed or shy about asking for condoms, especially if there were other customers in the store, so they used this signal. We usually gave them Sheiks unless they asked for one of the other brands. And I can still remember Mr. Miller's embarrassment one day when a woman asked for "safes" (condoms). He hesitated, fearing he hadn't heard right, but when she repeated her request, he sold her the goods. When he came back into the dispensary, his face was beet red; it was the first time this had ever happened to him in his long years at the store. But I guess it was a sign of the changing times.

Graydon's had a basement that extended the length of the entire store, and it was a wonderful place to explore. At one time, a loading ramp had extended from the alley to the lower area but this had since been filled in. Yet the double doors were still in place and I always wondered what was behind them. They were hard to get to, as the space in front of them was used to pile empty cardboard boxes. One day, I took matters into my own hands, cleaned away the boxes, and pried the door open slightly. Imagine my disgust when all I found was a solid wall of clay and gravel.

In another corner of the basement were some rusty old German relics from World War I. There was a belt buckle inscribed "Gott Mit Uns," a potato-masher–type hand grenade, a cloth wedgie hat, and a few other items. The only British object was a helmet. I was captivated by these relics and wondered why they were abandoned in the basement to rust away. I asked Mr. Ferris (hoping he might say, "Take them") and he explained that they belonged to a former employee. A war veteran, the man had spent a few years at Graydon's and one day he simply didn't show up for work. This was in the 1920s. As far as Mr. Ferris was concerned, they still belonged to that man and until he came to reclaim them, they would stay where they were. I suspect they went under the bulldozer when the building was destroyed, as in later years neither Mr. Ferris nor Mr. Miller knew what became of them.

Considering that we were just on the fringes of the depressed areas near 97th Street, the drug store was remarkably free of trouble. There was never a robbery during my five years there and we seldom had beggars or derelicts in the store. A few denizens of St. Elmo's Hotel, a block away, sometimes came to get prescriptions filled, but they were usually sad, elderly men who were down on their luck. Most customers were businessmen or women who passed the store when walking to work, or people who lived in the various rooming houses and apartments in the district. Others who had once lived in the area still patronized Graydon's but did so by phone. These were the people to whom I delivered orders, including the widow of George Graydon, who lived at the far west end of Jasper Avenue.

———∞———

At school, I managed to squeak through Intermediate (later called Junior High) with passing grades but I found myself slipping farther and farther behind in classes. I still hadn't adopted a discipline of study and my feeble attempts to memorize math tables and scientific formulas were dismal failures. Only in English, social studies and art did I continue to excel.

In 1944 I graduated into high school. Like my fellow classmates from McCauley, I lined up to register at Victoria High School and found the hallways packed with students. A bunch of us who had chummed together at McCauley gravitated to each other in this plethora of strangers and found ourselves assigned to the same room. After the second day, we were notified that the school was overcrowded and arrangements had been made for us to transfer to McDougall Commercial High School, five blocks away.

McDougall! That was a girls' school where they taught bookkeeping and stenography! But rules were rules, so forty-four boys and sixteen girls trooped off to the sedate world of female education. We were divided into two classes, all the girls going into one room with fourteen boys, and all the rest of the boys – including me – in another room. That was a mistake; even a couple of girls would have made our room less rowdy, but as it was, we became the terror of the school. The poor women teachers, unaccustomed to handling a roomful of recalcitrant youths, were unable to cope during the first few weeks. On at least two occasions a teacher fled from the room in tears.

The school had a distinguished history. Its principal was J. Percy Page, who had coached the world famous Grads basketball team and later became lieutenant-governor of Alberta. He was absent for part of the year and his duties were taken over by Clare Hollingsworth, who I believe was his son-in-law, and also coached the Grads. As the weeks passed, we gradually slipped into the school routine, but as the only academic classes in a school dominated by commercial courses, we were the outsiders. A few boys excelled both in classroom and sports activities, but we were really in the wrong place.

My closest friends during that year were Eddie Andruko, Howie Carey, Ken Riddle, and Julian Buchanan. Some of us had nicknames: I was "Cuke," Ken was "Maggots," and Julian was "Judd."[5] Actually, the latter may have been a family name, for in later years when he became Minister of Indian Affairs & Northern Development, he was the Hon. Judd Buchanan. During his tenure in office he remembered our earlier association when he appointed me Alberta member of the Historic Sites & Monuments Board of Canada.

Patriotism ran high during my time at McDougall. The Allies were finally on the offensive and the end of the conflict was near. The school had competitions between classrooms as to which could sell the most number of War Savings Stamps, money was collected to buy chocolate bars for veterans in local hospitals, and lists were published of former students killed in action. In music class we sang patriotic songs such as "Rule Britannia," "White Cliffs of Dover," and "The Maple Leaf Forever." If someone suggested "O Canada" or "God Save the King," we had to rise and stand by our desks. That was all right, but I could never understand why we had to stand while singing "I am an American," or why we didn't sing the revised version, "I am a Canadian." Maybe it was the strong American military presence in Edmonton that caused the teachers to defer to the Stars and Stripes.

I graduated from Grade X a few days after the war ended in Europe in June 1945. My three brothers were in the RCAF, one overseas, and I bitterly resented the fact that at fifteen I was too young to join up. Now I'd never be a war veteran.

———o﬈o———

There had been some big changes in my life over the winter of 1944–45. Most importantly, we moved to a house on 76th Avenue, on the South Side. It was a nice two-bedroom bungalow with a big yard and a garage, even though we had no car. It was nine blocks from the streetcar line, but as I had a bicycle the distance never bothered me. Even when I had to use the streetcar, I simply rode my bike to Whyte Avenue, parked it beside a shoe repair shop, and picked it up on the way home.

When we moved, the big questions were my school and my job. I was registered at McDougall and had been there for several weeks but now the school was about four miles away, with the Saskatchewan River valley separating us. Similarly, I was now a couple of miles from Graydon's. I guess there never was a question, for even with the river valley, the distance was not great for a cyclist. There were many people who walked that distance every day. So for the rest of the winter and into spring, I rode my bike down Scona Road to the Low Level Bridge, then carried it up the long steps below the Macdonald Hotel. I then rode to Graydon's, cleaned the sidewalk, and got to school in time for classes. The return route was similar, although sometimes if I was lucky, I grabbed the end of a slow-moving vehicle and was pulled up Scona Hill instead of pedalling.

I had managed to pass from Grade X into Grade XI after dropping trigonometry. In the Christmas exams I had the dubious honour of having the lowest mark in the school, some 16 per cent, a clear indication that the sciences weren't my field. I wasn't much better in algebra, chemistry, or physics but I continued to be an honours student in English, art, and social studies. My one passion continued to be art. I was now into water colours, wood carving, and oils. During my senior high school years, I earned extra money by making hand-painted ties featuring pinup girls, and making school crests and other adornments out of felt. I became quite proficient with my mother's sewing machine and found a ready market for my products, particularly crests featuring Walt Disney characters like the Big Bad Wolf.

During the summer of 1945, when I was fifteen, I left Edmonton on my own for the first time. This was the first of three expeditions that I made over the next three summers. It took me to the interior of British Columbia where I had planned to spend the summer picking apples. However, one look at the hovel that was supposed to be my living quarters made me so homesick that in just two days I was back in Edmonton. I don't know what my parents must have thought when their adventuresome son came home with his tail between his legs, but I still admire the fact that they recognized my independent spirit and made no attempt to limit my actions, no matter how foolish or unrealistic.

A year later I decided to hitchhike to Winnipeg, stay with my brother Harry, and get a job for a month or so. The trip was a memorable one. I caught a number of rides that took me through Calgary and on to Lethbridge. Next day I made it to Maple Creek for the night. When walking out of town early next morning, I met a young boy named Jackie who was also hitchhiking. I thought I was rather adventuresome, travelling all the way to Winnipeg, but he was younger than me and his destination was Toronto. We stayed together all day and by the time we were dumped off at Whitewood, Saskatchewan, the town looked like it was closed down for the night. When we went to the hotel – the only one in town – the owner had gone to bed, but we woke him up and asked for rooms. He told us there was only one left, with a double bed, and a bathroom down the hall. It would cost us a dollar each. That was fine by me, and if Jackie hesitated, I didn't notice it.

We crept up to our room through a darkened hallway and once we were inside, I started to get ready for bed, as I was dog tired. Jackie, however, just stood in the middle of the room, his packsack on the floor in front of him.

"I've got something to tell you," he said.

I paused as I rifled through my duffle bag, looking for my pyjamas.

"What is it?"

"I'm not a boy, I'm a girl."

"What?!"

Yes, she told me. Her name wasn't Jackie Jackson, it was Judy Dwyer. She was eighteen years old and on the way to Toronto to meet her boyfriend. She had cut her hair short and disguised herself as a boy so she wouldn't be hassled by truck drivers.

I was speechless. Here I was, sixteen years old, no experience with girls, and thrust into a bedroom in the middle of nowhere with someone who was presumably a nubile young woman. Before I could say a word, she picked up a towel, said, "I'm going to the bathroom," and was gone. When she got back, she said, "It's your turn," so off I went. When I got back, the room was in darkness and she was already in bed. I undressed, joined her, and after a few exploratory probes, I found that all she was wearing was a shirt and panties. But although I had a general idea, I really didn't know what I was looking for, where to find it, or what to do next. All I knew was that I was sixteen with lots of hormones. But that didn't help, for as soon as I crawled into bed she rolled over on her stomach and started snoring. Even for a neophyte like me, the message was clear.

Next morning when we went for breakfast, it was as though nothing had happened. She even took my little diary and in a crisp clear hand, recorded our journey of the previous day. She was still dressed in blue jeans, shirt, and cloth cap, and could quite easily pass for a boy. But now that I knew what she was, she was quite willing to talk about herself. However, the more she talked, the more I realized that she was just spinning me a wild story, either because I appeared to be so gullible or because she had a screw loose somewhere. She claimed she was a courier, carrying heroin from a dude ranch on the Ghost River in Alberta to her boyfriend in Toronto. She told me that the drugs had been delivered by another courier from Vancouver and she was taking them the rest of the way. As immature as I was, I knew it didn't make any sense. If she was a courier, why didn't she take a bus instead of facing the uncertainty of life on the road? What would her contacts think when she was out of touch for days at a time? And, most important, why would she be telling me all this, when all I had to do was to stop the closest Mountie and have her arrested? She was a nice girl and a good travelling companion but it was obvious she had mental problems of her own.

Then our luck seemed to change. We sat at the side of the road from 7:30 a.m. until noon without a ride. Plenty of passenger cars roared past us, but it was July 1st, Dominion Day, and the usual truckers were nowhere to be seen. It was as though Jackie's transformation to Judy had cast a spell over our previous good fortune. So we sat and talked, as the girl went on and on about her fictional life. I rather enjoyed it, as it sounded almost like a dime novel, and it certainly passed the time.

At noon, a trucker came down the road and when he saw us with our thumbs out, he stopped in a cloud of dust. He called out from his window, "I'll take the little lady, but that's all." It took Judy half a second to make up her mind. In spite of the fact that he had seen through her disguise, and in spite of the fact that he was a truck driver, she was fed up with sitting by the road. She waved me a hasty goodbye and, with a spin of the tires and a shower of gravel, the truck headed down the highway.

I sat there until evening without a ride and when I saw a Greyhound bus looming into view, I decided I had had enough. I waved it down, paid my fare to Winnipeg from my meagre holdings, and spent that night comfortably ensconced in my brother's house in West Kildonan.

I never saw the girl again, but there was a footnote to the story. Four years later, when I was with the *Edmonton Bulletin*, I went with police reporter Brud Delaney to see two Mounties from Regina who were staying at the Macdonald Hotel. They were involved in a drug education program, and when they invited Brud up for drinks, I went along. While we sat around swapping tales, I couldn't resist telling about my little incident with the so-called courier. Instantly, one of the Mounties became serious.

"What did she call herself?" he asked.

"Jackie Jackson."

He looked at his fellow officer. "That was the alias used by Judy Dwyer," he said.

"That's right," I said. "She told me that was her real name."

"You travelled with Judy Dwyer?"

"Sure."

"When she told you about the drugs, why didn't you tell the police?"

"Look," I said, "if a perfect stranger comes along and starts telling you about carrying heroin, are you going to believe them? I thought she was just stringing me a line."

The Mountie asked me to tell him everything I could remember. When I mentioned the dude ranch as a contact point, he said they had never heard of it. I said all this had happened four years ago and couldn't possibly be of any use, but he took notes anyway. He explained that the woman had been part of a major drug network and was well known to the authorities. So it turned out that everything she had told me had been absolutely true.

Wow!

During my short stay in Winnipeg, I couldn't find a job and ended up trying to sell encyclopaedias. I quit after a week with no sales and when I couldn't find anything else, I decided I'd better get back to my 30 cents an hour at Graydon's. This time I didn't try to hitchhike; my brother loaned me the money for bus fare.

My third foray into the unknown occurred just a year later when I was seventeen. This time I decided to hitchhike to Vancouver where my brother Bill lived. The trip west was relatively easy and my stay was quite pleasant. The return, however, had its share of adventures, including spending the night in a deserted wartime internment camp, and then meeting a mountain lion on the highway at 6 a.m. He looked at me and I looked at him. Not knowing what to do, I decided to do nothing. I propped up my duffle bag to use as a chair, and sat on it, and just watched. The mountain lion stood at the side of the road, looking at me while its tail moved in slow rhythm. At last it walked across the highway, went up a slope, and disappeared into the trees. Strangely enough, I wasn't the least bit scared. I was curious and cautious, but I really didn't see the animal as a threat. I remained where I was for another fifteen minutes, and then continued on my way.

I was dropped off at a mosquito-infested area at Kinbasket Lake on the top end of the Big Bend road, where I curled up against the wall of a shed, pulled a coat over my head, and tried to sleep. But it was hopeless. It was a warm night, and if I covered my head I suffocated, but if I left it uncovered, the mosquitoes tried to eat me alive. Over the next several hours, I must have moved a dozen times, walked around, futilely swatted at the attacking insects, and barely slept a wink. I was on the road about 4 a.m. and walked for three hours before I got a ride. I finally made it back to Edmonton and that ended my hitchhiking adventures.

By this time, from 1945 to 1947, I was a student at Strathcona High School. Living on the South Side, it was impractical for me to stay at McDougall High, so at the beginning of the next school term I had switched schools. I kept working for Graydon's, but now I left my bike at the store and went to and from work on the bus. In both years, I managed to have my last class of the day as a spare so I could slip away early. It was against the rules but I was never caught.

---

In general, my high school years were more memorable for what I didn't do than what I did. I didn't study; I didn't get good marks in the sciences; I didn't join any clubs; I didn't go to any dances or graduation exercises; and I didn't enjoy school. It has been said that our high school days can be the happiest of our lives. It didn't happen to me, or perhaps I should say I didn't let it happen to me. I seemed to have been driven by some unfathomable work ethic that grew out of my experiences in the Depression. Now that times were more prosperous, my father was working steady and all my brothers were gainfully employed as civil servants, yet there seemed to be an almost desperate need on my part to be sharing in these times. And it certainly wasn't for the money alone, for I spent most of it on junk food, stamps for my collection, art supplies, and other nonessentials. The little bit I saved was for Christmas presents and summer holidays.

The result was that I was a poor student. It would be easy to blame my parents for not being tougher on me, not forcing me to study and develop a positive attitude towards school, but I had only myself to blame. I had made up my mind that school was simply preventing me from getting on with my life, and I wanted it out of the way as soon as possible. After one year of Grade XII I was still far away from matriculating, but I announced to my family that I was going to quit and get a full-time job. I had always wanted to be an artist and now I would do so.

# 2

*Off to Work*

My decision to quit school came just a few days before the starting of the 1947–48 fall classes. Now that the die had been cast, I had to decide what to do next. There obviously were no jobs for apprentice portrait painters or fine artists, so my first step was to look in the yellow pages, where the only category which even came close to my goal was that of Sign Painters. So early on a Monday morning, I mounted my bicycle and began to make a tour of the paint shops in Edmonton. At each one I was either told there were no openings or to leave an application. Finally, I reached Artcraft Signs, just off Jasper Avenue on 102nd Street, and – lo and behold! – they needed a painter's helper. I was hired on the spot at a wage of $18 a week.

Artcraft was a typical sign shop. It did everything from billboards to gold leaf, from showcards to window displays. Initially, my task was to help build signs, undercoat and surface-coat them in readiness for the painters, and to do any infilling on large images. I also helped to build screens for silk screening, string canvas banners over streets, and install window displays. One time I even helped paint the backdrops for an Icecapades show at the Edmonton Gardens and worked all week in changing sets between shows.

My boss was Leo McKinnon but my mentor was Vic O'Neill. He voluntarily took on the task of teaching me the business and was extremely patient with me. He showed me how to hold a showcard brush between my thumb and finger so I could make smooth curves by giving it a gentle twirl. He taught me how to use round-ended pens for showcards and during quiet times he made me practise on sheets of old newspapers. He was, in my view, a real artist and had a well-deserved reputation of being one of the finest gold leaf specialists in the West. He not only did all of Artcraft's work in putting gold leaf signs on doctors' and lawyers' doors but he did subcontract work for other sign shops that lacked this skill. But what really impressed me was his ability to produce illuminated scrolls and presentation pieces. One time, I watched in fascination as he prepared a frontispiece for an ancient book owned by a Catholic order of nuns. Using gold leaf and his own mixture of oil paints, he created an illustrated page in gold, enamel, and ink which followed the ancient traditions of the Catholic Church.

Under Vic's tutelage I was soon given the task of producing cards for Kresge's department store. They had tabletop counters for most of their wares, and each section had a 1 x 4–inch card indicating the price. Every week, a hundred or more of these had to be produced with a round-ended pen. From there I graduated to laying out showcards and doing penwork, but not brush work. That Christmas, I was given the task of designing and installing a window display for Mike's News Stand. It consisted of a cutout Santa poised to climb down a chimney while in his pack were popular magazines of the day.

The guys at Artcraft were a great bunch to work with. The carpenter/painter was an old German who mixed his paint from white lead and was single-minded about the care and cleaning of brushes. A couple of sign painters, plus Vic, Leo, and I, rounded out the crew. I knew I had been accepted when one day I was sent to another shop to borrow their board stretcher. Leo explained that a completed sign was a little too small and had to be stretched to size. I didn't give the matter a second thought and went traipsing off to the other shop. The manager called to one of his men, asking where he'd put the board stretcher. He said he'd loaned it to a third shop, so I was sent there to pick it up. When that shop was in the process of sending me to yet a fourth place, I saw a flicker of amusement in the eyes of the manager and suddenly realized that I had been suckered. My common sense took over: how in hell can a board be stretched? I arrived back at Artcraft amid unbridled laughter from the entire staff and was needled about the incident for weeks after.

I was often sent to other shops to borrow things, as the sign painters seemed pretty friendly with each other. Usually it was a can of showcard paint or a special type of cardboard that was needed on a weekend or after the wholesalers were closed. One Saturday I heard my boss phoning around looking for some sheets of acetate used in silk screen work. He was obviously having no luck, and in desperation he phoned a shop which he normally ignored. After a short conversation, he called me over.

"Hugh, I want you to go to their shop and pick up some acetate. But be sure to look at it to make sure it isn't dried out. We've had some trouble with these guys in the past and I don't trust them."

With that caveat in mind, I went to the shop in question and found the acetate rolled up and waiting for me. Conscientiously, I peeled back the wrapping.

"What are you doing?" asked the manager.

"Oh," I said innocently, "I'm just checking to make sure the acetate's fresh."

He gave me a dirty looked and stomped into the back of the shop. The acetate was okay so I took it back to Artcraft and the incident was forgotten.

A couple of months later, in the spring of 1948, the boss informed us that our company had been sold and the new owner was waiting to interview us individually. When I went into the office, I saw it was the manager from the other shop.

"You're the smart ass kid who thought he was an expert on acetate," he snapped. Then, before I had a chance to explain, he added, "You're fired."

So there I was, less than a year into my illustrious career as an artist, out on the street. I knew there was no point in trying the other sign shops so I was at a loss as to what to do next. I considered going to Winnipeg or Vancouver to look for work, but my former boss, Leo McKinnon, talked me out of it. When I concurred, he wrote me a letter of reference in which he said, "I am very glad that you decided to sever your connections with the sign business. With your ability and competence, you certainly can achieve more in some other line. Talent like yours is wasted in this concern."[6] Those were nice words but they didn't put bread on the table.

— ⊗ —

One of my hobbies since about the age of seven had been stamp collecting. I had become something of a Canadiana specialist, was a member of the Edmonton Stamp Club, and really took the hobby seriously. One day when I was in Wevill's Rare Stamps, a shop facing the Macdonald Hotel, the owner offered me a job as clerk. I loved being around stamps, so I immediately accepted. And it was a fun job. Besides normal clerking duties, I helped evaluate collections, prepared first day covers, and made up nickel packets of stamps for beginners.

Harold Wevill was an interesting man. He was a war veteran, and the gossip was that he got his start by an incident which occurred during the liberation of Holland. I was told that he was in a tank that "accidentally" ran into a post office and somehow their stamps and money disappeared. I don't know if it was true, but Wevill seemed to have unlimited sets of fifteen stamps that made up the 1944–45 liberation issue, and piles of ten-guilder banknotes. Yet in all the months I worked there, I never saw him gyp a customer. More than once, someone came in with an old album with no idea of its value and his price was always fair. After he bought an album, he removed all the valuable stamps, then tossed the book onto a table where everything was two cents each. If the stamps were glued down, as many were, I had to tear the album part, soak off the stamps, and put them into stock books.

One time I saw a stamp which I thought might be valuable and pointed it out to the boss. "If it's on the two-cent table," he told me, "it's yours." Over the next several weeks I bought scads of nineteenth-century low-denomination stamps and quickly filled my tiny album. I bought three Suez Canal stamps which according to Scott's catalogue were very valuable; Wevill took one look at them and said, "They're fakes." I still have them and he was probably right. On another occasion, a hodge-podge collection contained two envelopes with bisected Canadian stamps on them. They weren't in the catalogue so again he pronounced them as fakes and again I bought them. Even today, some of my purchases probably aren't worth much more than I paid for them, but it was a lot of fun. Other stamps proved to be good investments but these weren't on the two-cent table. I was still getting a minimum wage of $18 a week, so I was limited in the number of good stamps I could buy. Yet I did develop my Canadian, Dutch, and Irish collections to a point where I could be proud of them.

Working at Wevill's was almost like being on a holiday, but like most holidays, it didn't last. Late in October 1948, Wevill told me I was through at the end of the month. I was shocked. I thought I had been doing a good job and he certainly needed the help. But it turned out to be my age, not my performance, that was the problem. On November 7th I would become eighteen years old and according to government regulations my minimum wage had to increase to $20 a week. He didn't feel he could pay the added amount, so twice in one year I found myself out of a job.

❦

Over the next few days, I checked the want ads and followed up anything that looked promising. I seemed to have put my creative juices on the back burner while I concentrated on simply getting a job. One of the ads that I answered was from Sun Life Insurance, which had offices at the corner of 101st Street and Jasper Avenue. I was pleased when I was called in for an interview and I must have made a reasonably good impression as I was contacted a couple of days later and told I was on the short list. My father was extremely pleased. If I couldn't get a government job like the rest of my brothers, at least I could get into something substantial like an insurance company.

When I went for my second interview, I was taken in to see the manager. He explained that if accepted, I would begin in the general office, writing policies, and eventually I would be directly involved in selling insurance. He said the field had been narrowed down to six candidates, of which I was one. After outlining the responsibilities of the position, he took me on a tour of the place. When we entered the general office, I saw row upon row of desks, people with their heads down, diligently writing or shuffling pieces of paper. Suddenly the whole scene came crashing down on me. It was as though I could see a chain strapping every clerk to his desk and someone standing over him to make sure he didn't smile or laugh. I just couldn't see myself in that situation, so I quietly excused myself and said I wasn't interested in the job. My father was furious. He couldn't understand how I could pass up a position which offered so much security and prospects for future advancement. He couldn't understand that I needed something which appealed to my imagination and sense of adventure. Maybe I didn't understand it myself, but I did know that I didn't want to spend my life being tied to an insurance desk.

A few days later I was walking somewhat despondently along Jasper Avenue when I met Vic O'Neill. He told me he had quit Artcraft Signs shortly after me and was now a reporter with the *Edmonton Bulletin*. Vic was quite a guy. Not only was he highly respected as a commercial artist, but he had the same reputation as a reporter. Somebody once called him a tramp reporter but I don't know if that was true or not. He was a loner with a drinking problem and might disappear without warning, then reappear and easily find work in either the newspaper or sign painting business. And he was a man with a heart of gold. When he learned that I was out of work, he took me to see the managing editor of the newspaper. They already had a copy boy but Vic convinced his boss they needed another one and so they hired me.

Sometime later, Vic quit the *Bulletin*, borrowed a packsack frame from me, and said he was heading for the Northwest Territories. I never heard from him again. My father, who was unhappy that I had taken such an insecure job as working for a newspaper, was also incensed that I had loaned my expensive pack frame to Vic. He didn't understand that I never expected to see it again and that I was so grateful to Vic for steering me into my new profession that I would have given him anything he asked for.

In all the years that I thought I wanted to be an artist, I had obviously misdirected my creativity. I was never a very good artist, but deep in my heart

I knew I wanted to create things. With my limited knowledge and experience, I thought that creativity meant being an artist. However, after I was with the *Bulletin* for only a few weeks I knew what I really wanted to be: a writer. My school marks in English grammar, my proficiency in spelling, and the fact that I had read virtually every book in the children's section of the Edmonton Public Library before I was a teenager had been clear signs of my literary interests, but I hadn't seen them. Now, by pure chance and the actions of a good friend, I was cast among people who wrote for a living.

My job of copy boy covered a multitude of duties. I arrived at 7 a.m., alighting from my bus at the Macdonald Hotel and walking east along Jasper Avenue to a point where it curved to follow the edge of the river bank. I passed Graydon's Drug Store, where the old apothecary jars still decorated the window. On my first day at work, I saw that the sidewalk had been swept clean, so I knew their new boy had either come in early, or old Mr. Miller had done it himself.

The *Edmonton Bulletin* was right at the bend in the road, on the south side of the avenue next to the Zenith Block. The advertising department was on the main floor, but to get to the newsroom, you had to go to a door near the east side of the building and mount a long flight of stairs to the upper floor. As you walked through the entrance, you stepped into the newsroom, which was a clutter of editors' desks, teletypes, and individual desks of the reporters. The women's department and sports department occupied the front area where the windows overlooked the street, while flanking the west side of the newsroom were doors leading to the managing editor's office, the provincial news room, and the morgue.

Out through the swinging doors at the back was the noise and organized chaos of the composing room, where linotype operators sat in front of their machines, typing lines and then casting them in hot lead. In the centre of the room were large metal tables, used to sort the lead slugs into pages, while nearby were the proofing presses, matrice makers, and proofreaders. One floor beneath them were the presses, which were built so close to the ceiling that a pressman had to bend over as he walked along the upper tier.

When I arrived in the morning, I sometimes had to step over a drunk sleeping in the doorway. On one occasion, the drunk turned out to be a tramp reporter, and when he later wandered into the newsroom, everyone seemed to know him. He worked on the rewrite desk for a couple of days and then disappeared again.

Once I opened up the newsroom, I grabbed a jug and went across the road to Fawn's Cafe to get a supply of coffee for the staff. Meanwhile the other copy boy, John Holinsky, began tearing the overnight output from the Canadian Press and British United Press teletypes. These he sorted and tossed into the appropriate baskets of the city editor, news editor, sports editor, and women's editor. By the time I got back with the coffee, the editorial staff was drifting in, the reporters writing up their late night assignments and the editors looking over the teletypes and the layouts for the morning edition.

For the next two or three hours, John and I were running back and forth to the composing room. As soon as an editor put something in the "out" basket, it was picked up and rushed to the composing room, where the foreman gave it to one of the linotype operators. As soon as something was set in type, a galley proof was made and either John or I rushed it to an editor's desk. Then another editor might call for a photograph from the morgue and one of us dashed off to tell librarian Mollie Stanger. All this time the teletypes kept churning out the stories and every once in a while a bell would ring to indicate something important was on the wire. Everything during those first hours was rush, rush, rush.

I went back and forth to Fawn's Cafe for coffee as often as necessary while John, who was older than me, sometimes visited the liquor store to make sure that our news editor, Bill Lewis, had his coffee cup filled with his favourite beverage. Another of our duties in the morning was to service the local bookmaker. I was told that the only reason we had a British United Press teletype was because it carried the race results from the United States. The *Bulletin* was owned by Max Bell of Calgary, and it was said the bookies dealt directly with him. In any case, when the morning scratches came in, one of us phoned them to the bookie, a swarthy man whom I knew only as John. If we couldn't get through because his lines were tied up, we had to deliver the scratches in person. Conveniently, his headquarters were right across the street next to Fawn's Cafe. To make a delivery, we rang a doorbell and stood so that we could be seen from the top of the stairs. We heard a click, opened the door, and went to the top of the stairs where another door, this one with a peep hole, stood open for us. Inside was a large room, with chairs piled on gambling tables for cleaning the floors.

During the rest of the day, every time race results came in, we had to phone them across to John. There was a tacit understanding among the editors that this service took precedence over everything, even if we were sitting on a deadline. The bell on the teletype rang for every race result, and as soon as we heard it, Holinsky or I would drop everything and rush to phone the results. The bookmaker gave us a tip of five dollars for our services from time to time, which was a nice bonus over and above my pay of $85 a month.

Our managing editor was Reg Hammond, who left a few weeks after my arrival and was replaced by Len Tilley, followed by Alex Janusitis. Bill Lewis was the news editor, Charlie MacFarlane the city editor, and his wife Dolores the women's editor. When Charlie left, he was replaced by Ken Liddell. Stan Moher was the sports editor and Eric Bland the chief photographer. At any one time, the editorial department had a staff of about thirty, but because of low wages there was a frequent turnover.

I soon discovered that if one didn't mind the wages, their rise at the *Bulletin* could be meteoric. Shortly after my arrival I expressed an interest in writing, and before the end of 1948 I was doing obituaries and minor rewrites of press releases. Then, after being on the job for less than two months, I was permitted to cover the annual meeting of the Edmonton Stamp Club, of which I was a member. The published item – my first – appeared in the January 3, 1949, issue of the *Bulletin*.

A week later, I was sent to cover a speech that Mayor Harry Ainlay was giving on the future of the oil industry, and the experience terrified me. I don't know why I was chosen to go – likely no one else was available – but I knew this was something usually handled by a senior reporter. After the meeting, I came back to the office and wrote a 300-word account of the mayor's speech and put it into the city editor's "In" basket. Next morning, as I pursued my normal duties as copy boy, I kept a close eye on my story. When at last Charlie MacFarlane picked it up, I expected him to call me over and tell me to redo it. Instead, he simply glanced at it, wrote a head, "Ainlay Traces City Growth" and tossed it into the "Out" basket.

Oh no, I said to myself, he didn't read it! He didn't know it was written by his inexperienced copy boy! I'm gonna get fired! In a daze, I took the item to the composing room and later brought back the galley proof. Again I expected the city editor to fix it up before it actually went into the paper. But he didn't and later that day, January 13th, there it was in black and white for everyone to see. I waited for the inevitable explosion, but none came. The managing editor didn't roar over to the city desk demanding to know who had written that terrible article, and no one called from the mayor's office demanding a retraction. Gradually I relaxed and later in the day I even got up enough nerve to read the article. Not bad, I finally concluded, not bad at all.

A week later, I got my first byline for a story on a school operetta, and so it went. During the day I was a copy boy and occasionally after hours I was a cub reporter, covering stories relating to schools, art classes, and winter carnivals. In the summer of 1949, I took on the added duties of being a liaison between the editorial and advertising departments. It was a bottom-of-the-barrel assignment but one which I embraced with enthusiasm. Whenever a new company opened for business, the advertising department tried to sell a page of congratulatory ads and a portion of the page was left for a so-called "news" story about the opening. Over the summer and autumn I waxed eloquent upon the merits of such firms as Avenue Furniture, Marr's Fashions, Nu-Way Cleaners, and Milky Way milk bar.

I was still willing to do more so I was given the task of writing so-called "reviews" of upcoming movies. I never saw the shows; I just did rewrites from their press releases and wrote captions for the glossy photographs they provided. Besides these assignments were the ever-present obituaries, club meetings, and minor rewrites. And as with Artcraft Signs, Vic O'Neill was there to help me during my first months. He taught me the pyramid style of writing where one put most of the essential facts into the opening sentences, i.e., the top of the pyramid. As the story progressed, the information became more voluminous but less important. This style had two advantages: if readers lost interest after the first paragraph, they still got the essentials, and if the article was too long, an editor could lop it off anywhere at the bottom and not lose anything important.

I also learned that the opening sentence – which was often a paragraph in itself – had to be as dramatic, pithy, and fact-loaded as possible. Often, that first sentence was the hardest part of the whole article to write. Another lesson was conciseness. One time I wrote an article and Vic told me to take it back to my typewriter and cut it by one third. I found this to be difficult, for all my words seemed like pearls of wisdom. But at last I succeeded and proudly returned it to him. He looked it over briefly and told me to go back and cut it by another third. I protested. He insisted. And he was right. I struggled over the piece, concluded that my words weren't as sacrosanct as I believed, and in its final form the article was far better than the original submission.

———— ❧ ————

Late in 1949, at the age of nineteen, I was officially promoted from copy boy to reporter soon after Ken Liddell took over as city editor. I was given the weather beat, which sometimes was as little as writing a daily summary of local temperatures or as much as doing major stories on storms and weather conditions. I also did the travel guide, which was a daily schedule of trains, aircraft, and highway conditions. To that, Liddell later added the hotel beat, which meant daily tours of the Macdonald and other leading hotels to see if anyone important was in town. And for the first time, my bylines identified me as a "*Bulletin* Staff Writer" as I covered such stories as Christmas mail pileups, hibernating bears, and the Robbie Burns night at the Macdonald Hotel.

But bylines are funny things. On January 2, 1950, in addition to my other duties I started to write a daily children's column, and even though I produced some 130 columns of 700 to 800 words each, no one ever knew who I was. A couple of years earlier, the *Bulletin* had started the Tawasi Club, where children could get membership cards and badges and have their names published on their birthdays. The main activity of the club was to offer crossword puzzles, pictures to colour, a locally written children's story, and the syndicated children's columns Uncle Wiggly or Burgess Bedtime Stories. The idea had been the brainchild of Edith McLellan, a mother of three who wrote under the pseudonym of Ruth Barry. Early in 1949, she left and was replaced by Eleanor Page, who wrote under her own name for less than three months before she was replaced.

At this point, the editors felt that these changes were having a detrimental effect on the continuity of the Tawasi Club, so they opted for the generic name of "Joan Walker" for all future columnists. During the rest of 1949, a couple of people were involved in writing the stories and at the beginning of 1950, I officially became Joan Walker.

Over a period of time, the Club became little more than the daily column and birthday greetings in a corner of the comic page. In April 1950 it was reduced to three times a week, alternating with a Whipper Watson Safety Club column written by Edmonton sportsman Tiger Goldstick. I continued to write the Tawasi Club column until the end of August 1950, at which time I was promoted and the whole club was discarded in favour of a crossword puzzle.

When I look back over my old scrapbooks, I can see that the experience as Joan Walker was good for me, not just in writing but in learning how to do research. I started off with Aesop's fables, then haunted the public library searching for good children's stories. But my best source proved to be a children's illustrated encyclopaedia I had bought at an auction sale when I was about thirteen. All ten volumes were picked up for 25 cents, and I had a devil of a time carrying them home in the basket of my bike. But they were now a godsend, providing information on the origin of names of months, Egyptian hieroglyphics, Roman ruins, discovery of tea in China, and a host of other assorted data.

But as time went along, I became more and more interested in local stories and Indian legends. Even as a child, local scenes captivated me. Hunting birds with a bow and arrow, imagining myself back in the "buffalo days," and feeling a sense of the past while working for Graydon's Drug Store, all evoked within me a romantic feeling about the past. I wrote about such topics as Alberta place names, an Indian battle at Fort Edmonton, the formation of the North-West Mounted Police, and adventures of Father Lacombe and other missionaries. In the field of mythology, I used such authors as George Bird Grinnell, Diamond Jenness, and John Maclean to tell Blackfoot stories of Scar Face, the girl who married the Morning Star, and others.

My writing style for these columns was somewhat cloying at times, and I also did quite a bit of moralizing. For example, I wrote, "It's wrong to suppose the early Indians of Canada were cruel and hated all white men. They had been moulded by conditions in the forests and were superstitious of anything unusual. They were never guilty of low or mean vices and before the coming of the white man with his 'firewater,' they had quite a high sense of morality."[7]

The beauty of writing this column was that I had a completely free hand. None of the editors bothered to read it, and my copy went straight to the composing room. Mind you, if I had ever strayed beyond my mandate, I would have soon heard of it. But over the months, as I became more and more aware of Canada's Indians and their problems, my columns (or rather Joan Walker's) reflected this interest.

Like most writers, I promised myself I would get a dozen or so columns ahead but I never did. Hours before a deadline, I would be rushing around, looking for a topic and dashing off my short essay. This work was in addition to my regular duties as a reporter but I loved it.

During this time, I mixed with an interesting bunch of fellows. Probably the most outrageous were Stan Burke and John McLean, who lived in a basement apartment which they called "The Towers." They were wild, irreverent, and the most likeable pair that one could ever hope to meet. Once, one of them (I won't say which) was invited to a swank garden party in the West End. As a guest he brought a hooker whose social conversation was limited to shop talk. Needless to say, he wasn't invited back. Also, Burke was probably a better cartoonist than many of those who supplied the *Bulletin*. Satirical and humorous, his drawings graced the walls of the newsroom and two even found their way into my personal collection. One shows Burke entering a maternity delivery room with a plumber's helper in his hand while nearby a nurse says, "A difficult case. Dr. Burke, the specialist, is being called in."

All in all the *Bulletin* news staff were a great bunch. The newspaper was far behind the *Edmonton Journal* in circulation, so to sell papers everything was done to make it bright, cheery, and sensational. About this time, for example, the *Journal* placed wooden seats at bus stops; they were painted dull green and inscribed "Rest and Read the Journal." The *Bulletin* responded with wood and concrete seats, painted bright orange, and inscribed "Wide Awake People Read the *Bulletin*." That reflected the competitive, upbeat attitude of the *Bulletin* and its staff.

Jack DeLong, with the face of a prizefighter, was just as pugnacious in his daily column "On the Town." Brud Delaney was the police reporter, while Harlo Jones was our specialist on the rapidly expanding oil industry. Spud Murphy covered the city hall beat, Jim Sherbaniuk the university, and Ted Horton the legislature. Others such as Eunice Hoffman, Pat McVean, Paul Hurmuses, Don Flach, Art Etter, Ivers Kelly, and Don Travis were general reporters or had their own beats. In the sports department were a bunch of jocks, including Jim Algeo, Ernie Fedoruk, Jim McCurdy, and the loudest of the bunch, Dick Beddoes.

Those reporters who worked on Saturdays often gathered in the managing editor's office after he had gone home and spent the afternoon drinking and swapping stories. To me, the room had a nice atmosphere, as all the walls were taken up with books and huge volumes of the back issues of the paper. It was as though we were surrounded by history. People came and went during the afternoon, and by evening the diehards retired to Fawn's Cafe or to one of the Chinese restaurants on 97th Street.

I had never been much of a drinker, but while at the *Bulletin* I acquired a taste for rye and Madame Brizzard's blackberry brandy. The Saturday afternoon sessions usually centred upon rye or scotch. In later years, one of the editors told me I looked like a scared fifteen-year-old when I started at the *Bulletin*, instead of a worldly eighteen-year-old. But she also said that after a year, I looked my age, which says something about life at the *Bulletin*.

One of my duties as copy boy had been to make deliveries and pickups from our engraving plant, which was located about four blocks away. There I became good friends with Ed Jackson, the engraver, and spent a lot of my spare time there. I learned quite a bit about the engraving business at a time when everything was shot on zinc plates which had been covered with dragon's blood and then etched in acid. Next door was the *Bulletin's* photo lab under

Eric Bland, who immediately impressed me with his red MG sports car. I got to know the other photographers, Chuck Ross, Bud Dixon, Laddie Ponich, and Danny Scott, and later worked with Chuck Ross when I was with the Alberta government.

I was still painfully shy and although I had had two or three girlfriends during my high school years, there had been nothing serious. At the *Bulletin*, I found female companionship in the waitresses at Fawn's Cafe. One shift ended at 7 p.m. and I would sometimes take a girl to a movie but more often I was able to get free tickets from the Sports Department for boxing or wrestling matches. If I had an extra ticket, I would give it to my brother Glen. In later years, Glen said he went to the matches as much to find out what kind of a woman I was bringing as to see the show itself. I know that some of them were pretty tough but I was still a very innocent youth.

Interestingly, I never went out with the same girl more than two or three times and in most cases our relationship seldom got beyond a goodnight kiss. I suspect they were all much more experienced than me and were wise enough to understand that I was too shy to be much of a threat. I guess I was something of a change from the usual guys who tried to pick them up.

Four waitresses stand out in my mind – Beryl Black, Marie Trembley, and two others whom I recall only as Ann and Marg. One evening, Ann and I left Fawn's and were en route to the Dreamland Theatre when a man jumped out of an alley and pointed a knife at me. He told me I was stealing his girl. Before I had time to act (I don't know what I would have done), Ann lit into him with a tongue that was far sharper than his blade. She backed him right into the alley and although I didn't hear exactly what she said, I do know he took off like a frightened rabbit.

"That was my old boyfriend," she said, matter-of-factly. "We split up."

"What are we going to do now?" I asked.

"Why," she said, "let's go to the show, of course." And we did. I must confess that I was looking over my shoulder when I walked her home, and we never went out again.

Marg was a waitress who told me that she hated her work; she wanted to be a stenographer but couldn't afford to take a typing course. She was a farm girl and none of the commercial courses had been available at her one-roomed school. So I got a bright idea. During evenings after work we went into the business office of the *Bulletin*, where I gave her typing lessons. We became quite good friends, and although she had the best of intentions of bettering herself, I found she simply didn't have the necessary education. After about a week, Marg realized this herself and was more disheartened than if she had never tried. A short time later, she told me she was going back to her parents' farm. Perhaps that was best, as the life of a waitress so close to notorious 97th Street could be dangerous for an impressionable young girl.

Beryl, on the other hand, was quite a hard case. We saw a couple of sporting events together and sometimes went to the Bulletin's engraving plant to drink beer. But like other dates, it lasted for only a short time.

As for Marie Trembley, that was a whole different story. Early in 1950 I dated her a few times and then moved off to other fields. In April, when the *Bulletin* carried a story about a woman named Marie Smith being arrested for the murder of a Chinese merchant, I didn't think anything of it, but when I saw her picture in the paper I knew it was Marie Trembley. According to press reports, Marie had innocently stopped to buy groceries and was attacked by the merchant. She resisted and stabbed him nineteen times. At this time she was living about a mile away and did not seem to know the man, yet when I knew her she roomed less than a quarter of a block from the store and must have shopped there. Anyway, she was found not guilty.

# 3

# The Indian Association of Alberta

A simple action or event can change the whole direction of a person's life. That's what happened to me on February 4, 1950. The previous day, city editor Ken Liddell had called me over to his desk and handed me a piece of paper.

"The Indian Association of Alberta is having an executive meeting at the Bissell Institute tomorrow," he said. "I want you to cover it." Glancing at the paper, I saw the message had been sent by a man named John Laurie, secretary of the organization. Thinking that I might save myself the trouble of actually attending the Saturday meeting, I looked in the Edmonton telephone book for John Laurie's number to see if I could interview him over the phone; it wasn't there. I also checked for the Indian Association of Alberta, and had no luck. I phoned the Bissell Institute but they knew nothing about the organization, other than that its members were from out of town. Reluctantly, I concluded that I had no option but to actually go.

When I got to the meeting on Saturday afternoon, I was immediately impressed by two things. One was a group of Indians conducting a meeting along strictly business lines and following all the parliamentary forms of procedure. The other was a beautiful girl sitting in the front row. The Indians were dressed in a variety of garb. Most had business suits with vests; others wore jeans, woollen shirts, and mackinaw coats. Some of the women had kerchiefs and wore moccasins. At the front of the room was a table where a white man was busy writing, while beside him was a tall, distinguished man who was conducting the meeting. Later, I learned that these were secretary John Laurie, a Calgary schoolteacher, and president James Gladstone, a Blood Indian farmer.

I was told that the Indian Association of Alberta (IAA) had been formed some years earlier but had been reorganized in 1944 to make it a province-wide political organization. Its purpose was to address many of the problems facing Indian people as a result of policies of the federal Department of Indian Affairs and the Alberta government. The executive meeting had been called in Edmonton to discuss changes to the Indian Act which were being contemplated in Ottawa. The revisions were being made without consultation with the Indians and fears were expressed that the new legislation would be even more repressive than the old, and that Native concerns would not be considered.

As the day wore on, I became a convert to the Indian rights movement. I heard stories about traditional hunting rights being violated, fishing nets seized, and the failure of the federal government to listen to Indian concerns about education and health. During a break, I interviewed George McLean, a Stoney Indian who was better known to tourists as Walking Buffalo. He told me how he had gone to the Methodist orphanage at Morley in 1880, and then went away to learn the trade of carriage maker before returning to his reserve to become its chief. He told me, "The Indian has been taken away from the things that are familiar to him – the forests, steams, and life on the plains. He is taken into a world of trains, automobiles, airplanes and television, and must learn to live in this new life."[8]

The meeting was conducted in English but translated into Cree, Blackfoot, and Stoney for the benefit of the older members. I watched as people such as Dave and Daisy Crowchild, Joe Bull Shield, Peter Burnstick, Mark Steinhauer, and Frank Cardinal rose to address the meeting, little realizing that they would later become my good friends. At the same time, I kept an eye on the gorgeous girl in the front row and, while it may not have been love at first sight, I was certainly attracted to her.

When the meeting was over, I introduced myself to John Laurie, who greeted me with warmth and enthusiasm. He was fully aware of the importance of the press in the association's battle with the government and was pleased when I offered to help in any way that I could. While we were talking, he introduced me to the president, who in turn took me over to meet his wife and his daughter, Pauline. She was the lovely girl in the front row. I had only a few moments with her to learn that she worked for the Edmonton Indian Agency, then I was called away by John Laurie and introduced to other delegates. The next time I looked, she was gone.

I left that meeting full of enthusiasm, and even today I cannot explain why. My association with Indians until that time had been virtually nil. When I was about nine, my father had been a clerk at the Edmonton Indian Agency at Winterburn for a few weeks and came to know a few of the people there. In later years, they sometimes came to our house to sell firewood or fish, but

I never took any particular notice. And during the months I had been writing the children's column, I had included some Indian legends, but these seemed no more important than my columns on sea serpents and Japanese flowers.

The possible explanations are twofold. First, as I sat in the meeting, I saw people with limited education and limited finances who were utterly devoted to their cause. Yet in spite of their years of mistreatment, they weren't a bunch of wild-eyed radicals, but men and women who followed all the rules and procedures of Canadian justice. But not only were they not receiving Canadian justice, they weren't even getting a hearing. This seemed grossly unfair. Also, I was drawn to the president's daughter, and one way to get to know her would be through the Indian association.

For the next several weeks, it was business as usual for me, providing daily reports of Edmonton's weather conditions and writing news stories on everything from blind bowlers to Boy Scout awards. Then, early in May, I read that a Blood Indian artist named Gerald Tailfeathers was having an exhibition at the Edmonton Museum of Arts. I thought there was a chance that Pauline Gladstone might attend so I went to the opening and, sure enough, there she was. I found out later that she had gone to St. Paul's Indian residential school with both Gerald and his wife Irene, and they were close friends.

I introduced myself to the Tailfeathers but monopolized the attention of Pauline. And the more I talked to her, the more I liked her. I was just getting up enough nerve to ask her for a date when she suddenly saw that Irene and Gerald were leaving. Without even a goodbye she scurried away like a scared rabbit. She told me in later years that she was terrified that her friends were going to leave her with "that white man."

―――∞∞∞―――

Early in June, I received a letter from John Laurie, inviting me to attend the annual meeting of the Indian Association on the Blood Reserve. I already had made plans to take a week's holiday about that time so that Ed Jackson and I could hunt for the Lost Lemon gold mine. We had read all the available literature on the subject, and after scanning a number of maps, we decided to search in the Mist Mountain region, west of High River. So I made arrangements with Ed to meet me in Waterton Park after the two-day meeting was over.

On the morning of June 8th, I caught the slow train to Calgary, stopping at every small town and milk run along the way. I was armed with my trusty duffle bag, pencil, pocketful of copy paper, and Laurie's letter giving directions to the Blood community hall. I transferred to another train at Calgary and by the time I arrived in Macleod, it was already late in the evening. The railway station was about a half mile from town so I took a room in a dingy hotel close to the station. And dingy it was. The door to my room had been smashed so many times that it could barely close and for some reason, the bottom had been cut off almost a foot from the floor. To add to the decor, it had been painted orange. I heard a few drunks during the night but I had a good sleep and next morning I began to search for a way to get to the Blood Reserve. I had expected some form of bus service to be running between Macleod and Cardston, but there was none. While I was pondering my next move, I noticed that a large truck filled with Indians had stopped at a restaurant. When I enquired, I learned they were a delegation of Crees from Hobbema who were on their way to the meeting and were glad to give me a lift.

I climbed into the box with the others and found a handy corner where I could stretch my legs. Beside me was a man named Soosay who was suffering from a severe toothache. The only way he could get relief was to jam the point of a safety pin into the cavity and hold it there. He was in agony every time the truck hit a bump on the gravelled road but once he got to the Blood Reserve, a local dentist extracted the rotten molar.

I couldn't see much as we travelled, as clouds of dust swirled up into the dry summer air. I felt us bump across a couple of bridges and sensed we were on the reserve, but the landmarks would have meant nothing to me, even if I could have seen them. At last the truck rolled quietly onto a grassy field and the dust disappeared. As I struggled to my feet, I saw that we were parked beside an old World War II army building which had been converted into a community hall. But that wasn't what impressed me. The image which became indelibly imprinted on my mind was that of a dozen or more young men playing softball in front of the hall. I would swear that every one of them seemed six feet tall, slim, muscular, and built like Apollo. Heretofore, my impression of Indians had been based on the few I had seen on the streets of Edmonton – mostly short, nondescript, and dissipated. These ballplayers were handsome, cleared-eyed men who personified the James Fenimore Cooper image of the "noble savage." Some had braids and wore cowboy boots or running shoes. They were laughing and calling out to each other in Blackfoot as the game progressed.

The hall was in the bottom of Bullhorn Coulee and around it were scattered the white tents of delegates who would be camping there for two days. A whole row of saddle horses were tethered beside the hall, while farther away were wagons, buckboards, hay racks, trucks, and cars. Obviously every kind of transportation available was pressed into service.

Inside the hall, I renewed acquaintances with John Laurie and Mr. and Mrs. Gladstone. Unknown to me, Pauline and the postal service had kept her family up to date on what was happening with "that *Bulletin* reporter," so they took a special interest in me. I think they suspected that my interest in their daughter was more than just a passing fancy. Anyway, they took me in tow and when they learned I had no place to stay, they invited me to their farm for the night. As I was living out of my duffle bag and had made absolutely no plans beyond the moment, I was glad to accept.

John Laurie had hoped to have a draft of the new Indian Act in hand before the meeting, but as it had not yet been tabled in the House of Commons, this was not possible. Instead, the association passed three major resolutions in anticipation of what the legislation might contain. It came out strongly against the right to vote, individual land allotment, and involuntary withdrawal of Indian status. At first, opposition to the right to vote puzzled me, until Laurie explained that Indians viewed it as the thin edge of the wedge. If they were given the vote, the next step of the government would be to introduce taxation and to take away their legal rights as Indians.

Other resolutions came from individual reserves, sometimes dealing with local problems but often broaching broader issues such as hunting and fishing rights, and the need for Indian-controlled traplines. An angry outburst came from one delegate who had been told that old age pensions for Indians would be limited to eight dollars a month because they weren't taxpayers. "We Indians were the owners of Canada before the white man came," he explained. "Even the mineral rights were ours, but we got nothing for them. So, in that sense, we have already paid our taxes."[9]

I wrote a long article and a number of sidebars on the meeting which Laurie later praised as being "a piece of fine factual reporting."[10] Meanwhile, I struck up friendships with Dave Crowchild, Percy Creighton, Peter Burnstick, and a number of other delegates. At the end of the first day, the Gladstones invited me to stay over and attend church services at the Indian residential school.

That proved to be another interesting experience. As we left the farm, I could see the residential school tucked into the rolling foothills a couple of miles away, while behind it was the rugged range of the Canadian Rockies. And dominating the skyline was the distinctive mass of Chief Mountain. As we approached the school we passed under a wooden archway and parked near the huge three-storey brick structure. Around it were well-kept lawns, flower gardens, and pathways. A short distance to the north was the white wooden church, its steeple projecting into the blue summer sky. Quite a number of the parishioners had been at the IAA meeting so I didn't feel like a stranger. All the students had to attend church, and again I was impressed by the handsome boys and attractive girls from the Blood tribe. After services, the principal, Canon Samuel Middleton, showed me around and introduced me to the staff. And when I met an attractive teacher named Jenny Fraser, I must confess that I monopolized her during most of the teatime. I found out later that Pauline learned all about "the reporter and the teacher" long before I got back to Edmonton. On the tour, I saw the classrooms, play rooms, kitchens, and rectory; the whole place impressed me as spotlessly clean, institutional, and drab.

After church, the Gladstones drove me to Waterton, where they were going for a picnic, and there I met *Bulletin* engraver Ed Jackson. We toured along the foothills for a couple of days and then made a futile attempt to look for the Lost Lemon mine. We got past the Sentinel ranger station and followed a trail up the Highwood River, but we soon realized that we would have to walk a greater distance than we had anticipated. We cached the car and plodded westward, panning in the various streams that ran into the Highwood. In the evening, we pitched our war surplus tent and had a good feast of bacon and beans before settling down for the night. We had been told there were plenty of bears in the area so I took the precaution of stashing our food high up in a nearby tree. As I was doing this, Jackson was doing the dishes. When I came back to the camp, the aroma of bacon was heavy in the air.

"Where's that smell coming from?" I asked.

"Oh," said Jackson, "I dumped the bacon fat on the fire."

"On the fire?! The smell will attract every bear within ten miles!"

I had a restless night as the bacon odour seemed to hang heavy in the mountain air, but no bears visited us. Next morning, with Mist Mountain shrouded in the distance, we did some more panning and found absolutely nothing. We discussed going deeper into the mountains, but somehow we knew that if the Lost Lemon mine really existed, it wasn't anywhere near Mist Mountain. So we abandoned the search and simply enjoyed camping until it was time to go back to work.

That summer was one of the most enjoyable I ever experienced. I now had several good friends at the *Bulletin* and spent most of my spare time with them. Often it was nothing more than an extended coffee break at Fawn's, but at other times we haunted Chinatown or took in the local sights. One memorable evening consisted of visiting a small carnival to play games and go on the rides while drinking Cointreau and using beer as a chaser. With that mixture, I had enough sense to stay off the Ferris wheel. On another occasion, I went with Stan Burke, John McLean, Jim Sherbaniuk, Brud Delaney, and several others to spend the weekend in Jasper. It was late in the season and most of the camps were closed, so we ended up in tents near Pyramid Mountain. That was the time when McLean taught me a lesson in gambling. He had just finished a bottle of rye, holding it upside down until the last drop was drained.

"Do you think this bottle is empty?" he asked me.

"Sure."

"Is there any more whisky in it?" he asked, handing me the bottle. I looked at it. The whisky had been drained.

"It's empty," I said.

"Would you give me a dollar for every drop I got out of the bottle if I promised to give you five dollars if it's empty?"

"Sure," I said confidently, "that's easy money."

All this time the bottle had been sitting in an upright position. "Then you'd lose," he said. Tipping the bottle, several drops came quickly and then slowed down, but I counted ten of them.

"I guess I owe you ten bucks," I said.

"No," he said. "I was just trying to show you something. If someone wants to make a bet with you, ask yourself why. It could be a sucker bet, like this one." It was a lesson I never forgot.

———⚬⚬⚬———

Back at the *Bulletin*, the city editor asked me in July if I wanted to cover a religious pilgrimage to Lac Ste. Anne. I still had no car of my own, but the photographer assigned to accompany me had wheels so I was glad to go. I hoped I might meet some of the Indians I had visited at the association meeting. However, the pilgrims turned out to be a completely different bunch, strong Catholics with little or no interest in politics. Almost all were Cree speakers and the majority were Metis, rather than treaty Indians. I interviewed a family that had travelled three days by wagon to attend the services, but other than that, the pervasiveness of Catholicism was so overwhelming that I felt completely out of place.

Upon my return to Edmonton, I was sent to cover a fair in St. Paul and to write feature stories on Camrose and Stony Plain. I didn't know it at the time, but I was being tested to see if a city boy could effectively cover the rural beat.

I must have succeeded, for in the first week of August 1950, I was promoted to the position of Provincial Editor. This gave me the sole responsibility for a daily page of rural news, an occasional bylined column entitled "Country Club," and a retinue of correspondents to keep happy. And this pleased me, if for no other reason than my salary increased to $200 a month, a far cry from the $85 I had received twenty months earlier as a copy boy. Also, I was flattered when the managing editor told me that at the age of twenty I was the youngest editor on a daily newspaper in Canada.

One of my first tasks was to review the list of correspondents from various parts of our marketing area. There were about fifty, but when I examined their accounts, I found that some of them were virtually dormant, having submitted nothing during the previous six months. Also, when I checked the list against the towns and villages of area, I discovered there were many important centres which were unrepresented.

Correspondents were local teachers, administrators, housewives, and others who were prepared to gather news for the *Bulletin* and be paid by the inch for whatever we published. Some had a real eye for the news while others couldn't see beyond social teas and Boy Scout meetings. Over the next few weeks, I began a letter-writing campaign, asking the dormant correspondents if they wanted to continue, and seeking new representatives in towns not currently covered. One undertaking which ultimately had dramatic results was my attempt to gain correspondents in the far north. When I took over, we had only two northern representatives, a clergyman in Aklavik and an office worker in Yellowknife. Considering Edmonton to be the "gateway to the north," I added such places as Upper Hay River, Lower Hay River, Fort Norman, Fort Smith, Fort Resolution, Atikameg, and Fort Chipewyan.

I still have a few letters from the correspondents, as they opened a strange new world for me. For example, Joseph Hyde wrote from Fort Resolution that mink were selling for $50 a pelt and that "this wave of prosperity saved many a hard trek by dog team to attend Midnight Mass here on Xmas, and chartered airplane flights were not uncommon from Snowdrift, Roche River, etc."[11] Jennie Wright wrote from Atikameg, "We are really an isolated community, 60 miles from the railway. Our only link with the outside world is a very bad trail through muskeg country."[12] She went on to describe the problems in trying to travel over corduroy roads and through virtually impassable mudholes.

But by far the most interesting correspondence came from Mrs. Alicia Humphries, a teacher at Fort Chipewyan. She admitted that she wanted to be a writer and sent graphic descriptions of life in the north. In a 4,000-word diary essay – impossible to publish in a newspaper – she told about the people and conditions that she had encountered during her first two months at the village. This included the arrival of the caribou herds, which she described as follows:

> *November 1* – The caribou came to-day, hundreds of them. Small bunches from the big herd ran right through the village. My students went almost wild when about twenty of these animals ran right in front of the school. I could not have kept them in if I had wanted to....
>
> *November 4* – The caribou are still "running" but not quite so close to the village now. They say now there are thousands, but people are not supposed to kill more than they need and not to feed caribou meat to the dogs...
>
> *November 6* – The Mountie's wife was out with her binoculars to get a good look at those marching on the lake when, to her utter surprise, about thirty came in sight over a little rise and raced directly for her, the village dogs after them. The small herd was thoroughly frightened. The Mountie's wife turned and ran screaming toward her home which was no great distance away. Her husband and his aide ran out when they heard the screams and then the caribou swerved sufficiently to miss the terror-stricken woman.[13]

These northern contacts really paid off during the autumn and winter. In fact, during the month of September I seemed to be writing as much for the front page as for the rural page. It started when the correspondent at Rycroft, in the Peace River area, wired me that a tornado had struck the town. With that information and telephone interviews, my writing was on the front page of the *Bulletin* for the first time, under a banner headline "Tornado Hits North District of Rycroft." A week later, our correspondent at Elk Point told us that Francis Moocheweines, a Cree Indian from Frog Lake, had murdered his sister-in-law and was the subject of a manhunt. I was quickly on the phone to the RCMP and local people to find out what was happening. Luckily I was already becoming acquainted with Native life and questioned people in the community when they kept referring to Moocheweines as a "breed," and to all the people at Frog Lake as "breeds." When I pressed them, they admitted these people lived on an Indian reserve, but from their own discriminatory viewpoint, they were still "breeds." I kept track of the story but it ended tragically when the heavily armed fugitive committed suicide.

A week after that, I received a call from Newbrook, a town a hundred miles north of Edmonton, that their town was being threatened by a forest fire. We determined that our rival, the *Edmonton Journal*, knew nothing about the occurrence, so the newspaper went all out. I was assigned to accompany Stan Burke in a light aircraft which the *Bulletin* chartered for the trip. As we approached the town from the south, we could see flames surrounding it on three sides, the closest not more than a few dozen yards away. There was no airstrip so the pilot set the plane down in an open field on the south side of town.

For the next three or four hours, Burke took photographs of the fire and the work of local volunteers, while both of us interviewed the locals. Burke decided that I should fly back with the photographs and notes while he would stay overnight to be on hand in case the town had to be evacuated.

That's when I became an item of news on the front page of the *Bulletin*. The story began, "*Bulletin* provincial editor Hugh Dempsey and pilot Jim Radford escaped injury yesterday when their plane crashed in an attempted takeoff."[14] I had climbed into the single-wing aircraft and relaxed as it taxied down the bumpy field. Then the pilot revved the engine, roared ahead, and had just barely cleared the ground when one wheel hit a clump of earth. It spiralled the plane around, snapped the undercarriage, then damaged a wing and the propeller before coming to rest. Neither of us was hurt and the only thought that went through my head as the plane was spinning around was how was I going to get back to the *Bulletin*? The solution was simple. I had been an able hitchhiker in my teens, so now was the time to test my skills. On the edge of town I was picked up by a salesman who had come to look at the fire. Two other rides brought me into Edmonton just after midnight and in plenty of time for the morning edition.

As a result of that little adventure, I concluded that the average person never experiences more than one plane crash in their lifetime, and I already had mine. In succeeding years I travelled by jet, large and small propeller craft, and helicopter, and seldom worried. And my philosophy came sharply back to me many years later in Newfoundland when I had a chance to enter any one of three aircraft waiting on the tarmac. I chose the first one and it took off safely. The second one crashed and all aboard were killed.

---

The rest of September was taken up with other news, including a suspected arson north of High Prairie, a new gas well at Meeting Creek, and the announcement of construction of the Valleyview highway. But probably my most "creative" story came in December when I received a 55-word radiotelegram from a new correspondent at Hay River, at the south end of Great Slave Lake. It simply stated that four fishermen in a Bombardier had gone through the ice at Caribou Point and two had drowned. On the basis of this, I wrote a 200-word "news" story for the first edition, my imagination taking over where the facts left off. I also wired the correspondent to interview the survivors. He responded with an excellent first person account which we tacked onto my story for the second edition. Later, I learned that my expanded version of his telegram had been right on the mark. So much for creative journalism.

My interest in Indians, and a certain Indian girl, had not abated during the summer and fall. Just about the time the IAA was meeting on the Blood Reserve, Ottawa was introducing Bill 267 as a revision to the Indian Act. When the IAA received copies, Laurie, Gladstone, and the others were shocked at its contents. It permitted the government to expel Indians from reserves if their status was in doubt, dispose of a band's capital or revenue funds without the consent of the Indians, enfranchise entire Indian bands, and arrest persons engaged in pressing claims against the government on behalf of an Indian band. At the same time, the legislation failed to respond to Native requests for gradual self-government, protection of hunting and fishing rights, and honouring the intent of the treaties.

Laurie immediately sent a note to me, stating, "You should see the terms of the proposed new Act. Its only equal is the miscegenation laws of the deepest south."[15] He also contacted other newspapers, Native groups, politicians, and interested people. The result was that the Bill did not get beyond its first reading before summer recess. In August 1950, the IAA met in Calgary to discuss details of the legislation and I wrote an article for the *Bulletin* based on a wire service story. Then, in September, Laurie wrote to me again enclosing a copy of a letter the IAA had sent to the Minister of Indian Affairs, detailing criticisms of the proposed changes. Copies also went to every Member of Parliament. I responded with an article in the *Bulletin* entitled, "Indians Send Protest to Federal Minister,"[16] As a result of the IAA campaign, Bill 264 was scrapped and the Minister announced that Indians would be consulted before any changes were made to the original Act. When a meeting was held with federal bureaucrats a few months later, Gladstone was one of the leading delegates.

While all this was happening, I decided to try again to see if I could make a date with the president's daughter. After a bit of planning, I "accidentally" met her on Jasper Avenue during a noon hour and asked her if she would go with me to a wrestling match. Her response was quick, unequivocal, and explicit. "I hate wrestling," she said and stomped off, leaving me standing on the sidewalk like an idiot. Then in October, I was assigned to cover a variety program featuring George Formby, an English comedian and banjo player. I thought to myself, if she doesn't like wrestling, maybe she likes music, so with tickets in hand, I resolutely marched to the Edmonton Indian Agency office to try again. I was still extremely shy but I was not to be dissuaded. With office workers looking on with some amusement, I asked her for the date and – oh joy! – she accepted!

On that first date, we found we had a lot to talk about. By now we had mutual friends, mutual interests, and seemed to like each other's company. She was a nice, friendly, and beautiful girl whom I loved to be with. In fact, for a long time after we were dating, I could never quite accept the fact that such an attractive girl could love someone as gawky and introverted as me. But she did, and so began a courtship. At the time of our first date, Pauline roomed with two Cree girls, Eleanor Seenum and Rose Schott, not far from the Royal Alex hospital. Over the next few months, I became part of their world, visiting Indian patients at the Charles Camsell Indian Hospital on weekends and socializing with Irene and Gerald Tailfeathers and other Indians living in the city.

The Camsell was an interesting place. I was told that during the war it had been used by the American Army to house people who were building the Alaska Highway. The Canadian Army had it for a while and in 1945 it was turned over to Indian Health Services to be used as a hospital for Native tubercular patients. At that time the disease was rampant on many Alberta reserves and during the early years with Pauline and at the Camsell I had to take precautions, including T.B. tests. I was very impressed with the hospital. Some patients had been involuntarily admitted but most soon accepted the fact they were there for their own good. Everyone we knew survived their treatment there and in a few years, the incidence of tuberculosis was dramatically reduced in Alberta.

─────

As the world moved into the year 1951, my future seemed bright. I was an editor on a lively newspaper, courting a gorgeous girl, and discovering an increasing interest in Indians and history. My usual working routine was to put in a six-day week – as did most of the staff – taking Saturdays off and working Sundays to get my provincial page ready for the Monday morning edition. On

Saturday, January 20th, I was still lazing around the house when I received a phone call from one of the reporters.

"Hugh," he said, "were you planning to come to work tomorrow?"

"Of course," I replied.

"Don't bother," he said with a bitter laugh, "the paper just folded."

"Wha–at?!"

I hurried down to the *Bulletin* office and when I arrived, there was confusion everywhere. A security guard refused to let me in until I showed him my press card. Inside, people were standing around in small groups while a couple of women in the social department were quietly crying. As I joined the others, I learned how the announcement had been made.

Apparently when the morning edition was being prepared, publisher Hal Straight ordered that a two–column space be saved on the front page, and that the banner headline be left open. When everything else had been plated and on the presses, Straight went directly to one of the linotype operators. The man gulped as he read the announcement, then set it in lead type as the publisher stood over him.

"Don't move from your seat until the paper is out," Straight told the man. Undoubtedly the publisher was afraid that if the composing room or press room heard the news ahead of time, the paper might never make it to the press. He then picked up the type, placed it in the font himself, added the lead type bearing the banner headline, and sent the whole thing off to be cast. The first people to read the front page were the pressmen and, except for Straight and the linotype operator, they were the first to know the paper had folded.

"The *Bulletin* Ends Publication Today," read the banner headline. In the announcement, Straight indicated that the rising costs of materials and labour had made it impossible for the *Bulletin* to continue, in spite of the fact that it had made "the largest percentage gain in circulation and advertising of any paper in Canada. Restricted newsprint supply, building and mechanical expansion limitation, forbid *The Bulletin* to handle this extraordinary growth, so we have to discontinue publication."[17]

According to the story I was told, the *Bulletin* presses were capable of handing a run of 16,000 newspapers, but because of the oil boom and resulting prosperity, the circulation had expanded to 32,000 for its Saturday edition. In order to increase the output, it would be necessary to add another level to the existing presses, but as they were already up to the ceiling, this was impossible. This forced owner Max Bell to choose between two options. He could pay approximately a million dollars to construct a new and enlarged building and press, or he could close the newspaper and invest the money in the burgeoning oil industry. It was "no contest" for the *Bulletin*. The Leduc and Redwater fields had been discovered only three years earlier and fortunes were being made overnight in the oil industry. On the other hand, the *Bulletin* was the second-place competitor to the Southam-controlled *Edmonton Journal*, so an investor could expect meagre profits on his investment in the face of rising costs. Max Bell had a family tradition in the newspaper field and still controlled the *Calgary Albertan*, but business is business, and so Alberta's oldest newspaper went down the drain.

As the day wore on, a number of interesting events occurred. From the streets, we learned that many paper boys had dumped the last edition into the garbage, rather than delivering it, so there was a steady stream of people knocking on the *Bulletin*'s doors, trying to pick up one of the last editions. We also were told that some of the *Bulletin* delivery trucks were simply abandoned with their boxes still full of papers. In the newsroom, a few reporters tried to make long distance calls at the expense of the *Bulletin*, either looking for jobs or phoning relatives, but the phone company wouldn't accept any out-of-town calls. And at one point during the afternoon, I saw a reporter lowering one of the *Bulletin*'s typewriters by a rope out a back window while a compatriot waited below.

Most people's terminations were effective immediately, but I was given an extra week to clean up the rural accounts. Meanwhile, reporters were allowed to come and go as long as they took nothing except their personal belongings. My only souvenir during that time was my editor's shears, a brass and steel instrument that dated back to the early years of the newspaper.

As I tallied up the accounts, I began receiving letters from my correspondents. Some were quite bitter. A man from Rocky Mountain House suspected a deal had been made with the *Edmonton Journal*. "You know," he wrote, "that *Journal* hasn't had a correspondent here for months. They just swipe the articles from the *Bulletin*... I suppose that is the way to save money and become the only paper in Edmonton."[18] From Stettler came some flattering comments after I suggested to the correspondent that she contact the *Journal*. "Frankly, Mr. Dempsey," she wrote, "I'm a bit spoiled for working with anyone else now. I can't see just anyone being so patient with my foibles and my notes. I enjoyed writing for your page too. It seems to me so many of the other papers print local items that are so cut and dried. It must be your sense of drama."[19] In Vegreville, the correspondent was Jim Sherbaniuk, a former *Bulletin* reporter. He commented, "It'll sure seem funny going to Edmonton now and not stopping off at the *Bulletin*. It was sort of a home to me for the past year and a half. All those times you and I had this last summer are sure going to mean an awful lot to me now."[20]

⌘

A few days after the closure, we were visited by a public relations officer from Canadian National Railways, offering reporters and editors a free one-way pass anywhere on their line. It was a nice gesture, and one which was very much appreciated. A few staff had already found work and made good use of the tickets, while about half a dozen of us thought this was a good way to have a holiday before settling down to job hunting. Sitting in Fawn's Cafe for the last time, we decided to go to Vancouver. We tumbled into a day coach late in January and set out through the wintry landscape, bound for Lotus Land. I sat with Barney McKinley, who already had a job lined up on the West Coast. That night I had a terrible time trying to sleep on the tiny seat, and next morning I became vaguely conscious that the train wasn't moving. I pulled on a pair of moccasins and trudged through some snowdrifts to the front of the train. We were near Boston Bar in the Fraser Canyon and our progress had been halted by an avalanche. I picked up a shovel and pitched in to help the CNR employees who were trying to clear the line. After about an hour's work, the line was open and I happily relaxed in my seat as we got moving again. It turned out that I was the only passenger who had tried to help, so I got some nice words from the train crew. Seeing that I was travelling for free, I thought it was the least I could do.

Once in Vancouver, I dutifully left job applications with the *Sun* and the *Province*. Interestingly, I was offered a reporter's job in Trail, but I wasn't interested. I told my pal Garth Hopkins about it and he went after it instead. While in Vancouver, I took time out to visit Masie Armytage-Moore, redoubtable publisher of the *Native Voice*. I had been writing freelance articles for her ever since the first IAA meeting and we had become good friends. I soon found there was no prospect of a job, but she did give me a press card and also a pass to the Arctic Club, a private club. One day I took a couple of *Bulletin* pals with me and, as the liquor laws in the province were quite restrictive, they were very impressed. We were all in our twenties, and I recall one of the reporters looking at a woman who was drinking alone. She was clearly in her thirties. "I'm going to try and pick her up," he told us. "When they get that old they think that every lay will be their last." I can't remember if he tried or if he succeeded with the "old" woman.

I also promised Pauline that I would visit her sister Nora, who was a nurse in Victoria. My plan was to take the midnight ferry, spend the afternoon with Nora, and then return later in the day. That evening, a bunch of us went to a speakeasy called The Penthouse, run by someone called Philliponi, whom I was told was a rather unsavoury character. Our crowd were all *Bulletin* types – Hugh Watson, Brud Delaney, Garth Hopkins, Danny Scott, and me – and we were collectively in an alcoholic fog when somebody called out, "Hey, Hugh has to catch the midnight ferry and it's already 11:30!"

There was a mad rush for the door as everyone took it as their solemn duty to get me on the boat. By the time we reached the dock, the ferry was just about ready to leave, but amid shouts and well wishes, the *Bulletin* bunch poured me on board. That was the last time I ever saw most of them; they were a great bunch. The combination of whisky and turmoil, plus my inability to handle liquor, made the bathroom my first port of call. Once on the toilet seat I passed out, but sometime later I was startled into wakefulness by a sixth sense which warned me of danger. Opening a bloodshot eye, I saw the blade of a knife being inserted between the door and the frame, and the latch slowly being raised. Instinctively I slammed the latch down and moments later I heard someone running away. Obviously I was about to be robbed.

Staggering to my feet, I decided to see the purser and get a room for the night, but when I reached his office, everything was in darkness and no amount of knocking had any effect. By this time the ferry was well out to sea and everyone had gone to bed. Concerned that my attacker might still be around, I went into the salon, pulled three chairs together and made a sort of bed for myself. There I spent a most uncomfortable night, and when the boat docked at Victoria in the early morning, I was tired, sick, and hungover. I left the ferry immediately, walked along the dock and found a Salvation Army hostel where I thankfully got a room. Up at noon, I wandered into their thrift shop and saw a nice silver pin I thought Pauline would like. A few years later, a North-West Coast specialist looked at it and said it had been made from a Mexican silver dollar by Charlie Edenshaw. So I guess the 50 cents were well spent.

I was in no condition to meet Pauline's sister, so I moved over to the YMCA and arranged to meet her the following day. I don't know what Nora thought when she met her younger sister's bedraggled boyfriend, but we had a nice visit and before long I was back on the ferry, then on the train (at my own expense), and was welcomed home with open arms by Pauline and my parents. It seemed strange to be in Edmonton without the *Bulletin*, and even more unsettling to be without a job.

⸙

Over the next few weeks, I papered the city with applications. At one point I thought about going east, but already the spectre of an inadequate education was rearing its ugly head. When I went to the CBC offices in the Macdonald Hotel, I was told that they would not consider anyone without a university degree, while one of the other radio stations said that college courses in journalism were a prerequisite to employment. And I was a high school dropout.

Each day I scanned the want ads and put in my applications, no matter how inappropriate. I applied to the city police, fire department, provincial government, city hall, and the CNR. And when a job opening at Canadian Western Natural Gas was advertised, I was quick to submit my application, complete with resume. A few days later, I got a call from their personnel officer to come in for an interview. However, any hopes I held of getting the job were dashed when the officer said, "The reason I asked you to come in, was to tell you why I'm not hiring you." That was a twist. He went on, "Look at the work you've done – sign painter, rare stamp dealer, and reporter. Those are all creative jobs. You'd be just wasting your time if you took a nine to five office job here." In later years, I appreciated his kindness, for he was perfectly right. He went on to suggest that I go to the Alberta Department of Education and take an aptitude test. I did, and it showed that I should go into a creative field, like art or journalism. Great.

In the middle of April, after being out of work for two and a half months, I got a call saying that I had been accepted as a trainee by the Edmonton Fire Department. I hardly remembered applying for the job, but now I was thrilled that at last someone wanted me. I showed up with the other new recruits and was told we would get two weeks of classroom and practical training before we were assigned to fire halls. We were issued rubber boots, a slicker, and other paraphernalia, and I settled down to learn the skills of being a fireman. The classroom stuff was fine, but the practical training was hard. I was just too weak and skinny to be a good fireman. I could jump off a moving fire truck with the best of them, and wrap the nozzle around a hydrant as the hose was unfolded. But when the water was turned on, the hose was like a savage snake beyond my control as it twisted and turned under the strong water pressure. I had no trouble entering a burning building, but when it came to chopping a hole in the floor, I just wasn't up to it.

But I stuck with it. Our final test was the use of a safety net. We were to be taught how to catch people jumping out of windows, and then each of us was to jump off the top of the Edmonton Gardens into a waiting net. We knocked off early on the day before the test and as I went home, I didn't relish the thought of what tomorrow would bring. As I went into the house, my mother told me there had been a call from the Publicity Bureau of the Alberta government, asking if I was still interested in a job. Was I! I got right on the phone to Ed Bryant, the director, and had an interview that afternoon. Before advertising the job, Bryant had checked for any existing applications and found mine. I was the only candidate and he hired me on the spot.

Next morning, I showed up at the fire department's training station and told the instructor I had another job. I don't think he believed me, and thought that I had chickened out, but it was the truth. On May 1, 1951, I became a publicity writer for the Alberta government.

# 4

# With the Government

The Publicity Bureau was located in the basement of the Legislative Building, right under the dome. The professional staff consisted of only three people: Ed Bryant, the director; Sid "Robbie" Roberts, editor of *Within Our Borders*; and me, a publicity writer. Besides us, there was H.E. "Bert" Nichols – who had some sort of title but really looked after Social Credit propaganda – and a secretarial staff of two or three people. We were part of the Department of Economic Affairs, which also included the Film and Photographic Branch across the hall from us, the Economic Development Branch, the Tourist Bureau, and perhaps a couple of others. Our deputy minister was Ralph R. Moore, and our Minister, A.J. Hooke.

Although my boss was Ed Bryant, I worked directly under Roberts. He was a fine, easygoing fellow and we got along very well together. Our main responsibility was to produce the monthly four-page illustrated tabloid *Within Our Borders*. When I started, it had a circulation of 14,500 and was sent free to anyone who asked for it. Besides that, copies were mailed to daily and weekly newspapers with the comment that any of its contents were free for republication. And, as a matter of fact, the information was used quite frequently by the Alberta press.

When we were not busy with the tabloid, Robbie and I did any tasks that were assigned to us. I prepared annual reports, press releases, promotional booklets, fact sheets for conferences, tourism handouts, and even wrote the first Alberta drivers' manual. The usual routine was to be contacted by another government department, write whatever was needed, and send it back for their approval. With the newsletter, the ideas came either from us or from other departments, but the routine was slightly different. *Within Our Borders* was considered to reflect official government policy and therefore came under the scrutiny of Premier Ernest Manning's office.

When we completed plans for the next month's issue, we had a meeting with Pete Elliott, the premier's executive secretary. Each proposed article was discussed and approval received. We then contacted the appropriate government departments, wrote the articles, and submitted them to their deputy ministers. Most of the time this was simply a routine, but once in a while a deputy with his own agenda made life difficult for us. When this happened, we simply told Pete Elliott, who phoned the minister, and any opposition quickly disappeared.

After the articles had been written and photographs selected, we had another meeting with Pete, who carefully read every line. He seldom had any complaint and was good to work with. Not only that, but because of his position we were able to circumvent a lot of government red tape.

It was interesting to see Pete in action. I would swear that he had more authority than any cabinet minister, and the mandarins were either in fear or in awe of him, as they never knew whether he was speaking for himself or for the premier. I think Pete deliberately kept it that way in order to maintain his own effectiveness.

There were only a few instances where a deputy really gave us trouble. One time, I was assigned the task of summarizing assistance available to the aged, disabled, and widows. It was pretty straightforward, but when I presented it to the deputy minister of public welfare, he rejected it, saying it was too long. When I tried to pin him down about any mistakes, he would not be specific. His complaint seemed to focus on the belief that if the article was too long, it would come to the attention of too many people who might qualify for help. Puzzled, I returned to my office and read the article again. It was bare bones; there was nothing to cut. Then I got a brilliant idea. The original article was double spaced, so I retyped it single spaced, resubmitted it, and the deputy approved it! On another occasion, a deputy changed my article so much that it was both unrecognizable and inaccurate. When I showed both versions to Pete, he said "to Hell with the deputy" and told us to use my version. It was nice to have that kind of muscle behind us.

I quickly learned that my experience at the *Bulletin* made the job a snap. The deadlines were once a month, instead of daily, and I often had space in the newsletter to write long feature articles. The only problem, from the standpoint of ego, was that nothing was signed; there were no bylines. This was a firm departmental policy. If any credit had to be given, Deputy Minister Ralph Moore was listed as the author.

My assignments for *Within Our Borders* took me to many parts of the province. The first of these was to accompany a busload of Members of the Legislative Assembly (MLAs) who were touring the irrigation areas of southern Alberta. The tour had been arranged a year in advance by local politicians who wanted to stress the need for more irrigation to combat the perennial problems of drought. The only problem was that when the tour was held in June 1951, it had been raining steadily for so long that the irrigation ditches were filled to overflowing and drought was the farthest thing from anyone's mind.

The tour started with a little holiday for MLAs in Waterton, so I was not needed until the bus arrived in Cardston. This was fine with me. I went to Macleod, where Pauline's folks, together with Clarence Melting Tallow and Stanley Healy, were waiting for me at the station. Pauline had tipped them off that I would be coming, perhaps to keep me away from the schoolteacher at St. Paul's. So we drove to the Gladstone farm and found we had a lot to talk about. That was a wonderful thing about the Gladstones. Her dad and I shared the same interests – Indian politics and history. He had a keen mind and could recall the most minute details of his experiences in residential school in the 1890s and many other aspects of life on the Blood Reserve.

Next morning, I was standing with the Cardston brass band when the MLAs wheeled into town for a tour of the Mormon temple. I took my seat on the bus and was their public relations officer for the next week. We were wined and dined all the way across southern Alberta, and treated royally everywhere we stopped. However, the rain rarely let up and I think the message of the importance of irrigation lost some of its impact.

During this period, the Social Credit party had a massive majority in the legislature and I don't believe that any opposition members were included in the tour. One day while we were on the bus, an MLA asked me about my political affiliations. It wasn't any of his business but I didn't mind telling him that I voted Social Credit provincially and Conservative federally. When he heard this, he really lit into me, saying that it was because of people like me that Social Credit could never implement its monetary policies. The creation and distribution of money, he said, was a federal responsibility and voters were preventing them from fulfilling their real destiny.

When he asked me what I knew about Social Credit, I mumbled something about the A plus B theorem whereby the government could create money based on the value of its resources. This led him into a protracted monologue which delved so deeply into Social Credit monetary theories that I didn't have the foggiest idea what he was talking about. When he finally asked me what I thought, I equated the running of a government with that of looking after one's own personal finances. A good provider, I said, spent only his assured income, paying off small expenses immediately and extending large expenses such as a house or car over a period of several years. I thought the government should do the same – operate within a balanced budget each year and amortize major capital expenses such as highways and buildings. At this, the MLA snorted that I obviously understood nothing about government financing and abruptly left me alone for the rest of the tour.

———— ⬢ ————

A task of the Publicity Bureau was to interview winners of Master Farm Family awards but without letting them know they had won. When visiting their farms, we were supposed to tell them we were interviewing the three semi-finalists, but I don't think they believed us. These trips gave me a chance to see some excellent Alberta farmsteads and to learn of the struggles facing many farmers during difficult economic times. When I got back to the office, I wrote press releases for newspapers and feature stories for magazines, all to be released when the official announcements were made.

A number of rural visits also were made for other purely agricultural stories. For example, Alberta was the only major area to be free of rats, thanks to an aggressive campaign along the Saskatchewan border. Regular patrols ferreted out any creatures hiding in barns or granaries and poison traps kept them from invading Alberta farmlands.

Coyotes, on the other hand, were a constant pest to sheepman and ranchers. When a new poison named Ten-Eighty was developed, the Crystal Springs Hutterite Colony south of Lethbridge volunteered to experiment with it. After the poison had been in use for a few weeks, I was sent there with photographer Bill Marsden to cover the story. We were kindly received by the black-garbed, bearded Hutterite sheep boss and taken on a tour of the poison sites. Afterwards, we were invited to the boss's room for a glass of wine.

Hutterite wine! I'd never tasted anything like it. The boss, Bill, and I each had two glasses from a recycled whiskey bottle, and it was delicious. The homemade grape wine was very smooth and seemed almost as mild as milk, but by the time we left the colony, Bill and I were flying high. I never knew the alcohol content, but neither of us should have been driving as we wove our way back to Lethbridge.

Bill and I became good friends during our work with the government, and remained close until his death in 2006. One of our most memorable assignments occurred in 1952, just after the Mackenzie Highway had been opened. This stretch of gravelled road extended 384 miles from Grimshaw in Alberta to Hay River in the Northwest Territories. Bill and I started out early in September just as the country was taking on its mantle of autumn colours. Our first stop was Peace River which, considering the condition of the roads, was a long day's drive. Next day, we went north to Manning, where we saw the Lambert family, who were up for a Master Farm Family award. We had the bad luck to catch them right in the middle of harvesting, so we had to wait until after nightfall for a short interview and a bunch of pictures. Manning itself was a lovely place near the lower end of the Mackenzie Highway. It had a population of six hundred and boasted the only hotel on the entire road.

From Manning, Bill and I drove north to High Level at Mile 183, our next port of call. As I wrote to Pauline, "High Level consists of just a clearing cut in the forest on which a store-café, two auto court bungalows, and a gas pump are located. There is no power, no radio, no nothin'"[21] The whole place was run by James Jones, who had owned three trading posts in the Arctic and decided to come south when he heard the highway was being built. It turned out that he knew my brother Harry when he had worked for Northern Traders at Aklavik in the late 1930s.

Jones broke the news to us that a full-blown rabies epidemic was raging through the fox, coyote, and wolf populations in northern Alberta. Immediately my reporter instincts took over, as I was aware that no news about this outbreak had appeared in any "southern" newspapers. I only wished the *Bulletin* had still been around so that I could have broken the story through them.

At this point, Bill and I ignored our mandate to publicize the Mackenzie Highway and began to cover the epidemic. Jones told us that earlier in the day a fox had attacked a passing car and had been killed, so Bill and I went over to look at the carcass. It was in pretty good shape, so I posed with my .22 rifle as though I had just shot it. It turned out to be a good publicity picture. We then turned east and followed a gravel road towards Fort Vermilion, interviewing people who had had experiences with rabid animals. The first person we met was Dick Olsen, a homesteader, who said that he had been grubbing roots in a new clearing when a timber wolf had approached within a few yards of him and had to be turned away with an axe.

Olsen also told us about his neighbours, Mr. and Mrs. Steve Kowal, whose farm had been ravaged by a rabid wolf. It had attacked a dozen hogs and a cow before turning on the family's log home. As I later wrote, "The animal, which weighed 150 pounds, gashed at the wood on the entranceway and hurled all its weight forward in an attempt to open the door. It took the combined strength of Mr. and Mrs. Kowal to keep the mad beast out and at one stage it was reported to have wedged its head through the door opening."[22] Next morning, Kowal's son shot the wolf and skinned it. At the time of our visit, the boy was undergoing treatment in case he had contracted the disease.

Because of the condition of the roads, we weren't able to visit these farmers but the stories came to us thick and fast. A man named Art Simmons was reported to have been working on his tractor when a wolf attacked its wheels and had to be driven off. Another farmer heard a yelping sound and found a fox attacking his dog. He pried the animal's jaws apart and killed the fox, but his dog had to be put down and the man had to take anti-rabies shots. And Jones told us that two rabid foxes had been killed with clubs right at his auto camp.

With the story and pictures in hand, Bill and I continued our northern trek. The land was a virtual wilderness and there was practically no traffic on the highway. There was a deserted Hudson's Bay Company store at Indian Cabins and nothing at Upper Hay River, so in order to have a meal we had to pull over to the side of the road to build a campfire. Wieners and beans cooked in the can tasted pretty good among the spruce and tamarack trees of the North. Beyond High Level we never saw a cabin or a side road, only trees, bushes, and muskeg. It had a wild beauty that captivated me and kept Bill busy with his camera. At Mile 350 we came upon the majestic Alexander Falls, which looked to me like a not-so-miniature Niagara Falls. The broad Hay River dropped 109 feet at this point and fell into a sheer canyon. In order to get a good shot of it, Bill had me stand at the very brink of the falls, looking down into the churning chasm. Later, when I saw the picture, I thought I must have been nuts to get that close to the edge.

We were only a few miles inside the Northwest Territories when a man waved to us from the side of the highway. He proved to be a Metis who had a sick boy that he wanted us to take to Hay River. Of course, we obliged, as we were the only car we'd seen along the road in the past four hours. The Metis family had their tent pitched near the road and the whole scene was uniquely northern. They had moose meat smoking on racks while more meat was being boiled in a pot. Nearby, they had a moose and a caribou hide staked out on the ground in preparation for tanning. The man offered us some moose meat, but we were going in the wrong direction for it to do us any good.

We got to Hay River, the northern terminus of the Mackenzie Highway, later that day and after we dropped off the Metis lad we checked into the town's only hotel. It was owned by Calgary Brewing & Malting and the only beer available in the bar was a Calgary brand. And the prices! Beer was 50 cents a bottle, or more than double the price charged on the outside. And in order to drink in the bar, one had to get a one-dollar Territorial permit. The rest of the prices were equally high. Soft drinks were two bits and in one store, all the canned goods were 25 cents each, regardless of contents.

Hay River settlement was spread out for about two miles along the river but its only main street was about a block long and consisted of five or six businesses. Its population of 250 people included about a hundred Metis, 50 treaty Indians, 75 people who worked for the government, and the rest involved in transportation, commercial fishing, and other occupations. My impression of the place was that it consisted of a lot of log shacks, plenty of dogs, big Arctic ravens, unimproved roads, and a polyglot population. I had the feeling that it could be a rough town and this was confirmed when I went into the bar's washroom and saw blood splattered on the walls. On enquiry, I was told there had been a fight the previous night between fishermen and loggers.

Our plan was to spend the night in Hay River and, after getting a bunch of pictures, to head back south. But that's where my luck ran out. Shortly after our arrival, Bill encountered an old buddy of his, Larry Mitanski, who was doing some aerial prospecting. He had a float plane and was living on a boat named the *Pilot II* which usually plied the Mackenzie River. That night we attended a wild party on the boat which featured overproof rum – a highly alcoholic beverage found only in the Northwest Territories. I didn't (and still don't) like ordinary rum and I found the overproof stuff to be absolutely unpalatable. Even when it was diluted with Coke it tasted like kerosene, so I was amazed to see some of Mitanski's northern pals drinking the stuff straight from the bottle. I knocked off early and went to the hotel and next morning Bill announced that he and Larry were flying across Great Slave Lake to Yellowknife, which boasted the only liquor store in the North. Larry wanted to stock up and Bill was anxious to see the northern capital. There wasn't room for me, so Bill promised he would be back next morning at daybreak so we could get as far as High Level that night.

Next morning, I checked out of the hotel at dawn and drove to the docks where I waited, and waited, and waited. By mid-afternoon, I realized there was no way we could get to High Level that day even if Bill did arrive, so I went back to the hotel and was chagrined to learn that they were fully booked. No rooms. I had no recourse but to spend a miserable night in the car, periodically starting the motor to keep from freezing in the 30°F temperature. I saw the false light of early dawn, and then watched with growing impatience as the sun gradually crept over the horizon. As I told Pauline in a letter, "I've had absolutely nothing to do. There are no shows, no radios available, no magazine stores and, in short, absolutely nothing to do but wait."[23]

As soon as the town was astir, I went for breakfast then returned to the docks to continue my vigil. Finally, late in the afternoon I heard the welcome roar of the float plane as it landed on Hay River and taxied to the dock. Bill was apologetic but it soon became apparent that Mitanski had been the culprit and convinced my companion to stay with the bright lights of Yellowknife rather than returning to his job. I was furious, and my temper didn't improve when I learned that the hotel was still full. It was too late to head south, so we had to spend the night on the *Pilot II*. That might have been a pleasant experience, but with Mitanski's liquor supply replenished, all his pals were back for another night of revelry.

But party or not, Bill and I were on the road shortly after daybreak the following day and reached High Level by noon. We made a side trip to Fort Vermilion so that I could interview a doctor and get some statistics and reports of other wolf attacks. We also stopped to do a little duck hunting and accompanied a Norwegian homesteader on a short but unsuccessful deer hunt. That night in High Level, I slept like a log. Even the howling of wolves near the cabins failed to disturb me, although they shook Bill out of a sound sleep.

As we wended our way south, the debacle at Hay River took on humorous undertones and soon Bill and I were laughing about it. That the hotel should be full in that northern wilderness was surprising, and as a plus I was able to display four pencil sketches I had made of the town and the docks during my protracted wait.

We had only one more assignment before returning home, and it proved to be a fascinating one. Virtually all homesteading land in Alberta had been taken up long before World War II, but in 1951 the Alberta government surveyed a wilderness area on Blueberry Mountain and decided to open it for some good old-fashioned homesteading. This meant that an applicant could file on the land, improve it over a period of three years, and buy 320 acres for a token $300. More than a hundred farmers had accepted the challenge, and our task was to interview some of them.

Our first stop was at the log home of Herman Hindmarch, who had taken off his first crop that fall and was planning to spend a second winter on the land. He had been raised in the Peace River area, so grubbing the land was nothing new for him. Not so with Andrew Clarke, a prairie man from west of Calgary. He was living in a trailer with his wife and baby daughter and had brought in heavy equipment for clearing the land. His nearest neighbour was ten miles away so they had a lonely season ahead of them. The roads were unimproved but there was plenty of game to tide them over the winter months.

By this time, I was already deeply immersed in my studies of western history, so I was struck by the seeming anomaly of the situation. Here was a homesteader doing what other settlers had done in 1912 or 1920, but not in 1952. It was as though we had gone back in time, yet the portable trailer and heavy equipment reminded me that we were very much in a modern era. And I didn't see much romance in the situation. The Clarkes and others would have a long, hard, and expensive struggle before them if they expected to gain title to their homestead land.

When I got home from this extended trip, I set to work and wrote a general press release about the rabies epidemic. However, I didn't get to "break" the news, as a local correspondent at Fort Vermilion for the *Edmonton Journal* beat me to it. But I did write a feature story for *Within Our Borders*, as well as two or three extensive articles on the Mackenzie Highway and the Blueberry Mountain homesteaders.

---

The years with the Publicity Bureau were happy ones for me. I was working with a nice bunch of people, my job was enjoyable, and by superiors seemed to appreciate my outside interests in Indians and history. As it turned out, the first couple of years with the government were the most pivotal ones of my life from the standpoint of family, career, and personal interests. These years set the tone for what became the three passions in my life: Pauline, Native culture, and history.

The most important of these was my love for Pauline. After our first date in 1950, we began going steady, but our first several months were filled with doubts and concerns on both our parts. My worry was that I was a shy, insecure homebody who was completely different from the outgoing and vivacious Pauline. After losing my job at the *Bulletin*, I was also afraid that I might be forever confined to some menial job and could never properly look after a family.

Pauline's concern, as expressed to me, was much more basic. The problem as she saw it was that she was an Indian and I was a white man. She could envision my future being jeopardized by marrying someone of another race, and perhaps in the future I might have regrets that I didn't marry someone "of my own kind." My answer to her in a letter was, "You are 'my own kind.' You can't measure it on race alone. I might find a girl of the same race but who would never have the qualities that you have. My own kind of girl would be measured for her love for me, her likes and dislikes, her personality and friends, not on her race, her religion or her doubts."[24]

I got some idea of the seriousness of the situation when Pauline told me that one of her roommates had seen me on Jasper Avenue chatting with friends. She told Pauline she didn't say hello because she thought I might not want to recognize her on the street because she was an Indian. I was flabbergasted to say the least.

I told her that I would prefer to face any problems as they arose, rather than trying to predict them. I expressed a willingness to seek employment with the Indian Affairs Branch if she thought that would keep me in contact with Native people on a regular basis. Thank God that didn't happen!

But as it turned out, the problem simply didn't exist. I became a part of her world and she a part of mine. My mother and Pauline became lifelong friends who always enjoyed each other's company, while her dad was like a father to me. In later years we laughingly said if we ever got into a big fight, we were sure my mother would support Pauline and her dad would side with me. It was that kind of relationship. Also, my friends and hers accepted us without reservation and we quickly felt at home wherever we went.

---

From the time of the fateful meeting in 1950, I was also enamoured with Native history. Shortly after the *Bulletin* folded, I blanketed the world with letters in a search for more information. I got anthropological books from the American Museum of Natural History in New York, Blackfoot language studies from The Netherlands, transactions from the Royal Canadian Institute, Native studies from the American Ethnological Society, reports from the British Association for the Advancement of Science, and Indian photographs from the RCMP, Royal Ontario Museum, CPR, and Hudson's Bay Company. I also launched into a lifelong friendship with John C. Ewers, who was then Associate Curator of Ethnology at the Smithsonian Institution in Washington, DC. My first letter in 1951 was a formal one but after we met in Browning a couple of years later, it was "Dear Jack" and "Dear Hugh." As time passed, Jack and Marge became great friends as we visited each other in such places as Browning, Cody, Washington, and Calgary. I now prize almost fifty years of correspondence with Jack filled with a wealth of information on every imaginable aspect of Blackfoot and museum work.

About the same time, I opened correspondence with Claude Schaeffer, Curator of the Museum of the Plains Indian, in Browning, Montana. This also was the basis for another lifelong friendship but a tragically short one. Claude left the museum in 1954 because of ill health and lived in Oregon for a few years before returning to his old job in 1960. He retired a short time later and died of a heart attack in 1969. Claude was a quiet, kindly man. I got along fine with him, while his wife Halina and Pauline were good friends. Claude was a meticulous researcher among the Blackfoot and Kootenay but he seldom published anything. He was always waiting until his research was complete but, of course, it never was. At the time of his death, he had just agreed to write a history of the Kootenays for the University of Oklahoma Press. I learned of his passing when Halina phoned me from Seaside, Oregon. She said that Claude had told her if anything ever happened to him, she was to turn his research papers over to me. A few days later, I made the sad flight to the West Coast and brought back to the Glenbow Museum as fine a body of Native interviews as one would ever see. It made me sad that Claude had never taken that next step.

Another person I contacted in the early 1950s was Douglas Leechman, anthropologist for the National Museum of Canada. We, too, started writing to each other and ultimately he was to have a major impact upon my career.

With all of the information about Indians pouring in, my writer's instincts took over. In the spring of 1951, I decided to interview Percy Plain Woman, one of the tubercular patients at the Charles Camsell Indian Hospital. He was an artist who painted under the name of Two Guns. Percy and I had become great friends over the previous few months so I was pleased to write his life story and to see it published in *The Native Voice*.[25] This made both of us happy, as the story helped to bring in more orders for paintings.

I must tell a little story about Percy which occurred sometime after he was released from the sanatorium. At that time he was living on the Blood Reserve, just on the outskirts of Cardston. Pauline and I were going to Montana for a holiday and I had brought some beer with us, as Cardston was a dry Mormon town. Just as we were leaving, I remembered that we still had half a dozen bottles left and we couldn't take them across the line into the States. We were parked on Main Street so when I noticed Percy coming our way, I dumped the bottles into a paper bag and handed them to him.

"Here, Percy," I said. "It's a half a dozen beers. Maybe you could use them."

Without giving the matter any further thought, Pauline and I headed south for our holiday. When we got back, I met Percy in the Old Chief Café and the first thing he said to me was, "Dempsey, you scared the shit out of me. I've bought bottles from bootleggers in back alleys but that's the first time anybody gave me the stuff right on Main Street. After you left, I was almost too scared to walk home with it, and I was sure I was going to be stopped by the Mounties."

I had completely forgotten that Indians were not allowed to either drink or possess alcoholic beverages, and if Percy had been stopped, he would have been sent to jail for at least a month. He never tired of reminding me that I was the boldest bootlegger he'd ever met.

---

Later that summer I decided that my first major literary effort should be a book on the life of Pauline's grandfather, Joe Healy, or Flying Chief. All I knew about him was that his parents had been killed by enemy Indians in Montana in the 1860s, that he had been raised by whisky traders, and that Pauline had loved him very much. A few newspaper accounts slightly expanded his biography, but not enough for me to make any sense out of the confusing stories. In one account, the white Joe Healy, for whom Pauline's grandfather had been named, had been a soldier who had saved the boy's life. In another, a man named John Healy had been the rescuer, but he'd been a whisky trader.

This set me off into another facet of my career. At Christmas 1951, I was invited to spend the holidays on the Blood Reserve with Pauline and her family. I gladly accepted, not just to be with Pauline, but to be part of her family. I can still remember us travelling over the snow-covered prairies and being told that the Bloods were experiencing one of their worst winters on record. When we turned off the main highway, we couldn't travel on the secondary road as it was choked with snow, so we had to follow a winter trail along a ridge that led down to the Gladstone ranch. When we approached, I saw that the whole place was ablaze with lights and the reflections from the windows shimmered across the frozen snow. Coming closer, we passed some Gladstone cattle huddled together near the shelterbelt, their backs encrusted with snow. I found the whole experience to be exhilarating.

On the day before Christmas, I asked if I could speak was some of the elders about Joe Healy. This led us to the Marquis Café in Cardston, where I interviewed ninety-four-year-old Iron, who revealed the real story of how Joe Healy's parents had been killed. He also told about Healy having been struck by lightning, and another time being in a shack which was attacked by white horse thieves. When he finished his stories, Iron added, "Many men told lies about their experiences and that was why they are now dead and I am still alive. I tell only the truth."[26] All of this was in Blackfoot, with Pauline's father interpreting. We then moved to another table where Pauline's aunt, Rosie Davis, was sitting. She was the eldest of the family. She repeated the story of the attack by Pend d'Oreille Indians, adding a few more details about Healy's life.

As it turned out, I never did get enough information for a book, and not until 1994 was I able to tell Joe Healy's factual story in *The Amazing Death of Calf Shirt and Other Blackfoot Stories*. But the experience taught me about the wealth of oral history that existed among the Indians, particularly those who spoke no English and prided themselves on the accuracy of their information. I came to appreciate the fact that storytelling and history were inextricably intertwined, that elders told their stories both for entertainment and to pass on the history of their tribe.

The first Christmas on the Blood Reserve left me with a multitude of memories. From the front porch of the Gladstone house I could get an unobstructed view of Chief Mountain, huddled at the Alberta-Montana border in all its massive glory. Slightly to the west, St. Paul's school was nestled in the foothills while between it and the house were a few Indian homes, those of Ken Tailfeathers, Henry Standing Alone, and Harry Mills. There were two houses at the Gladstone farm – the main one and the old original cabin which was now occupied by Pauline's brother Fred and his family. To the north were the barn, corrals and – for me a new experience – the outhouse.

I was given a comfortable room under the eaves of their two-storey house and became accustomed to the workings of the household. This included being jolted awake at 7 a.m. when Pauline's dad turned on the radio full blast. I was accustomed to sleeping in late while on holidays but it was impossible at the Gladstones. By the time I struggled down to breakfast, most of the family had eaten and gone about their chores, but Pauline had waited for me to avoid leaving me in the embarrassing position of eating alone. Pauline's mother was an excellent cook, so there was lots of bacon, eggs, and pancakes in the morning.

Pauline's dad had a small office just off the veranda where he kept all his Indian Association and farming files. After a short while at the ranch, I became accustomed to a steady stream of visitors who came calling. Some were relatives, some fellow Anglicans, and a few were neighbours. All of them were Indians and mostly they talked politics and local gossip. I don't think I saw a white person during my entire visit, except at church and in town. There was a certain amount of holiday drinking, as the nearest bootlegger was never very far away. This caused some boisterousness but only one time did I have any concern. This occurred when Pauline's uncle David arrived very drunk and in a fighting mood. Later, I was told that at one stage he had to be forcibly restrained, but by this time I had gone to bed.

On Christmas Eve everybody had a few drinks but no one was drunk; they were all boisterous and happy. At midnight, they began opening their presents. While I was growing up, we didn't open our presents until Christmas morning, so this experience was entirely new for me. Not only that, but because of the drinking, the opening of parcels was sometimes a hilarious affair.

Next morning the women were up early preparing the turkey while the men went about their chores. By suppertime the house was filled with good odours and a bunch of adults and kids. Besides Pauline's brothers Fred and Horace, and her sister Doreen with her New Zealander husband, there was Pauline's Aunt Suzette Eagle Ribs, her Uncle David Healy, neighbour Harry Mills, and his son Buster who worked at the farm. Most of them had kids with them. The meal itself was the usual turkey, stuffing, vegetables, giblet gravy, and several kinds of pies and cakes. All the Gladstones had attended St. Paul's residential school, where they had learned everything they needed to know about English and Canadian cooking. I was told that at one time Pauline's grandfather used to include flaming plum pudding with the meal.

Pauline had talked about me being with "my own kind," but on the reserve that season I felt completely at home with her folks and her friends. And that's the way it turned out to be over the years. I can honestly say that on a social basis I have felt more comfortable among Indians than among white people, and throughout my lifetime the majority of my closest friends have been Indians. That first holiday on the reserve simply confirmed the fact that, as far as I was concerned, Pauline and I had nothing to worry about. If we ran into discrimination from time to time, that was somebody else's problem, not ours.

Back in Edmonton, I threw myself wholeheartedly into my work. Over the months, it became common knowledge that I was interested in history, so enquiries that came to the Tourist Bureau or to our department were passed along to me. Then, early in 1952, the deputy minister asked me to prepare a report on historic sites for him to take to a federal-provincial conference in Ottawa. I jumped at the chance, and after considerable research I produced a thirty-six-page report dealing with every major site in the province. When the deputy got back from Ottawa, he was ecstatic; the report had far surpassed anything from other provinces and had been warmly praised at the meeting.

A few weeks later, when a federal bureaucrat who had co-chaired the conference visited Edmonton, she asked to meet the author of the report. While the three of us – the bureaucrat, the deputy, and I – were standing in the deputy's office, the federal official said, "Mr. Moore, this report is too good to put on the shelf. Why don't you have it published?"

"That's a good idea," he responded. And, looking at me, he said, "You look after it, Dempsey."

Then the Ottawa official, with a twinkle in her eye, added, "And surely, Mr. Moore, you're going to give this young man credit for writing it."

The deputy was momentarily taken aback but then, knowing he had been cornered, good-naturedly added, "Of course."

And so it was that I broke with the department's policy on anonymity. The booklet came out in mimeographed form under the title *Historic Sites of the Province of Alberta* and bylined by me. It was such an instant success that it went into a second edition before the end of the year, this time as a typeset and fully illustrated booklet. Ultimately it went through ten printings over the next twenty-five years, with some 25,000 copies being circulated. It was my first book and nothing since then has ever attained that kind of distribution. The fact that it was free and distributed by the Tourist Bureau may have had something to do with it.

The response was astounding. For many years, Alberta had been languishing in the backwaters of Canadian historical publishing, even though there was considerable local interest in the subject. As a result, people were delighted when the Alberta government did something historical. Over the next few months I got friendly letters from a raft of people whose names didn't mean too much to me at the time. Among them were Grant MacEwan, Norman Luxton, G. Rider Davis, J.E.A. Macleod, George Heath MacDonald, Morden H. Long, George Edworthy, and Walter N. Sage. All were extremely laudatory.

This project, interestingly, led me into another facet of my career. In 1953, Ed Bryant introduced me to an engineer named Jim MacGregor and said we were going to help his group, the Historical Society of Alberta, publish a quarterly journal. The government had agreed to mimeograph, collate, and bind four hundred copies free of charge.

And so began the *Alberta Historical Review*. Four years earlier, Jim MacGregor had made publishing history when his book *Blankets and Beads* was published. It was one of the first ever written about Alberta by an Alberta author and produced in the province by a commercial publisher. Because of the publicity surrounding the book, MacGregor had become president of the Historical Society in 1952 and began an aggressive campaign to promote Alberta's past. Professionally, Jim was general manager of Canadian Utilities Limited and was chairman of the Alberta Power Commission.

This society had been organized by an Act of the Alberta legislature in 1907, right after the province was formed. It had functioned off and on for years, offering meetings in Edmonton, marking historic sites, and generally trying to raise an awareness of Alberta's history. Although supposedly province-wide, in the beginning it was purely an Edmonton organization.

Shortly after his election, MacGregor wrote to several local historians throughout the province, stating that, "It has occurred to me that we might be able to start publication of a monthly or quarterly bulletin devoted to Alberta history. What would you think of such an effort?"[27] Encouraged by the response, he asked the Rev. W. Everard Edmonds, a retired high school teacher, to be the editor, then contacted our department for assistance in launching the new publication.

I was designated the liaison person in seeing the magazine into print. For the first issue, the Society decided to produce seven hundred copies, of which four hundred would be paid for by the government. This first issue, released in April 1953, was mimeographed, thirty-five pages long on legal-size paper. It included four lectures that had been given at society meetings and contained a brief history of the organization. Copies were sent to the ninety-one members of the Society while others were widely circulated to libraries, newspapers, and interested persons throughout the province.

This first issue surpassed all expectations. Shortly after it was released, MacGregor wrote to the editor, "The reception given the *Review* has been most gratifying. Mr. George [the treasurer] advised that we have received 130 new subscriptions and he has sent me dozens of complimentary letters which he has received."[28] This more than doubled the previous membership and there was no sign of a letup. As a result, the first printing was soon gone and it was necessary to reprint another hundred copies and to order 500 copies of the number two.

Fairly quickly, Edmonds and I slipped into a routine. He gathered the articles (mostly papers given at earlier meetings) and carefully prepared everything else in handwritten form. He then delivered to me at the Publicity Bureau a bundle containing the articles and news of society happenings. I organized it, had it typed by one of the secretaries, and delivered it to a company which printed and bound the copies. When I received the invoice, I deducted the cost for the first four hundred (later increased to five hundred) and sent an invoice to the Historical Society for the remainder. I also began contributing articles to the magazine, starting with "Story of the Blood Reserve" in 1953, and "Fort Ostell and the Riel Rebellion" in 1954.

Because of my involvement, I soon found myself recruited into the society by Jim MacGregor. At the annual meeting in February 1954, I was elected to the executive committee before I had even become a member. My task, besides working with Edmonds on the editorial side, was to arrange for newsstand sales of the magazine all across Alberta. At its peak, we were selling more than a hundred copies through the news outlets.

A year later, when looking at the invoices, I realized that we were paying a lot of money because of the amount of mimeograph paper we were using in the cumbersome magazine. On a hunch, I checked with some friends at Douglas Printers and learned that we could get a professionally printed, glossy, illustrated magazine, 7 x 10 inches, for approximately the same price we were paying for the mimeographed ones. A quick change was made and everyone was happy. We now had a format which was kept for the next thirty-seven years, changing the name to *Alberta History* in 1975, and switching in 1992 to the format and size used today.

In 1956, I officially became associate editor of the magazine even though I had actually been filling that role since 1953 and would continue to guide its production throughout my career. When I moved to Calgary, Edmonds and I continued to work together at a distance, but two years later he was obliged to resign because of ill health. I then took over as the editor, a role I accepted with pleasure and continued to pursue in my spare time during all my years at Glenbow.

My involvement in the Historical Society opened a whole new vista for me in the way of interests and friends. I attended meetings, heard interesting lectures, and became friends with many of the members. Jim and Frances MacGregor visited back and forth with Pauline and me, and I came to know people like Bruce Peel, Lewis G. Thomas, Ernie George, Sam Dickson, and Jean McCallum.

My responsibilities at the Publicity Bureau also increased when the Historical Society convinced the Alberta government that it should launch a historical sign program, similar to the one which was so successful in Montana. I was given the task of looking at the recommendations, making suggestions to the deputy, and arranging for the placement of the highway signs. In the early years, I wrote virtually all of the text myself, selected the sites in conjunction with an engineer from the Department of Highways, and attended the official unveilings. These signs, commemorating such events as the Frank Slide, arrival of the North-West Mounted Police, Jerry Potts, the Frog Lake Massacre, and the first irrigation ditch, became very popular tourist attractions.

---

My interest in history naturally led to freelance writing. At first my sights were set high on such major magazines as Macleans, Argosy, and True, but after a few rejection slips I concentrated on more local publications. I launched a long association with the Montana Historical Society in 1953 when they published my article, "The Amazing Death of Calf Shirt,"[29] and also had stories in Scarlet and Gold[30] and Western Canada Police Review.[31] Actually, my start with Scarlet and Gold – a magazine for RCMP veterans – had been an accident. It started in 1951 when I read an article by Philip H. Godsell dealing with the pursuit of a Blood Indian named Charcoal.[32] I was disgusted when I read that Godsell had the Indians speaking Cree instead of Blackfoot. By this time, I was already appreciating the pride that many Bloods had in themselves and saw the article as an insult to the tribe. I wrote to the editor of the magazine, venting my spleen and was surprised when I received a response, asking me to contribute an article. I was also told that Godsell had been reprimanded by the editor for his undue liberties with historical fact. Little did I know that a few years later I would be working with Godsell at the Glenbow Foundation. At that time he immediately made it clear that he did not forgive nor forget my earlier criticism, and indicated he had no use for me. That was fine, as the feeling was mutual.

One of Pauline's good friends in Edmonton when I met her was Father Antonio Duhaime, an Oblate priest. He had been a teacher and coach at St. Mary's school on the Blood Reserve and met Pauline and her friends at the

Camsell Hospital when he was transferred to Edmonton. Tony encouraged my Native studies and in the summer of 1954 asked me if I would like to prepare an English edition of *Le Grand Chef des Prairies*, a biography of Father Albert Lacombe, written by Father Paul-Emile Breton. A brother at Lac La Biche had made a word-for-word translation into English but it was unpublishable. When I agreed, Tony took me to see Father J.O. Fournier, the Provincial Superior, who gave me a $100 contract to write the English edition. He also gave me free access to the Oblate Archives, which were not open to the public.

For the next four months, I laboured over the manuscript in my spare time and enjoyed every minute of it. I checked quotations against their originals, particularly the ones written in English, added details from letters in the archives, and put the manuscript into literary form. Father Fournier was a delightful man who regaled me with stories of the early missionaries and some of their foibles. One day, he had Father Devique (an elderly priest who was looking after the archives) dig up a letter in which the bishop had instructed a priest to "get that sixteen-year-old girl out of your room." I think Father Devique was scandalized by the idea of a Protestant having access to his beloved files, but even more so when his Provincial Superior was revealing the order's deepest secrets. But it was all in good fun, and Father Fournier succeeded in putting a human face on the missionaries of the past.

Late in 1954, the manuscript was finished and published in Montreal under the title *The Big Chief of the Prairies*. In the front, I was pleased to read, "Acknowledgement is given to Mr. Hugh A. Dempsey who translated and revised the text."

During this period of research and writing I was still living at home and being outrageously pampered by my mother. I slept late on Sundays, spent countless hours on the phone with Pauline when I couldn't be with her, and devoted my spare time either to writing or painting. My father had retired from Canada Customs and was actively pursuing his interests as an elder of the Presbyterian Church and as a gardener. He was a man of strong principles, strong ideals, and with a firm sense of what was right or wrong. I never knew anyone who could see the world in black and white, without shades of grey, the way he could.

He was a faithful adherent of the Loyal Order of Orange and had demonstrated a number of prejudices over the years, including opposition to French-Canadians and the Catholic church. He had even been a member of the Ku Klux Klan for a short period in the late 1920s, but had quit when fellow Klansmen wanted to burn a cross on the lawn of the Catholic Church in

Edgerton. He abhorred such overt actions; he had joined the Klan simply as an outlet for agrarian protest, as an interim stopgap between his support for the Progressives of the 1920s and Social Credit of the 1930s.

I was pleased that his prejudices did not extend to Indians. In fact, the opposite was true as he welcomed Pauline and her folks into their house on many occasions. I believe his brief experience as a clerk with the Edmonton Indian Agency in the 1930s had given him a positive outlook on Indian people generally, and later to Pauline in particular. So Pauline felt just as welcome in our home as I did in hers.

⚬⚬⚬

Pauline and I became engaged in 1952, and that summer I learned something about the extended family. In white society, a "family" usually consists of one or more parents and their children. In the Indian society, the word can mean parents, children, grandparents, aunts, uncles, cousins, foster children, adopted children, and even friends and adopted adults.

During the summer, for example, I was visiting the Gladstones while on a government assignment and met Mr. and Mrs. Charlie Revais, from Browning, Montana. Charlie was introduced to me as Mr. Gladstone's father. This puzzled me greatly, as I already knew quite a bit about the family and it did not include a handsome elderly Indian from Montana. Only later did I learn that many years earlier Pauline's father had befriended an Indian cowboy who had been hurt in a riding accident and had put him up for the winter. He was Charlie's brother, and the following spring, Charlie came to the Blood Reserve and expressed his gratitude by adopting Pauline's father as his son. There was no blood relationship but both families took the "adoption" quite seriously.

A similar situation existed between Pauline's dad and Joe Bull Shield, except in this case they were brothers. When they were in residential school together, Joe's father had taken Pauline's dad as his son and gave him the name of *Akainamuka*, or Many Guns. As a result, Joe and Pauline's dad always considered themselves to be kin, in an Indian sense.

During the early summer, Joe and Dorothy Bull Shield visited us in Edmonton and we took them for a tour around the city and out to the Winterburn Reserve. When we were parked, Joe, who was sitting in the front seat beside me, spoke to Pauline in Blackfoot, "Does my son-in-law have an Indian name yet?" He used the term "son-in-law" because of the close relationship between him and Pauline's dad.

"No," she said. "He hasn't."

"Well, my son-in-law suits my name better than I do. I'll give it to him." He then turned to me and said in English, "Here, I'm giving you my name of *Piksi'nee*. Take it." In saying this, he cupped his hands and "threw" the name at me. Following Pauline's instructions, I made the motion to "receive" the name.

"*Piksi'nee*," I repeated. "What does it mean?"

Dorothy and Pauline laughed and Pauline said, "It means 'Skinny.'" They explained that this had been his young man's name. Now, truthfully, it fit me perfectly, as I was as thin as a rail, while Joe was expanding with age. Ever since then, *Piksi'nee* has been my personal name, the one used by my family and close friends. I have received other "official" names but this one has always been my personal name, the one that Pauline uses when she says something to me in Blackfoot.

Then, a few months later while on assignment in Fort Macleod, I was taken aside by Pat Bad Eagle, patriarch of the Peigan tribe, and given the name of *A'sitapina*, or Young Chief. Pat also took me as his adopted son. We had first met at the Camsell Hospital, where a number of his grandchildren had just been confined. When Pauline and I arrived at the hospital, Pat and his wife were outside, looking up at one of the windows and crying. Pauline was able to calm them down and learned that they were not allowed to visit their grandchildren until some initial tests had been done. They didn't understand this; they thought they were permanently banned from seeing their young ones. Over a period of time, Pat and I became good friends, and from that time on, the Peigans always referred to me as Young Chief.

That Christmas, 1952, Pauline and I were back home on the Blood Reserve for the holidays and this time the family announced that we were all going to the Christmas dance. After supper we followed the Blue Trail across the prairie and then went along the snow-covered Glenwood road until we came to the Bullhorn community hall. This hall was the same one where I, as a stranger, had attended the Indian Association meeting only eighteen months earlier. It seemed like a lifetime ago. At the hall, we saw pickup trucks, cars, sleighs, and saddle horses scattered everywhere and from inside we could hear the tum-tum-tum of the drum.

Two big dances were held during the holiday season. On Christmas night it was sponsored by the Horn Society, the most sacred religious organization on the reserve, while the New Year's Eve dance was put on by the Magpies, an age-grade society of young men. Little did I realize that within a few years,

I would be inducted into their group. At both of these gatherings there were chicken dances, owl dances, round dances, honouring dances, and chiefs' dances, all to the beat and singing of the drum group at the far end of the hall.

I learned that the Bloods had retained from the buffalo hunting days some vestiges of their warrior age-grade society system. There were eleven societies, each based upon the ages of the men involved. The youngest were the Magpies for men under the age of twenty-eight. Next oldest, in five or ten year groupings, were the Small Change, Skinny Horses, Eagles, Red Belts, Crazy Dogs, Tall Hats, Big Holes in the Ear Lobes, Fast Horses, Shell Earrings, and Crow Indians. At that time, Iron was the only surviving member of the latter group.

While at one time these societies had a role in protecting the camps and performing ceremonies, they now limited their activities to sponsoring dances. There was great rivalry among them, with all even-numbered societies considering each other as allies, and all the odd-numbered ones as their competitors. That year, the Magpies had the New Year's Eve dance, the Small Change the pre-Lent dance, and Skinny Horses the Easter dance.

There were at least a thousand people jammed into the hall, and the only white people I saw were priests or teachers from the residential schools. At one stage, a fair red-headed child stopped in front of me, and I looked around for her parents. Then she burst forth with a torrent of Blackfoot to her friends and ran away laughing. I don't know if she could even speak English.

Wise to the ways of Indian pow-wows, the Gladstones had brought their folding chairs with them. They found a place with the Joe Bull Shields and Fred Tailfeathers families while Pauline and I paired off with Irene and Gerald.

Very quickly I learned there were rules that had to be followed. If anyone was dressed in their Native outfits, they had to join the chicken dance if one of the Magpies came along and tapped their legs with his whip. The owl dance was for couples, and three rules were that the women asked the men to dance, the men could not refuse, and wives could not dance with their husbands. Perhaps these were good rules to make people circulate, but they could also be the cause of considerable jealousy, especially if an old girl friend persistently asked a man to dance while his wife looked on.

About midnight, the Magpies had a feast for the crowd, handing out sandwiches, soft drinks, and cookies. At the same time, gifts of money and blankets were given away to visitors. Finally, about 2 a.m., while the dance was still going strong, we headed for home. I was told the dance would last until dawn, but it had been a long day and we were all tired.

A week later, we were back for the New Year's Eve dance. I was pleased to notice the complete absence of drunks at both dances, and when the Mounted Police patrols showed up, they had nothing to do except watch the dance for a few minutes and continue on their way.

On our return to Edmonton, I mentioned the dances in one of my letters to Douglas Leechman at the National Museum of Canada, and he thought it was a subject worth pursuing. He said if I wrote it, he would see if he could get it published in one of the scientific journals. This was a new experience for me, but I wrote the manuscript, "Social Dances of the Blood Indians," and it was eventually published by the *Journal of American Folklore*, a prestigious American periodical.[33] This was my first experience with the professional world of ethnology, but over the next several years I had other papers published by such periodicals as the *Journal of the Washington Academy of Sciences, Plains Anthropologist, American Anthropologist, Natural History,* and others.

———— ⚭ ————

With a growing interest in Native history, I remembered that a Cree named John Rabbit had invited me out to his place on the Louis Bull Reserve. This invitation occurred at one of my first Indian Association meetings. So one spring day Pauline and I drove out to his log house in the Bear Hills, and after some visiting the storytelling began. John was there with his wife and his friend Tom Bull. Perhaps the most interesting story came from Mrs. Rabbit. She told us that when she was a young girl she saw the Little People playing in the Red Deer River. These were the *Maymaykwaysiuk* believed by the Cree to inhabit the lakes and sandhills. She said they were about eighteen inches tall, with big bellies and white faces. "Their ears were big too," she said, "and they were something like little bears."[34] She ran down for a closer look but they went into a whirlpool or eddy and disappeared.

At this point in the story, John Rabbit reached into his vest pocket and took out an arrowhead that was about two inches long. He said he found it on a hill said to be frequented by the Little People and he wanted me to keep it. I have it still.

I found out later that stories about the Little People were common. They were said to have made all the stone arrowheads used by the Crees. They left them on rocks or in open areas for the Crees to find.

After the storytelling, John took me out to an old Sun Dance camp that was still standing. He let me take a picture of it, also of the buffalo skull that had been used in the ceremony, and the frame of a nearby sweatlodge. He then showed me a deep rutted trail and wallow that he said had been made by buffalo, not cattle.

After I bid goodbye to this kindly man, Pauline and I were making our way back home when we became hopelessly stuck in a mudhole on the reserve. The nearest house wasn't far away, but we were worried as we could hear sounds of revelry coming from it. Regardless, I knocked on the door and was greeted by some happy drunks. When they learned of my predicament, they hitched up a team and promptly pulled us out. When I tried to offer them money, they just laughed and went back to their party. This was quite an introduction to the Crees, their friendliness and their hospitality.

<hr>

After a long engagement, Pauline and I were married on August 31, 1953. The decision was made – at my urging – that we should be married in St. Stephen's Anglican church in Edmonton, and have the reception at St. Paul's school on the Blood Reserve. My thinking was that many of our friends, as well as my family, would not be able to make the long trip to Cardston, while on Pauline's side they were all a bunch of travellers. Pauline agreed, but only after it was all over did I learn that she had had her heart set on being married on the Blood Reserve. She wanted all her old school chums to be there to send her off in grand style. I just wish she had told me beforehand but by then we were already married. One of my many faults was to see something as being logical and assume that everyone else would see it the same way. I did not take into account that emotion can be just as important, if not more so, than logic.

We were married in Edmonton, with Rev. J.E. DeWolf, missionary on the Blood Reserve, coming north to conduct the services. My brother Glen was my best man while Irene Tailfeathers was matron of honour and Naomi Foster and Audrey Pilling were bridesmaids. It was a very ecumenical wedding in many ways. Pauline, Irene, and Naomi were Anglicans; I was Presbyterian (but soon to turn Anglican); Glen was United Church; and Audrey was Mormon. And we were driven to the church by Tony Duhaime, the Oblate priest who was a long-time friend of ours. However, ecumenicalism had not progressed to the point where Tony could enter the church. Instead, he sat in the car reading his Bible until we emerged amid rice and confetti.

A few months earlier, I had purchased my first car, an old 1941 Ford sedan which was a piece of junk when I got it and was still a piece of junk when the transmission gave out a year or so later. With this as our transportation, we made our way to Cardston for a big reception and supper in the church hall. The place was jammed with Indians, government and school staff, local ranchers, and old friends. Master of ceremonies for the evening was Ralph D. Ragan, the Indian agent. The toast to the bride was given by Canon S.H. Middleton, who recalled that the first wedding he ever performed on the Blood Reserve was that of Pauline's parents. A toast was also proposed by Mike Mountain Horse, a long-time friend of the family and the husband of Pauline's Aunt Mary. Other speeches were made by Pat Bad Eagle and Many Guns, who had come from the Peigan Reserve. After a huge dinner prepared by the staff and students, the evening ended with dancing to a live band, the Rhythm Ramblers.

Fearful that my old Ford wouldn't make it back from the honeymoon, Pauline's dad insisted that we use his car. We had intended to go to Glacier Park that night but the dance lasted so long that we got to the border a few minutes after the customs office had closed. As a result, we spent the first night of our honeymoon in a dingy tourist cabin at Carway. But it really didn't matter, as we were together. For the rest of the honeymoon we had a wonderful time as we wended our way over Logan Pass, through the mountains, and on to Spokane.

On our return to Edmonton, we rented an upstairs suite in an old house just off Jasper Avenue. The landlady, Miss Paul, was a spinster who kept to herself and treated us well. I don't know what she thought of the steady stream of Indians who came and went from the house but she never complained. We stayed there a year until we had enough money for a down payment on a small house on the South Side. That year was the only time I had ever lived in anything but a detached house. I didn't mind it, but I was glad to get our own place.

---

Now that we were together, Pauline and I were seldom without house guests or visitors. Pauline's mom and dad visited us regularly and stayed for days at a time. It was delightful having them, as Dad (I guess I can call him that now) and I never ran out of things to talk about. More and more, I became immersed in the activities of the Indian Association of Alberta, attending annual conferences, helping to write resolutions, and watching the directions of the political winds. This was particularly true of the Alberta government, for I was in an ideal position to see what was going on. I told the premier's executive assistant, Pete Elliott, about my interests and more than once he phoned me to find out what was happening on the Indian side.

Once, I interviewed E.S. Heustis, Alberta fish and game commissioner, for a *Within Our Borders* story on beaver ranching. I had been led to believe that he was an ogre who had always hated Indians. I knew that he had prevented them from killing female game for food, even though they had a treaty right to do so, and that he considered any fishing with nets to be commercial fishing. After the meeting, I wrote to Pauline, "I had a long talk with Mr. Heustis and … drew him out on his policy with Indians. It gives me a slightly different impression of him now. Here are a few of the things he said, word for word: 'I just can't understand those people. For years, I tried to play fair with them, but all I got for it was headache and heartache. So I've just about given up. Sometimes I'd like to kill every God-damned one!' That is word for word, so you can see, and I felt it, that he is bitter and disillusioned. He gave me examples, too. Apparently beaver control is one of his favourite projects. He said he cooperated fully with the Indian Department to stock beaver on reserves. But he said it did no good. Instead of only trapping a limited quota each year and allowing them to become established, they would clean them all out the first year. But I will say his reasoning for the female game problem doesn't hold water."[35] The information did not make Heustis any easier to deal with, but at least there was some indication of why he was reacting the way he was.

On the matter of female game, one time in 1952 I was tipped off by Ivor Eklund, fur supervisor for Indian Affairs, that the Alberta government had made an illegal seizure. Four members of Paul's band, near Wabamun, had an elk and two deer carcasses seized by a provincial game officer. Not only that, but the officer didn't have enough room in his car, so he made the Indians transport the meat to Entwistle so it could be sent to the Edmonton residential school. The action left the families of the hunters stranded in the bush with only bannock and tea for food. As the IAA was involved in contesting another female game case at the time, I was able to pass the information along to give the lawyers more ammunition to fight illegal actions of the Game Branch.

But perhaps my most dramatic involvement between the Association and the government occurred over the question of provincial old age assistance. In 1952, the federal old age pension scheme was extended to include Indians over 70 years of age, but assistance for the 65-to-69–year group was a responsibility of the provincial government. John Laurie, secretary of the IAA, asked whether this program, too, would be extended to Indians but was told that a decision had not yet been reached. In fact, the Alberta government intended to provide old age assistance, but details of a federal cost-sharing arrangement were still being negotiated. Laurie, however, took the delay to mean that the

Alberta government was refusing to participate. As it happened, the annual meeting of the Association was taking place on the Blackfoot Reserve when the delay occurred, and Laurie told the press that "the Province of Alberta has so far refused to grant old age assistance."[36] He also drafted a resolution which attacked the government for its "punitive laws and all restrictive regulations."[37]

On the second day of the conference, Laurie phoned Premier Manning's office and learned that old age assistance for Indians had been approved and would become effective retroactive to January 1st. He immediately announced the news at the general meeting and left the impression among the press that the government had been a reluctant participant but that Laurie had won them over.

The premier was furious when he read the newspaper accounts. I was in Pete Elliott's office when the incident occurred and Pete asked me, "Who in the hell is this John Laurie?" I explained his role in the IAA and Pete said he'd pass the information along to the premier. Later that day, I wrote to Dad, saying "The Indians almost didn't get the old age assistance. Apparently an Order-in-Council was ready to go before the Executive Council at least three days before the IAA meeting, and Mr. Laurie's remarks at the convention almost made the premier tear up the bill."[38] I don't know if my comments were of any help in that particular situation but they did explain what was happening within the IAA.

Don't get me wrong. John Laurie was the best thing that could ever have happened to the Indians of Alberta. He was utterly devoted to the cause of improving the lot of Indian people and he knew how to make best use of the press, opposition Members of Parliament, and sympathetic organizations to get action out of Ottawa. He may have had a high profile in the newspapers, but within the IAA he made it clear that he was simply their secretary and did not try to run their meetings. He sat at his table taking minutes, and if he felt the meeting was getting off the track he simply passed a quiet comment to Dave Crowchild, who proceeded to set things straight.

Laurie was a Calgary schoolteacher who came to the attention of the Association after he had helped the Stoneys get new reserves at Eden Valley and Bighorn. When the IAA was close to folding in 1944, Laurie stepped in and gave it the kind of business organization and political clout that it needed. I admired and liked the man from the first time I met him. While I was still living at home, he was a guest at my parents' house for dinner and we found that both of us shared a lively interest in Native history. During all the time I was in Edmonton, we corresponded with each other and a number of times when I was with Dad we visited him in Calgary.

Politically, Laurie was a left-wing member of the CCF party, but most of his lobbying was with the Conservatives. Doug Harkness, the Conservative MP from Calgary, was the Indian Affairs critic in the House of Commons and Laurie was one of his closest confidants. Laurie was extremely suspicious of the federal government, and rightly so. He questioned their motives on just about every action they took and firmly believed that their secret agenda was to divest themselves of any responsibility for Indians and to force them into Canada's mainstream population. For that reason, he opposed Indians getting the vote. He was also opposed to the extension of liquor privileges to Indians, but this was more from his Calvinist background than from politics. In these two areas – the vote and liquor – he interfered blatantly in IAA policies, but otherwise he left them alone.

One of Laurie's greatest contributions had occurred in 1950–51, just as I was getting involved. In 1950, the federal government introduced a new Indian Act which was even more restrictive than the old. With only a few days in which to organize a campaign before a quick third reading of the bill, he used all his contacts to flood the Liberal government offices with complaints from Native and white groups. As a result the bill was tabled and, for the first time, the government agreed to consult with Indians before bringing forth a new Act. They partially kept their promise, calling conferences of mostly handpicked people, but the IAA could not be ignored and managed to see that the new Act, passed in 1951, was more equitable than the old one.

Once Pauline and I were married and ensconced in our own apartment, we became kind of a crossroads for people who were personal friends of the family. Sometimes they were on their way to IAA executive meetings while at other times they were simply visiting friends or relatives in the Charles Camsell Hospital.

———— ∞ ————

After the positive experience of interviewing Iron and Rosie Davis in 1951 I was anxious to pursue more oral histories. Because of the distance between Edmonton and the Blood Reserve, I was limited to summer and Christmas holidays. However, I had been visiting patients at the Camsell Hospital with Pauline for a couple of years and had made some good friends. Among them were Percy Plain Woman and Albert Wells from the Blood Reserve and Jack Black Horse from the Blackfoot. When I asked Albert any questions, almost every answer was prefixed with the comment, "Jack Black Horse told me..." As a result, I decided to interview Jack. The only problem was that he spoke practically no English and, while Pauline was completely fluent in Blackfoot, she had never tried interpreting. But always game, she accompanied me to the Camsell on a couple of weekends after our honeymoon so that I could speak with him.

Jack explained that he was a son of Big Meat Eater, who had died in 1928 at the age of ninety. His information had come from his father. Jack decided that he wanted to tell me about the origin of the Sun Dance and of the four people who contributed to its success. These were Beaver Man, Scar Face, Night Rider, and Tail Feathers Woman. Patiently, he explained how Beaver Man had been given the beaver bundle on the shore of Waterton Lake; how Scar Face had visited the Sun and received the Sun Dance ceremony; how Night Rider (also known as Scabby Round Robe) had been befriended by beavers; and how Tail Feathers Woman had married the Morning Star. In the end, according to his account, these four people came together to put up the first Sun Dance.

Everything went well as far as the translations were concerned, except for one amusing incident. We were at the point in the story where Scar Face and Morning Star went to hunt birds along the lake shore. Black Horse said the birds were *Sai-eeks*.

"I don't know what they are," Pauline told me. "Maybe they're geese or swans."

"No," interrupted Black Horse, "They're ducks."

That was the first time that either Pauline or I knew that Black Horse could speak English. He didn't consider himself proficient in the language so he spoke it only when he had to. From that time on, I found that I could visit him without Pauline there, as he really did not need an interpreter. It became even easier to visit him a short time later when the hospital authorities moved Albert Wells to the adjacent bed.

On another visit later in 1953, Black Horse told me that he wanted to sing a song for me. It started on a high note then gradually went lower and lower until I thought his voice must have been coming from the bottom of his feet. By this time, I had heard a lot of Indian songs and while I have no ear for music, I found this one to me dramatically different and very melancholy. After he was finished, he explained through Albert Wells that it was a ghost song.

He said that long ago, a Blackfoot Indian had become lost in a blizzard and was almost dead when he stumbled onto a lone tepee. When he went inside he saw it was a burial lodge. Opposite the doorway on a scaffold were the skeletons of three dead Indians. Frightened, he was about to leave when one of the skeletons called to him.

"Come and build a fire," it said. "We won't hurt you."[39]

The man did as he was told and when he was warm, the skeleton said they would teach him a song and a dance.

"They began to sing the Ghost Dance Song I have just sung," Black Horse told me, "and showed him the dance. They would get up and dance a slow step, moving their fists in front of them, sit down, then get up and repeat it again. After the warrior watched them for a little while, he joined them and soon learned the song. He stayed with the skeletons all that night and in the morning, when the blizzard ended, he returned to his people and brought the Ghost Dance and song with him."

"This is not a legend," Black Horse assured me. "It really happened."

It was certainly nice having friends like Percy Plain Woman and Jack Black Horse. Both were released from the Camsell a few months later but that didn't end our friendship. I have in front of me a letter which Jack sent to me a month after he was released. It was obviously written for him by a member of his family. "You know," he said, "since I ever got back home now here on the Blackfoot Reserve, seems to me everything is been changed. Every Sunday, they have rodeos, and lot of people attended it.... I give you a big hello to you and your wife. I miss both of you. Hope to see you in the future."[40] Similarly, Percy wrote from the Blood Reserve, "I'll send you a nice painting some time next month. I just got started again the last two weeks. My rheumatism was bothering me all summer, especially the weather, but I am O.K. now. I am sending Pauline a little pair of moccasins and a little doll for you.... Well, my dear friends, I close now with the best of luck."[41]

I experienced this warm friendship time and time again as I ventured deeper into the Indian community. By the time Pauline and I were married, I had pretty well concluded that there wasn't enough for a book on her grandfather, but discussions with her dad, members of the family, and correspondence with Jack Ewers opened up several new fields to explore. In particular, I became curious about Blackfoot traditional leadership and the biographies of some of the leading chiefs. It's strange, but right from the first I was more interested in the lives of people than I was in religious practices, mythology, material culture, and all the other topics that are near and dear to so many ethnologists.

The interest in biographies started innocently enough when I began borrowing letter-books of correspondence from the Blood Indian Agency for the period from 1880 to 1900. Ralph Ragan, the Indian agent, generously allowed me to take three or four volumes at a time, and I laboriously copied out any reports and letters that seemed interesting. In a letter to Jack Ewers, I mentioned an incident in 1882 where a Blood chief named Running Rabbit had given up his leadership and moved south to become a chief of the South Peigans in Montana. Ewers was interested, as most of his work had been among the Montana Indians; he was familiar with a great leader named Running Rabbit but was unaware of any Canadian connection. As it turned out, there were two Running Rabbits, an American one and a Canadian one. However, by the time I learned this, I had already become interested in the identities, careers, and politics of Blood chiefs.

I learned that the Blood tribe had been made up of bands with distinctive names such as Fish Eaters, All Tall People, Lone Fighters, etc., and each was led by a chief. Soon such personal names as Red Crow, Seen From Afar, Bull Back Fat, and Father of Many Children were floating past my eyes, each seeming to be a subject worthy of study. Excitedly, I planned (with Pauline's blessing) to devote part of our summer and Christmas holidays speaking with elders. Dad was free and agreed to be my interpreter.

And so began the most active year of my life in the pursuit of oral history. During July, October, and December I spoke to more than two dozen people, many of them unilingual, and all of them wondering why a twenty-three-year-old white man would be interested in their stories. During this period, the only white people to regularly visit their homes were missionaries, Indian Agency employees, or bootleggers. I didn't fit any of these categories and under normal conditions I would have been greeted with considerable suspicion. But because I was the son-in-law of *Akainamuka*, they could immediately pigeonhole me and welcome me as a guest, and later as a friend. More than once, elders complained that no one listened to their stories any more. Their children were too busy and their grandchildren simply weren't interested. As a result, they were not only willing, but anxious to talk of the "old days" and to share the information that had been passed down to them.

The usual procedure was to drive up to a person's place and for Dad to go inside to explain my mission. Often they asked us to come back later, and it didn't take me long to realize that they wanted to tidy up the house and get tea ready for their unusual visitor. When we entered, I shook hands with everybody in sight. That was another lesson I learned. If I missed someone, like an old lady sitting in a dark corner, she'd never forgive me.

Some homes were of log or frame construction on a small plot of land. Others were tiny cabins in the newly established village of Moses Lake, on the northern outskirts of Cardston. And in a few cases, the interviews took place in a tent, or in a tepee at the Sun Dance. Sometimes, if it seemed to be the right thing to do, the elder was brought to the Gladstone farm for a visit and a meal.

I quickly learned that there were certain protocols to be followed. For example, if I entered a door from the east and saw a stove in the middle of the room and the elder on the far side, I knew the room had been laid out in the same fashion as a tepee. This meant that the fire, i.e., stove, was in the middle, the owner of the lodge was at the back, and his altar was in front of him. Female members sat on the south side of the room, and men on the north. The altar consisted of a shallow box of clay holding such holy objects as *iniskim*, or buffalo stones, and the ashes of a fire. Beside the box might be a piece of braided sweetgrass while nearby were his pipe, fire tongs, and bags containing tobacco, paint, and other items needed for daily ablutions and ceremonies.

It was important never to go between a man and his altar, or between the altar and the stove. If, for example, I had a photograph that I wanted to show someone sitting to the right of the elder, I walked all the way around the stove and handed it to them.

Once we shook hands, often nothing happened for quite a while. It took a few visits to realize that this was an accepted practice among the traditionalists. The elder would point to our seats, and Dad might open a package of cigarettes and pass one to the elder. They would light up (I never did smoke) and sit pondering the floor. In many cases, the elder was obviously curious about my visit, but he was too polite to ask. Finally, the silence would be broken when Dad started speaking quietly in Blackfoot. The conversation had nothing to do with my visit. Often he asked about the man's cattle or horses, or commented on the condition of the hay crop. Or the elder might ask about the Indian Association or enquire whether anything had been done about interest payments or grazing leases.

After a reasonable amount of conversation, Dad switched over to the reason for my visit, explaining who I was and why I was interested. To this day, I have no real knowledge of what was said, for the conversation was entirely in Blackfoot. But as they spoke, the elder would look at me from time to time, as though confirming some comment that had been made about me. Then, at last, Dad would lean back and say to me, "Okay, what do you want to ask him?"

I never learned regular shorthand but I did use a method picked up at the *Bulletin* whereby I would write down the key words of a conversation. Besides, there was always time while Dad was interpreting for me to polish my notes. And I made a point of typing them as soon as possible while the conversations were still fresh in my mind.

Dad was a wonderful interpreter. He knew how to ask the right questions, often taking a different approach than my enquiry if I happened to be on the wrong track or was violating some aspect of the culture. He had an extensive knowledge of the language, both ancient words and modern ones. He also knew sign language so if he really got stuck, he could still make himself understood. In speaking to me, he gave me everything that was said, including the conversations. That was one thing I noticed about Blackfoot storytelling. Even though an incident might have occurred two or three generations earlier, the informant would speak as though he had been there, complete with conversations. And, among those elders who proved to be reliable, the conversations when compared with government reports or other documents proved to be strikingly similar. This simply pointed out the importance of accuracy among a people with no written language. One could be confident among good informants that the story was being passed along just as he had heard it.

Sadly, not all elders were reliable. Sometimes Dad warned me about them, while at other times I had to learn for myself. Some had shown no interest in history or culture while they were young. They were too busy being cowboys, chasing women, or getting into trouble with the law. Others simply had bad memories. If they happened to live to an advanced age, they started to take on the mantle of an elder but it didn't change the fact that they didn't know anything. To make matters worse, such people sometimes were inclined to invent something rather than admit that they didn't know. I could name half a dozen people like that, but naturally I won't, as their memories are revered among their families, even though they may have left a litany of misinformation for future generations. Happily, they were in the minority.

Over a period of time, I developed a couple of methods for determining the accuracy of elders. For example, I would pick out nine or ten statements of fact from an elder and compare them with different sources, such as statements of other elders, fur trade records, and government documents. If I could find comparative data for even half of them and they checked out, then I knew the elder was reliable. Also, if an elder told me something that was extremely important, I might run it by another elder without giving the source. If he verified it, I knew it was true.

Speaking of truth, someone once asked me how I could believe all the stories about ghosts, visions, animals taking human form, and other supernatural events. The answer was simple. The information was the truth as far as the elder was concerned, so I accepted it as his truth. I did not question its logic but felt that if the elder believed it then I believed him. But more important, these tales fitted perfectly into the beliefs and customs of the tribe. To understand the Blackfoot, one had to understand their perceptions of the world and everything in it.

Some of my best male informants were Jim White Bull, Jack Low Horn, John Cotton, Charlie Pantherbone, Bobtail Chief, Harry Mills, Percy Creighton, George Calling Last, Frank Red Crow, Big Sorrel Horse, Iron, Laurie Plume, Rides at the Door, and Shot Both Sides. Among the Blackfoot were One Gun, Ben Calf Robe, Paul Wolf Collar, Ayoungman, and Heavy Shield, and with the Peigans were Pat Bad Eagle, John Yellowhorn, Good Rider, Joe Potts, and Joe Crow Shoe. Among the women were Suzette Eagle Ribs, Rosie Davis, Jennie Duck Chief, and Vickie McHugh. There were lots of others, but these stand out in my mind.

The only reason I didn't interview more women was because I had a male interpreter. If we had pursued some of the possible informants, we would have been the subject of gossip, and this I wanted to avoid. Pauline made it clear that she didn't particularly want to interpret, and because of the mother-in-law taboo, I really couldn't ask her mother. Most of the women we did interview were relatives or old friends of the Gladstone family.

A word about the mother-in-law taboo. In traditional families, a son-in-law was not supposed to speak directly to his mother-in-law and avoid even staying in the same room with her if this was possible. When Pauline's eldest sister, Lucy, married Wilton Frank, the mother-in-law taboo was honoured as much as possible. However, the second girl to marry was Doreen, and her husband Max was a blond, blue-eyed New Zealander. When they came to the farm, Mom tried to follow the taboo custom but after a couple of days, Max stopped her in the kitchen and said, "What's the matter, mother? Are you mad at me?" Everyone started to laugh and the taboo ended right there. However, the unease remained, and when Pauline and I were married, Mom didn't avoid me but neither was she openly talkative and chatty as she was with her female friends.

From time to time, I wrote down personal observations about the elders as I was interviewing them. For example, when I saw Jennie Duck Chief, she was ninety-three years old. I noted that "she was reclining in her iron cot which was covered with mattresses and an array of blankets and quilts. She wore a black knitted coat and had a kerchief pulled tightly around her hair. Lying on the bed was her willow walking stick, its end blackened by poking the fire."[42] Of Bobtail Chief I commented, "He is blind and speaks no English. He sat cross legged in the middle of his bed, with a jam can beside him for an ashtray and spittoon. Behind him a tent canvas was nailed to the wall on the west side to keep out any drafts, and his medicine bundle was hung over his bed."[43] While interviewing Charlie Pantherbone (or Sinew Feet) I noted he was "as thin as a ghost, very mild in appearance, and with one of the most kindly faces I have ever seen."[44]

And the stories these people told! As they talked, I could envision White Wolf when he was surrounded by Crows and dared them to attack. I was with Running Wolf as he crouched in a coulee while his comrades were dying all around him. I listened with interest to the story of a feud between Seen From Afar and Big Snake with all its supernatural overtones. And I was impressed when White Calf cursed Calf Tail after the government had made him a chief and heard how had he died a few days later.

Not all stories had been passed down from earlier generations. Shot Both Sides told me of his own raids against enemy tribes. John Cotton described his tribe's last buffalo hunt and how he'd been too scared to kill a buffalo calf. And Big Sorrel Horse let me know what it was like to farm a small patch of land using only a few crude hand tools.

I discovered that there had been five major bands in the Blood tribe, and from them came another thirteen offshoots. The two leading bands in the mid-nineteenth century were the Fish Eaters under Seen From Afar and the Followers of the Buffalo under Bull Back Fat. The politics were intriguing, and it was fascinating to hear how the Fish Eaters gradually gained ascendancy until by the time of Treaty Seven in 1877 they utterly dominated the tribe.

But by far the most engrossing story I heard that year came from Jack Low Horn. Just before sunset, Dad and I had driven to his home on the edge of Bullhorn Coulee. After the usual preliminaries, Jack asked me if I wanted to hear about the reincarnation of his father. Did I?! Wild horses couldn't have dragged me away. Jack spoke for almost five hours, with Dad carefully interpreting every word. What emerged was the saga of a Blackfoot chief who had been killed by Crees in the 1840s. At the moment of his death, Jack's father had been born, his ears already pierced for earrings and his body bearing the scars of musket ball wounds. He was given the name of Only Person Who Had a Different Gun, but when he was about five years old, he revealed to his family that he was the reincarnation of Low Horn. When this was determined to be true, he assumed the name of the dead warrior and went on to become a leading medicine man in his tribe. In 1899, when Jack was a teenager, his father had been killed when his wagon overturned into a muddy ditch. Low Horn had told everyone he had the power to come back to life if a ceremony was performed immediately after death by his oldest wife. Unfortunately, she was at the Timber Limit collecting tepee poles at the time of the accident, and by the time she got back, it was too late.

Jack told the whole story – the powers of the original Low Horn, his battle and death, the birth of Jack's father, the discovery of his real identity, his own mystical powers, and his ultimate death. Later, I found ample documentation in fur trade records, Indian Agency files, and other sources which backed up almost every statement he made, but added materially to my knowledge of the two great Low Horns. This story, with the added documentation, was published in my book *The Amazing Death of Calf Shirt and Other Blackfoot Stories*.

By the time 1954 was ending, I had notebooks full of stories, and files of typed transcripts to supplement the books, Indian Affairs letters, and other pieces of information I had amassed. I wasn't quite sure what I was going to do with the material but I knew that much of it would end up in print, either in books or articles. But more important, I knew it was information which was fast disappearing, and that if I didn't collect it no one else would.

And that was only the beginning, for in the ensuing five or six years, I used every opportunity to interview elders and collect their stories. During that time, Dad was out of office at the Indian Association so he had plenty of time to take me around to all his old friends and associates who were now elders of the tribe. In retrospect, I wish I could have done more, but when I look through my files of interviews, I am amazed at what I did do in my "spare" time.

During these years I met a number of Stoney Indians at Indian Association meetings and at the Calgary Stampede, but I was not really close to any of them. This was because I was a "Blackfoot," i.e., I was closely identified with the Blackfoot tribes who historically had been enemies of the Stoneys. Even today the intermingling of the two groups is very limited. The people were always polite and friendly to me, but not on a basis that made me feel like pursuing research or collecting stories among them. I did enquire one time about writing a history of the Stoneys but it never went anywhere.

———∞∞∞———

One of the most spectacular and gratifying interviews took place during the Christmas season of 1955. During the course of conversation one day, Dad mentioned that Joe Potts, a son of the famous scout Jerry Potts, was a next-door neighbour of Charlie Revais, Dad's adopted father. They lived in cabins along the Two Medicine River on the Blackfeet Reservation in Montana. When I asked if we could go and see him, Dad agreed, and we set out from the Blood Reserve in the early morning of December 30, 1955. The weather was cold and clear and the roads were all snow-packed. I didn't know it then, but many people limited their travel on the Cardston-Browning road to warm chinook days when the ice was melted off the roads.

, We set off in Dad's car, with Dad and I in the front seat and Mom and Pauline in the back. That was one practice that never changed. The women always sat in the back. Even after many years of marriage, Pauline insists in sitting in the back if there is another male in the car. I gave up years ago trying to argue with her about it. Anyway, we set off from the farm and I noticed we had the road virtually to ourselves all the way across the line to Babb and then to St. Mary's. The roads were snow-packed and there were high drifts on each side, but travel itself was no problem as long as one drove slowly and carefully.

From St. Mary's we went up the long hill to the top of the ridge that divides the watersheds of Hudson Bay and the Gulf of Mexico. I was moving along at a nice pace, gauged for the snowy roads, when we reached the summit and made a hairpin turn to go down the hill on the south side. However, I failed to appreciate the fact that the winter sun was beating down on the south side and the snow on the road had turned to sheer ice. Not only that, but at the hairpin turn and down the slope there were no fences or barriers of any kind. On one side were high snowdrifts hugging the bank, while on the other side of the road was nothing but a sharp incline to the bottom of the canyon.

As we hit the ice, I had enough presence of mind to cut the wheels sharply and almost in slow motion, the car skated down the slope, reaching the edge of the precipice and then slowly swinging towards the bank. There were four collective sighs of relief when the car finally bumped against the snowbank and stopped. If I had had my choice, I would have turned back right then and given up any idea of seeing Joe Potts. But we were sitting several yards down the slope of an icy hill with no way of getting back up. The only alternative was to keep going. Cautiously I turned the wheels and felt the car moving of its own accord on the icy surface. After a few yards, I cut the wheels again so that we bumped into the snowbank and stopped. I repeated this all the way down the hill, and by fits and stops we successfully reached the bottom.

But the problem was far from over, or so I thought. Ahead of us was a long stretch of road along a valley, then up over another dangerous mountain ridge that led down to Cutbank Creek. From there the highway split, one staying in the mountains to join up with the road to East Glacier, and the other going straight east to Star School. With more than my usual share of trepidation we crossed the valley and up over the next ridge. There I was overjoyed to find that my fears had been groundless. This piece of road was at a lower altitude than the Hudson Bay Divide and the area on the south side was dry and bare of snow! At the river, we cut east towards Star School, getting out of the mountains and back on the snow-covered roads of the prairies.

After a brief stop in Browning we continued on to Two Medicine River, where there was practically no snow. Dad took us to Joe Potts' cabin and we were pleased to find him at home. He was a kindly quiet man, and although he could speak English, he preferred to talk in Blackfoot with Dad translating. I learned that he had been twenty years old when his father died, and that he had left Alberta in 1901 when the North-West Mounted Police had a warrant for his arrest for horse stealing. He ultimately became a member of the Blackfeet Tribe and never moved back to Canada.

The interview itself was a revelation. I had read everything available on Jerry Potts, but virtually everything had come from the Mounted Police and gave only the white man's viewpoint of the man. From his son I got the whole Indian story and much of the other side too. I learned about Potts' parents, the murder of his mother, his experiences as a warrior.

"I was very young when my father related his war experiences at a Sun Dance at Brocket," he told me. "There was an Indian with whom he had a friendly feud of long standing and the main reason he counted his coups was to show that he was a greater warrior than his rival."

By the time we left, I had a picture of Jerry Potts that was two-dimensional, not the cardboard image that came from the Mounted Police stories. In addition Joe told me that he had a half-brother named Charlie who worked for the Carnation Milk company in Seattle. I hoped I might interview him as well, so I contacted him. He wrote a very nice letter saying he was only six years old when his father died and knew nothing about him. He did say that an old-time surveyor named Johns had his father's gun but when I tried to track it down I had no luck.

Needless to say, I was quite excited about all this new information about Jerry Potts, so when I got back to Edmonton I wrote a lengthy biography of him. I submitted this to *Argosy* and *Canadian Cattlemen*; the first turned it down without comment and the second because it was too long. So I sat on it for a few years and ultimately it was published as an Occasional Paper by the Glenbow Foundation. Since then, the Indian-based stories I got from Joe Potts have been "lifted" by numerous authors around the country. Grant MacEwan once told me I should enlarge the Occasional Paper into a full-length book but I didn't think there was enough there to do it. A local writer named Long did take my material and made a book out of it but, as I expected, it didn't work and the book was a flop. There was another so-called biography in 2005 that also borrowed heavily from my work.

⊶⊷

I was enjoying my publicity work for the government, but my interest in history took me in a new direction in January 1954 when Ed Bryant received an invitation to speak to the Canadian Club in Calgary. He could not attend so he suggested that I go instead. I agreed, and as a topic, I selected "Calgary in the Buffalo Days." Although the meeting was at noon, the only way I could conveniently travel was on the midnight CPR milk run. I never did sleep well on a train, and this time was no exception. We arrived in time for breakfast and then I wandered over to the Calgary Herald to visit Garth Hopkins, my old pal from the *Bulletin* days. After I left him, I looked into Jaffe's Bookstore, and finally asked a man where I could find the Club Café. He pointed to a prominent downtown landmark.

When I went inside, the waiter directed me around the corner to the main meeting room. Up to this time, I'd never really given the matter much thought. I assumed the club consisted of a dozen or so men and that we would be meeting in a small cafeteria room.

Imagine my surprise when I walked into the room and found it packed with close to four hundred people! I learned later that it was one of the most prestigious clubs in Calgary, strongly supported by the local business community. I was welcomed by W.H. Herriot, the chairman, and Mel Shannon, the secretary, and escorted to the head table. We had a fine lunch and I gave my half-hour talk on the whisky trading posts which had existed in southern Alberta before the arrival of the Mounted Police.

When I was finished, the chairman asked me if I would entertain any questions. There were a couple of random queries, then a man arose and said, "You mentioned that William Gladstone was the carpenter who built Fort Whoop-Up. I knew a lovely Indian nurse named Nora Gladstone who came from that part of the country. Do you know if they were related?"

"Yes," I said, "They were. And I'm married to Nora's younger sister."

That brought more delighted laughter and applause than my original speech.

Strangely enough, while I sat at the head table during the meal, looking over the sea of four hundred faces, I was not the slightest bit worried. Nor was I nervous when I arose to speak or to field the questions afterwards. For someone as shy and introverted as I was, this seemed to be an anomaly and I often asked myself why it was. In all the years I spoke to large conventions or small school groups, appeared live on television or before any group of people, I was never really nervous.

There were only two exceptions. One occurred when I gave the convocation address at the University of Calgary, and the organizers insisted I provide them with a written copy of my speech and that I not deviate from it. This was hard, as I never used a written speech. My method was to make a few notes on a piece of paper (often the back of an envelope) and pace myself to meet the allotted time period. At the university, I found that reading the talk was very unsettling, resulting in an unfamiliar nervousness.

The second incident occurred when I stopped at the bus depot café in Fort Macleod for lunch. As I was ordering, a number of local friends walked by and said hello. Obviously they were going to their noon Rotary Club meeting. I was halfway through my meal when Abs Swinarton came over me. "Hugh," he said, "We've got a problem. Our speaker hasn't turned up. Will you fill in for him?"

"Sure," I said, thinking I would take a few minutes to organize my thoughts, make some notes, and give them a short talk. However, as soon as I walked into the room, there was a round of applause and the chairman introduced me to speak. At that moment, I didn't even have a topic selected. I don't remember what I spoke about, but it was accompanied by a nervousness that was apparent to me, and likely to everyone else.

But those were the only times. I came to the conclusion that my lack of nervousness came from the confidence I had in my subject and the knowledge that I knew more about it than the people I was speaking to. But whatever the reason, it was a godsend for me, because of the hundreds of speeches, lectures, and interviews I gave during my career.

⎯⎯ ∞ ⎯⎯

In the autumn of 1954, Robbie Roberts and I were talking one day about Alberta's upcoming fiftieth anniversary. Except for the construction of auditoriums in Edmonton and Calgary, nothing much seemed to be happening. We agreed that when politicians and the public realized that the anniversary was almost upon them, there would be a mad rush to get things done, and we'd probably be caught in the middle. We knew that daily and weekly newspapers liked to produce special editions on occasions like this, especially if they could sell lots of advertising. We also knew they would have many blank columns to fill with historical data and would expect the Publicity Bureau to provide it.

In order to avoid the rush, we began working on feature stories and mimeographing them by the dozens. I wrote articles on the formation of the province in 1905, Alberta's first legislature, early trails, the fur trade, and any other subject that seemed appropriate. I also looked through the Ernest Brown photographic collection and selected a number of pictures I thought could be used to publicize the event.

A few weeks later, there was an emergency meeting in the deputy minister's office and, much to my surprise, I was asked to attend. It turned out that the premier's office had been receiving enquiries about the anniversary and in turn the premier wanted to know what the Department of Economic Affairs was doing. Not much, it seemed. Then suddenly, the work that Robbie and I had been doing took on great significance, as it was used as evidence to show that the department had indeed been planning for the anniversary year. The upshot was the formation of a five-man Alberta Golden Jubilee Committee, of which I was a member.

Within a short time, the committee had a full list of projects to be undertaken during the year. The celebrations were to begin on June 5th, with September 1st being Inauguration Day. With nothing scheduled for the first five months of the year, we had plenty to time to get organized. There were school programs, bumper cards, posters, play-writing and song-writing competitions, grants to municipalities, and all sorts of other events. I had five highway signs planned for the year, and these suddenly became part of the golden jubilee. In addition, an Ontario publisher was given a contract to publish an anthology of Alberta writing and one of my articles was included.

My involvement in the whole celebration was neither administrative nor honorary. For the next year, I was up to my eyeballs in work, all in addition to my regular duties. And I loved every minute of it. As the program moved into high gear, a number of subcommittees were formed. I was placed on the Historic and Senior Citizens Committee and was also made responsible for any museum-related activities. This included designing an Alberta Golden Jubilee Caravan as a travelling museum and installing museum displays in a newly built exhibition building in Fort Macleod. Keep in mind that there wasn't a single museum of consequence in Alberta at that time, except perhaps in Banff, so I was venturing alone into uncharted waters. In fact, in 1955 there were only forty-two significant museums in all of Canada, mostly in central or eastern Canada. Most of these were run by provincial governments or universities. So our travelling museum and museum displays were something new to Alberta.

Fortunately, I had access to the Ernest Brown collection, which was stored in the basement of the School Book Branch. It contained the remnants of an old private museum Brown had operated in Edmonton during the 1930s. It had a lot of wonderful stuff and was the basis for both exhibits. But besides that, I scoured the country looking for more artifacts. I borrowed a broad axe and treaty box from the Edmonton Indian Agency, an iron pot from Pauline's Uncle George at Pincher Creek, a frying pan from Norman Luxton, and other items that came to my attention.

The travelling museum trailer was about thirty feet long and designed with closed display cases down each side, with pictures and artifacts on the walls, and a large display space at the far end. There were Indian dresses, back rests, snow shoes, and parfleche bags; coffee mills, scythes, swords, chaps, and buffalo skulls; pictures of missionaries, sports teams, and politicians. Considering the sources of material, it was a hodge-podge, but the public loved it. During the summer of 1955, it toured fairs and celebrations throughout the province and had people lined up to see it wherever it went.

In the summer of 1955, I moved to Fort Macleod for a week to install the exhibits at the Tourist Bureau. A building had been constructed for the occasion; it consisted of three rooms viewed from the outside, like department store windows. One I furnished like a pioneer home and included a Mountie in full uniform. The next was a modern room with furniture borrowed from Eaton's, and the third consisted of exhibits such as a beaver pelt, guns, iron kettles, and historical photographs. This also was well received, especially by American tourists.

While in Fort Macleod, I took a side trip to Pincher Creek to complete arrangements for another project. The committee had lined up a stagecoach and four-horse team and needed somebody to drive it. The idea was for it to travel from Fort Macleod to Edmonton, picking up and delivering messages from the mayors of the various towns and cities along the way. I had been told that one of Pauline's distant relatives, a man named Charlie "Chink" Reviere, was good with a four-horse team. I went to see him in Pincher but he was so drunk that I couldn't even talk to him. But I tried again, and this time I caught him when he was sober and we made the necessary arrangements. He was a tall, gangly chap who looked the part of an old-time stagecoach driver. He also got a local pal, Ralph Vroom, to ride shotgun for him. We were warned that Reviere was unreliable and too fond of the bottle, but he proved to be a gem. He was perfectly sober (or almost so) as he raced the four-horse team into each new town and impressed everyone with his down-to-earth western mannerisms. He may have quaffed a few at the local beer parlours in the evenings, but he was always on time and ready to go the next day. The stagecoach project was one of the many success stories of the jubilee.

One proposal that came before our committee was for illuminated scrolls to be given to any Albertan who had lived in the province since 1905. I pointed out that every Indian over the age of fifty would qualify, and suggested that we should also do something special for those over the age of sixty-five. The committee agreed and we designed a zinc-plated medal which was presented at the Calgary Stampede and at other ceremonies. I had the pleasure of being involved when the medals were presented to Black Sleeps and others at the Camsell Hospital.

During all this time, I continued to pour a steady stream of articles into *Within Our Borders*, dealing with everything from historic sites to game counts, telephone books, and oil and gas regulations. Then, in the autumn of 1955 Robbie Roberts resigned to take over a newsletter for the Department of Northern Affairs in Ottawa, and I became editor of our magazine. It seemed sometimes as though events were moving so rapidly that I could hardly keep up with them. At one stage, I seriously considered quitting my job to live off Pauline's income while I went to university to seek a degree in anthropology. Jack Ewers was against it. He wrote, "I believe you are now much better qualified to make something out of anthropology than the average person entering college with a yen to become an anthropologist – your published work would show that."[45] However, it all became academic when the University of Alberta indicated it had no desire to accept a high school dropout into its ranks.

So I settled in as editor of *Within Our Borders* and it looked as though my future was secure as a publicity man for the Alberta government. I was twenty-six years old, married to a wonderful woman, living in our own house, and quite contented in my work. I was having a great time studying and writing about the Blackfoot Indians and much of my personal life revolved around the Gladstones, the IAA, and our mutual friends in the city. It was, to all intents and purposes, a very comfortable life.

Two of Hugh's friends, Buck Alton and Ray Bulger, are seen here in 1942.
A bunch of kids, they called themselves the Fifth Street Gang. (Author photo)

On Saturday afternoons, after the *Edmonton Bulletin*'s publisher had gone home, some staff gathered in his office for drinking and high jinks. Here in 1950, left to right, are news editor Bill Lewis, oil reporter Harlo Jones, and reporters Stan Burke, John McLean, and Don Travis. (Author's files)

Hugh's 1947 hitchhiking venture from Edmonton to Vancouver took him through the United States. A family that had picked him up photographed him at the border south of Vancouver. (Author's files)

This is the group that Dempsey met when he first went to a meeting of the Indian Association of Alberta. Seated at centre is President James Gladstone. Immediately behind him, left to right, are John Laurie, George McLean (Walking Buffalo), and Dave Crowchild. At left of Gladstone is his old companion Joe Bull Shield. Others in the group include Albert Lightning, John Callihoo, Peter Burnstick, and Frank Cardinal. (Author's files)

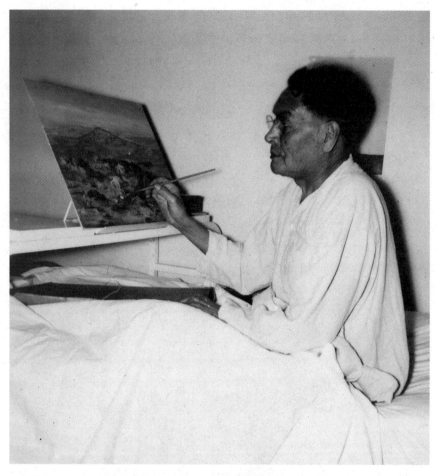

Percy Plain Woman, who painted under the name of Two Guns, became friends with
Hugh Dempsey while a patient in the Charles Camsell Hospital in Edmonton. Their
friendship continued when he returned to the Blood Reserve. Percy is seen painting
from his hospital bed in 1951. (Author photo)

Hugh Dempsey and Pauline Gladstone in 1952, a year before their marriage. Dempsey is wearing one of his hand-painted ties. (Author's files)

Dempsey recalls that this was the Blood Sun Dance when he first saw it in 1952. It was a sight he never forgot. It was taken looking west from the slopes of the Belly Buttes. (Author photo)

In 1952, Pat Bad Eagle, Peigan elder, took Dempsey as his son and gave him the name of Young Chief. At right is Mrs. Janie Gladstone, later Hugh's mother-in-law. (Pauline Dempsey photo)

Close friends of the Dempseys were artist Gerald Tailfeathers and his wife Irene, seen here in Edmonton in 1953. Pauline had gone to residential school with them. (Pauline Dempsey photo)

In 1953, shortly after his wedding, Hugh climbed Chief Mountain, on the Alberta-Montana border, with Jim Black Plume. Dempsey is seen here on the saddle of the ridge. (Jim Black Plume photo)

Two of the most sacred societies of the Blood tribe are the Horns and the Motokix. The Horn double lodge is seen here in 1955 and the Motokix, or Old Women's Society, in the background. Dempsey has been permitted to enter both. (Author photo)

One of Dempsey's assignments during the Alberta Golden Jubilee was to design and install a travelling museum, seen here in Calgary in 1955. (Author's files)

Jack Low Horn, Blood elder, became one of Dempsey's favourite storytellers. (Glenbow photo NA-1757-1)

When Dempsey moved to Calgary in 1956, he helped to form a Calgary branch of the Historical Society of Alberta. Seen here are the Calgary executive members in 1960. Left to right: President Benton Mackid, Sheila Johnston, Sheilagh Jameson, and Hugh Dempsey. (Author's files)

# 5

# The Glenbow Foundation

Since my first letter to Douglas Leechman at the National Museum in 1952, we had maintained a fairly regular correspondence. I had arranged for him to be a guest speaker at the Historical Society and Pauline and I entertained him while he was in Edmonton. Then, in the summer of 1955, he sent us a change of address postcard indicating that he had moved to Calgary, where he had become Director of Western Canadiana for the Glenbow Foundation.

The Glenbow had appeared on the scene in 1954, when it was established as a charitable foundation by Eric L. Harvie, a lawyer and oil man. Like philanthropists of old, such as Guggenheim, Carnegie, and Getty, Eric Harvie wanted to put his fortunes back into where he had obtained them. His personal interest was in collecting, so his foundation was geared towards western Canadian history and art. It did not start off as a museum, but as an agency for collecting and preserving the past.

I had already heard of Glenbow, for a few months earlier, George H. Gooderham, formerly Regional Director of Indian Agencies, had retired and joined that organization as its first employee. He had been Pauline's "big boss" and they always got along very well. I had met Gooderham and we, too, had become friends.

George was born on an Indian reserve in Saskatchewan and spent almost his entire life in the Indian service. He took over as Indian agent on the Blackfoot Reserve in 1920 when his father, the former agent, died suddenly of a heart attack. George was one of the "good guys." He was sincerely interested in the Indians and worked hard on their behalf. There were a number of times when he had to defy his own bosses when be believed that some intended action was detrimental to them. He liked the Blackfoot, visited their homes on a social basis, and had many lifelong friends among them. He was a natural candidate for the position of Inspector of Indian Agencies for Western Canada, but his liberal views towards the treatment of Indians had alienated such people as Inspector W.M. Graham, and the promotion never came. Only in the latter years of his career was he placed in charge of Alberta reserves.

Not only did we like George, but he was so fond of Pauline that he used to call her his daughter, Indian-style. She gladly accepted this honour and over the years we spent a lot of time together. When George died in 1977, Pauline sat in the chapel as part of his family.

George's initial duties at Glenbow were to identify a large number of pictures taken by Arnold Lupson, an Englishman who had lived with the Sarcees and had married Chief Big Belly's widow. After that, George was a liaison between Glenbow and the Indian Department, and with the Indians themselves. He was a great guy.

---

Late in 1955, I received a request from Leechman, asking me if I would examine the Harry Pollard photographic collection to determine its historical and financial value. Pollard had moved to Calgary in 1899, and his collection of Indian and pioneer photographs was reputed to be comparable to the Ernest Brown collection of Edmonton, which the Alberta government had recently purchased for $40,000.

During my Christmas holiday, I spent two days with Pollard but the results were somewhat disappointing. He proclaimed that he had 50,000 negatives, but any time a person visited him, he showed them only his prize pieces. These included Indian portraits taken by a predecessor, Alexander Ross, about 1886. Pollard started that way with me too, but when I asked to review the entire collection, he grudgingly agreed. It turned out there were 50,000 negatives all right, but 20,000 were studio portraits, mostly of routine customers, and another 3,000 were group shots of military graduating classes. There were 5,000 international views, beautiful stuff but not pertinent to Alberta, and another 10,000 commercial negatives which had a few interesting pieces but consisted mostly of flower shows, advertising shots, and window displays.

In the end, I estimated that the historical part of the collection consisted of about 10,000 negatives, not 50,000. But those 10,000 were wonderful pictures, for there was no doubt that Pollard was a first-rate photographer. I recommended to Glenbow that it try to acquire all the "oil photos, Klondike gold rush, early Lethbridge, early Calgary, a few Indians, historical portraits, some ranching, farming and irrigation."[46] I believed the entire collection was inferior to the Ernest Brown collection, both in size and content, and accordingly was worth far less than the $40,000 paid for that collection.

I think Glenbow offered Pollard $10,000 and he became so angry that he sent them a bill for the two days I had spent with him. Pollard insisted that his collection was just as big and as important as Brown's, and he demanded the same amount the government had given to the Edmonton photographer. At one point he even threatened to destroy the collection, but in the end it was sold to the Alberta government. I was rather sorry, as I would liked to have seen it remain in Calgary.

<hr>

As a result of this assignment, I was asked by Douglas Leechman if I would like to join the staff of the Glenbow Foundation. Next to my marriage, this was probably the most momentous decision of my career, and I agonized long and hard over the offer. I also sought the counsel of others. Pauline – bless her heart – said she'd go wherever I chose to go. She loved Edmonton and had lots of close friends there, but on the other hand, Calgary was halfway to the Blood Reserve. When I wrote to Jack Ewers, he replied, "I personally feel that it is a field you might do very well in – your interest in art and in history and ethnology might very well be combined in a museum career. Lord knows Alberta could use some new museums. And there is no doubt but what there is no end of fascinating material on Alberta history and Indians that could be used."[47]

My father, on the other hand, was completely against the idea and could not understand how I could even consider it. Currently, I had a government job, with good pay, security, and medical and pension plans. Glenbow offered me a slight raise, no security, no medical plan, and no pension plan. In fact, leaving my job for a rich man's hobby seemed to my father to be an entirely foolhardy prospect. Besides that, I learned that there was going to be a division of duties within the Department of Economic Affairs, with advertising being split off from publicity, and there was more than a good chance that I would get a sizable raise and promotion within the year.

I did what I always did at decision time. I made a list of positive and negative factors on both sides. In the government job, the pluses were security, a good chance of promotion, good pay, and good working conditions. On the minus … there weren't really any. For Glenbow, the minuses were lack of security, having to sell our house and move away from Edmonton, and going into an organization which could be terminated at the whim of its benefactor.

In the end, there was one big plus for Glenbow that won the day – spending my full time working in the field of western Canadian history. So I accepted.

Eric Harvie then announced he would not hire me unless the Alberta government agreed to let me go. If they were opposed, the deal would be off. A few days later, I was on tenterhooks when I learned that Hod Meech, president of Managers Limited, Harvie's umbrella company, was coming to see our deputy minister. I had worked well with Ralph Moore, but to me he was a typical senior civil servant and I wasn't sure how magnanimous he could be in this kind of situation. I found out later in the day that I had grossly underestimated him. When he called me into his office, the first thing he did was to congratulate me on being accepted by Glenbow. He made it clear that the rumoured promotion for me was true if I decided to stay, but he would do nothing to interfere with my ambitions. When I left, I was extremely grateful and relieved.

The next few weeks were a blur, as I arranged to start work in Calgary on April 1, 1956. We had our house to sell, but this proved to be no problem, as my mother and dad wanted it. Then I was off to Calgary, travelling around with real estate salesmen looking at houses. There was a good prospect in the Highwood district of northwest Calgary, so Pauline came down to give her opinion. The place was a nice little two-bedroom bungalow for $8,000. We had almost decided on it when the salesman told us of another house a block away. It had three bedrooms and was available for $12,000. A family had put a down payment on it but had been unable to meet the loan requirements and it was back on the market. We took one look at it and decided to buy it. The house was far too big for our purposes but we were always having visitors and hoped to have a family some day. It turned out to be a wise choice, as we were still living in the same house when I retired from Glenbow thirty-five years later.

After the farewell parties and good wishes, Pauline and I and a furniture van headed south for Calgary. I suppose I should have been homesick, leaving Edmonton for good for the first time, but it didn't turn out that way. I had Pauline with me, so my home was wherever she happened to be. I often said that I changed from being an Edmonton Eskimo football fan to a Calgary Stampeder supporter when we reached Red Deer. Not so with Pauline. Although she was a southern girl, she had loved Edmonton, her friends, her hockey and football teams, and was loath to give up any of them.

Fortunately for us, Irene and Gerald Tailfeathers had moved to Calgary some time earlier and we immediately picked up our old friendship. Gerald was a draftsman for an oil company and lived only a couple of miles from us, so we were visiting back and forth all the time. Similarly, Bill and Sally Marsden were living in Calgary where Bill was running a Calgary studio for the government. He lived only three blocks from our new house, which was one of the reasons why we chose it. So four of our best friends had preceded us to Calgary.

Obviously, Glenbow was very new when I joined it in 1956. When oil was discovered at Leduc and Redwater in the late 1940s, Eric Harvie held a number of leaseholds which made him a wealthy man. His interest in collecting apparently came from his old hunting partner, Norman Luxton of Banff. Luxton had amassed a large collection of Indian artifacts, and in 1951 he decided to open a museum; Harvie became involved and ended up financing the deal. However, Harvie was known as a man who liked to have complete control over any business he was involved in, and in this deal, Luxton was running the museum. Harvie's solution was to establish his own Glenbow Foundation in 1954.

––––––––⊶⊷––––––––

On my first day at work, I didn't know what to expect. Until this time, any business I had conducted concerning my employment had been at Harvie's business offices, Managers Limited, which were located in the Michael Building on 9th Avenue. However, I was instructed to show up for work at the Hull House, on 12th Avenue. On the morning of April 1st, I walked about a mile to the nearest bus stop (my old car had been sold for junk), went downtown, transferred to the Belt Line, and ended up in front of an old brick mansion. Inside, I was directed to Leechman's office which had once been the parlour. After some pleasantries and general discussions, Leechman reached into a filing cabinet and handed me a pile of manuscripts and photographs.

"Here," he said, "You are the archivist of the Foundation."

I knew the meaning of the word "archivist," but that's about all I knew. However, the prospect of looking after all the documents and photographs collected by Glenbow seemed like a thrilling one. Until that moment, I had no idea what my duties would be or what position I would hold. I was then directed to a tiny room in the back area of the second floor. This had been the maid's quarters in palmier days and now would be the archives.

The Hull House was a wonderful building. It had been constructed for merchant W.R. Hull in 1904 in relatively close proximity to the homes of Sir James Lougheed and Senator Pat Burns. It consisted of a three-storey mansion on huge grounds, with a carriage house and greenhouses near the back of the lot. It had a number of ingenious features. For example, the chandeliers were equipped to use either electricity or natural gas. The house had a well in the basement (long since sealed up), and a vacuum system which was activated by plugging a hose into one of the many outlets along the baseboards. It had the finest hardwood on the floors, fabric wallpaper in many places (I believe it was Japanese), and fireplaces of marble imported from Italy. I was told that there was a secret compartment near one of the fireplaces but none of us could ever find it.

Even outside there was an original innovation in the watering system. The yard was surrounded by a fence made of iron tubular railings set between sandstone pillars. The bottom railing was in fact a water pipe and had outlets for watering the lawn. And in the garden at the back was a huge archway which I was told was actually a pair of mammoth tusks.

When I joined Glenbow, I brought the staff complement at Hull House up to eight. Besides Leechman and Gooderham, there was Nina Napier, the librarian; Eleanor Ediger, in charge of the art collection; D.T. Smith, business manager; and secretaries Dorothy Wardle and Hazel Boswell. There also were four groundsmen and maintenance staff. Working away from the building on a part-time contract basis were Margaret and Isobel Loggie in the Peace River area, John Laurie and Philip Godsell in Calgary, and perhaps a few others. In addition, Dr. Marie Wormington of Denver had been conducting archaeological surveys on behalf of Glenbow.

The layout of Hull House put Leechman and his secretary on the main floor, with Gooderham occupying a study near the rear, and with a few paintings decorating the walls. On the second floor were more offices, the archives – such as it was – and Eleanor Ediger's office. On the upper floor was the library, and in the basement was the art storage area.

My immediate task was to set up a filing and cataloguing system. There were no archives in Alberta, and the only collection I had ever seen was in the Montana Historical Society in Helena. I got permission to revisit Montana and to make a trip to Regina to see what they were doing there. After extensive study and considerable reading, I concluded that the system devised by Lucile M. Kane at the Minnesota Historical Society was the best on the continent so I adapted it for our own use. It proved to be quite effective in handling a small volume of papers, but twenty years later it had to be discarded when Glenbow's collections became too large to organize on the basis of topic and Cutter numbers.

At Regina, I learned about proper storage boxes, acid-free folders, and the importance of temperature and humidity controls. Some of these were little more than a dream in the old Hull House, but they made me aware of the requirements in handling documents.

From the beginning, I realized that incoming documents had to be properly documented. As soon as they arrived, I recorded the date, source, size, and other pertinent data. Anyone who examines the old handwritten accession book I started in 1956 will note that the first few acquisitions show no date and no source. These were the documents handed to me on my arrival. I never could find out where they came from.

The cataloguing of photographs was a different matter. I checked Helena and Regina, read the few pieces of literature available on the subject, and even examined commercial studios for systems, but none satisfied me. I then devised a temporary system for recording new collections but waited until many months later, when I was able to travel to archives in Winnipeg, St. Paul, Chicago, Toronto, Ottawa, and other centres to examine their systems.

I observed that some archives filed their photographs subject-wise and made cross-entry cards, but to my mind this didn't work. For example, at one archives I looked in a folder entitled "Farming" and found a few items, but there were other farming pictures filed under the names of individual farmers. In some cases these were cross-entered but in most cases they weren't. In another archives, prints were made instead of cross-entry cards. This meant that if there was a picture with ten identified people in a group, then ten prints were made and filed under their names. I found most of these systems were awkward and unworkable for larger collections.

Finally, I pulled together all of my notes and, based partly on the system used in Minnesota, I devised our own system. This divided collections into two groups – prints with no negatives, and collections with negatives. There was a further division on the basis of the size of negatives which made storage and retrieval much easier. Within each of these categories, collections were simply filed consecutively in the order received. With negatives, a print was made and mounted on a small card with the identification and other information on the back. Then cross-entry cards were made on the basis of Library of Congress headings.

The system worked. In fact, it was copied by a few other institutions, and over the years the archives received many compliments on the accessibility of its photographic collections.

During the first few weeks at Glenbow it seemed as though we were riding on a roller coaster. New staff were coming in thick and fast. By June, O.S. Longman, former deputy minister of agriculture, and his assistants, were working on agricultural history in Edmonton; Nick Wickenden, a university student, was studying steamboats; Eleanor Luxton was working at High River; and William Rodney was studying the life of John George "Kootenai" Brown. Meanwhile, Dick Forbis had joined the staff a month after me and set up an Archaeology Department out back in the carriage house.

Besides setting up the archives, my activities during 1956 included being Eric Harvie's speech writer. As soon as I joined the staff, I was put to work interviewing oil pioneers and writing a speech which Harvie used during a tribute to the oil industry. No sooner was that out of the way than I began research into the history of the Calgary Highlanders, of which Harvie was honorary colonel. This resulted in a speech Harvie gave at the retirement of Lt. Col. Mark Tennant.

By comparison with later years, the tools for archival and research work were archaic. Old Underwood manual typewriters were the standard, and I also had a small portable I had picked up at an auction sale. This was useful when travelling. Wet paper and thermal copying machines were just coming on the market. I experimented with a Thermofax machine but found it to be useless because of the temporary nature of the copies. I then tried two wet copiers, Contoura-Constat and Cormack. They were messy and the copies tended to turn brown because of the chemicals, but at least they did make copies. We stayed with a Contoura Scout for a couple of years until dry copiers came on the market.

Tape recorders were not yet in general use, but we did have a Webcor wire recorder, which was better than nothing. A few years later, any wire copies we had were transferred to tape. As for microfilms, they were readily available but Eric Harvie was opposed to having them in the archives. He wanted originals, not copies. I quietly collected everything available on microfilm but a couple of years passed before I could get permission to buy a microfilm reader.

As archivist, I was anxious to get out in the field and start collecting, and in this I was encouraged by both Leechman and Harvie. At first, I used leads which I had brought with me. But the biggest early project was one which involved the old Indian Department records. As soon as I arrived at Glenbow, I told Leechman and Gooderham about the rich collection of correspondence at the Blood Indian Agency and suggested that the same kind of documents might exist in other agencies and should be preserved. This set in motion a series of events which ultimately involved Indian Affairs Branch in Ottawa and the Public Archives of Canada.

Leechman wrote to W. Kaye Lamb, the Dominion Archivist, and suggested that Glenbow salvage all historical records in the various Indian agencies and provide a list to the Public Archives. Lamb could then select those documents to go to Ottawa and the rest would stay at Glenbow. While we were waiting, Gooderham and I toured all the major agencies, making an inventory and in some instances borrowing the records in hope that something would be resolved.

At the end of 1956, I sent a memo to Jack Herbert, our director of research, complaining that negotiations had stalled and that in my opinion the Indian Department records were "the most valuable material that could ever be obtained by the Archives of the Foundation."[48] As a minimum, I recommended that 131 letter-books, 140 diaries, 64 treaty paysheets to 1900, 66 Shannon files to 1900, 45 ration issue and account books, 16 bundles of loose files, and 16 files of vouchers be salvaged.

My suggestion was to obtain permission to pick up this material, with Glenbow keeping on deposit what it wanted and sending the rest to the Public Archives. Also, Glenbow could request microfilms of anything in Ottawa and Public Archives could do the same for the records in Calgary. It was asking for a lot, I know, but in view of the fact that Glenbow would be incurring a considerable expense performing a service that the Public Archives couldn't do, it was worth a try.

When Lamb demurred, Jack Herbert suggested that the situation be reversed: the good stuff would go to Ottawa and microfilms given to Glenbow, and the discards would stay with Glenbow. Lamb felt that this was a workable arrangement and suggested it be handled on a trial basis.

All these discussions had been taking place without the involvement of the Indian Affairs Branch – deliberately – as both sides believed that its director, Col. H.M. Jones, could throw a monkey wrench into the whole thing. Lamb was sympathetic to Glenbow and told us that the Indian Affairs Branch was one of his biggest problems. Officials refused to turn their old headquarters records over to the archives and insisted that there was nothing in the field offices worth saving. When Lamb finally approached Colonel Jones, sure enough, the bureaucrat was ready to screw up everything. In his own lofty manner, Jones informed Lamb that his department and not the Public Archives would decide what would happen to its papers. Then, after a bit of sabre rattling, he approved a pilot program, reserving the right to call the records into Indian Affairs Branch rather than the Public Archives if he so wished.

When Lamb passed the news to us, he added a statement that at last gave Glenbow some leeway. He stated, "I may say that if we find that certain of the records of interest from your point of view are not required in Ottawa, the Indian Affairs Branch would have no objection to our placing them in your custody."[49]

The matter dragged along for another several months, but it got a shot in the arm in November 1957, when Jack Herbert had a call from a friend of his, Doug Light in Battleford. Doug had been visiting a federal government office when he saw the caretaker piling a bunch of records in the back yard, ready for burning. When he learned that these were old Indian Agency records, he salvaged what he could and then asked Herbert what to do with them. Jack told him to put them in boxes and ship them to us.

With some pleasure, we used this incident to show Lamb just what was happening to Indian Department field records. We sorted the documents, sent the list to the Public Archives, and asked them what they wanted. These were shipped and the rest we kept.

However, it wasn't until the spring of 1960 that the matter was resolved, and not entirely to my satisfaction. By this time, Colonel Jones could no longer deny that there were valuable records in the field, but instead of giving us or Public Archives a free hand, he decided to send a pair of bureaucrats from Central Registry to collect anything important, and to destroy the rest.

I immediately wrote to Jones, expressing my concern "that there may be a tendency to consider the administrative rather than the historical importance of some of these documents." I asked him if the men could set aside anything they didn't want and to let us take anything we wanted before any destruction took place. Jones agreed, stating that his two agents, P.F. O'Donnell and A.A. Goulet, would inform me after every inspection.

The men arrived in June 1960, but the program soon turned sour. At the Sarcee Agency, we were given only a couple of days to pick out the leftovers and were amazed at some of the things they left. There were death registers, ration lists, and other items that could be very important to the history of the tribe. I was travelling a few days behind the Indian Affairs men (at their request) so I never saw them.

My next trip, immediately after picking up the Sarcee records, was to the Blood Reserve. I knew these documents well, as I had prowled through the Indian Office in Cardston and an attic full of records at the farm headquarters.

When I got to the reserve, I met my brother-in-law, Horace, who was in charge of the farm headquarters.

"I've come to pick up the Indian Department records," I told him.

"Sure," he said, "but there's practically nothing left. We burned two truckloads of papers a couple of days ago."

My worst fears were realized. Send a couple of bureaucrats out from Ottawa and you're sure to have a disaster. Horace said that the two men picked up some old records in town, then came out to the farm headquarters, selected a few random files, and ordered the destruction of the rest. They stayed at the scene until two truckloads of papers were piled on the ground and burned.

As it happened, I had been working on these files a few weeks earlier. I had made a list of those I hoped to preserve and when I checked what was left I found that over half of them had gone up in smoke. As it was, they left behind some excellent correspondence files from the early part of the twentieth century. Thank God these survived, as they have been a boon to historians. But I am equally distressed at what they destroyed, especially as Glenbow supposedly had a deal with Indian Affairs.

At the time, I was told that the Central Registry people had picked up all the old records from the office in Cardston, but I later discovered they had taken only the letter-books. There were several dozen treaty paysheets and interest payment books dating back to the 1880s which were left behind, and these too were destroyed. Apparently these men said that the paysheets were all duplicated in Ottawa, but this was a lie. The ones in the field office were working copies, with all sorts of side notations, while the copies the agents sent to Ottawa were clean.

A few days later, I went to the Peigan Reserve. Here is what I say in my diary: "We saw [Harold] Woodsworth [the Indian Agent] and I picked up what few records he was willing to part with. I feel certain that there was more allotted to us by the Central Registry boys but Harold would not part with them."[50] All I got was a voucher book for 1896–1914 and a ration issue book for 1883–95. I knew there was a pile of stuff in the attic next door to the office but Woodsworth wouldn't let me near it. In the end, the Peigans were the losers, for an edict came from Ottawa and the files were destroyed.

My next trip was to the Blackfoot Reserve, where I was not surprised to find just a handful of papers. Again, the Ottawa crew had taken the letter-books, but I knew that almost everything else had been destroyed by a zealous Indian agent some years earlier. Similarly, Hobbema did not have much to offer, and I was told that everything was gone from the Edmonton Indian

Agency long before we started our campaign. My final trip was to Saddle Lake, where a few good records had survived.

I suppose I should be satisfied with the final results. There is no doubt in my mind that if Glenbow had not started the ball rolling in 1956, that nothing would have survived. By and large the Indian agents didn't care, and in some cases it was only by accident that the records had survived as long as they did. I am sure that when the administrative structure of Indian Affairs changed and agents were moved into nearby cities, the final destruction would have quietly taken place. So at least the letter-books survived in Ottawa, and these, now on microfilm, are a rich source of history, particularly for Native people.

There is one sad footnote. During a trip to Winnipeg in 1960, Gooderham stopped off at the Indian office to visit with Ralph Ragan, who was regional supervisor for Manitoba. During the course of conversation, Gooderham asked if any of the old Inspectorate files had survived. In the late nineteenth century and well into the 1930s, the headquarters for the prairie division of Indian Affairs was in Regina, and later in Winnipeg. Ragan said there had been a fire in Winnipeg "four or five years ago" and that most of the records had been destroyed. However, those that survived were in the basement of the federal building. Gooderham inspected these and, among other things, he found annuity payment books back to the 1870s. He then telephoned the regional supervisor in Regina and learned that they had a bunch of old files and letter-books in their basement.

For some reason, Gooderham never mentioned these to me. He simply wrote to the Public Archives, informing them that these files existed, and left it at that. Gooderham had been, after all, a career civil servant, and I think he expected that something would be done by Ottawa. I suppose he thought that if he told me, I'd raise a big fuss as I had been doing with the Alberta records. And he would have been right. As it is, I can find no record of the Winnipeg and Regina inspectorate files ever reaching Ottawa. I have no idea what became of them.

⁂

During the early years, the staff was encouraged to undertake research projects, and I was no exception. Because of the enjoyment I got from interviewing Joe Potts and writing a long biography of his father, I decided that I liked the biographical approach, so I looked around for someone else to consider. Soon after, I attended a meeting of the Indian Association of Alberta and on one of the breaks, I sat with Frank Medicine Shield, a member of the Blackfoot tribe. When we started talking about history, I told him I was curious about something.

"Why is it," I asked him, "that the Blackfoot consider Crowfoot to be such a hero? From what I can understand, he helped the Mounted Police, convinced the other chiefs to sign Treaty Seven, and sided with the government during the Riel Rebellion. He sounds like a toady who did everything he could to please the white people."

Medicine Shield glared at me for a moment, then his look softened. "Dempsey," he said, "if you weren't such a good friend, I'd beat the hell out of you for what you just said. I don't know about that other stuff but Crowfoot was the greatest chief we ever had."

Thoroughly confused, I decided there and then to study the life of Crowfoot to determine how a man could do virtually everything the white men wanted and yet be a hero to his own people. With the blessing of Glenbow I toured the Blackfoot, Blood, and Peigan reserves over the next several months looking for stories about the chief. I spoke to a woman who had lived in Crowfoot's lodge and had been eighteen years old when he died. I spoke to his grandson, Joe, and to people like One Gun who remembered the chief. And when the opportunity arose, I examined the Indian Department and Mounted Police records in Ottawa, and other documents around the country. I also wrote to Lucien and Jane Hanks, who had done research on the Blackfoot reserve in the 1938–41 period, and was grateful when they loaned me some of their field notes.

By the time I was ready to write my story, I had the answer to my question. In fact, the answer not only told me about Crowfoot but addressed the whole question of Indian-white relations. It was perfectly true that Crowfoot had done all the things that writers had given him credit for, but they had completely misunderstood his motives. Crowfoot never did anything for the white man; everything he did was for his own people. It just happened that their goals were the same, so the white man, looking at the situation from the lofty perch of superiority that seemed to go with his race, said, "Aha, Crowfoot did this because he was our friend." Actually, he did it because it was in the best interests of his people.

He welcomed the Mounted Police in 1874 because the chiefs had lost control of their bands and the whisky traders were killing his people by the score. The traders were like grey wolves following a herd of buffalo, picking off the weaker ones as they lagged behind. And there was nothing the chiefs could do. Then in 1877, Crowfoot had signed the treaty because he could see the buffalo herds disappearing and had the foresight to realize that the Blackfoot would need the white man's help to survive in the future. And he stayed out of the Riel rebellion because he had paid a visit to Winnipeg a few months earlier and knew there were thousands of white people at the other end of the railway line who could utterly destroy the Blackfoot in a matter of days. Crowfoot may have sympathized with the rebels, and was aware that his adopted son Poundmaker had been drawn into the fray, but he also realized the rebels would be defeated by a numerically superior army. And he did not want to see the same fate befall his own people.

Other facets of Crowfoot's life were revealed to me as I continued my research, and they indicated that he wasn't all that friendly with the white man. He was opposed to the Canadian Pacific Railway passing through his lands. He was strongly against the introduction of ranching, and he made no effort to become a farmer. And when the Mounted Police tried to arrest one of his councillors, he strongly resisted them to a point just short of violence.

This was my first lesson in Indian-white perceptions. I became aware of how people often drew conclusions based upon their own experiences, without realizing that someone from a different culture may have an entirely viewpoint. It wasn't always a cultural difference; sometimes it was based on a person's biases, or his superiority complex. But the end result – particularly where Indians and whites were concerned – was that two people could be talking to each other without each person really understanding what the other meant.

I came to the conclusion that in the latter part of the nineteenth century most Indians did not understand the significance of the treaties or the allocation of reserves. And when it came to religion, the first converts really accepted Christianity in addition to their own beliefs, not in place of them. Also, when they encountered something they did not understand, they were usually too polite to say anything. As a result, the person speaking to them assumed they were fully aware of any consequences of the discussion. Time and time again, I could find rational explanations for seemingly divergent actions when I placed each side of a question into its own cultural milieu.

I finished the Crowfoot manuscript in 1958 and, full of hope, I sent it off to several publishers. That's when I learned of the state of Canadian publishing. In most cases, without even reviewing the manuscript, the publishers said there was no market for Canadian history, especially western Canadian. The University of Toronto Press said that my work was not academic enough for them and that I should go to a commercial publisher. The closest I got to a bite was from Macmillan of Canada, which said if I would cut it by two-thirds and turn it into a children's book, they might be willing to take a look at it.

Instead, I put it on the shelf and turned my attention to other things. It looked as though my book publishing career was over before it had started.

—∞∞∞—

The first few years at Glenbow were exciting and fun. We were like the big family that Eric Harvie wanted us to be and most of us got along pretty well together. I stayed clear of Godsell and Eleanor Luxton, but worked quite close-ly with the other researchers. I saw Harvie quite often and was a frequent guest for lunch at his special dining room at the Michael Building. I was very im-pressed with that dining room. It had a large table with a sheep's head centre-piece denoting his role of honorary colonel of the Calgary Highlanders, while around the room were some of Harvie's favourite paintings and sculptures. In particular, I remember a pair of porcelain swans by Hans Achtziger and some miniature British military figures.

There was usually a business reason for the meeting, but Harvie was al-ways the gracious host, talking about his interests and drawing others into his conversation. I soon learned, however, not to take the meetings too seriously, as Harvie had a tendency to dream out loud. One time he talked about moving the Luxton Museum outside the Banff gates, and setting up a huge park which would have Indian villages from the various culture areas of Canada. He told me to follow it up, and I had put quite a bit of work into it before I discovered that he hadn't been serious. After a while, I learned to send him a confirming memo after I got back to the office, asking for more direction. If I didn't get an answer, I knew that Harvie had only been chatting.

In our day-to-day work at Hull House we had to adjust to the way that Harvie wanted things done. For example, he was entirely opposed to putting nails in the walls for any reason. Paintings were hung from wires suspended from picture rails and anything else had to lean against the wall or simply be placed elsewhere. Neglecting this edict was one of the reasons why Vera Burns was fired from the Foundation. Mind you, with those beautiful walls, many of them covered with imported rice paper, I can understand Harvie's feelings.

There were other rules that had to be followed. One was that only letter-size paper could be used, and if a memorandum was written that took less than half a page, then the paper was cut in half and the blank part used at a later date. Of course, what happened was that the paper was cut in half and the un-used part thrown in the garbage. I also had a problem in that initially, Harvie's people would not let me order legal-size file folders and storage boxes. When I explained that many of our collections had legal-size documents in them, I was told to fold them over so they would fit. This would be highly detrimental to the documents, so I demurred until I finally got my way.

Harvie also directed that every desk had to be completely cleared off at the end of the day. As a former journalist accustomed to a mess of paper I found this very difficult, but as time went on I became very thankful, for I was forced to organize my material and my mind so that a clear desk became the norm at quitting time. This practice continued long after Harvie was no longer involved. Another Harvie rule was that nothing should ever extend beyond the edge of a table or desk. A file folder could not stick out into an aisle and nothing could be laid on a table that was larger than the table itself. On one occasion, Harvie came into a room where file folders were sticking out from a number of desks. As he walked by, he simply knocked the folders to the floor and the files scattered everywhere. He didn't say a word; he didn't need to.

He had a habit of prowling the offices and work areas at night or on week-ends. If anything was amiss, we heard about it the following day from one of his people. One person who got caught up in this was an artist/naturalist named Terry Walton. He got a dead porcupine and decided to mount it. He knew there was a rule that no unapproved personal work was to be done at Glenbow but he did not think that Harvie would be around on the weekend. But just to be sure, he hid his work in the women's bathroom, believing that Harvie's sensitivities would keep him out of that forbidden area. But Walton was wrong. Harvie came in during the weekend and included the women's washroom in his tour of inspection. Walton wasn't fired but he was sure read the riot act.

Some of these requirements may have been mere Harvie foibles but most of them were based on good solid logic and business practices. But whether we liked them or not, we had to put up with them.

Harvie did take a personal interest in his staff. He wanted to meet Pauline soon after our arrival, and when he learned that I didn't have a car, he arranged for Glenbow to loan me the necessary funds and to deduct it from my payroll. And near Christmas 1956, he invited Pauline and me to visit him at his ranch, just east of Cochrane. It had been a very open winter and both of us were impressed when we saw farmers still harvesting in mid-winter.

The ranch house was big and homey, but what really attracted us was the view. Standing beside the house, we had a clear vista of the Bow River valley clear to the Rocky Mountains. It was the most breathtaking view we had ever seen.

After a very enjoyable afternoon, we were just about ready to leave when a strange car pulled into the yard. The driver looked at Pauline and me – obviously a couple of city folk – and then at Harvie, who looked like a hired hand.

"Can you tell me who owns this place?" he asked.

Without even the hint of a smile, our host said, "It's a man named Eric Harvie."

"They tell me there's an old stone quarry down by the river," responded the stranger. "Do you think he'd let me drive down to see it?"

"I don't think so," said Harvie, "but you can check with his office in town."

The man drove away without ever suspecting that he had just talked to the owner, and to one of the richest men in Alberta.

During the summer of 1956, D.T. Smith, Glenbow's business manager, had to resign because of ill health. In fact, he was sick when I arrived so I hardly knew him. He was replaced in August by Jack D. Herbert, formerly Director of the Historic Sites Branch for the province of Saskatchewan. He was given the title of Director of Research, so all of a sudden Glenbow had two directors. I don't know if this was by accident or design but it had all the earmarks of a "divide and conquer" strategy that never left one person in charge. When Leechman departed in 1957, Clifford P. Wilson was hired to jointly run the Foundation with Herbert. Cliff had been long time editor of *Beaver* magazine for the Hudson's Bay Company. Later, when Herbert resigned in 1959, the leadership was split between Wilson and Eric McGreer. But I guess we all knew there was only one boss – Eric Harvie.

Although Smith had been a business manager, Jack was brought in to take charge of the rapidly expanding group of researchers. He was a young Turk when he joined the organization and had the idea that he was going to reform it overnight. I think he looked upon Leechman as an old fuddy-duddy and was inclined to ride roughshod over him. And instead of fighting back, Leechman tended to draw into himself and took on the role of senior statesman. During this time, I had a twinge of panic when Jack announced that he was going to professionalize Glenbow and that all department heads would have to be university graduates. He told me I should consider my position of archivist as "temporary" until his master plan was drawn up and implemented. When I started at Glenbow, I had been offered a two-year contract but I had refused. My philosophy was that if Glenbow didn't want me, I wouldn't want to stay around. Naive, perhaps, but it made perfect sense to me at the time.

But contract or no contract, Jack had overlooked a couple of points. First, Eric Harvie showed a decided dislike for anyone flaunting his university degrees and tended to judge people on the basis of their performance, rather than their academic credentials. And second, I had developed a good working relationship with Eric Harvie and he made it clear that he had confidence in both me and my work. In any case, Jack soon learned that Glenbow could not be run like a government department or a profit-making business as Eric Harvie was too personally engrossed in every aspect of its operation. Nothing was too small or insignificant for him to be involved.

If Jack had been given a free rein, perhaps he would have turned Glenbow into a professional organization a decade or two before it really happened, and I might have been out on the street. But it didn't happen, and pretty soon Jack learned that he had to do things Harvie's way if he was going to survive.

In spite of my initial jitters, Jack and I got along well. In my view, he was Glenbow's finest director in the years when it was still a foundation, and would rank second or third in the overall history of Glenbow. He had a keen mind, good administrative talents, and could instill fierce loyalty among his staff. We became good friends over the years, and when he later became Director of the Manitoba Museum of Man and Nature, he wanted to hire me as the assistant director. It was an attractive offer but the museum was too far from the Blackfoot and too close to the Manitoba winters.

Although Harvie did not consider Glenbow to be a museum in the usual sense of the word, he did have the propensity to be a packrat. I remember once he called the staff together and told us to go out and "collect like a bunch of drunken sailors." But at this time we had no curators of artifacts, except perhaps Eleanor Ediger's responsibility for paintings and sculptures. But Harvie couldn't resist the temptation to accept the offer when friends asked him to install an exhibition for the opening of the Southern Alberta Jubilee Auditorium in the summer of 1957. I think that Jack and I were the only two who had had any experience in mounting displays, so much of the task fell to us. I remember that Jack, Eleanor, and I worked into the wee hours of the morning getting everything in place for Glenbow's first show. When it was opened, the press treated us kindly, commenting favourably on the books, documents, Indian dioramas, argillite carvings, paintings, and the artifacts from Dick Forbis' archaeological excavations.

By 1958, the growth of Glenbow in the previous two years had created a situation whereby we had a lot of inexperienced people going their own way without too much direction. When Jack suggested adding three new researchers – Tom Petty, Bill Jacobson, and Everett Baker – he also recommended that Glenbow hold its first staff training program. When this was approved, the Banff School of Fine Arts was chosen as the location.

Each of us department heads was instructed to give a talk, outlining the scope and procedures of our operations. In addition, I was asked to introduce my friend Jim MacGregor, who agreed to be guest speaker at the windup banquet.

On Sunday, April 27th, George Gooderham and I shared a car to Morley, where we stopped to pick up John Laurie, who had been staying with his protege, Eddie Hunter. In Banff, we were housed at the school, where I shared a room with Pat McCloy. He had succeeded Nina Napier as our librarian. Eric Harvie and the Managers Limited staff stayed downtown at the Mount Royal Hotel.

The meeting started next morning with a welcome from Eric Harvie, after which Jack Herbert explained that the staff needed to be more familiar with the workings and objectives of the Foundation. I led off the staff discussions with a review of my department. "Although the archives have been operating for a relatively short time," I said, "we have already gathered the nucleus of a very fine collection. We have priceless documents, records and photographs which would be an asset to any archival institution. At the present time we have approximately 40,000 pages of documents, 60,000 photographs or negatives, and over 100 microfilms."[51] I bragged about some of the particularly important pieces, and went on to tell how to collect, document, store, and provide access to archival materials. One of the things that bothered me, which I expressed at the meeting, was that too many of our field workers were content to borrow a document, make a typed copy of it, and return the original. "With a little more effort," I told them, "we should be able to obtain the original documents." This criticism was aimed primarily at the Loggie sisters, who seldom collected anything original, and Eleanor Luxton, whose High River material consisted mostly of typed copies.

In the afternoon, Dick Forbis, Bill Marsden, Cliff Wilson, and Eleanor Ediger all spoke about their particular areas of expertise. Of these talks, Eleanor's was the most notable, for it got her into hot water from which she never fully recovered. When describing the art department, she commented,

"We have a large collection of buffalo paintings by Frederick Verner, T. Mower Martin, Paul Kane, and others. These we refer to as our Bloody Bison collection." Everyone roared with laughter – except Eric Harvie. He had collected each and every one of those paintings and after the conference, word seeped back that he had been extremely angry about her comments. Perhaps this was why she never gained the same level of independence or responsibility as other department heads.

Next day Pat McCloy spoke and then a panel was held to discuss problems experienced by field workers. It turned out that their greatest difficulties stemmed from the fact that few people had ever heard of the Glenbow Foundation and were therefore suspicious of it. But this wasn't new, for we faced this problem constantly in Calgary. Glenbow had no public face and Eric Harvie had no desire to put us in the limelight.

We had three guest speakers during the conference – Saskatchewan archivist Lewis H. Thomas, University of Alberta librarian Bruce Peel, and Jim MacGregor.

That was the conference, at least on the surface, but what went on behind the scenes was equally interesting. On the last night, a number of us were invited to Leechman's room for drinks but pretty soon we were just sitting around while he dominated the gathering, telling one story after another. Then I noticed that the crowd was starting to thin out; a few of the staff had planned a strategy whereby one person at a time slipped away. Leechman never noticed. He kept on and on until there were only a couple of us left, and when he awakened to the fact that his audience had deserted him he was obviously embarrassed. He said something about going to bed, so the rest of us left. I thought it was pretty sad.

When I got outside, I learned that the others had gone to Jim Fish's room at the Mount Royal. Jim was part of Harvie's managerial staff. I joined them and we had a roaringly good time until about 3 a.m. when the night clerk pounded on the door. "Keep the noise down," he said. "The people next door are complaining!" His comments were greeted with whoops and laughter until Jim Fish said, "Do you know who's next door? Eric Harvie."

That put a damper on the party right away. By the time I got out on Banff Avenue with Andy Russell, everything was dark and quiet. We walked back to the school and it too was in darkness. I had no idea where the rest of the party had gone, so I went to bed. Next morning I learned they had broken into the swimming pool at the Upper Hot Springs and had gone skinny dipping. There were well-founded rumours of other happenings, and afterwards, when the story got around, more than one wife wanted to know what her husband had been doing that night. I never did get an accurate count of who had been in the pool but I have a good idea.

I understand that the rumours of the debauch also got back to Eric Harvie. In any case, that was the first and last all-staff conference ever held at Banff by the Glenbow Foundation.

I mentioned Bill Marsden being at the conference. He was still with the Alberta government when Pauline and I got to Calgary, but it was clear that his government job was going nowhere. We needed a photographer at Glenbow so arrangements were made to hire Bill and to have use of the government darkroom. This worked pretty well for a while until Bill finally went into private industry. While he was with us, he arranged to film the Blackfoot Sun Dance, and once we went on a photo tour and succeeded in getting portraits of a number of Bloods, including Jim Shot Both Sides, Rides at the Door, and Bobtail Chief.

As for Jack Herbert, he fought the wars in favour of professionalization as long as he could, but finally left in the spring of 1959 to join the Historic Sites Branch in Ottawa. I was sorry to see him go, as our ideas always seemed to be on the same wavelength. Eric McGreer, who was the administrator, took over many of Jack's duties. He was a different type altogether. He was simply an administrator and nothing more. He had no vision and no understanding of what we were trying to do. With him, the Glenbow became so bogged down in petty details that at last Eric Harvie decided that he had to go, and he went.

Meanwhile, I found there could be nothing more rewarding or exciting than to be an archivist in Alberta in the 1950s and early 1960s. It was an untapped field, and rather than running into resistance from people wanting to preserve their old records, I more frequently encountered the problem of families and businesses wondering aloud why anyone would want all that old junk. Apathy, rather than acquisitiveness, was my usual dilemma.

———⟨∞⟩———

Very early in my career, while still living in Edmonton, I showed a great interest in photographs as a means of viewing and preserving history. This continued at Glenbow when I set out on an organized campaign to obtain photographic collections. Soon I was touring photographic studios, buying their old back files. Studios like Atterton's in Cardston, Cameron's in Lacombe, and R.A. Bird's and Cadman's in Calgary – the latter holding the Bill Oliver negatives – were added to the collections. But two of the biggest and most important collections came from Edmonton. These were the McDermid Studio collection and the *Edmonton Bulletin* collection. I don't recall exactly how we made contact with McDermid's but I knew them well as the studio right next door to the Edmonton Journal building in the downtown area. At my first contact, I was shown hundreds of negatives that were stored in the basement, many of them within inches of a huge old furnace. In some instances, the jackets were so brittle that they crumbled at the touch, and with a few negatives, the emulsion had lifted from the acetate. Later, we found that some of these weren't acetate negatives at all; they were nitrate films and highly combustible. Two of the active ingredients in such films are nitric acid and glycerine. It doesn't take much imagination to figure out what they can become!

However, the McDermid negatives were in remarkably good condition. We found that over the years, the studio had done a lot of work for the *Journal*, so there were plenty of news pictures as well as studio work. After that first visit, I made repeated trips to the studio over the years, picking up more and more of their back files until the whole collection became one of our best resources.

The *Edmonton Bulletin* collection was another story. I, of course, knew about it when I worked there. The studio was at the Bulletin Printers, in a separate building from the newspaper, so I thought there was a chance that the negatives might have been left behind when everything else closed. Sure enough, when I checked, there were the complete files from 1948 to 1951, giving a good cross-section of social and economic life in western Canada in the post-war era. The building was owned by Max Bell so I spoke to Mr. Harvie, he spoke to Max Bell, and a few weeks later I picked up the collection, filing cabinets and all. I was sad some years later when Glenbow, in its wisdom, donated the whole collection to the Provincial Archives (or the Edmonton archives), as it contained a lot of material that wasn't local in nature and could have been profitably used by people coming to Glenbow. It's nice to share, but not at the expense of your own holdings.

Another major collection which arrived about the same time was the Lomen Brothers collection from Nome, Alaska. Harvie bought this from Shorey's Bookstore in Seattle, and it provided to be a gold mine of views of Eskimos, mining towns, and northern events at the turn of the century.

I also began borrowing pictures wherever I could find them and having copies made. Many were from other museums, private collections, and a goodly number borrowed from Indians who were friends of mine. Our researchers also helped considerably as they brought in their share of photos from pioneer families and a host of other sources. Within a short time we had a major archives of photographs that fitted nicely into the cataloguing system that I had developed.

During the first year or two I began a crusade looking for old newspaper files to microfilm, and found some excellent ones in places like Fort Macleod and Pincher Creek. This became the nucleus of what proved to be a large newspaper collection on microfilm. Later, I got the co-operation of the Legislative Library in Edmonton to microfilm some of their holdings of rural weekly newspapers. But the big surprise came when I visited the Manitoba Legislative Library. I had been told that they held many nineteenth-century newspapers from western Canada from a time when Winnipeg was the main business centre of the West. When I asked to microfilm such newspapers as the *Calgary Tribune* and the *Medicine Hat Times*, I was told by the librarian, Marjorie Morley, that these and other non-Manitoba newspapers were extraneous to their holdings. If we would microfilm them and give them a copy, we could have the originals! I was quite excited for two reasons: it is always nice to have an original rather than a copy, and I had been having a hard time convincing Harvie that we should be collecting newspapers. He didn't like microfilms so this became an ideal chance to sell him on the whole idea. And it worked, so that over the years we amassed quite a collection of old newspapers.

My one disappointment was the *Calgary Herald*. When I approached them, they told me they already had a Toronto firm microfilming their back issues. When I asked if we could get the originals as well as a set of microfilms, they agreed. Imagine my surprise and disgust when they started to arrive. The Toronto firm, Preston Microfilms Ltd., had done no advance work to get the newspapers organized in chronological order and the microfilming itself was the shoddiest work I have ever seen, before or since. Many pages were overexposed, underexposed, or had uneven exposure so that a page was light at the top and so dark at the bottom to be almost unreadable. I was further disappointed when we got those originals that they hadn't already destroyed. I found they had taken the bound copies, chopped off the binding with a paper cutter, then microfilmed the loose pages. These were tossed helter-skelter back into the outer cover, and that's what we got. Later examination also revealed that they had missed some volumes, and Glenbow still has a few originals but has never microfilmed them. The later years of the *Calgary Heralds* were okay as I don't think they were done by Preston. From time to time I have hinted that Glenbow should redo the entire early years as these are heavily used, but this has not been a high priority item.

During this time, there seemed to be manuscript collections galore that were just there for the asking. At first I used my old government contacts to find archival material, but then leads started to come from George Gooderham, the Harvie organization, and people who simply dropped by for a visit. These visitors formed an impressive list. Before long I was having coffee (or tea, in my case) with the likes of historians George Stanley, Grant MacEwan, Dr. A.O. MacRae, Kerry Wood, and Montana historian Merrill Burlingame; and local personalities like Benton Mackid, Colonel Macleod's son Norman, lawyer J.E.A. Macleod, Ken Coppick, and naturalist Andy Russell. Then there were the politicians and international figures Harvie paraded through the place. During the late 1950s I recall such personages as Viscount Montgomery and his entourage. In my diary for September 30, 1957, I comment, "M.J. Coldwell was in with George Gooderham and [Lester B.] Mike Pearson with Mr. Harvie. I had a chat with both of them. Not too impressed with the latter, although he knew more about Archives than Coldwell."

As for Indian visitors, there was no end to them. Some came to see me because of the Indian Association or because we were friends, and others came to see George Gooderham and dropped by to chat with me. In the late 1950s these included such people as Joe Crowfoot, One Gun, Ben Calf Robe, and Frank Medicine Shield.

As a result of the various leads, I spent a lot of time travelling to cities and rural parts of the province. Often my trips were a mixture of Glenbow business, Historical Society meetings, and Indian Association matters. To me, they all seemed to blend perfectly and to the advantage of everyone.

⸻ ⊸⊸⊸ ⸻

One of the great things about being the archivist for Glenbow in the 1950s and early 1960s was that I was pretty well given a free hand. Because I wasn't costing Glenbow much money to buy things, and because archival items weren't as sexy as paintings and rare books, Eric Harvie tended to leave me alone when it came to day-to-day gifts and acquisitions. It was only when I wanted to buy something or travel that I ran into problems, as permission was required to do just about everything. On the organizational side, there were no other archives in Alberta and those across Canada were mostly all government agencies that did not seem to be too open to innovative ideas. That meant I pretty well had to start from scratch, and this was fine with me.

However, whenever there was a chance to learn more about archival science, I was anxious to go. In 1959, the Public Archives of Canada in association with Carleton University put on a five-week archives training course in Ottawa and I received permission to attend. The course itself was the first of its kind ever offered in Canada and had an impressive student enrolment. The only problem was that it was really a training session on how the Public Archives did things. The theory seemed to be that there were only two ways to run an archives – the Public Archives way or the wrong way. This became a running joke among the students, but I will say we all learned a lot about archives, both from the teachers and from our fellow students. I had a chance to meet some of the best archivists in Canada – Hart Bowsfield of Manitoba, Allan Turner of Saskatchewan, and Andre Vachon of Quebec, among the students, and W. Kay Lamb, Bernard Weilbrenner, Kay Storey, and others on the staff. Hart, Allen, Andre, and I hung around together, which was convenient as Andre had a car. One of his goals, he said, was to learn English, so he had plenty of chances. However, during many an evening while sitting in a beer parlour he would suddenly proclaim that he couldn't take any more English and to speak to him only in French. As Hart was fully bilingual, he took on those duties for the rest of the night.

That course, together with my travels to other institutions, gave me a good idea of what was happening – and what was not happening – in the archival field. I found there was plenty of room for innovation as long as one followed the basic principles of archival science. The most important of these were the proper documentation of collections, and their care under the most optimal conditions available.

Over the years, I found that collecting required a combination of salesmanship, sincerity, and knowledge. This was particularly true in the early years when no one had ever heard of the Glenbow Foundation. As a result, I name-dropped shamelessly to give my request some credibility. Sometimes I invoked the names of friends in the Historical Society, sometimes the Indian Association, and sometimes people at Glenbow – whatever worked. I also found that a bit of advance research also helped so I could talk about a family or company with some modicum of intelligence. Contacts came from Glenbow staff, from friends, from newspaper reports and obituaries, and as a result of the multitude of speeches I made to service clubs, local groups, and anyone else who would listen to me. As a result, the collections began to flow into the Archives and more and more time was needed to process and catalogue them.

On one occasion, I was instructed to contact Mrs. Lillian Graham, the only surviving daughter of missionary John McDougall. I believe the original contact had been made through Eric Harvie. In any case, I found her living in the old family home in the eastern part of downtown Calgary, a section of the city that was destined for destruction under an urban renewal program. She was living by herself in this big old house with only a Dutchman as a boarder. I found her to be a very interesting lady, but one who had strong opinions and did not seem to get along with her relatives, particularly those from the David McDougall side of the family. I don't recall the exact arrangements with Glenbow, but I went to see her to obtain a collection of artifacts, photographs, and documents that she possessed. There were some fine items – a "silk" buffalo robe, the knife scabbard her grandfather had been wearing when he died in a storm in the 1870s, an unpublished manuscript, and a quantity of Indian and missionary material.

I struck up a friendship with Mrs. Graham and used to visit her from time to time. We had some wonderful chats together but for some reason I never tried to interview her. I believe I just looked upon her as a friend. In the 1970s, she was admitted to a nursing home and one day she asked me if I would stop at the house and pick up some clothes she had left in the basement. The Dutchman let me in, and while I was downstairs I began prowling around. There seemed to be nothing of interest until I opened a cardboard box and found it full of dockets – letters folded into little packets. When I opened a few of them, I was surprised to find files of correspondence of Richard Hardisty while he had been chief factor of Fort Edmonton during the 1860s to 1880s. I was absolutely flabbergasted, as Mrs. Graham had assured me that she had given me everything of value. She was permanently in the nursing home and the old house was destined for demolition, so these papers were just waiting to be destroyed. I put them in the trunk of my car, picked up Mrs. Graham's clothes, and immediately went to see her. I told her I'd been poking around in the basement and explained what I had found.

At first she was puzzled, as she could not recall having any such papers. And then it came to her. When she had married Fred Graham many years earlier, it had been his second marriage. His first wife had been a daughter of Richard Hardisty and when she died he had inherited the papers. He had brought them along when he married Lillian and when he died she had inherited them. She was glad that I had found them and was quite pleased to give them to Glenbow. Isn't it amazing how one little incident can have such far-reaching consequences? If Mrs. Graham and I had not become friends, if she had not asked me to get her clothes, if I had not been so nosey – the papers would have been lost.

I was very sad about Mrs. Graham's last days. She had invested her money in an annuity that was supposed to assure her a private room in the nursing home for the rest of her life. However, when I went up to visit her one day, she wasn't there. When I enquired, I learned that she was in a public ward and was distraught with grief. She was a lonely woman but also a very private one. That is when I learned that her money had been used up and she was now in a basic ward provided by government welfare. I was shocked. I immediately took the problem to Eric Harvie and he said if I would find out the difference in cost between the public ward and the private room, he would personally make up the difference. I started to make arrangements but the whole experience had been such a shock that Mrs. Graham died before the change could be made. As I noted in my diary on October 23, 1973, "She was 89 and a very lonely woman."

The search for archival material led me into a number of interesting situations. One day I heard that Atterton Studios was closing down in Cardston. When I went there I learned the building was going to be torn down and managed to get a small collection of negatives from the old man. As we were talking, I noticed a trapdoor in the ceiling and asked him if there was anything in the attic. He said he hadn't been up there for years but if I wanted to look, I could go right ahead. I got a ladder and when I pushed the ceiling lid aside the attic looked like the usual dusty area of joists and rafters. But then I noticed something sitting on one of the rafters, and when I checked, I found it was a pile of glass plate negatives. There were quite a bunch of them perched on the rafters and when I brought them down Atterton recalled that they had belonged to his predecessor, a man named Arthur Hensen, and had been up there for thirty years. There were some very good studio portraits of settlers, Chinese merchants, and local farmers, but the real prize was a previously unknown portrait of plainsman John George "Kootenai" Brown.

Another interesting adventure occurred early in 1961 when I had a call from a man working in the Legal Department at City Hall. He told me that he was looking out his window and below him he could see an old City building being cleaned out before being demolished. He said that workmen were carrying out piles of old records and files. I rushed down there and, sure enough, there was a low one-storey building abutting the east side of City Hall and it was being abandoned. By the door was a large garbage truck loaded to the top with file boxes and file folders. I grabbed the first box I could find and saw it contained old correspondence from the turn of the century. The garbage men were just about ready to drive away but when I begged for a chance to climb into the box and go though the pile, they said they'd stop for coffee and then they'd have to leave. I climbed into the back of the truck and feverishly went through the pile, tossing onto the ground anything that looked promising. I had gone through most of the pile before they got back but I knew there was some I had missed. Shortly afterwards another truck arrived but by this time I had had a chance to go into the building to see what was left. Most of it was recent tax files but on one shelf I found some wonderful material that dated back to 1884.

Somehow W.R. Castell, the City Librarian, learned that I had taken the files; he said they were the property of the City and inferred to the local newspapers that I had illegally taken them. Perhaps I had, who's to say? But I responded by saying that if Mr. Castell wanted the records back he should contact me and give some assurances that they would not be destroyed. I never heard from him and so we kept the papers for many years until the City established its own archives, at which time they were returned to them.

Another time I was told by one of our researchers, Bill Jacobson, that there were some old records in the PFRA (Prairie Farm Rehabilitation Act) office in Vauxhall. When we went there, we found that when the PFRA had been formed as a federal agency, it had taken over the private business papers of Canadian Wheatlands, Grand Forks Cattle Company, Southern Alberta Land Company, and Canada Land & Irrigation Company. This collection of some fifty boxes was now collecting dust in the basement, but when I asked the manager if he would donate them to Glenbow, he was unsure if these were now federal records. I tried to convince him that when they took over the private companies, their papers were just physical assets, like chairs and filing cabinets. He suggested that he write to headquarters but I dissuaded him, as I knew the papers would either be destroyed or shipped off to the East. He told me he'd think about it, and we left it at that. This happened in the spring of 1961. When I didn't hear back, I assumed we had lost out. However, two years later I got a phone call from this same manager. He said he was retiring at the end of the week and if we wanted the papers to come and get them the next day. His idea was that he was leaving anyway so he wouldn't get into trouble if he was wrong.

There was only one problem. By this time we had a new director, an ex–military colonel named Benny Greene. To him, a word from Eric Harvie, even a passing one, was like an order from his commanding general: it was not to be questioned but to be obeyed. Earlier, Harvie had indicated that some important visitors would be coming to the Foundation and he didn't want anyone leaving town during the month. We all knew when the visitors would be arriving, but to Colonel Greene, an order was an order. When I sought permission to make the pickup, I was refused.

If I didn't go, we would lose the collection, so next morning I rented a truck and left at dawn. I got to Vauxhall at noon, loaded up the truck, got a receipt, and arrived back in the city in the early evening. Next morning I learned that Greene had been suspicious about me and had phoned the Archives off and on all day. My secretary and others did a wonderful job in stalling him, saying I was out of the office, at a meeting, etc. At one stage he asked point blank if I had left town and my secretary said she just didn't know. Next morning I was summoned to Greene's office and he went up one side of me and down the other, threatening to go to Eric Harvie and having me fired. I don't know if he ever tried but I never heard anything more about it. I have a feeling that if he did raise the question and Harvie learned what I had collected, he would have been on my side. At least I'd like to think so. And a chewing out was a small price to pay for such a valuable collection.

Then there were the Canadian Pacific Railway records. In 1961 I went to Montreal for a meeting of the Archives Section of the Canadian Historical Association and was elected vice-chairman. While in the city I took a letter of introduction from Eric Harvie for Fred V. Stone, vice-chairman of the CPR, and was taken on a tour of their Montreal facilities. In the bowels of the old building I saw a shredding machine working full days destroying CPR documents. And in a private vault I saw ten feet of personal papers of Sir Edward Shaughnessy. I was told they were scheduled for destruction because none of the family wanted them and they were not CPR records. I also saw a good collection of letter books dating back to the 1880s. I wrote in my diary for June 9th, "The whole picture does not look encouraging in finding out just what they have in the way of records and what steps are being taken to preserve them. I feel our best contribution would be to find a way to encourage them to establish a proper records management program, particularly as it affects pre-1900 records." Perhaps this had some effect, for a few years later an archives department was created under the leadership of CPR publicity manager and railway historian Omer Lavallee.

When I went to see the librarian, he showed me some of original tickets used on the first transcontinental run of the CPR in 1885. There were three sets, each having first class, coach, and tourist tickets, all properly stamped. On an off chance, I asked him if we could have one of the sets, and he gave them to me on the spot. I continued to go through the scanty files and whenever

I found a duplicate booklet or other item, he freely gave it to me. I really appreciated his generosity.

Another positive feature that came out of the trip was that I got permission from headquarters to look through the files in Calgary to see if I could find any duplicate material of value. Pat McCloy and I went to the Natural Resources Building and went through filing cabinets of immigration literature where we found a quantity of CPR pamphlets in various foreign languages that had been used to entice settlers. A number of them were completely unknown so Pat was very pleased.

We kept in touch with the CPR in Calgary, letting them know we were interested in their old records. One official who seemed particularly sympathetic informed us that they would be moving out of their old downtown quarters and into a building constructed a little farther east for Marathon Realty, one of their branches. We looked over the material and found 1½ tons of large ledger books containing records of all their land sales since the 1880s. The man was willing to turn them over to us and I drafted a formal letter which was signed by both parties.

A short time later, he said there were more records which Marathon was planning to discard. They were located in a repair shed on the railway right-of-way. When I went there, I found an old wooden building with the ground floor used for motor repairs; there was enough grease around that the whole place could have gone up in smoke in an instant. Upstairs were shelves loaded with files from their old Colonization Branch. I spent the next several days going through records of irrigation projects, farm lands promotions, and other valuable material relating to the settlement of the West. I divided the files into two piles, one for us to keep and the other to discard. When I was finished, some CPR officials looked them over and gave us most of what I had put aside. The only exception was a nice pile of records relating to land sales and town plans for southeastern British Columbia, around Cranbrook. I learned that there was some litigation in progress and these documents would be kept by Marathon. We were pleased to get the rest of it; I tried to keep track of the Cranbrook material and traced it to the new Marathon office but I eventually lost sight of it.

Some years later, a couple of lawyers came to the Archives and demanded to know why we were in possession of CPR records, implying that these had been illegally taken from their Calgary offices. They were very hard-nosed and officious, but when I produced the agreement signed by one of their top officials (since retired), their faces fell. They asked for a copy and said they'd be back but we never saw them again.

⸎

Three years later, I was in Winnipeg looking for some Metis material when I phoned a woman who worked for the Canada Northwest Land Company. I recalled that they had been the agents for land sales for the CPR so I asked her if they had anything. She said there were some old records in the vault but that the office was going to be closing down. I went in and saw her boss and, as a result, I picked up a number of old plans and legal agreements. Among them was a document that I like to call a Bill of Sale for Calgary. In 1884, in order to subdivide and sell the land on Section 16, which became the downtown part of Calgary, the CPR "sold" the property to its subsidiary, the Canada Northwest Land Company, and we got the document. By the time we were finished, I was quite pleased with the amount of material we got from the CPR. Not only that, but we seemed to have established good relations with them and over the years Sheilagh Jameson, Doug Cass, and others were able to add to our CPR holdings.

We were not so lucky with the Alberta Provincial Police records. Earlier we'd had Don Tannas working for us and in 1961 he was with the provincial government on their historic sign program. One day he noticed a load of papers being taken from one of the vaults in the basement of the Legislative Building and upon examination he saw they were headquarters and detachment records of the Alberta Provincial Police that operated from 1916 to 1931. There were daily diaries from the detachments, correspondence, wanted posters, and other important files. He tried to convince the Attorney General's Department that these were historical documents and tried to prevent their destruction but he was chewed out by one of the bureaucrats. Don told me about it and I phoned the deputy minister. I was assured that these had been nothing but personal case files and had already been destroyed. It was a lie that they were confidential case files but true that they had been destroyed – about five truckloads full.

Similarly, when Doug Light and I were on a field collecting trip to Saskatchewan in 1963, I learned from our interpreter, Wilfred Chocan, that the old Fort Pitt trading post business had been moved to Onion Lake after the 1885 Riel Rebellion and that the widow of the last store manager, a woman named Mrs. Al Blower, was living in the old residence. When we visited her, she gave Wilfred a warm welcome and announced that she had just returned from her first visit to Hawaii. When I asked her about the old Hudson's Bay

Company records from Fort Pitt and Onion Lake, she said that a pile of old papers had been stored for years in a back room in her house. However, when she decided to go to Hawaii, she was afraid these might be a fire trap, so she had taken them out in the yard and burned them. These records had sat there for decades and we missed them only by a couple of weeks. That was really heartbreaking.

One of the strangest situations I ever encountered concerned the papers of Joseph F. Dion, a Metis schoolteacher who lived near the Kehewin Reserve. In 1960, while gathering information for a history of the Indian Association, I was told that Joe had been one of the group's first organizers. When I visited him in his log home, I was very impressed with the man. Not only did he tell me a lot about the early years of the Association, but he showed me a series of articles he had written for the *Bonnyville Tribune* on the history of the Cree Indians. I also learned that he was extremely knowledgeable about Cree material culture so I asked him if he would be interested in doing some contract work for Glenbow. When he agreed, I applied to Glenbow for approval and when it came, I wrote to him to arrange the details. But it never happened, for just after I had written to him, I learned that he had died of a heart attack.

A month later I had business in Edmonton, so I continued on to Kehewin, where I saw Joe's widow and arranged to buy all of his manuscripts and papers. These included the early drafts of some of his published articles and a number of others that were as yet unpublished. It proved to be an important collection of papers.

The story might have ended there, but now we jump to 1976, when I was appointed to the Alberta Indian Treaties Commemorative Program, organized by the Alberta government to provide funds for marking the anniversaries of Treaty Six in 1876 and Treaty Seven in 1877. A good chunk of money was earmarked for publications and I suggested that Glenbow should publish a history written by Joe Dion. When I got approval, I got legal copyright releases from Dion's two daughters, then gathered Dion's writings together and published them in 1979 as *My Tribe the Crees*.

There's more. A few years later I received notice that Glenbow and I were being sued for infringement of copyright. The editor of the *Bonnyville Tribune* claimed that he, not Joe Dion, had written the articles that we had published. He said that Dion would visit him at his newspaper, tell him stories, and the editor would write them and publish them under Dion's byline. I pointed out that this was ridiculous, as we not only had first and second drafts of some of these articles in Dion's own handwriting, but we also had letters from the editor to me in which he stated clearly that Dion had done the writing. I showed these to our lawyer and he spoke to the editor's lawyer, but the editor was adamant and wouldn't back down, not even in the face of this evidence. The matter went all the way through examination for discovery and other legal processes until it finally came before a judge in Edmonton. I was supposed to have been there, but my plane was grounded by fog in Calgary and I missed it. Our lawyer later told us that the judge took one look at the evidence then bawled out the editor's lawyer for letting it go that far. The lawyer explained that his client wouldn't back down, so the judge hauled the man up in front of him and read the riot act to him. I knew from the beginning I had all the documentation on my side but it is still very unsettling going through weeks of legal proceedings.

There was one other time in my career that I was threatened with a lawsuit, and it was just as specious. In 1988, while attending the opening of Glenbow's Olympic exhibition, *The Spirit Sings*, I was served with papers suing me for defamation. Here are parts of the press report:

> Buff Parry has filed a statement of claim in Court of Queen's Bench in Edmonton, alleging he was defamed in a letter Dempsey sent to the governor general's office. Parry said after the June 25, 1985, letter he was refused funds for research into origins of Cree Indian writing.

> Dempsey ... advised the governor general, whose office controls the funds, that the writing form was invented by a Methodist missionary named James Evans, not the Cree. Dempsey recommended against supporting Parry's search for an inscribed tablet, that Parry says the explorer LaVerendrye buried in southern Alberta. Parry said finding the tablet would prove that the Indians, not the missionary Evans, invented their own writing form.[52]

I was absolutely furious when I got the news. My report to the governor general's office had been sent in complete confidence, but they had passed a copy of it along to Parry. I have done scores of assessments of funding requests for many agencies but this was the first time my report had actually gone to the person that I was recommending against. I got on the phone and burned up the wires to Ottawa, but in typical civil servant fashion they denied ever sending my report. When I asked them how else he could have obtained it, they had the temerity to suggest that I might have sent it! I screamed as much as I could, but it was to a stone wall of bureaucracy that said deny, deny, deny, so there was nothing I could do.

As for the request for funds, I had plenty of evidence to support my position. I had copies of James Evans' notes while he was labouring in Ontario, showing his experiments with different symbols for his syllabics. When he moved to Norway House, in Manitoba, he perfected these and introduced them to the Cree. And as far as LaVerendrye was concerned, this was completely inaccurate, as that explorer never got any closer to southern Alberta than the Black Hills of South Dakota. Contrary to popular mythology, he never did see the Canadian Rockies.

As it turned out, the situation was all sound and no fury. After a year, Parry had failed to pursue the case and it was abandoned.

At Glenbow, our search for Canadiana took us to many homes and businesses, but one of the strangest incidents occurred right in Hull House. George Gooderham and I were discussing aviation when one of our caretakers overheard us. He said he had some old pictures in his trunk and we could have them if we wanted them. It turned out that he had once worked for Alexander Graham Bell at Baddeck, Nova Scotia, at the time when experiments were taking place with the Silver Dart and other aircraft. The caretaker had obtained proof pictures showing some of these experiments and some aquatic ones showing their use of hydrofoils.

Then there were times when our searches created some unusual situations. For example, I was quite interested in the history of the Social Credit party, which had been in power in Alberta since 1935. I managed to find some excellent collections, including the papers of Bert Nichols, whom I had worked with at the government. This led me to search for an anti–Social Credit newspaper called *The Rebel*. I traced it down to a man named J.J. Zubick who was still living in Calgary and was an ardent Conservative. I got to know him fairly well, but I must admit I was surprised in 1959 when he said he was a member of the Conservative nominating committee and asked me to be a candidate for Calgary North in the next provincial election. I was flattered but I was too heavily involved in other matters to give it serious thought.

I was never that interested in politics but I did like public speaking. When television first came to Calgary, everything was live; there was no taping of shows. In 1960, CFCN-TV invited the Foundation to appear in a weekly series to tell what we were doing and to talk about western history. I was surprised when Eric Harvie agreed, and we started our first show in December with a round table discussion including our president, George Crawford, Moncrieff Williamson, and me. The first show was a real laugh. The interviewer was obviously very inexperienced and so were we. He started off by asking Crawford a question but didn't follow it up. In the ensuing silence, Crawford didn't seem to know what to do so he kept talking, and talking, and talking. I could see that he had a tiger by the tail and couldn't shake it loose. Finally the interviewer got into the act but by then our part of the program was over. Crawford saw the humour of the situation but said he'd leave the rest of the series to us. I appeared in January 1961 and had a nice fifteen-minute talk about archives. Just as in my public speaking, I wasn't the least bit nervous and over the years I had dozens of other interviews, some lasting as much as an hour. And as long as I had something to say, I didn't mind talking.

---

When Dick Forbis joined Glenbow a month after me, we became very good friends and colleagues. I had already shown an interest in archaeology and earlier in the year I had my first paper published on the subject; through the help of Jack Ewers, the *Journal of the Washington Academy of Sciences* had published my "Stone 'Medicine Wheels' – Memorials to Blackfoot War Chiefs."[53] Dick and I travelled to the Blood and Blackfoot reserves to look at tepee rings and other sites that seemed to have archaeological interest. Then in 1960, I accompanied Dick and his crew on a three-day trip into the Porcupine Hills to look for a site mentioned by explorer Peter Fidler and to search for possible Kootenay Indian sites. I had great fun camping out with the crew and became quite enthusiastic about archaeological work.

Dick and I had also discussed a site on the Blackfoot Reserve that had been mentioned by an artist named Edmund Morris. We went out there one day with Dad, and I arranged for One Gun to take us to the site. He told us the history of this fortified village which was located beside the banks of the Bow, saying it had been built by strangers who had come from the south; he called them Earth Lodge People. Dick believed they were Crows while I thought they might be Hidatsa. In any case, Dick thought the site was worthy of study, so we worked together to get approval from the tribal council and eventually Glenbow did a full archaeological excavation of the site.

There were a couple of unexpected sidelights. One was Dick's insistence that the entire non-professional crew be Blackfoot, under a Blackfoot supervisor. When he decided to hire Matthew Melting Tallow for the job, George

Gooderham was entirely opposed to it. As former Indian agent for the reserve, Gooderham considered Matt to be unreliable and difficult. In my mind, that meant Matt thought for himself and would not do everything he was told to do by the Indian agent. So Dick hired Matt and he proved to be excellent. And not only was he reliable, but on many mornings he got up early and rounded up the crew himself, rather than waiting for them to come in to work. Of course, I was prejudiced as I always liked Matt and I believe I had suggested him in the first place.

An amusing incident occurred one day while I was visiting the site. We got talking and Matt mentioned that there was a stone effigy nearby that marked the sleeping place of Napi, the mythical trickster-creator of the Blackfoot Indians. He rounded up One Gun and we drove to a spot just south of the grain elevator at Crowfoot Siding. One Gun searched around in the grass for a while and finally found the site. It consisted of a human figure made of stones laid out on the ground in outline form. The figure had a head, body, arms, legs, and a penis so long that it defied description. This was in keeping with the legends of Napi and his ability to extend his penis to any length. Even the rainbow was known in Blackfoot as "Napi's penis."

Virtually all the interviews I had conducted in the past had been with Dad as my interpreter, and there are some strict rules of protocol within the Blackfoot community regarding father-in-law and son-in-law relations. One of them is that the subject of sex is never discussed when they are together. So it came as quite a surprise to me when a bunch of ribald remarks were tossed back and forth by these Blackfoot as we looked at the Napi effigy. Finally, One Gun reached into the centre of the figure, picked up a stone the size of a tennis ball, and as he handed it to me he said with a laugh, "Here. I am giving you Napi's belly button." I treasured that moment and I still have that "belly button" in my possession.

Dick and I were involved in a number of archaeologically related projects. We went together to the Head-Smashed-In Buffalo Jump north of the Peigan Reserve and I gave him a copy of a letter I had received from Boyd Wetlauffer, who had done some work at the site years earlier. This letter proved to be the only "report" ever produced for that dig. I also went to the Peigan Reserve and got some of their traditions relating to the site. Another place we visited was the site of Rocky Mountain House, and after some searching in farmers' fields we located some good prospects. Dick later excavated the site and I prepared a historical report which was published along with the findings of the dig.

Dick stayed with Glenbow until 1963, when Eric Harvie gave the whole Archaeology Department to the new University of Calgary and Dick went along as a professor. I'm sure he wished that the program had stayed at Glenbow, for he loved field work and did not really enjoy teaching. But he inspired a lot of people with his publications, teachings, and excavations and was appropriately called the "father of archaeology in Alberta."

While at Glenbow, Dick married Marge Chown, one of our secretaries. They bought a house in Bowness, on the banks of the Bow River, and this became quite a gathering place. They liked to mix their friends for social events, so there were academics from the university, artist friends of Marge's, pals from Glenbow, a few of the social elite from Bowness, and just plain friends. We always had a wonderful time at their place, where conversation flowed freely. Marge was *very* English and Dick was a Montana boy so they made an interesting couple. Dick later took out Canadian citizenship and Pauline was very proud when he asked her to be his sponsor.

———

Although I seemed to have my fingers in a lot of pies, I was still archivist at Glenbow. In 1960, when Cliff Wilson resigned as director of the Foundation, I was given the first of the many "temporary" duties that came my way over the next few years. I was informed in April that I was now "temporarily" in charge of the research program, the museum collections, and the photographic department. That meant that besides the Archives, all the field workers and researchers had to report to me, and the hodge-podge museum collections were now under my tender care. The only areas not reporting to me were the Library, Art Department, Archaeology, and Administration.

This came at a time when I was up to my eyeballs in archival work. For example, I had been working with an old pioneer named John McHugh to write his reminiscences. George Gooderham had brought him in one day and I learned that he was a member of an old ranching family that had owned the H2 Ranch. John, or J.O. McHugh, had been considered to be the poor relative in the family and had been virtually ignored all his life. He had worked for the railway, I believe, and was now living in a small room in the downtown area. As he spoke, I thought he had an interesting story to tell, so I suggested he write out his reminiscences. This was in the days before the popularity of tape recorders. McHugh admitted that he had time on his hands but he couldn't afford the paper and pencils needed to do the work. I happily supplied these and a few days later he returned with his first stories. They were fascinating but because of his limited education his spelling and grammar were poor and he asked me to "fix them up" for him. So I edited his writings, got my secretary to type them up, and gave them back for him to check. He made corrections where needed and a final draft was prepared. This was the beginning of an association that lasted for several months, with us supplying the materials, him doing the writing, and us producing the finished product. By the time he finished, we had a book-length manuscript of stories of the ranch and detailed descriptions of Calgary at the turn of the century. He called the finished product "The Adventures of H2 Jack." We bound up a couple of copies of the manuscript and gave one to him. The beauty of all this is that when he showed it to his nieces and nephews (he had no children) they began to see him in a new light and he was no longer their poor uncle. For the last few years of his life I think he was very happy as the manuscript helped to strengthen his ties with his family.

Here is a brief description of a couple of typical weeks for me at Glenbow. First, *Calgary Herald* columnist Ken Liddell and I waited on the mayor, Harry Hays, to urge him to establish a City of Calgary Archives and Historic Sites Committee. This was on January 19, 1960. At the time I was encouraged by the response we got from the mayor for an archives, but nothing came of it at the time. I then started on a program to collect the records of the Great West Saddlery from its various branches across the west, and then drove to Nanton to get the papers of George Coote, a former MP and member of the "Ginger Group." This was followed by a quick trip to Edmonton to pick up some papers of Norman B. James, one of the "original" Social Credit MLAs of 1935, and the papers of John J. Bowlen, a former lieutenant-governor. All this happened within a few weeks and doesn't include the time taken up helping such researchers as Grant MacEwan, Robin Harvie and the ladies from Glendale who were writing a local history, Iris Fleming of the *Globe & Mail*, lawyer Webster McDonald, cartoonist Stu Cameron, Rev. J. Ernest Nix, Kerry Wood, and a host of others.

A little later, Cliff Wilson announced his resignation just as I was leaving for an extended trip to the East. I stopped in Winnipeg to pack and ship the early newspapers that the Manitoba Library had agreed to give us, then to Toronto to discuss a possible Glenbow publishing program in co-operation with the University of Toronto Press. Nothing came of that. The next day saw me in Ottawa, where I arranged to microfilm the early paysheets for the western Indian reserves.

But my main objective in Ottawa was to see the Commissioner of the RCMP, C.W. Harvison, about their early papers. Dominion Archivist W. Kaye Lamb had told me earlier that he had had absolutely no luck in getting the police to transfer any of their records to the Public Archives. I contacted Eric Harvie about it and an arrangement was made for me to follow it up. On arrival at the headquarters, I was taken to a storage area in the basement and left to myself. As I wrote in my diary, "I began the mammoth task of trying to study and roughly list about 125 linear feet of old records which are in absolutely no order. The idea is to make the RCMP aware of the historical value of these records and induce them to appoint someone to look after them and make them available for research, or to turn them over to the Public Archives."[54]

I spent two days in the basement, prepared a rough inventory, and then went for my meeting with the Commissioner. His aide told me we had ten minutes but the visit lasted for almost an hour. Harvison looked over my list and wondered aloud what all the secrecy was about, and stated that these records should be in the Archives. He advised me that the only reason the police had denied access to them and refused to transfer them was that they didn't know what was in them, and it wasn't a high enough priority for anyone to take the time to find out. But now that he had my inventory, he said he would see what he could do. I passed the information along to Lamb and negotiations were opened that finally resulted in the transfer of the records I saw, and many others, to the Archives. As one who made good use of these records over the years, I was very pleased with the results.

I had just returned from Ottawa when I learned that Eric Harvie had launched a new idea to make his senior staff and family more interested in what was going on at Glenbow. He called them all together and told them they each had a thousand dollars to spend on something for the Foundation and they would get together in six months to have "show and tell." Immediately two people came to see me. To George Crawford, president of the Foundation, I suggested that he commission a dozen historical paintings from Gerald Tailfeathers. When he agreed, I had the task of coordinating the whole thing. And to Jim Fish, treasurer of the Foundation, I suggested microfilming a collection of theses. Again, when this was approved I had to prepare lists, contact universities to borrow the documents, and have the microfilming done.

Part of our regular routine at Glenbow was to hold weekly meetings of department heads, with either George Crawford or Eric Harvie presiding. These were quite valuable as they kept everyone up to date on what was happening and gave the staff some idea of Eric Harvie's current thinking. In addition, I began holding a meeting every three weeks of our research staff, bringing them in from Edmonton, Lethbridge, or wherever they happened to be working. Here again, we had a good exchange of ideas. In light of all the extra work I was able to promote Sheilagh Jameson from her research position to that of assistant archivist. She was a good person to work with and I always admired her diligence and ability to deal with the public. One thing I insisted on from the beginning was that regardless of how private we might be at the Foundation, we still had an obligation to the public, and that meant treating people in a friendly manner, making them welcome, and doing whatever we could to assist them in their research. Sheilagh was a natural for this kind of approach and between us we established a pattern that persisted over the years and gave us a very favourable reputation among researchers and the general public. On the Library side, no one could beat Pat McCloy for working well with the public.

During the summer of 1960 I tried my best to put our museum collections in order. As I mentioned in my diary in late August, "Still working hard in trying to get things organized in the Museums Dept. I've had to start at the bottom and work right through the whole thing, including setting up a filing and accessioning system."[55] During my travels I had met Bill Fleming, who was curator of the museum in Fort Macleod. I was quite impressed with him so in the fall I had a meeting with the Glenbow executive committee – George Crawford, Hod Meech, and Jim Fish – to talk about the whole museum mess. I suggested that Fleming be hired by the Foundation but, as I said in my diary, "I did not get too far with that idea."[56] When this recommendation was turned down I asked to be relieved of any museum duties as I could not give that work the attention it deserved and so the whole problem was turned over to our administrator, Claude Humphreys. He was not a museum person but a good business head. He soon found he could not cope with the problem either, and at the end of the year he recommended that the Foundation follow up on my suggestion of hiring Bill Fleming as our museum curator. This time it was approved, but in the interim the whole mess was tossed back in my lap. Once Bill joined the staff I was finally able to get out of the day-to-day problems of that department, and none too soon, for later in 1961 Eric Harvie bought an entire ghost town from a carnival operator and we were suddenly into museum work in a big way.

That's the way things worked during the early years of Glenbow. If a person was willing to work, they could find themselves involved in just about any aspect of the organization. Yet there were two cardinal rules that had to be followed. The first was the recognition that there was only one boss – Eric Harvie. He owned the Foundation and, in effect, he owned us. Anyone who didn't accept this fact had a short-lived career with Glenbow. Jack Herbert found this out and so did art director Moncrieff Williamson. The second rule was that the staff collected western Canadian material and Eric Harvie collected whatever he wanted. Another one of our directors, Jim Garner, got that one wrong and he suffered for it.

# 6

# Glenbow, Indians, and Me

My personal, business, and professional activities were often so melded together that it was difficult to separate them. On any given week, I might go with Mom and Dad to an Indian Association meeting where I had some volunteer duties to perform, and at the same time visit with friends on a personal level, and have people approach me on Glenbow business. If I tried to keep this autobiography purely chronological, I believe I would be constantly jumping back and forth between these three phases of my life. So, for the early years at Glenbow, I will separate them, even though I may risk losing the significance of some events where the business, professional, and personal were all tied together.

My work as archivist had nothing to do with collecting Indian artifacts or being involved in Native rituals. But it happened anyway. It all started when Dad and I visited the Peigan Reserve in 1956 to conduct some Indian Association business. I told the Peigans about my new job and shortly after I got back to the office, I had a phone call from Bob Crow Eagle. He told me that his brother, Charlie, had embraced the Full Gospel Church and had come to the conclusion that Native religion was the work of the devil. He owned a beaver bundle and said he was going to throw it out the window and destroy it. However, his family convinced him that he should sell it to a craft shop in Browning, Montana. From past experience, I knew the shop would tear it apart, sell the showy stuff, and discard the rest.

Even at that early date, I had misgivings about acquiring religious objects that were required for ceremonial use. My feeling was that these objects should remain in the community where they would enable the tribe to carry on the rituals. But in this case, it was a question of preservation or destruction. I was able to get Charlie to come to the phone and I asked him if he would sell the bundle to Glenbow. He said he was leaving for Browning the following day,

June 22nd, but if I got there before he left, he'd sell it to us. I then had to dash around to get permission. Fortunately, Doctor Leechman was fully in accord with my plans and I had no trouble in getting a cash advance.

Next morning, I arrived at Charlie's place just before they were getting ready to leave, and I bought the bundle. I tried to find out about the songs and ceremonies that went with it, but Charlie said he didn't know them. All he could tell me was that the bundle had previously been owned by Jim Crow Flag, and he claimed that nobody on the Peigan Reserve knew the songs. He suggested I try the Bloods.

So I drove over to the Gladstone farm, where Dad told me that John Cotton had once owned a beaver bundle and would know the songs. John had been one of my best informants. He had recently retired as a member of the tribal council and I had written a long tribute to him in the *Lethbridge Herald*. He was an active supporter of the Indian Association and a good friend of the Gladstone family. John lived in a tiny house at Moses Lake, and when we contacted him, he said he would round up a crew and open the bundle. I had a Webcor wire recorder with me and got his permission to record the ceremony.

Next day, John Cotton, Jack Low Horn, Jim Many Chiefs, and Willie Eagle Plume came to the Gladstone farm, and we all sat in the porch while they went through the ceremony. This was my first direct involvement in a Native ritual and I was very impressed with the solemnity of it. Cotton explained at the outset that he had paid fifty head of horses for his beaver bundle, which he had held for ten years. He now remembered only some of the hundred or so songs that went with the bundle, but said perhaps he would remember more after he opened it.

Before he started, Cotton told me the story of the origin of the bundle. Back in the dog days, he said, there was an Indian who was an excellent hunter but he killed more animals than he needed. One day when he was camped near Waterton Lakes, a beaver spirit in the form of a man came from under the water and kidnapped his wife. When the husband found where she had been dragged into the lake, he was heartbroken and sadly returned to his lodge. That night, he had a vision in which the beaver spirit came to him and asked him if he would stop killing game unnecessarily in exchange for the return of his wife. The man agreed.

Next morning, a procession emerged from the lake. There was the beaver man, his wife, the hunter's wife, the Sun spirit, and his wife, the Moon. They were singing holy songs as they entered the hunter's lodge. After they sat down, the beaver man explained to the hunter that he would give him the beaver bundle in gratitude for sparing his children. Inside the lodge were the skins of many animals and birds. One by one, the beaver man took them and sang a song. When he was finished, these became the beaver bundle. It was, concluded Cotton, the oldest bundle in the tribe, and was given to the hunter in the days before horses.

When they were ready to begin the ceremony, Cotton sat with the bundle on his right while in front of him were his altar of clay, sweetgrass, and fire tongs. Each of the participants also had a rattle. The fire tongs were used to bring a glowing ember from the kitchen stove. It was placed on the altar and sweetgrass sprinkled over it. As the smoke curled into the air, Cotton began to sing and the others joined in. When they finished, each in turn said a prayer while holding the fire tongs in his hand. I had no previous experience with ceremonial prayers but I soon became accustomed to their length. Cotton prayed for five minutes and the others weren't much shorter. Cotton explained that they were now ready to open the bundle and explained to me that it was bound with a cord which was tied in seven places and there were seven songs for each knot.

The men picked up their rattles and began to tap them on the floor while Cotton took a bone whistle and made several piercing sounds. After he untied the bundle, he took a pipe from it while the others sang. He then took one item at a time and sang the song that went with it. He started with a beaver skin, placing it close to his face while he said a prayer, then wrapping it around his shoulder and placing it on his lap while he sang. He repeated the ritual with a second beaver skin, and again with the skin of a baby beaver, which he said was the most sacred of the three. Meanwhile, the others were singing and beating the floor with their rattles.

I was transfixed both by the holiness of the occasion and the wisdom of the men involved. Here, on the Gladstone porch, they repeated the songs and rituals which dated back for many generations. These same songs had been chanted while the buffalo still coursed the plains and in the days when the Blackfoot knew nothing of the white man and his way of life. It didn't take much imagination on my part to visualize the freedom and richness of life experienced by those who had sung these songs two centuries earlier.

In the next sequence of the ritual, Cotton sang specific songs as he picked up a badger skin, young antelope skin, a duck, the head of a crow, a woodpecker, another antelope skin, a weasel, and a handful of sticks bound together. The latter, he said, were used for reckoning time.

By now it was noon, so we stopped for lunch. Mom gave us a good feed, and then they started again. Although I had a little trouble with the wire recorder, I got most of it. Cotton resumed with a badger skin and after finishing the song he put it down, then picked it up again for a second song. It was clear that he was getting tired (after all, he was eighty-one years old) and was having trouble remembering the rest of the songs. He would pick up an object, hold it for a moment, then put it down. At last he looked at me and said, "That's all I can remember."

He took the pipe, placed it against each of his shoulders and said a prayer. Then he donned a buffalo hair headdress from the bundle and, shaking some hoof rattles, he imitated a buffalo shaking its head. Afterwards, they all sang for about fifteen minutes and the ceremony was over. Quietly, and without ado, John Cotton returned the objects to the bundle, handling each one with reverence and care. To me, it was quite an experience, and one which impressed me with the responsibility that I (and Glenbow) had assumed when we took possession of this ancient and holy object.

That was my first ceremony, but the second wasn't long in coming – only seven weeks later, to be exact. I started my holidays in late July 1956, and we spent them on the Blood Reserve. On August 4th, Pauline, Irene and Gerald, and Irene's sister Doreen Goodstriker, and I decided to go to the Belly Buttes to see if the Sun Dance had started. When we got to the camp, there were only four tepees and sixteen tents, so we knew nothing would be happening for a few days. But Frank Cotton told us that there would be a dance on the following day, so we decided to come back. This time, it was just Pauline, her dad, and me.

As the three of us were wandering along, I heard a voice calling, "Hey, Dempsey!"

Looking around, I saw Pauline's uncle, Jim White Bull, waving to us. I had interviewed him several times and we had become such good friends that he sometimes acted as my interpreter.

"I'm having a ceremony to transfer some songs to my new tepee," he said. "Why don't you folks join me?"

I was eager to accept, so the three of us followed White Bull to a brand new tepee. It had been painted with a blue background and was covered with a multitude of ten-inch white circles. Jim said it was the Blue Star design, *Otskwi-kukatosi-okoka*, and had been owned by his grandfather, Chief Standing in the Middle. The design had been inactive for years, but now Jim had revived it and was going to invite a number of elders to give him songs to go with it.

After we had settled down, Jim summoned Willie Scraping White, a leading ceremonialist of the tribe, and told him who he wanted to invite to the ceremony. Willie then walked through the camp, calling out the names of the persons, and telling them to assemble at White Bull's tepee. As they entered, each man wore a blanket and carried a wooden bowl in his hands while the women wore shawls and also carried bowls.

The first to arrive was One Gun from the Blackfoot Reserve; he was Jim's uncle. He came with his wife and was followed by two other Blackfoot, Jack Kipp and his wife. In twenty minutes, all had arrived and were assigned their places. Jim, as host, was at the back of the tepee, while in front of him were the fireplace, altar, and various objects he would need for the ritual – a buffalo stone or *iniskim*, paint bag, grease, sweetgrass, fire tongs, and fresh sage. To his left, in order, sat John Cotton, Willie Scraping White, Big Nose, Jack Kipp, One Gun, Black White Man, Mrs. One Gun, and Mrs. Kipp. To Jack's right were me, Jim's wife Katie, Dad, Wings, Steve Oka, and Pauline.

The ceremonial objects had been provided by John Cotton, and as he placed the *iniskim* beside the altar, he said to me in Blackfoot, "Have you ever heard the story of this buffalo stone?"

When I said no, he told it to me, with my father-in-law interpreting. The others relaxed quietly, some smoking their pipes or cigarettes and others reclining on the blankets and buffalo robes scattered on the ground.

"One time long ago," he began in Blackfoot, "there was a camp of Indians who were starving. This camp was in a river bottom and in it were a particular man and his two wives. One time his second wife went out for wood and passed close to a cutbank. She heard someone singing a medicine song and a voice said: 'Say, you woman, take me! I have power. The buffalo know me and know my voice.'

"The woman looked around and saw a stone had fallen from the cutbank. She picked it up and put it inside her dress. That night she had a dream and told her husband: 'I have power. I pity the people who are starving. Tell everyone in the camp to look for something to eat – anything, even a bit of grease – and bring it to me. Then go and build a buffalo pound.' The husband did as he was asked, and everyone searched through their empty bags until at last one woman found a tiny bit of grease. This was brought to the second wife.

"The woman then made an altar like ours. She took some incense and invited all the old people to her lodge. She sat where Jim White Bull is sitting now. The woman began to sing her medicine songs the stone had taught her. Then she took the buffalo stone from her dress and rubbed the grease over it.

She said: 'I will now stand this buffalo stone in front of the altar. If it falls over on its face, it is a sign of good luck and we shall have food.' She put the stone down and, as everyone sang, the people saw the stone fall on its face. The next day, the men went out on the prairie and found a herd of buffalo. These were driven into the pound which the woman had told them to build, and they again had food."

"That," ended John Cotton, "is how the buffalo stone came to us."

For the next two hours, I witnessed the song-giving ceremony. Only this time there was a difference, as I was a participant, not an observer. After Wings had placed a glowing ember on the altar and sprinkled it with sweetgrass, the women served the food which had been sitting in pots and saucepans near the stove. This is when everyone produced their wooden bowls, and I saw they had also brought their spoons. As Pauline, Dad, and I had come unprepared, Aunt Katie supplied our needs. Saskatoon berry broth was ladled into our bowls and each of us was given a piece of bannock. Before starting to eat, each of us picked a single berry from the broth and held it aloft while we prayed. There was a cacophony of humming within the lodge as each person said their own prayer quietly but aloud. I watched and as each person finished a prayer, they buried the berry in the ground, so I did the same. Afterwards we all began to eat. That's when I noticed the women had brought small pails into which they dumped their broth. I was told they were saving it for their grandchildren. I also learned that every bit of food offered during the ceremony had to be accepted and that nothing could be left behind. A person had to either eat it or take it with them.

After the incense was renewed, John Cotton gave rattles to Willie Scraping White, Big Nose, and Jack Kipp, keeping one for himself. These were used during the singing. After this, each person was painted. Here is what I wrote in my notebook:

> I moved up to a point in front of John Cotton after Mrs. White Bull had returned to her former seat. Everyone was singing. John Cotton gave a prayer and passed his hands over my face and passed them over the altar. He took some red ochre from the bag, rubbed it on his hands and rubbed it over my forehead, on my left cheek, right cheek, and chin. Then he painted my left wrist and my right wrist. I then returned to my seat and all began to sing.

I have been painted many times since then, sometimes at ceremonies and other times after bad dreams or when in need of spiritual help, but I will always remember the song-giving ceremony because it took place at the Sun Dance grounds, in a tepee, and included some of the most respected patriarchs of the tribe. It was, in every sense, a great honour. I appreciated it then, and appreciate it still.

In the next part of the ceremony, Cotton picked up the buffalo stone, rubbed it with grease (to feed it) and held it close to his heart while he prayed. He then passed it to his left and each person prayed with it until the stone came to the women. At this point, Mrs. One Gun asked something, and Cotton nodded. I learned later that she was asking for permission for the women to pray with the stone. I said my prayer in turn, and when the buffalo stone got back to Cotton, he greeted it with a hearty "*Oki! Iniskim!*" ("Hello! Buffalo Stone!")

The rest of the ceremony revolved around the transferring of songs. Each of the four men giving songs – One Gun, Big Nose, Black White Man, and Jack Kipp – in turn sang the song he was giving away. As I noted, "One Gun and others, while singing their own songs, made motions of 'tossing' something to Jim White Bull, who made motions of catching something and clutching it to his chest with crossed arms. This signified the 'giving' of the songs."

After the last song was sung, John Cotton collected his ceremonial items while everyone sat around and chatted. There was a happy atmosphere in the lodge because everything had gone so well. Gradually people drifted away. The last thing that John Cotton said to me was that I should not remove my paint until the following day.

"Any paint given to a person when the moon is in the sky," Dad translated, "cannot be removed until she has gone. The same is true in the daytime. If paint is given while the Sun spirit is overhead, it cannot be removed in his presence."

That practice has always been faithfully followed by Pauline and me, and by our children. A number of times I have stopped in a cafeteria in Fort Macleod or Claresholm while on the way home from a ceremony and had people staring at the paint on my face. But I didn't care; I knew why it was there.

—⚬⚬⚬—

During the late 1950s and into the 1960s, Glenbow did not have an Ethnology Department, so I was the one who always seemed to get involved where Indians were concerned. I guess that's because of my personal interest, the fact that people sought me out, and the fact that I was willing to take on the extra work. It started with the Beaver Bundle and went on from there. In 1957, for example, I was told there was a woman on the Peigan Reserve who had a Sun Dance or Natoas bundle that she wanted to get rid of. There hadn't been a Sun Dance on the reserve for twelve years and people said there never would be another. I went to the reserve and located Mrs. Man Who Smokes, who was more than willing to sell the bundle. She also had no hesitation in opening the bundle, putting on the headdress, and posing for a picture.

Over the years, I had quite a few adventures and misadventures. One example of the latter occurred in 1959 at an All Smoke ceremony on the Blackfoot Reserve. One day while I was out of my office, Ben Calf Robe came with some things to sell. He was sent to Jack Herbert, the director of research, and in their conversation, Ben asked if Glenbow would be interested in tape recording an All Smoke ceremony that was going to be held at his house in the middle of April. By the time the discussion was finished, Jack agreed – for a hundred dollars – to record the ceremony on tape and with a still camera. Because this was Jack's baby, he took charge of the whole affair. He arranged for two sound men and a photographer and delegated to me the task of making notes and observations.

Briefly, the All Smoke is a ceremony where a number of people get together to sing those holy songs they are authorized to use because of their membership in secret societies, or through their past or present ownership of certain sacred objects. Normally these can be sung only when their own societies are opening bundles, etc., but a special dispensation is made for the All Smoke ritual. It is usually held when someone has a sick member of the family and puts on the ceremony so that the songs and prayers may benefit them. To accomplish their goal, a human-like figure was made from two crossed sticks, like a body with arms outstretched. Attached to it was a calf skin, while at the top was a willow hoop with seven eagle feathers attached. At the end of the "arms" were sagebrush clusters. This figure represented an enemy warrior who would carry the songs and prayers of the evening to the Sun spirit. In Blackfoot it was called *Iki'tstuki*, or Offering to the Sun.

Most of the ceremonialists from the Blackfoot Reserve were there. Amos Leather was the leader, while others included One Gun, Dick Brass, Joe Good Eagle, Paul Wolf Collar, Tom Turned Up Nose, Anthony Pretty Young Man, Charles Raw Eater, Joe Cat Face, John Butterfly, and their spouses or partners. Ben arranged to have George Crow Chief sit next to me to let me know what was going on and to translate anything said in Blackfoot.

It started about 7 p.m. in Ben's living room at the Four Corners and lasted for almost seven hours. An altar was made of grey clay and decorated with symbols of the sun, moon, morning star, and sun dogs in yellow ochre outlined in black. Incense was burned, the people were purified, and their faces were painted. Finally the pipes were lit and passed to the participants. The smoking went on all evening, as did the burning of incense. The belief was that the prayers and songs were being drawn by the smoke into the offering. Each person sang his own song four times in order to complete a "round" before they had a rest. Then the whole process was completed three more times, which meant that each person sang fourteen songs. In between the songs were prayers. Among the songs were those for the Horn Society, Beaver bundle, All Brave Dogs, Prairie Chicken Society, medicine pipe, tobacco dance, bear tepee, antelope tepee, buffalo head tepee, and many more, for a total of 148 songs.

When it was finished, Ben told everyone to bow their heads and not watch the conclusion of the ceremony, which consisted of giving prayers and purifying the offering. We were then permitted to watch while the offering was shaken over the altar, indicating that there were enemies all around them and the Blackfoot were looking for one of them to kill. Then, while everyone gave loud war whoops, the offering was lowered and the feathers used to destroy the altar. This signified that the enemy had been killed and now would take their songs and prayers to the Sun spirit.

With the ceremony over, the Calf Robe family distributed canned goods and food to the people and our own crew began packing up their equipment and prepared to leave. This is when my problems began. I was loading some things in my car when Jack Herbert came over to me, the sacred offering in his hand. He told me he had bought it from Ben for $75 but didn't have room for it in his car. He told me to put it in my trunk and to deliver it to Glenbow next morning.

Frankly, I was appalled. The whole evening had been devoted to prayers and sacred singing that were destined for the Sun spirit. The offering was supposed to be planted at the top of a high hill and left there until it rotted. That we should take it was a downright sacrilege. I tried to argue but Jack Herbert was my boss and there was no changing his mind, so I had no other recourse but to do what he said. I think he believed that I was just being superstitious. When Pauline saw the offering in the trunk of our car, she said in no uncertain terms that it would not be going into our house.

The ceremony ended at 1:15 a.m. on a Wednesday. We stayed at a hotel for the rest of the night and then I took the offering to Glenbow. On Thursday I became so ill that I could not leave my bed. Five days later I tried to go to the office but had to give it up. Two days after that Jack Herbert resigned from Glenbow after a dispute about his lack of co-operation with the Harvie group. My sickness continued for another four days, at which time Pauline finally called the doctor. (They used to make house calls in those days.) He thought I had a stomach ailment that would soon pass, but three days later he was out again when I wasn't showing any signs of improvement. Two days after that, I noted in my diary, "Doctor out again. Seems worried. Me too." The next day I was taken to the hospital emergency ward and a second opinion was given by another doctor.

The problem was they couldn't find anything wrong with me. But Pauline knew what it was. And I knew what it was. Twenty-three days after the All Smoke ceremony I was well enough to stagger to the office, pay Glenbow the $75 that Jack Herbert had given for the offering, and take the object back out to the Blackfoot Reserve. I gave it to Ben Calf Robe and he promised to place it where it belonged. After that, my health improved rapidly and I was soon back at work.

As for Jack, a couple of things happened to him. First, he lost his job. Then, just after the All Smoke ceremony, his daughter began to suffer with foot problems. The way it was described to me, the tendons at the bottom of the foot tightened so that the foot became arched and it could only be cured by a serious operation. Significantly (if one follows Native beliefs) it had a name like "eagle's claw."

Word soon got around the Indian community and the general reaction was that I should have known better than to tamper with religious objects. I tried to explain that I had been an innocent party in the whole exercise, but my involvement in carrying the offering away from the reserve seemed enough to make me guilty. Some of the Bloods kidded me about getting into trouble with "those Blackfeet" but most of them took it quite seriously. And so did I.

A different kind of situation arose one day while I was walking down the main street of Cardston. I was stopped by Steve Oka, and he said he wanted to sell Glenbow his medicine pipe bundle. My first inclination was to turn him down so I told him I did not like to see holy objects taken out of use. That's when he told me his story.

He said that he had been a *minipoka* or "favoured child" and when he was small his father, Mike Oka, announced that he was going to get him a medicine pipe bundle. He went to the owner of the bundle to smoke with him; when this happens the bundle owner cannot refuse. And when he smokes, he automatically agrees to transfer the bundle. After their ceremony, the old owner told Oka to take the bundle and they would go through a transfer ceremony after the first thunderstorm in the spring. As the day approached, the two men got together to agree on the number of horses, money, etc. that would be paid for the transfer. Only they could not agree. Steve's father made an offer so low that the old owner was insulted and refused to have anything more to do him. When Mike Oka offered to return the pipe bundle, the man again refused, saying that when he had smoked the pipe he had given up all rights to it. As a result, Steve told me, he had inherited the pipe bundle as a young man but he had never used it as the rights had never been transferred to him.

On the basis of this information I concluded that the pipe bundle was inactive and could not be used by him, so I applied to Glenbow and was told to go ahead and get it. I returned to the Blood Reserve and picked up Ben Strangling Wolf to use as my interpreter. We went to Steve's house and now that he knew we were interested he turned out to be an astute businessman. He started at $600 and I deliberately started low at $150. Four hours later we finally agreed on $300. That may seem like a pittance by today's standards but it was a reasonable price for 1962. It was about this time that I saw a dealer offering a decorated Assiniboine robe for $200 while another dealer had Shot Both Sides' trailing eagle feather headdress decorated with porcupine quills and couldn't find a buyer when he offered it for sale for $1,000.

Even though I had been assured by others on the reserve that the medicine pipe was inactive, I wanted to leave an opening in case someone heard about the sale and found a way to place it back into ceremonial use. As a result, I included a clause in the agreement that stated Steve could reclaim the pipe bundle anytime within the next year by refunding the money that we had given him. I heard nothing from him during that time and then forgot about it.

In the 1970s, Steve Oka showed up at Glenbow, saying that he wanted to reclaim the pipe bundle that he had "pawned" with us and was prepared to return the $300. I was puzzled, so I asked him why he wanted the bundle when he couldn't use it. He now claimed that he did have the rights to it and wanted to have a ceremony for a relative who was sick. I told him I was sorry, but he had not "pawned" the pipe nor had he reclaimed it during the year provided in the agreement. I said that several years had passed and the matter was now closed.

I felt a bit guilty about it until someone tipped me off that Steve had been approached by a dealer who didn't know that the pipe had been sold or thought Steve could get it back from Glenbow. He reportedly offered Steve a thousand dollars for it. The vision of a $700 profit, I concluded, was what brought Steve to our door. However, he was a stubborn man and I had to make a point of avoiding him at dances or on the streets of Cardston, for he was sure to collar me and demand that I return his pipe. Now that I was armed with the knowledge that he simply wanted to resell it, I wasn't so sympathetic.

There is another story of a medicine bundle that has a less than happy outcome. In 1961, May Owl Child, the wife of Nat Owl Child from the Blackfoot Reserve, came to see me during the Sun Dance. She was desperately in need of money (I can't recall why) and was willing to leave her Old Women's Society bundle with me as security. This surprised me, as she had just joined the society at which time the bundle had been transferred to her from Mrs. Louis Running Rabbit. Her situation seemed serious enough that I agreed, for she only needed about $35, but I made it clear that I was doing this personally, not as a representative of Glenbow. I expected her to return the money and I had no intention of letting this active bundle fall into the museum's hands.

Several times in the ensuing months, either Nat or his wife contacted me with an urgent need to get the bundle back immediately. Sometimes it was needed to pray for a sick friend, and at other times for a meeting of the Society. Nat even wrote me a long letter in November 1961, saying they needed the "Godess Bundle" for a ceremony right away.[57] But each time they did not offer to repay the loan, so I turned them down. Finally, in the summer of 1963 Mrs. Owl Child came in with the money but told me she now wanted to sell the bundle to Glenbow.

I explained to her that I did not like buying religious objects that were still in use. I had a long talk with her, doing my best to convince her that the best thing she could do was to return the bundle to Mrs. Running Rabbit or go through a ceremony to transfer it to someone else. I stressed how important it was to keep the culture alive. She seemed to be convinced and said she would take the bundle back home. I must confess I felt a bit smug as I believed I had just helped to keep the *Motokix* active on the Blackfoot Reserve. However, I was less than sanguine some time later when I was told that she had gone directly from my office to a second hand store in East Calgary and sold it. When I checked with them, I was told a tourist had bought it.

This raised an ethical question in my mind. Had I done right in refusing to buy the bundle? If I had taken it, the object would have remained intact in

Glenbow's hands and would ultimately have been returned to the tribe. There was no way of knowing this at the time, but it did make me wonder. In the end, I concluded I had been right, even if the outcome had resulted in the loss of an important religious object. If I had bought it and the word got around, very likely others would have been in to sell their bundles, thus speeding up the disappearance of that society.

Often, Sarcee or Blackfoot Indians arrived at the front door of Hull House with a paper bag containing objects they wanted to sell. Sometimes they asked for Gooderham, and when this happened, he turned them over to me. On other occasions while attending a dance or other festivities on the Blood or Blackfoot reserve I would be approached by someone with an item to sell. People even collared me at Indian Association meetings. Sometimes it was just a pair of new moccasins or a roach headdress while at other times it might be a feather headdress or medicine bundle.

Right from the start, I had my own set of rules about religious objects, and I tried my best to impose these on Glenbow – with mixed success. First, I did not want to take a religious object that was still in use, particularly if it belonged to the Horn Society or the Old Women's Society. I would accept it in those instances where it would normally be replaced, such as a Prairie Chicken Society staff that was made new for each dance. I would do my best to determine that the object was actually owned by the person trying to sell it. In some instances, old society items were jointly owned by two partners, and if something like an All Braves Dog rattle was offered for sale, I would try to find out if it was still in use (on the Blackfoot Reserve it wasn't) and if it was jointly owned.

I also tried to arrive at a price that I thought was fair to both parties. Sometimes an Indian would come in with an object and ask an extremely high price, such as a hundred dollars for a pair of moccasins. I would explain that the going rate for moccasins was ten dollars but that I did not want them to sell if they thought the price was too low. Usually they sold and I concluded that they really didn't have any idea of the object's actual value and had pulled a round figure out of thin air. There also were numerous times when I told the person they were not asking enough. For example, they might ask two dollars for a pair of moccasins and I would tell them that they were worth more than that, and offer them ten. Fortunately, none of the bean counters at Glenbow ever heard me, as they would have said this was a poor way to conduct a business. But I was trying to be fair, rather than businesslike.

I also made it a point to get as much information I could about the object – its name in Blackfoot or Sarcee, its maker, line of ownership, its use, and what it was made of. Sometimes I even got some mythological or cultural stories that went with the item. Then, not trusting Glenbow's cataloguing system at that time, I drew a picture of the object and made a copy for my files. In later years, those drawings sometimes were the only means of identifying the objects I had acquired.

In some ways I felt like a voice crying in the wilderness about preservation, for even many Indians did not subscribe to the view that their religion and culture should be preserved. People today, particularly young Indians, cannot grasp what it was like in the 1950s and 1960s. There were no annual Indian Days, Sun Dances were sporadic, and pow-wows taking place in community halls had fewer and fewer people in Native dress. Even the Indian village at the Calgary Stampede was seen by some as an anachronism. An example of Native attitudes towards their religion was demonstrated in 1962 when I was one of the judges at the Stampede and we had to choose the best decorated tepee. Imagine my surprise when we went to the lodge of Johnny One Spot. He was the owner of the Peace Pipe Bundle, the only medicine pipe on the Sarcee Reserve. In order to compete for the prize, he had opened the bundle and spread the contents all around the floor of the tepee and hung the parfleche container over the doorway. As we went inside to make our inspection, we had to step over ancient ceremonial objects that were now nothing more than ornaments for the entertainment of tourists.

With the exception of the Bloods, most of the Indians I met felt that their culture was a thing of the past and if it hadn't completely died out, it was well on the way. Many people who sold objects to Glenbow did not do so entirely for the money – although in some cases it was a factor. Rather, these objects were relics of the past that had no roles in their lives and would have even less relevance, they believed, for their children. Yet they remembered enough of the old days to want to see these things preserved and Glenbow seemed to be the only place where this could happen. So the sale of artifacts was largely governed by these emotions, as well as a feeling on the part of some elders that if they didn't sell to Glenbow, their children or grandchildren would steal the objects and sell them to a second hand store for liquor money. This happened often enough for us to know that their fears were well grounded.

Generally, I would say the attitude was one of fatalistic acceptance that the white man's culture was now their culture, and that the white man's religion was now their religion. Many families refused to speak Blackfoot or Sarcee in front of their children because they didn't want to see them "held back" in gaining a knowledge of English. I have a note in my diary for April 29, 1962, that touches on this subject of religion and culture. "The Sarcees are a very difficult people and for a small tribe (330 people) are broken up into small cliques. There are the Crowchilds, Manywounds, Whitneys, and the Starlights (and maybe others) who seldom co-operate on anything. They seem to have lost much of their culture and when I spoke about reviving it as a means of working together, one man said the others would just laugh and make fun of them and make them shy."

The main reason many of the Blackfoot and Sarcees kept their beadwork and horse gear was because of the Calgary Stampede. That institution was, unknowingly, the aegis by which much of the Indian material culture was preserved. The tepee owners refused to part with their beadwork, buckskin outfits, horse gear, utensils, and other objects because they helped them to win prizes in the Indian village and in the parades.

I mentioned that the Bloods were an exception. I always felt that I was so lucky to be married into that tribe. Over the years they had maintained their pride when other tribes were losing theirs. They had retained their religious societies where others had abandoned theirs. They had maintained a lively interest in their past, their war exploits, religious practices, and mythology, when others had let theirs fall by the wayside. I always like to quote something a Mountie said in 1889: "The Bloods think they are the cream of creation." That summed it up.

After the resurgence of Native culture in the 1970s and 1980s, many young people could not understand how their parents or grandparents could have possibly sold their family treasures to Glenbow. The only obvious answers to them were that Glenbow somehow had stolen the objects, or that undue pressure from people like me had caused them to sell, or that poverty and starvation had driven them to it. None of these was true. Even some of the elders who had sold things to us years earlier could not understand why they had done so in light of the tremendous interest now being shown by their families. I had one lady from the Sarcee Reserve who came in one day to retrieve a dress she had "pawned" with us twenty years earlier. When we showed her the sales receipt she had signed, she still refused to believe she had actually sold the item. I had not been involved in that particular purchase, but I knew that this lady and her husband had been frequent visitors to Glenbow in the 1950s, each time bringing in items they wanted to sell. The subject of "pawn" had never been raised, for if it had been, Glenbow would have been quick to say that it was not a pawnshop.

But to return to my main point about museums, places like Glenbow were not trying to destroy Native religion or steal their culture, as some younger Indians claimed, nor were people forced to sell their objects because of abject poverty. At that time, poverty was a way of life on most reserves, and as virtually everyone was in the same situation, it was considered "normal." I know that after a short time I became quite accustomed to tiny welfare houses almost barren of furniture and log houses with earthen floors. I wasn't so conscious of that as I was of the fact that almost universally the houses were neat, clean, and well maintained within the economic limits of the householders. Sometimes broken windows were covered with cardboard or broken doors were fixed with plywood, but these were all the people could afford. At the same time, I never knew of anyone, man, woman, or child, to die of starvation, or to even have the haunting look of a person suffering malnutrition. Starvation wasn't the reason they sold to Glenbow. The loss of culture and a desire to see their artifacts preserved were more compelling reasons.

It might be useful at this point to describe the usual routine I followed when buying objects. Let's take a hypothetical situation which might not be a verbatim account of what happened, but is pretty typical.

When someone comes to Hull House I am summoned. We shake hands, talk about nothing in particular for a few minutes, then I ask them why they are here. They say they have something to sell and produce it. I find out all I can about the object then ask how much they want for it. Usually they say they don't know. I explain that under Glenbow's rules I must get an offer before I can name a figure. They eventually come up with something and I tell them it is either too high, too low, or just right. If too high, I name my figure but stress that they should not sell if they think it's worth more. Sometimes we negotiate but usually the person agrees. Once an agreement is reached, I write out a bill of sale and get the person to sign. I then get the cash from Accounting and pay them.

At first, this latter action caused a lot of trouble, as Accounting wanted the goods in hand, then a cheque prepared and mailed. I finally got it through to them that this was not the way to do business and we either had to do it on Native terms or not at all. Mind you, if quite a bit of money was involved, I sometimes had to get the person to return later in the day and give them a cheque. When this happened I sometimes had to go to the bank with them to identify them and approve the cheque. After a while, I was able to carry some petty cash in the Archives and remitted an accounting once a month. That turned out to be the best for all concerned.

One of the fairly frequent visitors was Mrs. Water Chief, the holy woman at the Sun Dance. She was a real contrast, for on one hand she was obviously very devoted to her religion and was involved in most of the sacred activities on the reserve, but on the other hand she was constantly coming in to Glenbow with holy objects such as the Natoas or Sun Dance bundle and holy woman's wristlets that she wanted to sell. George Gooderham didn't like her, as he had been forced to depose her husband as head chief because of his drinking. On the other hand, I found her to be a very pleasant woman who had devoted many years of her life to maintaining the sacred rituals of the tribe.

---

Speaking of the Sun Dance, I became a reluctant participant in a project to produce a film of the ceremony. Sometime earlier, Philip Godsell had entered into a discussion with the Blackfoot about making the film and convinced Eric Harvie that it was a good idea. Godsell got the backing of George Gooderham but no one approached me, presumably because Godsell and I didn't get along. This was fine as far as I was concerned. As I noted in my diary, "I hope I can keep out of this as I value my health and just can't afford to get involved with native religion. Look what happened to me for carrying the sacrifice from the All Smoke Ceremony."

In the spring of 1961 Godsell suffered a heart attack and Gooderham was given the task of seeing the project through. At the end of June he and Bill Marsden, our photographer, had a meeting with the Blackfoot and came to a preliminary agreement that Glenbow would pay the Blackfoot $1,000 for the right to make the film. They were to meet again during Stampede week to finalize the details.

But it seemed as though I was destined to get involved whether I wanted to or not. On the day of the meeting, Gooderham took sick and Marsden had not returned from Edmonton, so I went to the Indian village to tell the Blackfoot that the meeting was off. However, when I arrived, they were all sitting in the tepee of Clarence McHugh, head chief of the Blackfoot, waiting for the Glenbow representative and wanted to proceed immediately with the meeting. What could I do? Fortunately I knew everything that was going on, and also how far Glenbow was ready to go to finalize the deal. So, resignedly, I became the negotiating agent for the Foundation. The meeting lasted for 2½ hours, and when it was over, we had settled on a budget of $1,900 plus four sides of beef and a supply of beef tongues.

Once I was involved in the project, I couldn't get out. Gooderham begged off any further participation so it was left to Bill Marsden and me to proceed. Late in July, while I was otherwise involved, Bill went to another meeting on the Blackfoot Reserve, where the contract was presented for signing. With Glenbow's approval I had added the clause that the film would not be used for commercial purposes and would be shown only to Native groups and to others with a direct interest in Indians. Any exceptions would have to be approved by the elders of the tribe. At the meeting, Bill added $350 to the agreement and it was signed.

I then had the task of putting together a budget. The breakdown was as follows: All Brave Dogs Society and Prairie Chicken Society to get $350 each, Horn Society, $400, and Old Women's Society, $350. The holy woman was to get $500 and we would pay $10 per tepee at the Sun Dance to a limit of thirty tepees. That was the deal we had with the Blackfoot, but when I prepared the budget I added a large undesignated chunk of money to each society's total, knowing that it would be needed during the ceremonies. Meanwhile, other expenses appeared. Amos Leather rightfully wanted to be paid as the ceremonialist who would direct the whole Sun Dance. Originally, the money for him was supposed to come from the societies, but once the budget was approved they balked at it. Then there were a multitude of other expenses so that by the time I was finished the budget it had come to more than $3,000, not counting staff time, travel, etc.

I hired Adolphus Weasel Child as my interpreter but when Ben Calf Robe heard about it he was very angry. I learned later that he and Joe Bear Robe were the ones Godsell had discussed the project with years earlier but it had bogged down. When it was revived I guess Ben expected to play a major role, but I knew nothing about it. In the end I created the position of camp crier and gave him the job. He was responsible for going through the camp announcing when ceremonies would begin or when meetings were called. I always liked Ben and we got along well together over the years, but I had chosen Adolphus because I thought he was the best man for the job. He spoke good English, was a member of the Horns and the Prairie Chicken societies, and was contemporary in his outlook. Besides, he was Pauline's sister-in-law's brother-in-law, so that made him a relative and therefore easier to work with.

I don't think Ben held it against me for not hiring him, but he did complain in his book *Siksika, A Blackfoot Legacy* that Adolphus had not been able to do the work properly and that we had been obliged to call on Ben and Joe "to do the directing for certain parts."[58] Actually, Adolphus did an excellent job throughout the whole Sun Dance.

In order to properly oversee the project, it was decided that I would live at the Sun Dance camp while Marsden and the film crew would stay at a hotel in Gleichen. Glenbow owned the Wave Tepee that had been obtained from Mrs. Heavy Shield. We arranged to have it pitched on the west side of the camp, next to the Horned Snake Tepee of Head Chief Clarence McHugh, while behind us was the tent of Mark Wolf Leg. In all, there were twenty-eight tepees and fifty tents in the camp, and at its height some seven hundred people were living there.

Pauline and I arrived at the grounds on August 2, 1961, with our children, three-year-old Lloyd James and four-month-old Louise. Thus began two weeks of the most enjoyable time of my life. Our first activity was to install the linings, then furnish the lodge with the mattresses, blankets, folding chairs, cooking utensils, groceries, and other items. While we were getting set up we had a steady stream of visitors, mostly women who used the excuse of wanting to borrow some sugar or tea, or to bum a cigarette, but really to cast a critical eye on the way Pauline was setting up the lodge. After all, I was the only white man in camp and Pauline was from another reserve. But she hit it off right away with most of the women because of her personality and her fluency in Blackfoot. Mrs. Wolf Leg noticed that our little baby didn't have anything warm for night (it was August but we didn't realize how cold it could get after dark in the river valley) so she took some flannel she had and quickly made her a nice warm nightgown. She also showed us how to fashion an ingenious hammock by stringing ropes between two tepee poles, separating them with two sticks, then wrapping a blanket around the ropes. Once we tucked Louise in there she was happy for hours, any slight movement on her part causing the hammock to sway gently between the poles.

That first night was a most memorable one. As soon as it was dark we went to bed and the silence was almost deafening. For a while, some singers entertained themselves at Dick Brass's tepee but they finished about midnight. Then, according to my diary, "After about ten minutes of silence a new high-pitched voice came from the distance in a haunting night song. I thought it was a solo, but he was soon joined by a few other lower voices and the singing started again. They remained mostly on the east side and it was a beautiful sound as it floated over the camp and echoed down the valley. They carried on until about 2 a.m., when they reached our tepee and sang an Owl Dance song and some others. Then, led by the solitary quivering voice, they uttered the strains of the beautiful and familiar Sun Dance 'serenade' to end their performance. Almost a lullaby, the serenade was a restful climax to an interesting evening. After they finished, a solitary dog yapped from across the camp and we all slept."

These "lullaby singers" were young men who were following a practice that was generations old. They would stop in front of a tepee and sing until they were given food or gifts. They did it just for fun and everyone enjoyed themselves. They performed almost every night and after they finished in front of our tepee we would give them a couple of dollars or food and then hear them move on to the next tepee. But I enjoyed them the most when they were on the other side of the camp, as their distant voices were haunting and free as they echoed through the darkness of the river valley.

Next morning the camp began to stir about 5:30 a.m. and pretty soon it was a beehive of activity. It was a terribly hot day, so at midmorning Jack Crow dropped around and volunteered to build us a sun shade made of poles and canvas. When this was done, I drove to Gleichen to check in with the Mounted Police and to let them know our plans. Then I stopped at the local bank, where I drew out $550, mostly in one- and five-dollar bills. These small bills were a practical necessity. Whenever I gave out money, I knew it had to be shared so big bills would have been a problem and an inconvenience for the people. But there was another reason. I kept all the bills stuffed in my pants pockets and these made huge bulges that everyone soon recognized. This way, anytime I had dealings with a society, they knew they would be paid right away, and at the same time the obvious presence of this money was an incentive for some people to come up with innovative ideas for getting their hands on it. Over the period of the Sun Dance there were quite a few extra things that we filmed because of this money. I remember when someone from Glenbow saw me with all this money they asked me if I wasn't afraid of being robbed. I replied with the hoary old joke, "I'm not worried; there isn't another white man for miles."

By the time I got back to the camp, the first shipment of rations had arrived – about 400 pounds of beef and 175 loaves of bread. After some quick math, Adolphus and his helpers distributed ten pounds of meat and four loaves of bread to each family. That evening, I sat with Clarence McHugh and leaders of the various societies to lay out a schedule for the Sun Dance. It was all very neat and orderly. I had a program for each day with notations in my diary such as "Motokix to put up lodge & have 4 days of ceremonies," "Horns to have ceremony," and "Holy Woman comes out & Sun Dance lodge is built."

Often, nothing worked according to the schedule we had prepared, but rather, things happened when the group was ready. Sometimes events or ceremonies happened but weren't on the list. We had one photographer who almost went crazy because of the changes. He was a very orderly person and expected everyone else to be the same way. But Bill and I soon adapted to the situation, and he always tried to have a photographer on hand and ready to go even during those times when nothing was supposed to be happening. As a result, we didn't miss anything important during the entire two weeks.

The only sour note occurred that first night. People had received their ration payment of six dollars each and a bootlegger slipped past the Mounted Police patrols into the camp. Pretty soon the lullaby singers were being interrupted by raucous drunks and then things turned nasty when a young Blackfoot commandeered the drum used by one of the singing groups. It was finally returned but then the drunk went to the Wolf Leg tent immediately behind us and demanded the use of the family's truck. When this was refused, he threatened to take the truck and drive right through their tent. Pauline and I were laying in bed listening to all of this, realizing that if he drove over the tent he would probably also go through our tepee. This was a bit unsettling but finally the drunk was quietened down and there was no more singing for the rest of the night.

Those were the only troublesome drunks I saw or heard during the entire Sun Dance. In fact, I don't think I have ever been among a more law-abiding and helpful group in my life. They were co-operative, friendly, and were willing to do all sorts of things to make the ceremony a success. For example, on the day that a ceremony was to be held, everyone moved their cars and trucks out of the camp so they wouldn't show up in the film. Once when a car broke down and couldn't be moved, a bunch of young men went down to the river and cut some saplings. They piled these around the car until it was completely hidden from view. They did this on their own without any expectation of payment. Similarly, people went out of their way to provide our cameramen with the best viewpoint, while even the people taking part in the ceremonies co-operated by not looking at the cameras and by making sure they were providing an unobstructed view of what they were doing. It was a real pleasure to work with them.

It's not my intention to go through a day-by-day account of what happened during the two weeks of the Sun Dance. That is covered in a nineteen-page single-spaced report now at Glenbow that I produced after it was over.

But I would like to touch on some of the highlights and make some personal observations.

The first ceremony was held by the *Motokix*. It was supposed to start about noon but they were definitely on "Indian time" and it didn't get underway until nearly 6 p.m. As a result it was almost completely dark when their lodge was finished and our cameramen had their lenses open wide in the hopes that they would get something on film. This was followed by a grass dance in which everyone, including Pauline and Lloyd, participated. Everyone except me, as I am neither a dancer nor an Indian.

As the days wore on, the different societies would meet with me in the morning when their ceremonies would be held, and I would give them most of their allotted money. None of these society funds were ever used for personal purposes, that is, no individual benefited from them. The entire amounts were used to buy canned goods, bread, blankets, cloth, and other items for the giveaways. At the same time we discussed the day's activities and altered schedules where necessary to avoid any overlaps. By the number of meetings I held and the decisions made, it was clear that with the concurrence of Head Chief Clarence McHugh I had become the "straw boss" of the camp. And because I employed the only scout (at first it was Ed Turning Robe and later Norman Running Rabbit, Ken Yellow Fly, and George Leather), people were constantly coming to me to report bootleggers, drunks, family disputes, and other matters that required intervention.

By now my fears of religious retribution were quickly disappearing as I saw how the Glenbow program was providing an opportunity for a real resurgence of the ceremony. Ben Calf Robe, who thought the Sun Dance was dying out, later wrote, "The Blackfoot Elders agreed to have a movie made of the whole Sun Dance, so that future generations could see how it was. We knew that our old ways were nearly ended and that our grandchildren might never see the most important ceremony in the religion of their ancestors."[59] Several people told me that it was the best Sun Dance they'd had since the big Victory Sun Dance in 1919, right after World War I. Not only that, but we were able to honour any religious restrictions or limitations placed on us and thus avoided doing anything that might be considered sacrilegious or untoward. The only incident occurred during the Horn Society ceremonies when one of the photographers, Joe Rosettis, walked in front of the procession to get a good head-on shot. He was not aware that the pathway the Horns followed had become sacred and that he should not have been there. After the ceremony, the Horns called us in and told us of the infraction. They were not worried about the effect of such action on the Horns, but rather for the well-being of Joe. Some members wanted him to go through a sweatlodge ceremony but Adolphus convinced them that he should be painted. A couple of days later Joe took two cartons of cigarettes to their lodge, where he was painted and purified.

Mom and Dad and Pauline's nephew Jimmy joined us after the fourth day, so we readjusted our lodge to make room for them. Dad's presence added to our tepee becoming the centre of attention, as many Indian Association people kept showing up to discuss business with him. Not only that, but Mom had a lot of friends in the camp, particularly our next door neighbour, Vicki McHugh. The folks stayed with us for three or four days and had a nice time. Pauline and I were certainly glad to see them.

In the interval between the Old Women's Society ceremonies and the Horns, we were able to undertake some of the extra projects that had been suggested. I gave Dick Brass $75 to put on a medicine pipe ceremony which lasted for about two hours, $30 to Tom Yellow Sun for a holy hand game, and I put $20 into a pot for two teams wanting to play a hand game.

Then each of the societies performed their rituals, some inside their lodges and others outside. We saw the impressive Horn Society dance inside their double-sized tepee – a sight seldom seen by non-members – and their dance outside with their huge curved staffs and ancient headdresses. We saw two Blackfoot elders recite their war honours while holding the Horn staff, and the finale of the ceremony when one of the members fired a rifle into the air and a crowd of children fell down as though dead. We saw the Prairie Chicken Society members, mostly young people, starting their dance with low bows and rattling, then following each other in a haphazard line until a drum beat told them to stop. And we saw the All Brave Dogs being pressed into a small circle by two riders during their dance, and then the finale while the riders dismounted and joined the others.

Some of these ceremonies I had seen before on the Blood Reserve, but this was different for now I had a ringside seat and was directly involved. This was when all the nuances of the ceremonies were revealed to me because of my nearness to them and the explanations given to me, so I had a much greater understanding of the whole ceremony.

The culmination of the Sun Dance was the raising of the centre pole and the building of the brush lodge, and this was all new to me. Although the summer festival on the Blood Reserve was called a Sun Dance, it really wasn't. No holy woman promised to fast; there was no sacrament of beef tongues, and no building of the Sun Dance lodge in which the final ceremonies were held.

I had never seen such rituals so I was very anxious to witness the performance of the Blackfoot.

Early in the morning of August 12th, Ben Calf Robe paraded through the camp, announcing that tomorrow would be the big day. He told everyone to get ready, for all the men, women, and children to work together to made the Sun lodge a success. A short time later, people started heading out along the river bottom to cut trees and branches for the lodge. Each of the twelve bands that formed the tribe was responsible for cutting one upright pole that formed the foundation for the lodge. These were planted deeply in the ground in a large circle, members of the Horn Society directing the work.

Mrs. Water Chief had gone into her fasting tepee a couple of days before, and had allowed us to go in once briefly to see her cut the beef tongues for the sacrament and again to see her fasting. When she was ready, she led a procession outside and to a sweatlodge that had been made of a hundred willows. It was very impressive. The group was led by Amos Leather, as the ceremonialist. Behind him were Mrs. Water Chief (called the Holy Woman), Mrs. Rides at the Door (the Holy Mother), and two men, the Holy Man and the Holy Father. They prayed as they walked. I'd never heard anything like it before. It was a low mumbling sound almost like the buzzing of bees. The prayers were recited so quickly and quietly that they could not be translated. The procession stopped four times to pray, and when they got to the sweatlodge the men went inside while the women knelt to pray outside. A buffalo skull was then painted with the symbols of the sun, moon, morning star, and sun dogs, and then the men had a sweat bath. With that purification ceremony, everything was now ready for the big day.

You could feel the excitement in the air as people went about their duties beginning about noon the following day. First the members of the Old Women's Society went out to collect green branches and came back singing a joyful song and wearing green wreaths in their hair. A short time later, the Horns went into the woods to find a centre pole. I accompanied them and was very impressed with the ceremony. Mark Wolf Leg, as a warrior, went out in search of an "enemy," a forked tree. When he found one, he came back to the group in a zigzag fashion and gave the cry of a crane, indicating he had found the enemy. The Horns then went through the ceremony to attack the tree and when it was cut down, they dashed forward to count "coups" on it. After further rituals the pole was taken back to the camp and placed beside a hole that had been dug for it.

This was a big day for the Blackfoot but it also was a big day for me. Not only were Bill and I scampering around to make sure we covered everything, but this was the day that Eric Harvie and his entourage chose to visit. So I had to escort them, make the proper introductions to Chief Clarence McHugh and others, and make sure they had a good spot to view the ceremonies. I also had a lot of money problems to resolve. When the various societies had performed their dances a few days earlier, I had pretty well given them the whole amount that they had agreed upon. Now they were back, telling me that they had major roles to play in the Sun Dance itself and wanted to get paid for it. This was perfectly true, and I knew it before we started. That is why I had increased their allotments without telling them. For example, if I had told the All Brave Dogs that they had $500 instead of $350 in their budget, they would have demanded it all at the time of their dance. Instead, they got their $350. Now when they approached me, I reminded them of their agreed figure, told them that we had a deal, and made all sorts of noises, but in the end I gave them what they wanted and everybody was happy. Interestingly, these "final" figures were about what I had estimated.

But all this took time, and as I said sadly in my diary, "I found myself inundated with work – traffic problems, visits of Glenbow Foundation officials, etc., and as a result I was not able to observe many of the activities taking place or to properly record them." I did see the holy woman break her fast and go to a sun shade where she painted members of the Old Women's Society and blessed offerings that were destined to be placed in the forks of the Sun Dance pole. The real excitement came when the pole was being raised. It was nothing less than electrifying. The drumming, singing, shouting, war whoops, and firing a gun in the air all mingled to create a feeling of overwhelming exhilaration – for me at least. As the fervour mounted, the holy woman left her sun shade and walked with her helper to the base of the main pole. At this point (darn it!) I was called away so I could only see what was happening from a distance. Hundreds of excited people were crowded around the frame of the lodge, but even in their excitement they left a clear path so that our photographers could get everything. The climax was reached when the pole raisers, using long sticks in pairs with a rope joining them together at their ends, successfully raised the tree. When this happened, there was more gunfire, war whoops, and emotional cries.

Then suddenly the whole atmosphere changed. The rafters were run into place and then people dashed away to get greenery for the walls of the lodge. As I mention in my diary, "The ceremony became quite festive. When the vehicles returned, all participants were singing happily as children climbed on the trucks as they circled the camp.... Some of the young men bringing in the branches had their best girls behind them on their horses."

By the time the lodge was built, I was thoroughly exhausted, and so were many of the people. Next morning, things were slow to start. Mr. Harvie had obviously enjoyed himself the previous day for he came back at noon, this time in an airplane flown by his son Neil. They landed on a hill above the camp and I went to meet them. Shortly afterwards, the dances and ceremonies took place in the lodge but I didn't get a chance to see much of them. I was busy arranging for Jack Kipp to go through a simulation of the self-torture ritual (which caused great hilarity among the elders, as Jack used an elastic bandage instead of his skin and it stretched out to a ridiculous length). I also coordinated the honouring of Eric Harvie when he was paraded around the inside of the lodge amid singing and drumming.

Everything finished about suppertime, and the only sour note came when Mrs. Water Chief refused to put on a giveaway and Clarence McHugh had to do it on behalf of the council. Mrs. Water Chief was mercenary to the end. After the ceremonies she tried to sell me the sacred buffalo skull that had been placed at the base of the Sun Dance pole for the ceremonies. It carried the blessing of the Sun Dance and was supposed to remain there until it rotted. I'd already had my experience at the All Smoke ceremony so there was no way I was going to agree to buy that skull.

Within a couple of hours there were only about thirty tepees and tents left in the camp and the night became a festive one for those who had stayed. Long after dark I walked over to the main lodge and saw that the young people were having a good time. Boys and girls were walking around with blankets wrapped around them and often over their heads. Sometimes two or three were under a single blanket and not always of the same sex. They had an owl dance inside the main lodge until about 1 a.m.

The next morning, the last of the camp disappeared and our own tepee was packed away and shipped back to Calgary. My pockets full of money had almost disappeared and the few dollars I had left I gave to Adolphus for his fine work. By the time we got back to Calgary the entire family was so exhausted that we virtually collapsed and didn't do anything for the next five days but rest up.

Bill Marsden and I spent much of the winter of 1961–62 editing the film. I wrote the script and got both Adolphus and Vicki McHugh to do some small bits of narration, while the main text was read by a professional from Toronto. When it was finished, the film was a one-hour documentary entitled "Okan:

Sun Dance of the Blackfoot Indians." Jack Ewers described it as the best ceremonial film ever made in the northern plains.

As a footnote, in the spring of 1962 we had a special showing of the film on the Blackfoot Reserve. The Harvie family came, and afterwards Harvie announced that he would match any money raised to put on another Sun Dance this summer. Then there was an honouring dance at which time Harvie received the name of *Natósapi*, or Old Sun, after one of the great traditional chiefs of the tribe. When we came back to Calgary, Bill Marsden and I stopped at the Garrison Officers' Mess at Mewata Armouries, where Bill was a member. As we came in, Bill saw one of Harvie's old ex-law partners and told him that our boss had been named Old Sun. Snapped the ex-partner, "Old son of a what?"

———⁂———

Obviously Harvie was quite interested in Indians so I was encouraged to continue my work — even though ostensibly I was still an archivist. At the 1962 Sun Dance, Clarence McHugh had arranged to take over the leadership of the Horn Society and his wife joined the Old Women's Society. As they were close personal friends they were very generous in inviting me to their ceremonies. In May 1962 I attended a prayer meeting of the Old Women's Society held in Vicki's tepee, which had been pitched in her yard. I was not painted or purified but I did take part in the prayers and in making the offerings of meat and berry broth. A few weeks later I was invited to a sweatlodge ceremony put on by the Horn Society. I was asked if I wanted to go right into the sweatlodge but I demurred as I was shy, but I did have a chance to take notes on everything that happened. Then, during the late summer Pauline, our three children (we'd added John that August), and I went to the Harvie-supported Sun Dance. We didn't stay for the whole time, as in the previous year, but we were there long enough to know that it was almost as good as the one we filmed.

A delightful event occurred on the second day we were there. The Prairie Chicken Society had finished its dance when One Gun called me into the centre of the circle, where he conducted a naming ceremony, giving me the name of Calf Chief, *Onistaina*, his grandfather's name. Afterwards Clarence McHugh presented me with a pair of moccasins. This came as a complete surprise and its happening in the Sun Dance circle made it all the more important to me.

But that wasn't the end of it. Two days later, just as the Blackfoot were getting ready to raise the centre pole, Ben Calf Robe informed Pauline that he wanted the right to name our four-week-old son. Pauline rushed around and found a beautiful yellow blanket. When John was wrapped in it, I took him in my arms and Ben led us to the framework of the Sun Dance lodge. We stood in front of the sun shade where the holy woman was seated, while all around us were members Horn Society. As we stood in respectful silence, the Horns performed their traditional dance, ending with a "whooo" sound as they touched their fingers to the ground. During all this time, Ben was praying for our young son. Here is what I wrote in my diary: "After they finished Ben spoke. He said he wanted to name this child, giving him his own name as a boy. He hoped it would bring him strength and good luck, and also to the parents. The name is *Ninam'skoh'kitopi*, or Medicine Pipe Rider. He then gave me a push, intended for John, as a symbol of being humbled so that the naming would not make him swell-headed over the honour given him. I then gave Ben the blanket which had held the baby."

During the Sun Dance, Eric Harvie had raised a question about the beadwork and other objects and wondered if they were ever for sale. I told him that from time to time the Blackfoot came in to sell things but that we had never actually gone out seeking objects. Over the winter the matter was raised again, and as a result Harvie gave me a thousand dollars and told me to see what I could find on the reserve. Rather than going about it helter-skelter, I made a rough list of our current holdings and a "want list" of items needed to round out the collections.

As I noted in my diary, "I began checking the Indian artifacts and confirmed my suspicions that they are in an awful mess." In spite of my complaints, Glenbow was just not keeping proper records. The objects themselves were stored reasonably enough, but if someone other than myself acquired something, it just appeared on the storage shelves with no number or documentation. If I was lucky and noticed it early enough, I could find out the details and put a tag on the item. But too often, no one knew where the object had come from, who had purchased it, or what tribe it belonged to. This was particularly true of donations, where the items were simply accepted and put on the shelves with nothing to connect them to any documentation that might exist. True, we did not yet have an Ethnology Department, but we were getting more and more artifacts, both Indian and pioneer, and the record keeping was shabby at best. I couldn't help but to compare it to the Archives, where we had no trouble in documenting our collections, simply because we had a routine that we followed. In any case, hundreds of hours were spent in later years trying to match the collections with the documents, and far too many items were never identified. Yet it would have been so easy to have done so at the time.

Early in 1963 I set out to spend Eric Harvie's thousand dollars. Joe Cat Face and Olive Olds had evidently heard about the deal and they didn't wait for me to visit them. They showed up at Glenbow with a few items which I bought. Ben Calf Robe and George Runner also dropped by so I decided to wait until the weather cleared before tackling the snow-choked roads on the Blackfoot Reserve. Finally, I made my first foray at the end of January, a personal one on a Sunday for an Indian Association meeting that dealt with attempts of municipalities to tax non-Indians on reserve lands. I also went to see One Gun and Ben Calf Robe about a study I was doing on Blackfoot animal names. When a blizzard blew in, I decided to spend the night in the Cluny Hotel and next morning to do some Glenbow business. The blizzard was still blowing next day and once I had to get hauled out of the snow but I finally made it to Gleichen and to Clarence McHugh's house. There I found Dick and Emma Brass visiting them. I told them about the money for purchases and they promised to look around. Also, Dick offered to make reproductions of some of the sacred objects used in the tobacco dance. It was impossible to go anywhere on the reserve because of the storm, so I headed back to the safety and security of Calgary.

But I was back two weeks later when I picked up a fungus necklace and iron kettle from Vicki, six naval cord amulets from Cyril Olds, and the tobacco dance items promised by Dick Brass. The latter proved to be wonderful pieces. Included were a couple of painted bent sticks with tiny moccasins and bags attached to them. These are the "little people" who guard the tobacco fields during the summer. As soon as the Blackfoot leave the fields after a planting ceremony, these figures are believed to turn into little people who wear the moccasins, use the food stored in the bags, and guard the tobacco. Dick also made a rawhide bowl that was central to the whole ceremony. As I wrote to Jack Ewers, "The most significant is the raw-hide berry bowl which Schultz describes in great detail in *Sun God's Children*. The main difference is that the symbols on our bowl are the raven, two feathers, lizard, moon and Pleiades, scalp, and a hand. I just wonder whether this bowl is the type originally used when preparing food by the hot stone method?" I had no hesitation in taking these religious items as they were unblessed reproductions. At that point another blizzard rolled in so I hightailed it back to Calgary.

A week later I tried again, this time picking up Adolphus Weasel Child as my interpreter. I won't go into details, but by the time the day was over, I'd spent a good part of the money and had picked up a lot of items during visits to Mrs. Heavy Shield, Mrs. Water Chief, Jack Kipp, Mrs. Ayoungman, Tom

Turned Up Nose, Mrs. Gunny Crow, Mrs. Boy Chief, Jack Black Horse, and Dick White Elk. But it didn't end there. When word got around, I had visits for the next couple of months from such people as Rosary Duck Chief, Charlie Turning Robe, Alphonse Sleigh, and Joe Bear Robe. It was like a tap that, once turned on, couldn't be turned off.

—⚬⚬⚬—

An interesting sidelight occurred when I had visited the McHughs. After the 1961 Sun Dance the question had been raised by Indians about Glenbow filming the black-tailed deer dance, the tobacco dance, and other ceremonies. I said the door was open for discussion but nothing further came of it. But during my visit at the McHughs, Emma Brass said that there hadn't been a Ghost Dance on the reserve for twelve years but she and her husband were willing to sponsor one if we wanted to film it. I took the matter back to Glenbow and as we had lost our movie photographer we decided to record the ceremony on a sound tape and with still photographs. I went back to the reserve for a meeting with Dick and Emma Brass and with Cyril and Olive Olds, and we settled on a price of $85 and enough saskatoon berries to make the broth. Here again, one can see that the Blackfoot weren't in it for the money. The $85 would barely cover the cost of gas money and the giveaway. Rather, the Brasses, Olds, and all the others were motivated by a sense if preserving a dying ritual, of having Glenbow making a record of it before it disappeared completely. It was another sad example of the state of Blackfoot religion and culture in the 1960s.

During our discussions, Emma Brass told me the following story about the origin of the dance: "A man went to war with his comrades but they were attacked and he was separated from the others. On his way back, when nearing his camp at night, he came upon a lone Blackfoot lodge. Because it was dark he did not notice that it was a 'death lodge,' but thought it belonged to a family camped apart from the others. He entered the lodge and that night he was awakened when he heard people singing and bones rattling. He opened his eyes just a little and could see only some skeleton feet of ghosts who were kneeling as though they were playing a hand game. They sang four times and at the end of each song they tried to get up. After every dance the man could see a little more of their bones and during the fourth song, when they finally arose, he could see everything except their faces. They repeated this entire ritual four times. During the third dance a skeleton came in, danced by himself, and when he was finished he lit a pipe and gave it to the man. After he had smoked, the Blackfoot was told to take the ritual home to his people and to perform it when they wanted good health or good luck."

The Ghost Dance ceremony, or *Sta'ai-puska*, was held at the Olds' home on February 24, 1963. The Brasses and Olds were the sponsors and Ed Axe was the ceremonialist. Those participating were Clarence and Vicki McHugh, Mr. and Mrs. Jack Crow, Alex Breaker, Jack Black Horse, Gordon Yellow Old Woman, Ken Yellow Fly, Doris Stimson, and the wives of Teddy Yellow Fly and Charlie Raw Eater. The two "ghosts" were Francis Axe and Henry Backfat.

The ceremony itself re-enacted the events that had taken place many years earlier when the Blackfoot had entered the "dead lodge." The participants danced in the manner of the skeletons, and on the third round two masked figures entered the room and danced with them. It was important that the dancers not acknowledge the presence of these two figures, as they were supposed to be invisible. I won't go through the entire ceremony, as it was fully described in the monograph I wrote entitled *The Blackfoot Ghost Dance*, published by Glenbow in 1968. However, I must repeat what I've said before. Not only was I honoured at having the privilege of attending such a ritual but again I felt strongly about the need for the Blackfoot people to preserve their culture. During the ceremony I was very honoured when a special prayer was given for me. Pauline later translated it as follows:

> O You who pities us, the One we pray to
> May this white man have a long life
> He is working with us now
> Pity him, pity his body
> May he be skilful in his work
> Gather around me, Above People
> Bring good fortune to his children
> Help them to have a long life

In 1963, I commented to Glenbow authorities that we had very little from the Plains Cree in our collections. A short time later, I was given a purchasing budget of $500 and set out on a buying trip with Doug Light of the Luxton Museum. Doug had been raised in Battleford and had started collecting Cree artifacts while he was still a teenager. I got to know Doug quite well and in spite of a few misgivings, we got along pretty well.

We were on the road for nine days in east central Alberta and western Saskatchewan. During that time I had plenty of good opportunities to see various aspects of Cree culture and religion. I saw a lot of similarities but also many differences from the Blackfoot. I also learned that most people had never heard of or seen anyone from a museum but they treated us openly and without suspicion. It was soon apparent that these people had lost many aspects of their culture and religion to a much greater degree than the Blackfoot. I ascribed part of this to the fact that the entire Blackfoot nation was on just four large reserves while the Crees were scattered about on a lot of little ones. There they had been obliged to mix more with the surrounding communities, learned to speak English to get along with the shopkeepers, been heavily influenced by missionaries and by nearby Metis settlements and had few opportunities to get together in large groups to practise their religion. At the same time, I found the Crees placed a much greater reliance upon individual medicine men and that these people still exerted considerable influence. They were the ones who were willing to show us their religious items but were unwilling to sell them as they were still in use.

During our travels, it also came as a surprise to me – although it shouldn't have – to learn that the Blackfoot lost some of their battles. Over the years, the only stories I had ever heard were ones where the Blackfoot celebrated victories, so it seemed strange to listen to Cree stories about them losing.

Doug and I went first to the Saddle Lake Reserve to visit Ralph Steinhauer, who was a good friend of mine. The next day he took us to see Edward Cardinal, or Memnook, whose grandfather had been killed at the Battle of Frenchman's Butte in 1885. We got an eagle feather fan and a stone pipe from him while another member of the family sold us an old Ojibwa pipe. In these instances and during the rest of the trip, I tried to get the name of the object in Cree, its history, and significance. We picked up a couple of pipes and other such items, but we struck a real gold mine in William Half and his wife. She turned out to be a healer and produced a moose skin medicine bag which had belonged to her grandmother and was filled with roots, leaves, and other items used for medical purposes. She sold us the bag and shared a number of medicines with us, including those for sore throat, bleeding, throat constriction, menstrual problems, and for removing warts. She also sold us a beaming tool for tanning and obligingly posed for photographs of herself using it.

Our next visit was to the Onion Lake, where I hired Wilfred Chocan to be our guide. He proved to be a good choice and through him we found some excellent cultural material. One of the most interesting visits of our whole trip was to the home of Johnny Heathen. From him we obtained the Little Bear war medicine, or *Muska-sis*. It consists of a piece of bear skin decorated with coloured ribbons and with a piece of braided sweetgrass inside it. It was wrapped in a print cloth that was used as an altar during ceremonies. Here is the story that Heathen told me:

> Years ago when the Crees and Blackfoot were fighting, the Crees would win in battle because of the help and protection given by the Little Bear. It was hung from a tripod outside the tipi and three or four songs went with it. If the owner went to war, the Little Bear was brought inside and occupied his place in the tipi. The man would sing the songs on his way to war to bring the party good luck. If they fought the enemy and the owner was wounded, the Little Bear would groan in pain. The people at home would know what had happened and would appeal to the Little Bear to protect the owner and see that he came home alive. After hearing their pleas, the Little Bear would sit upright to indicate that the man would be saved or would fall down if there was no hope for him.
>
> Now those days are gone but the Little Bear still has power. After we settled on our reserves, it was used for curing sick people, protecting us, and was used in our ceremonies. I used it four times in the smoking lodge ceremony and tied a ribbon on it for each time.... Now if I sell the Little Bear to you, I still will have the songs and these will be used for curing people.

We asked him about "Cree medicine," sometimes called love medicine. Heathen said that he was a medicine man and admitted that some of the medicines he made could be used to render a person sick or insane but he also had antidotes that could cure such curses that had been imposed by other medicine men. When we asked him if he would sell us some of the Cree medicine, he refused. He said that when we got back to Calgary we might be curious about it and try to use it on someone. When that person got sick or died, the Mounted Police would ask us where we got the Cree medicine and we would say it was Johnny Heathen, and then the police would come looking for him. During the ensuing days we asked at just about every reserve for Cree medicine, but it was finally Solomon Bluehorn, a friend of Doug Light's, who supplied a small amount to us. He said that his was love medicine and could not be used to curse or injure anyone. He kept it stored in an old coffee can in the trees behind his house. He said it was made of 120 different roots, leaves and grasses, all reduced to a powder. He said to use the medicine, one must not look directly at it. You touch your finger to your mouth to dampen it, then touch it to the medicine so as to pick up a tiny amount. This is rubbed on your lapel and when you approach a woman, you walk once around her and from then on she cannot resist you. Another way to use it was to sprinkle it along the path where the woman (or man) walked.

To prevent it from working, some women carried anti-love medicine. We obtained an example of this too. It consists of a necklace made of large beads with two brass thimbles at the bottom containing the antidote medicine. When a woman wears this, no love medicine will work. Sometimes a woman acquired this, but often it was a jealous husband who got it and made his wife wear it.

The day spent at Onion Lake was highly successful, and by the time we settled down for the night at Cold Lake, we had a rawhide saddle, beadwork, tanning tools, drum, and other objects. Our visit to Cold Lake gave us our only contact with the Chipewyan Indians on this trip. I looked up Tom Beaverfoot, whom I knew from Indian Association meeting, and he agreed to take us around, in spite of heavy rains and almost impassable roads. These were purely woodland people and our collecting showed it. We picked up such items as snow shoes, a moose call, gun case, birchbark baskets, and bullet bags. When we drove from there to Meadow Lake the roads were so bad that we hit the ditch a couple of times and once we had to get towed out. At this point the country was so waterlogged that we had to give up and go on to Battleford, Doug's hometown.

The next day we picked up Solomon Bluehorn on the Little Pine Reserve. He knew everyone and had been everywhere, and I found him to be a thoroughly enjoyable companion. I interviewed him a bit and just wish I had had more time as I found him to be the most knowledgeable Cree on the whole trip in regards to history and culture. Under his guidance we found some important objects. One of these was a "spirit bundle," a type of bundle we had seen elsewhere but that no one would part with. They were, in effect, family protectors. They contained personal objects owned by deceased members of the family, going back several generations. In them we found quilled moccasins, hair cuttings, and even a rubber nipple from a baby bottle, each wrapped in print cloth. The bundle was supposed to keep the spirits of these people nearby to protect them. I understood that the owner of this bundle had embraced the Full Gospel Church and wanted to get rid of it.

Unquestionably the finest object that combined ceremonialism with creative art was a wooden *Pakakos*, or Bony Spectre, doll. It had brass studs for eyes, a white bead for a mouth, and was festooned with ribbons, beads, and cords. It was obviously very old. We also got a wonderful little brass object in the shape of a thunderbird that had been the war medicine of Loud Voice and had been worn in his hair. We then picked up a Prairie Chicken Ritual bundle from a young man who had inherited it from his father, but as he did not have the right to use it, he had left it out in the trees to rot. Fortunately we got there shortly after he had put it outside.

By the time we got back to Calgary we had obtained fifty-five items, including beadwork, drums, tanning tools, pipes, clothing, and religious objects. We were well over our $500 budget but nobody objected. I felt good in that we had not taken anything out of active ceremonial use, and in the case of rattles, etc., I was assured that these could be easily replaced. Also, the documentation was the most thorough of our entire Cree holdings, for most of the other objects had been donated by pioneer families or obtained from dealers with little or no information.

My last real collecting trip for Glenbow occurred in the spring of 1964. Because of the success of our Plains Cree trip, it was suggested that I go to northern Alberta and the Northwest Territories to collect material from the Chipewyans, Slaveys, Beavers, and other Dene groups. However, the decision was held up in Harvie's office and by the time I got approval we were in danger of encountering the spring breakup and getting caught for weeks in the North. As a result, approval was given for Doug Light and me to take $1,500 and make a return trip through Plains Cree country.

This time we went first to the Kehiwin Reserve, where I hired a young man named Lloyd Poitras. He knew the people well and by the time the day was over we had two medicine bags, a drum, two pipes, a rattle, scraper, moccasins, child's bow, moss bag, and a roach headdress. The next day we were on the Frog Lake Reserve with Fred Fiddler as our guide and obtained a spirit bundle, large drum, medicine bag, and a number of other items. One interesting piece was a little handmade wooden box, called a "joking box." When the top was slid open, it revealed a carving of *Wisakishak*, the Cree trickster, and when it was opened wider, a long penis suddenly sprang into view, controlled by elastic bands. I've never seen anything like it, before or since.

We tried the Onion Lake Reserve again, but as Wilfred Chocan was out trapping muskrats we had little success. On the Thunderchild Reserve we had Norman Sunchild as our guide and among the items acquired here was a stone "guardian spirit" in a parfleche bag made of buffalo skin. There was nothing for us on the Turtle Lake Reserve so we went to Little Pine, where we picked up Solomon Bluehorn and he found three or four beaded items for us. On his advice we returned to the Thunderchild Reserve to see John Noon. Here is what I wrote in my diary about John Noon:

> He had joined the Pentecosts and abandoned the old ways. Two years ago he set his father's material in the bush. He led us to the place, deep in the bush. It was well protected and damp but not damaged. In the box was ancient *Midewiwin* regalia including a wooden water drum, dog club, drum stick, rattle, wooden dish, and hide. Also there was a *pakahos* [bony spectre], 2 flat rattles, woman's rattle, 3 eagle claw tipi guardians, bear claw, eagle whistle, wooden medicine box, and Sun Dance feather. We bought everything.

Doug and I proceeded southward, picking up a few odds and ends on the Sweetgrass, Mosquito, Red Pheasant, Moosomin, and Saulteaux reserves, but there seemed to be very little available. James Baptiste, a leader of the Native American Church, showed us his regalia and tried to sell us a whip, but as it was being used in their ceremonies we didn't take it. We then went to the Moose Woods Reserve, which was Sioux, but found an election going on and no opportunity to see people. However, we did get a beautiful stone pipe from Bill Eagle.

From there both Doug and I were heading into unknown territory – the Cree, Ojibwa, and Sioux reserves of southern Saskatchewan. We engaged Doris Yuzicapi at Standing Buffalo to collect a number of Sioux items, including a navel cord bag, dentalium neck yoke, beadwork and tools. The next day we went to the Qu'Appelle valley, where we hired Bill Peigan and obtained a number of items from the Piapot, Pasqua, and Muscowpetung reserves. Among them were three stone guardian spirits, an eagle bundle, and two rattles. One item of particular interest was a shaman's mirror. I had read about them but had never seen one. It was a flat piece of board kept inside a decorated case. On the board was a small burn mark; the shaman stared at this and saw his vision on the face of the wooden "mirror."

But the greatest find of the trip occurred on the tiny Wood Mountain Reserve, home to descendants of Sitting Bull's refugee Sioux who had not returned to the United States. I looked up Pete Lethbridge, a saddlemaker who was a good friend of my brother-in-law, Fred Gladstone. He took us to the home of an elderly bachelor named John Wounded Horse. After a general conversation, this man told us that he had inherited a bunch of things after his mother died and he was willing to sell them to us. When he opened her trunk we were dumbfounded. The first things he brought out were a pair of moccasins fully covered with porcupine quills in bright red designs. Then, one after another, the quilled items appeared – a pouch, another pair of moccasins, a navel cord bag, and finally a huge cradleboard cover, the entire surface covered with quillwork. It was then, and still is, one of the finest pieces of quillwork ever produced in Canada. Besides this he had a headdress, bags, buckskin outfit, and horse gear. We bought them all.

Two weeks after we had set out from Calgary we returned with 113 objects that gave us one of the best and most well-documented collections to be found anywhere. It was a fitting conclusion to my years as a field collector for the Glenbow Foundation.

Those years had been beneficial both to the Glenbow and to me. They enabled the institution to gather objects that were important to the history and ethnology of the region at a time when Indians had been eager to dispose of them. There is no doubt in my mind that the majority of items I field-collected would have been discarded or sold to pawn shops with absolutely no documentation regarding their function or use. As for me, this period gave me the opportunity to learn of Native life and culture to a depth that otherwise I could never have achieved. I was both inspired and grateful for the knowledge that had been shared with me.

# 7

# *Adjusting to Calgary*

Life in Calgary was exciting for the two of us. We were midway between both sets of parents — one in Edmonton and the other in Cardston — and settling in to a brand new house. With it came all the tasks of buying new furniture, and generally doing the hundred and one things required when making such a move. At that time Calgary was a city of 180,000 people, and the Highwood district in which we lived was on the northwestern outskirts. At the end of our block was open prairie that led to the top of Nose Hill. During our first year it was not uncommon to see such creatures as rabbits and coyotes on their nocturnal prowls or to see Hungarian partridges and other birds wandering the streets. The nearest bus line was a mile away, although that soon changed. The city was still quite small; dominating the skyline was the Palliser Hotel, and when travelling south you reached the country almost as soon as you crossed Cemetery Hill.

As in most new subdivisions, we had all the work to do in landscaping, building a retaining wall, erecting a white picket fence, putting up a clothesline, and installing eavestroughs. It was a lot of work but it was a real adventure, creating something of our own in a new city.

Shortly after we arrived, Pauline got a job as secretary at Kendon Finance on Centre Street. Its office was above a car dealership and it mostly handled the automotive trade. She liked it there, but when a chance came in 1957 for her to become a secretary at the University of Alberta in Calgary, she jumped at it. The university was brand new and was housed in the old administrative building on the campus of the Southern Alberta School of Technology & Art. Pauline was secretary to Theo Finn, professor of elementary education. In fact, the total staff was not more than a dozen people, all in a Department of Education, with Dr. Doucette as the principal. During the several months that Pauline was there, the staff was planning a new campus that would eventually become the University of Calgary. Pauline is quite proud of the fact that the initial plans of the first building show an area that is designated as "Mrs. Dempsey's office."

But it was not to be. Shortly after our arrival in Calgary, a doctor said that the likelihood of us having children was not very good, so that we should consider adopting. Accordingly, in 1958 we went to the Alberta Government's Child Welfare Branch and asked for a baby who was comparable in racial background to our own, i.e., a mix of Blackfoot and white. When we were asked whether we wanted a boy or girl, we said it didn't matter, but for some reason the dim bulb clerk wrote down "girl" on the form. Over the next few months, we checked from time to time but there was no baby for us. We were told that most Native children had Roman Catholic mothers and as we were Protestants we did not qualify.

Then one day in March 1959, we checked again and were told there were still no girls available. When we asked why they mentioned "girls" we were told that that is what was on our form. We pointed out that we had never indicated a preference, and that either a boy or girl would be fine. That's when they told us that the perfect boy for us had been born five months earlier, September 20, 1957, and was in a foster home. We were absolutely flabbergasted and even all these years later I still get angry at that clerk who deprived us of the first five months of Lloyd's life, and that he was deprived of our love for the same period.

We made it clear that we wanted the boy and the matter was expedited. Although they never admitted it, I think they knew they had screwed up. Anyway, Pauline gave her notice at the University of Alberta in Calgary and on April 4th we went to a private home on the old Trans-Canada Highway west of the city and picked up the little boy whom we christened Lloyd James.

What a day to bring home a baby! Dad and I had gone to an Indian Association executive meeting at the Labor Temple and afterwards Howard Beebe, Steve Mistaken Chief, Jim Shot Both Sides, and brother Fred came to the house for supper. There were all there when Pauline and I came in with little Lloyd, and Pauline was handling him like he was made of egg shells. That evening, Gerald picked up Steve and Jim for the night while Howard, Fred, Mom, and Dad stayed with us. So for our first night with Lloyd we had a houseful.

I was the youngest of a family of four boys. I never had a baby sister or cousin around me and, in fact, I had never had anything to do with babies. It made me wonder how I would be as a father, but I needn't have worried. As soon as I saw the fat and happy little cherub in his crib my heart went out to him. I loved being a father, both for him and for the others that followed. The broad term of "family" had become important to me when I met Pauline and joined her extended family, but it now was a much more personal matter. As I always said, my priorities in life have been (in this order): family, career, writing.

James (he later chose to use his middle name) was the first of five children. He was followed two years later by another adopted child, Louise Diana, whom we got at birth, born April 5, 1961. She must have aroused some maternal/paternal instincts, for a short time later Pauline became pregnant and on August 2, 1962, she gave birth to John David. Now there was no stopping us, and on November 25, 1963, we had twin girls, Leah Suzette and Lois Pauline. Neither we nor the doctor knew Pauline was carrying twins until they were born. What a surprise! They arrived first thing in the morning and by noon I was addressing the Rotary Club in Red Deer, after which I had a meeting with the mayor, city council, library board, and old-timers association about establishing an archives in Red Deer. Now that I look back on it, I don't know how I did it.

For a while we had five preschool-age children, with three of them in diapers. We signed up for a diaper delivery service, and Pauline's folks bought us a washer and dryer so at least that part of the routine became manageable. It was a lot of work, but also a lot of fun. All our priorities immediately changed so that the children came first and we squeezed in everything else depending on our available time. However, Pauline's mother was a great help to us, and when we travelled, it was often with the whole herd.

---

Getting back to our first years in Calgary before the children, we already had a nice circle of friends when we arrived so we fitted in quite easily. We were frequently visited by Pauline's folks, and we were pleased when they stayed with us for several days at a time. We saw Bill and Sally Marsden quite frequently and were back and forth with Irene and Gerald Tailfeathers several times a month. Pauline and Irene never ran out of things to talk about. As for Gerald and me, we shared a common interest in things creative. We talked for hours about painting, history, and just about anything else that took our fancy. Gerald had a lively sense of humour and was great to be with. He liked starting a conversation with "Shucks...," which always got a laugh.

Gerald had a drinking problem but it was usually under control. He might go on a bender for two or three days, then stay dry for months. More than once, we searched for him in East Calgary after he had gone missing, but he always turned up safe and sound. I tried to avoid him when he was drinking, for he could easily become angry and vitriolic. At times like that, he seemed to hate the world. But, as I say, he usually kept it under wraps.

Often we talked about historical paintings and I was flattered when he sometimes turned to me for advice. There were occasions when I was able to find a photograph that met his needs, while at other times I offered criticisms on points of historical accuracy. But I had to be very careful, as Gerald was extremely sensitive and if he thought I was questioning the quality of his work he would become very defensive.

I remember three incidents involving criticisms that did not go well. Fortunately, none of them involved Pauline or me. In a painting he was doing for Glenbow, he showed some Blackfoot horsemen during a buffalo hunt. When Cliff Wilson saw it, he immediately objected to it because one of the hunters was using a woman's saddle. Obviously, he said, the artist didn't know what he was doing. Puzzled, I asked Gerald and he snapped, "Of course I know it's a woman's saddle. What I'm trying to show is that a big herd of buffalo has come close to a Blackfoot camp and every man is out hunting. This man didn't have a horse or saddle so he borrowed a horse and had to use a woman's saddle."

A more serious incident occurred when Gerald did a painting of some Indians getting drunk after they bought kegs of liquor from whisky traders. This had been commissioned by Glenbow, but when art director Moncrieff Williamson saw it, he refused to accept it. It's a cartoon, he said, and we don't buy cartoons. Unfortunately I was out of town when this incident occurred. I had seen the picture and loved it. Gerald explained that he had painted it in cartoon style because Indians acted like a bunch of cartoon characters when they were drunk. There was a deep meaning behind the picture that Williamson missed, nor did he ask the artist for an explanation. When I got back, I asked Gerald if he would sell it to me, but I was too late; the federal government had snapped it up for their art collection. Gerald wasn't mad at me personally, but he was so disgusted with Williamson and the Glenbow Foundation that he refused to do anything for them again.

The third incident came to our attention when Dora Plaited Hair phoned from Bowness to say that Gerald had been drinking and was angry. Pauline got him on the line and he told her that one of his customers had just refused an oil painting of Shot Both Sides that he had done on commission. He said he was getting ready to burn it in the backyard. Pauline rushed over to Dora's place and, sure enough, they had a bonfire going. However, Pauline was able to convince Gerald that the painting was a good one and that we would pay the price he was supposed to have received for it. In fact, it was not one of his best works, as oil was never his favourite medium, but it was a nice piece and there was no way we were going to let him suffer the humiliation of rejection. So we bought it and have displayed it many times in our home and in exhibitions.

Over the years, Pauline and I were in a position to buy some of Gerald's finest works. Too often we missed something because we couldn't afford it when it was available, but we still managed to obtain quite a few. Gerald never gave his paintings away nor reduced his prices. The only free painting I ever got from him was a small tempera for a Christmas present. Mind you, I agreed completely with this approach.

Right from the time we arrived in Calgary, our home was a way station for dozens of people. Besides Mom and Dad and other members of the family there were people from the Indian Association, distant relatives, and friends. A number of them were overnight visitors as Calgary became a halfway point between the Blood Reserve and Edmonton. People like Chris Shade, Jim Shot Both Sides, Ralph Steinhauer, and others often took one of the spare rooms or, if we were too crowded, they slept on the couch or on the floor in the living room.

I remember we were in Calgary for only a short time when Charlie Revais and his wife stopped for the night. He was Pauline's dad's adopted father from the Blackfeet Reservation in Montana and was on his way to Edmonton to visit someone in the Camsell Hospital. Next morning, before they pulled out, Charlie gave me a tobacco cutting board which had been made from the head of a whisky keg and was over a hundred years old.

I never tried to collect artifacts in competition with Glenbow, but if anything came to me as a personal gift through the family, it stayed with us. By the time I retired, two or three dozen items had come to us in this fashion. These included pipes, drums, beadwork, some ceremonial items, and a scalplock.

The scalplock ... I must tell you about that item and the dirty trick I played with it. Gerald had gone to the Blood Reserve and had stayed with his dad, Fred. While there, he was poking around an old trunk and found the scalplock. It was just a wisp of hair with a rawhide loop on the end. This could be attached to the end of a willow stick and used for dancing inside the Sun Dance lodge. Gerald learned that it had belonged to his uncle, Crazy Crow, who had taken it in battle. Fred let him have it and so Gerald took it home. A few days later, he came over to see me and told me what had happened.

"Ever since I've had that scalp in the house," he said, "I've been having nightmares. I'm scared to keep it any more. Do you want it?"

Of course I did, but I was afraid that if Pauline learned it was in the house, she might also start having nightmares. So without saying anything to her, I put the scalplock inside the pillowslip on her side of the bed and left it there for a couple of nights. When I finally told her what I had done, I thought she might be mad at me (I wouldn't have blamed her), but instead she laughed and agreed that it wasn't bringing any "bad spirits" into the house.

Also, if Glenbow rejected something, I didn't mind buying it. This happened when a son of Tom Wilson, an old Banff guide, came in with some fur trade books to sell. Glenbow already had them and turned them down so I bought them. They cost about $75 and today they must be worth more than $2,000. But that wasn't why I got them; they were, and still are, working tools.

This was also the time when I lost a great opportunity. While down in Cardston in January 1958, I went to see Jack Reed, a local gunsmith, and found that he had an original illustrated letter that Charlie Russell had written to him, thanking him for fixing his gun. He was willing to sell it for $1,000, so I took the information back to our art department and suggested they get it. Several months later, I happened to ask about the letter and was told that Eric Harvie had turned it down, that he thought Russell's works and prices were highly overrated. I was shocked, and although I couldn't afford it ($1,000 was a lot of money for someone taking home $350 a month) I decided that it was an investment that I couldn't pass up, for I loved Russell and his work. However, when I contacted Reed I found that he had already sold it to someone in the States for $1,500.

---

In the summer of 1956, just before Pauline and I left for our holidays, I got a letter from Jack Ewers telling me about Father Peter Powell, a Catholic priest from Chicago. Jack said the man was anxious to see a Blackfoot Sun Dance and he hoped that I might be able to arrange it. "I have met Father Powell," he wrote, "and am impressed with his genuine interest in Plains Indian religion. I don't know how the Indians might feel about having a Catholic priest view their traditional ceremony. I am not a Catholic. Nor do I have any prejudice against them. Father Powell appears to be a fine man."[60]

The Gladstones were strong Anglicans and there was no love lost on the Blood Reserve between the two denominations. However, Dad had many personal friends who were Catholics and said there was no reason why we couldn't entertain the priest at the farm and take him to the Sun Dance. We picked Father Powell up in Cardston and found him to be a very personable chap who told us of the work he was doing among the urban Indians of Chicago. In addition, he was extremely interested in Northern Cheyenne and Sioux religion. It was hard not to like him, even though he was from the "other side."

During the evening's conversation, he mentioned "Ginny" a couple of times. Finally, I asked him who Ginny was.

"Ginny is my wife," he said.

We were all taken aback. We knew Americans sometimes did things differently from Canadians, but the Roman Catholic Church wasn't all that different.

"But I thought you were a Catholic priest," I said.

"I am," he replied. "I'm an Anglo-Catholic priest."

"You're an Anglican!" exclaimed Dad.

Then it all became clear. Anglo-Catholics are a high order of Anglicans who recognize the Pope as the prelate of Rome but do not subscribe to other tenets of the Roman faith. Father Powell's ministry in Chicago was St. Timothy's Episcopal Church.

When I wrote to Jack Ewers and told him the news, he got a great chuckle out of it. Jack himself was a Protestant and his wife Marge was an Anglican. They had entertained Father Powell while he was in Washington but never suspected he was anything but a Roman Catholic priest.

Certainly he looked like one with his black suit and reversed collar. In fact, he told me that he almost got into serious trouble when he and his wife went on a research trip to Montreal. He had made hotel reservations ahead of time and when he arrived, he registered as Father and Mrs. Powell. The clerk was obviously surprised and politely suggested that the priest and "the woman" take separate rooms. Only after considerable discussion was the problem resolved, although the clerk never really believed the man was anything but a Catholic priest.

We learned all this on a Saturday night, and as the local minister was going to be away the following day, Dad asked Father Powell if he would take the morning service at St. Paul's. He had a bit of trouble with the pledge to the King and a few other differences in the prayer book but otherwise everything went well. Afterwards, we went to the Sun Dance and arrived there in time to see the dance of the Horn Society. Father Powell was tremendously impressed, and over the years he frequently harkened back to that wonderful day at the Sun Dance.

Father Powell made a return visit the following year and we met him at the North American Indian Days in Browning. Pauline and I had just returned from the All American Indian Days in Sheridan, Wyoming, where we'd gone with Irene and Gerald. We'd had a lot of fun there. Gerald kept poking fun at the announcer, for every time they had a parade, the man would refer to the Crows or Cheyennes by their names, but whenever the Sioux came on the scene it was always "the mighty Sioux nation." They didn't look any different than the others in the parade, so every once in a while Gerald would strike a pose and say he was from "the mighty Sioux nation." The only members of the Blackfoot nation taking part in the ceremonies in Sheridan were Stephen Fox and Albert Many Fingers from the Blood Reserve, and they won first prize for their tepee.

On our way home we stopped in Browning, where we met some interesting people. Prominent among these was Jessie Donaldson Schultz, the widow of James Willard Schultz. Her husband had entered the Territory in 1881, lived with the Blackfoot, and had been a prolific author of children's books. Jessie had just seen the *Motokix* dance at the Blood Sun Dance and had been very impressed. I also met Verne Dusenberry, who had written his doctoral dissertation on the Rocky Boy Cree. I was so taken with him that I was instrumental in getting him hired by Glenbow a few years later. I also met Mrs. Merrill Burlingame, who was working on a biography of whisky trader John J. Healy, so we had a lot to talk about. Father Powell and I further cemented our friendship a few years later when I stayed with him during my one trip to Chicago. He was the author of the seminal two-volume work, *Sweet Medicine: The Continuing Role of the Sacred Arrows, the Sun Dance, and the Sacred Buffalo Hat in Northern Cheyenne History*.[61]

---

Back to 1956. A few weeks before moving to Calgary I had been elected vice-president of the Historical Society and officially became associate editor of the *Alberta Historical Review*. I had been fulfilling that function since the beginning, and latterly I had been doing virtually everything except choosing the articles and writing the editorials. In the Spring issue of 1956, for example, I got Jack Ewers to write an article on the North West trade gun, drew information from an unpublished manuscript by Sir Cecil Denny, prepared an article based on the diary of Donald Ross, included some excerpts from the *Calgary Eye Opener*, and wrote some of the book reviews. I sent this material to Reverend Edmonds, who added an article on an Anglican missionary, and wrote a couple more book reviews. It was a nice co-operative arrangement and I thoroughly enjoyed it.

At this time, the only meetings of the Society were those held in Edmonton. In fact, it had really been the "Historical Society of Edmonton" until the magazine gave it a province-wide membership. In the first issue of the *Review* after my arrival in Calgary, I sent out an appeal to organize a branch in Calgary. "If there is sufficient interest and enthusiasm," I wrote, "plans will be made to hold the first meeting in September or October."[62] However, the response was so poor that I decided I had better things to do with my time, so I put it off until a later date.

At the 1958 general meeting in Edmonton I was elected president of the Society at the age of twenty-nine. I had never conducted a meeting before so I had to learn the rules of parliamentary procedure – and quickly. But before I had time to do anything, Reverend Edmonds announced that he was retiring as editor of the *Alberta Historical Review*. I had succeeded in talking him out of quitting once before but this time he was adamant. I agreed to take on the editorship but there was no way I could hold down the two most senior positions in the Society, so I had to resign as president after presiding over only two meetings.

This was a crucial time for the Society, for although it had broken out of its moribund state with the magazine, it now needed to expand beyond Edmonton if it was to succeed. Although I had failed to get any support for a Calgary branch on my first try, I made a second stab at it in the spring of 1958. Archie Key, director of the Calgary Allied Arts Centre, started things off when he offered monthly tours to historic sites in the region and I provided him with a copy of our Calgary membership list. The turnout was so good that Archie and I decided to hold some meetings over the winter of 1958–59. As I wrote at the time, "As the only Calgarian on our Executive, it fell to my lot to make these arrangements."[63] We took out an affiliate membership in the Calgary Allied Arts Council and held a few meetings over the winter at Coste House without having a formal executive.

The results were gratifying and in March 1959 we held our first election. This time I elicited some support from fellow workers at Glenbow and I got Jack Herbert to agree to stand as the first president of the Calgary Branch. Others on the executive were Benton Mackid, Bernie Toft, Sheilagh Jameson, Sheila Johnston, and members at large, T.R. Hicks, Una MacLean, Reg Gladden, Pat McCloy, Georgina Thomson, and me. As I commented in my diary on March 6th, "I hope now I can sit back and take it easy. I just have a seat on the Executive Committee." With this beginning, the Calgary Branch went on to become one of the leading parts of the Society, along with Edmonton, Red Deer, and Lethbridge, the latter being organized by Alex Johnston a few years later.

When I joined Glenbow, other staff members had contracts that restricted their right to publish, but Eric Harvie agreed that I could bring my Historical Society duties with me, and that included writing and editing. In addition to writing for the society's magazine, I did quite a bit of freelance writing. In 1956, for example, I had articles published by the *Journal of the Washington Academy of Sciences*, the *Calgary Herald, Lethbridge Herald*, and *Encyclopedia* Canadiana. During the early years at Glenbow, I was never actually reprimanded for my writing, but I knew that some of Harvie's administrative people didn't like it. I'm not sure whether this was because of their desire for a low profile as far as the Foundation was concerned, or whether it was simply an attitude that they "owned" the Glenbow staff, lock, stock and barrel. Or perhaps there was concern over my increasing public image. All I know is that over the years I wrote and published *in spite* of Glenbow, not because of it. Eric Harvie never mentioned the matter to me but some of his minions indicated that they were not pleased.

------ ∞ ------

On the home front, Dad had been defeated as president of the Indian Association in 1954 and had remained out of office for two years. However, he was re-elected in 1956 just as Pauline and I moved to Calgary, and we soon found ourselves immersed in Association business. Dad was back and forth to see John Laurie, and both Pauline and I helped him with some of the Association's paperwork. I attended the annual meetings wherever possible.

John Laurie had been glad to see Dad back as president. He had not got along with the outgoing president, Clarence McHugh, and didn't trust him. Clarence, at the same time, was not at all friendly with Laurie. Supposedly the problem had started when Clarence came with a delegation from the Blackfoot Reserve to the 1954 general meeting on the Sarcee Reserve. During the meeting there was some trouble with drinking, with both some Blackfoot and Sarcee delegates being picked up by the police. During the meeting, Laurie without proof blamed the Blackfoot for getting the Sarcees into trouble. Clarence became very angry and almost pulled out of the meeting. Instead, he stayed and saw himself elected president with John Laurie continuing as secretary.

I think that Laurie didn't like Clarence because he was too independent and outspoken and would not necessarily listen to Laurie's advice. He had been overseas during the war and knew his way around the white community. Clarence's whole life had centred around the Blackfoot Reserve and his later years were devoted to the betterment of his people, both as president of the Indian Association and as head chief of the Blackfoot tribe. I always liked Clarence and had a great admiration for him, so I was sad about Laurie's attitude towards him.

I recall one trick that Laurie played after Clarence was elected president. The whole Michel Reserve at Riviere Qui Barre, north of Edmonton, was enfranchising and it had become a hot political issue. The Association, I believe, was neutral as it was an internal tribal matter, but basically it was opposed to the idea. However, Laurie could not do anything as one of the main people in favour of enfranchisement was John Callihoo, former long-time president of the Association and resident of that reserve. John Laurie had tried to talk to him but with no luck.

Then John received a message from J.W. Pickersgill, the federal minister responsible for Indian Affairs, saying he would be in Calgary and wanted to meet with the Association officers. Laurie did not want Clarence there, as they had differing views on a number of matters, so he called Clarence and told him there was an important meeting taking place at Riviere Qui Barre and that he should attend. The day after Clarence left, Pickersgill arrived in Calgary and John Laurie and Dave Crowchild saw him. After Clarence came back he told me, "I found it was a wild goose chase. I'm convinced that John got me out of the area because he did not want me to see Pickersgill."[64]

Laurie got along all right with Clarence's successor, Albert Lightning, but he was pleased when Dad got back into office in 1956. Of course, Pauline and I kept up to date on all the news and gossip. Our home was frequently the site of informal meetings and the visitors were always talking politics – Indian politics – and I soon got to know pretty well everything that was going on.

In 1957, word was received that Prime Minister John Diefenbaker was going to officially open the Calgary Stampede. Dad suggested that a presentation be made to him at the Indian village, and when the executive agreed, a painting was commissioned from Gerald Tailfeathers. Dad agreed to make the presentation but only later did he learn that any Indians involved in ceremonies at the village had to wear a Native outfit. He didn't have one but borrowed one from a friend, complete with feathered headdress. I believe this was the first time in his life that he had ever worn a buckskin outfit and Mom had to show him how it was done. The presentation took place under the Medicine Tree at the Calgary Stampede and none of us realized at the time that the event was giving the prime minister a good chance to look at Dad.

Just three days later, word was leaked to the press that Diefenbaker intended appointing an Indian to the Senate of Canada, and that his choice had narrowed to three people – Gilbert Monture, a career civil servant from Brantford; Andy Paull, a lawyer from Vancouver; and Dad. Rumours were flying for the next several months, but nothing happened until January 1958 while Dad was attending an IAA executive meeting in Calgary. That evening, Pauline, Mom, Dad, and I went to visit John Laurie at his home. All evening our host seemed to have something on his mind, almost like a private joke. His eyes twinkled and he was quite animated but he gave nothing away. Four days later, I answered our phone and a secretary asked if Mr. Gladstone was there. I gave the phone to Dad and moments later he was talking to the prime minister!

When he got off the phone, Dad said he had been offered a senatorship but there was one problem. The law required that an appointee hold real estate to the value of $4,000 or more, and land held on an Indian reserve was questionable. Dad assured Diefenbaker that he would go right out and buy a house in Cardston. He located his son Fred, who was on an extended visit to Montana, sold some of their cattle, and bought a little house in Cardston for $7,600. By the end of the following day, he was back in our living room after wiring the prime minister and telling him that the deed had been done. Now he sat and waited for the call. At this stage, I can do no better than to quote my diary for this period:

> January 31, 1958 – Dad phoned Diefenbaker at 7.30 a.m. but he was tied up. He phoned back at 11 a.m. Said he was taking the matter to Cabinet and would likely phone in the afternoon. Asked Dad to have his headdress, etc. Phoned John Laurie and borrowed his leggings, moccasins, and jacket. Got a headdress from George Gooderham. No phone call came back. Very tense.

> February 1 – Phone call from Bill Gold, Calgary Herald, saying official news of the appointment had just come over the teletype. [Found later it was a phone call from Diefenbaker to the publisher.] Phone busy for the rest of the day. Gold and photographer Harry

Befus came over, CFCN made a telephone interview and sent Don Thomas over to make a 15 minute tape for Toronto. Phone calls from John Laurie, Mrs. Down, Dr. Johnson, Bill Marsden, George Gooderham, etc. and wires from Rev. Peter Kelly, Canon Cook, etc. In the afternoon we went to CHCT-TV. They did a miserable job. Dad did very well on all interviews except the latter, which was so badly handled I'm not surprised. Aaron Olsen was the chap in charge. Had a call from Horace and made plans. So Dad is now a Senator!

It was interesting later on to hear some of the stories and rumours that sprouted up about the appointment. One true story is that some of Dad's detractors on the Blood Reserve protested that they had not been consulted about the appointment nor did they have a chance to vote on it! There was a rumour that the appointment had been offered to John Laurie but that he had demurred in favour of Dad. This was untrue for the simple reason that Diefenbaker had made a campaign promise that he would appoint an Indian to the Senate, not a white person working among the Indians. Interestingly, John Laurie never claimed (to me or Dad, at least) that the appointment had ever been offered to him. In fact, he was highly elated that it had gone to Dad. I think the story arose because Diefenbaker had called Laurie a few days before the appointment to get his opinion about Dad. That was the secret he had been carrying when we visited him.

In any case, with that phone call our whole lives changed. For the next thirteen years, Pauline and I were Dad's secretaries, press writers, confidants, and companions. We helped him prepare for public appearances, accompanied him to ceremonies whenever possible, helped him draft letters to cabinet ministers about Indian problems, and did a hundred and one things that could never have been done by a secretary in Ottawa.

The activities started the day after his appointment, when we all went to church on the Blackfoot Reserve. Afterwards, Dad taped a speech in Blackfoot that was left to be played to future congregations. When we got home, a reporter from the *Toronto Star* was waiting for him. A few days later, Dad was off to Saskatchewan for a round of meetings, and from then on he was either coming to a meeting, leaving for a meeting, or waiting for the next meeting. When he and Mom finally went to Ottawa for the opening of Parliament, Pauline went with them and kept me up to date with daily letters telling of the adventures of the Gladstones in the nation's capital.

Pauline and I often accompanied Dad and Mom on their local journeys. One rather funny incident occurred later in the year when Dad was invited to open the Calgary Spring Horse Show. Fred was competing in town as a calf roper so when Dad was given an exclusive box at the show, he invited Fred and Edith, as well as Pauline and me, to join him. We sat there in the box with the high society of Calgary and flanked by two Mounties in scarlet uniforms. At the intermission, we were led to a reception room where we were treated to snacks and drinks. Remember, at this time treaty Indians did not have liquor privileges, and the possessing or consuming of liquor was against the law. When we entered the room, one of the Mounties took charge of the bar and, turning to Fred, he said, "What'll you have?" In all his years of drinking, Fred had never faced an experience like this. I think he gulped once before he said, "rye." I don't know if he expected the Mountie to handcuff him then and there, but nothing happened. Fred got his drink, as did everyone else, and we had a nice break until the show started again. I don't know if the drink helped, but Fred placed second in the calf roping event.

---

On April 6, 1959, two days after we had added Lloyd to our little family, we were saddened by the death of John Laurie. He had been in ill health for years but had still carried on his work, particularly for the Indian Association of Alberta. Just two days earlier, Dad and I had been at an Executive meeting while John Laurie was in hospital. I think everyone realized that he would not be able to carry on so Howard Beebe, the president, quietly asked me if I would consider taking his place. I told him I would think about it when the time came.

When I learned of Laurie's death, I phoned Dad to pass on the sad news to friends on the Blood Reserve. That afternoon I was interviewed by the *Calgary Albertan* and tried to give some insight into the man's dedication. That evening, I wrote in my diary: "Poor John! He had so many friends but he was so alone. No family, no children, no one to carry on his great name. He should have married that Stoney woman, Anna Beaver, in 1941. We had our differences of opinion but no arguments. Just where would the Indians be now if it weren't for him? He actually gave his life for them. His health had been broken for 12 years but he still carried on. The Indians have lost a friend and adviser that cannot be replaced. He was a great man whose name must go down in history as the champion of the people."

A few days later, Pauline, Mom, and I were asked to sit in the family section of the Pro-Cathedral for the funeral services and then we accompanied the entourage to Morley for interment in the cemetery on the Stoney Reserve.

After some discussion, I acceded to Howard Beebe's request that I be directly involved with the Association. The arrangement was eventually developed that Dave Crowchild would be corresponding secretary, Pauline the recording secretary, and I the honorary secretary. This meant that I would actually be doing Dave's work, just as John Laurie had done. I had been a card-carrying member of the Association since 1952, but as I am not an Indian, I was agreeable to the "honorary" status.

But now that Laurie was gone, the Indians had to deal with another problem, that of their volunteer legal adviser, Ruth Gorman. She was the daughter of a lawyer who had worked among the Stoneys and she too had obtained a law degree. During the Hobbema case in 1957, she provided her services to John Laurie and played a major role in publicizing the plight of some Hobbema Indians who were being ordered off their reserve. She waged a war with the Minister of Indian Affairs through the front pages of the newspapers while Laurie marshalled the various support groups to use their influence in Ottawa. In the end the Indians won their case, not because of the Association, but because the local priest conveniently "lost" some vital documents before the hearings and the case had to be thrown out. In any event, because of this incident, Gorman carried on as the legal adviser to the Association. This was fine as long as Laurie was alive, as he was able to control her, but once he passed on it became a different matter.

She may have done some good work, but her ideals and mine were so far apart that I had great difficulty in working with her. John Laurie always believed that he should work behind the scenes, and I agreed with him and operated the same way. In Association meetings, Laurie never tried to run things, but if he felt the discussions were going in the wrong direction, he would whisper his concerns to Dave Crowchild. If Dave agreed with him (which he usually did) he was the one who arose and tried to get things on the right track. Gorman was just the opposite. She liked to run things. She tried to be in control of the meetings, interrupted discussions, and seldom paid attention to the rules of parliamentary procedure. She tended to "tell" the Indians what to do, rather than listen to their views. I had no patience for such people.

Meanwhile, events were moving rapidly. Some time earlier, the federal government had responded to criticisms from the various Native associations across Canada by establishing a Joint Committee of the House of Commons and Senate on Indian Affairs. One of its goals was to listen to briefs from organizations and individuals, and the Association was gearing up for its presentation when John Laurie died. At the meeting in April, just before Laurie's death, Howard announced that the Association would seek repeal of the compulsory enfranchisement clause in the Indian Act and push for other changes that would place more of the decision making in the hands of the Indian people.

An executive meeting was held in late summer, at which time the decision was made to hold open sessions on five reserves in the province to give Indians a chance to express their concerns, to bring forward resolutions, and to indicate what should be contained in the Association's brief. The main meeting, a two-day affair, was scheduled in November for Hobbema, after which the results would be submitted to the annual meeting. I attended any meetings that didn't interfere with my job and then spent several days putting the resolutions into proper form for presentation at Hobbema. At the same time, Gorman dropped off briefs to me on various subjects such as welfare that had to be rewritten. When everything was in order, I had the resolutions and briefs mimeographed and bound for the Hobbema meeting.

The meeting was held on November 20 and 21, 1959, and it proved to be a turbulent affair. Here is what I said in my diary for the first day: "Arrived at Samson's Hall at 1.30 pm. It developed into a very stormy meeting during the afternoon, with Mrs. Gorman trying to run the whole show. It exploded violently during the liquor debate when Mrs. Gorman 'refused to accept' a motion (she was not the chairman, only an adviser) and clashed with Ralph Steinhauer. The delegates overrode Mrs. G. and withdrew the motion before adjourning. I had a talk with Ralph who says the Saddle Lake delegation threatens to pull out and prepare their own Brief unless Mrs. G. is controlled." On the following day I wrote, "There was another long session today. I caught Mrs. G. before going in and advised her to keep quiet and to speak only in explaining certain sections and if she didn't I warned it would probably split the IAA wide open. She was quite restrained all morning and all went smoothly. But she couldn't keep still and everything exploded again in the afternoon on enfranchisement. Finally, delegate Edward Cardinal asked who was running the meeting, the IAA or 'that woman.'"

After Cardinal made his statement (pointing to Gorman while he said it), she scooped her papers into her briefcase and stomped down the aisle of the hall. She was about halfway along when her briefcase popped open, her papers and other items were dumped on the floor. No one said a word. Then she gathered up everything and left the room. As soon as the door closed, Dad and Ralph rushed out after her. They spoke to her for quite a while and at last convinced her to return to the meeting. She did, and a number of people expressed appreciation for her volunteer work on their behalf.

By the time the meeting the over, the delegates had passed thirty-six resolutions on education, treaty rights, and self-government which provided the framework for the submission to the Joint Committee. But they had run out of time and still had not dealt with the resolutions on health, welfare, and other matters. In order to complete the work, the Association struck a committee consisting of President Howard Beebe, John Samson, Albert Lightning, Ralph Steinhauer, Peter Burnstick, Mrs. Nora Matchatis, Ruth Gorman, Dad, and me.

We met at our house about two weeks later. Steinhauer, Samson, Burnstick, Dad, Gorman, and I were in attendance. Ralph chaired the meeting and by midnight we had approved all the necessary resolutions, reviewed the drafts of the brief, and had everything needed to prepare the final report. It was nice, but even nicer was what happened next. As we met so late, Ralph, Johnny, Pete, and Dad stayed for the night and we were so crowded that Ralph slept on the couch. Next morning when I got up, Ralph said to me, "I didn't know that Lloyd could walk."

"He can't," I replied, "He can only crawl or stand up beside the furniture."

That's when Ralph laughed and said that when he woke up in the morning, the little boy came walking into the room. Sure enough, when we got him on his feet, Lloyd toddled along as fast as his chubby little legs could carry him. So Alberta's future lieutenant-governor was the first person to see Lloyd walk.

During the early weeks of 1960 I worked evenings and weekends on the brief to Ottawa. I wrote the historical introduction myself based on my earlier research and then Gorman provided me with her handwritten narratives which I rewrote and then appended the appropriate resolutions. It was long, tiring, and frustrating work, but I finally got the brief into shape and Pauline set to work to type five copies of it to send out for approval. When this was done, the copies were finally shipped off to Ottawa.

Some weeks later, an IAA delegation consisting of John Samson, Howard Beebe, and Ruth Gorman went to Ottawa to make an oral submission. Gerald Tailfeathers, who was there at the time, said that some of the Joint Committee members walked out on the first day because of Gorman's domination of the meeting. Gerald added, "But as time went on, Howard and Johnny Samson had more of an opportunity to talk and apparently did quite well (as we knew they would)."

In the end, I found out that we needn't have bothered. Even though Dad was a co-chairman of the Joint Committee, it proved to be a lion with no teeth. Submissions were heard from Native groups, governments, and interested parties over a period of two or three years. In the end, the recommendations the committee made were government-oriented, self-serving, and almost entirely without benefit to the Indian people. Not only that, but the final report was simply tabled and forgotten. So we could have saved ourselves a lot of trouble. In the end, it really didn't matter.

Once the Joint Committee was out of the way, the executive settled down to other business. Our new president was Ralph Steinhauer, and he set out to revitalize the organization. He was concerned about the lack of recruitment on most reserves and the fact that the total membership of the Association represented only a fraction of the treaty Indians in Alberta. In some cases, such as the Blackfoot Reserve, a once-active local had become completely inactive. Early in 1961 I accompanied Dad to the Peigan Reserve, where Bunny Grier agreed to reorganize that local. We called a meeting where about a dozen people showed up, including Chief John Yellowhorn, Samson Knowlton, Bob Crow Eagle, Joe Crow Shoe, and a number of young people. A week later, I met Pete Many Wounds and we called a meeting of the Sarcee Local at their community hall. There were seventeen people there, enough to hold an election, and Pete was named president, with Fred Eagle Tail as vice-president, Gordon Crowchild as secretary-treasurer, and his dad David as a director.

Pete Many Wounds was one of my best friends. We met because his wife, Muriel, was one of Pauline's schoolmates at Alberta College in Edmonton. Not only that, but she was the daughter of Ralph Steinhauer. When we moved to Calgary, Pauline and Muriel soon re-established contact and I immediately took to Pete. He was a man of limited education but great intelligence. We used to talk for hours about anything and nothing, from horses to the Indian Act to current events. After a while, we got into the routine of visiting on a weekend with all our children and they had lots of fun together. Often we would have a picnic down by the creek below Pete's house while at other times we had them over for supper. It was all very enjoyable.

But back to the Indian Association of Alberta: Howard Beebe volunteered to tackle the reorganization of the Blackfoot Local. We went there in February 1961 and were pleased when more than a hundred people were gathered at the church hall. I was really impressed with Howard. He made a speech which was more than an hour long, entirely in Blackfoot. I couldn't understand more than one per cent of what he said, yet he held my attention during the entire time by the force of his oratory, by his hand and body movements, and by the way he impressed the audience. I had heard historically how orators had transfixed their audiences but this was the only time I actually saw it happen. After Howard there were others – Steve Mistaken Chief, Dave Crowchild, Joe Crowfoot, Matthew Melting Tallow, Ben Calf Robe, Clarence McHugh, Charlie Royal, and others – all speaking in Blackfoot. I also made a short speech (in English) outlining the good the IAA could do for them. In the end, a new local was formed with Adam Solway as president.

Ralph also decided that the 1944 constitution of the Association was out-dated and did not reflect its current role and responsibilities. At his suggestion I prepared a draft copy of a new constitution, a committee was struck, and they met at our house a week after the Blackfoot trip. Those present were Ralph, Dave Crowchild, Steve Mistaken Chief, his brother Fred, Mike Devine, Pete Many Wounds, Rufus Goodstriker, Wayne Beebe, and Mary Dover. The members went over the proposal clause by clause, with Steve and Pete voicing the loudest criticisms and asking for revisions which, for the most part, were very positive. In the end, I had an approved outline which I was able to put into final form so that it could pass at the next general meeting. Later, I had these printed and distributed to all members.

During all this time I was busy with IAA matters but I was having great fun. Ralph was an excellent person to work with and had the best grasp of the Association's goals of anyone I knew. Over the next six years, my role as "hon-orary" secretary was anything but honorary. I sent out notices of meetings, so-licited resolutions from the locals, rewrote resolutions and gathered them into mimeographed form, made up the agendas, sent out accreditation forms, made delegate ribbons, attended the annual and executive meetings where Pauline usually took the minutes, and I wrote up the final minutes. I also wrote letters to ministers, premiers, the director of Indian Affairs, Indian Health Services, and any other places from which the Association was seeking the redress of their problems. Later I had to take their replies and put them into a narrative form to send to all the members. If it sounds like a lot of work, it was.

My name seldom appeared during these years because I worked behind the scenes. Most of the letters were sent out under Dave Crowchild's name and I was not mentioned in the minutes because I had no speaking role. Like John Laurie, if I had something to say, it was usually to people like Ralph Steinhauer or John Samson. As I always said, I considered myself to be the extension of a typewriter, providing the Indians with a service they needed. I was not there to give advice or direction as they were perfectly capable to doing this themselves.

The 1961 meeting was held on the Alexis Reserve, west of Edmonton. At that time, Ralph retired and Howard Beebe returned to office as president. Pauline was sick so I had to take the minutes as well as doing everything else. When it was over, I was so tired I slept for two days. Afterwards I reflected in my diary, "I can see that the Indians are still painfully short of leaders. Among those who have anything really useful to offer on a provincial basis are Ralph Steinhauer, Pete Burnstick, John Samson, Pete Many Wounds, Gerald Tailfeathers, and possibly a few more. I can see a hope for some of the younger ones but it will take time."[65]

The first day of the meeting went well, but just after the election on the second day, Ruth Gorman arrived. Ralph could always restrain her but Howard Beebe could not. As I wrote in my diary, "She began breaking all the rules again and held up the works, rewrote and misworded her own ideas for amendments, etc."[66] There were rumbles of dissatisfaction but nothing came of it.

The following few years ran only slightly more smoothly. The annual meeting in 1962 was held at Morley, where John Samson took over as the new president. The following year at Alexander's Reserve he was re-elected and I commented, "the meeting was one of the smoothest I have seen in recent years."[67] The following year the meeting was held on the Blood Reserve when Howard was elected president, but this time the legal adviser was there and the dissatisfaction was apparent.

As Ralph wrote to me in 1965, "We should meet in Calgary the week of June 6 and talk over the whole problem of Indian organizations in Alberta. ... it seems that IAA has fallen apart altogether and for one reason, I think, is that our legal adviser is trying to exercise too much authority and dictate the organization's every move. Saddle Lake is very disturbed with the way she conducted herself at Cardston last June and as a protest they, Saddle Lake, have reorganized the local and have quite a large membership. They also plan to bring to Cold Lake [annual meeting] a resolution protesting the conduct of the legal adviser."[68] However, the days of domination by white people were almost over, as Native people were taking more and more control over their own destiny.

In 1966 I was unable to get away for the annual meeting at Cold Lake and the next two as well. I still helped Dave Crowchild with the minutes and put the packages together, but my work at Glenbow was taking up more and more of my time. I did, however, continue to work closely with Ethel Taylor, of Red Deer, who had been named chairman of the Association's Advisory Committee. Perhaps by this time I saw the handwriting on the wall, for one of the young people who took an active role in the 1966 meeting was Harold Cardinal, a university student. He had all the qualities that people like Taylor and I had been hoping for. He was dynamic, intelligent, well educated, and an effective speaker. Also, his approach to the Association was entirely different from that of people like Crowchild, Samson, Burnstick, and the others. While they rejected any thought of receiving government money and were adamant about maintaining their independence, Cardinal firmly believed that government money could be taken without compromising the role of the organization.

In 1968, Cardinal was elected president of the Association, and a short time later he let it be known that they did not need an advisory committee, a legal adviser, or an honorary secretary. Both Ethel Taylor and I were extremely pleased, for this is just the goal we had been working towards, but I must say that some in the group were not happy and complained about a lack of appreciation for all their efforts. I felt that our goal from the beginning should have been to work our way out of a job. If that happened, we knew we had been successful. That's the way I felt then, and it's still the way I feel today. It was a pleasure to be fired.

***

During all these years, Pauline was also active in Native issues and I was sometimes involved, just as she shared my interest in the IAA. Her first major commitment was to young Indians coming into Calgary in 1959. In that year, the federal government became fully committed to integrated education but, like so many things they did, it was strictly a short-sighted bandaid approach. The policy was to get Indians into senior high schools, so an arrangement was made with the Calgary School Board to accept students and for the government to provide a monthly living allowance. The Indian Department never took into consideration that these were all reservation Indians who, for the most part, had had no experience with city life. They just dumped them in the city and left them.

Let me give you an example. One day geologist Bill Gallup was driving to work when he saw one of the students walking to school, and he realized that she still had miles to go. Because he knew her and her family, he picked her up and as they were driving to school he asked her why she hadn't taken the bus. She finally admitted that she had never been on a bus in her life and didn't know how to buy or use tickets. She was too shy to ask so she was simply walking to school.

Some time after the opening of the fall term, it was obvious that these young people were completely lost in the city. After some discussion, they said they'd like a place where they could meet other Indian students and get to know them. Pauline came up with a solution: form an Indian social club. She called a meeting on November 2nd and among those who turned up were Betty Crowfoot, Alex Janvier, David and Shirley Healy. Arrangements were made to hold meetings at our house or other private homes until sometime later when Tony Karch got the YMCA to agree to let them use one of their rooms. Indian Affairs co-operated by providing a list of all students in Calgary.

And so the Calumet Indian Club was formed. I believe it was the first Native organization in Calgary. After a few meetings a formal constitution was passed and an election held. Alex Janvier became the first president and Lila Healy the vice-president. The routine was to hold weekly meetings, usually on a Monday evening. The gathering opened with a meeting and after the business was over a dance was held. There were times when the entire Indian student population turned out – Blackfoot, Blood, Peigan, Stoney, Sarcee, and Cree. In later years, it was interesting to note how many of its young members went on to become leaders. Some of them were Alex Janvier, Delphine Black Horse, Matthew Ayoungman, and Edward Fox, just to name a few. Besides these regular meetings, the club also had craft sales, special events, and formed a basketball team that competed all over southern Alberta.

The club was designed much along the lines of the Indian Association, in that its membership was entirely Indian, both youths and adults, while interested white people formed an advisory committee. I was a member of the latter group, and from 1961 to 1964 I edited their monthly newsletter, the *Calumet Moccasin Telegraph*. The club worked closely with other Calgary organizations, such as the Council of Community Services, which was under the capable direction of Tim Tyler. Pauline also worked with the YWCA and helped them form the Ninaki Girls Club.

The situation began to get complicated in 1961 when the Council of Community Services held a series of workshops and meetings to see if there were any needs of Indian people that should be addressed. As Indian centres were becoming popular in places like Winnipeg, Edmonton, and Vancouver, the question was raised as to whether one was needed in Calgary. Independent investigations were made by Pauline and by a white person and they both came to the conclusion was one was not needed. While the other cities had large

Native populations, Calgary at that time didn't have more than about two hundred Indians and perhaps a thousand non-status people with Indian blood who were in various stages of acculturation.

The following year, the question was raised by Grace Johnson and Ruth Gorman, representing the Local Council of Women. Ignoring the earlier decision and without consultation, the Local Council passed a resolution indicating that some kind of an Indian shelter "was a necessity." They envisioned "a bathroom, telephone and a room where Indians can meet or rest"[69] and began to plan a facility to be located in East Calgary. Early in 1963, I noted, "This evening I went to a meeting of the Council of Community Services regarding an Indian centre. It was a hot and heavy affair but accomplished little. The Local Council of Women want to put up a place in east Calgary with toilet facilities while most other groups are opposed. Among the Indians present were Pete Many Wounds, Mrs. and Mrs. Lawrence Whitney, Mrs. Phyllis Bennink (nee Eagle Child), and Andrew Bear Robe."[70]

At that time I had no strong feelings about it one way or the other, just as long as the Indians were being consulted and their voices heard. From this meeting, it was obvious that this wasn't happening and the women were forging ahead with their own ideas. The Calumet Club held a meeting and decided to send a protest to the Council of Community Services. They asked me to write the letter but when it was sent to the Council, Mrs. Johnson tried to discredit it by saying it was written by a white man and also that the club was made up of young Indians who were not representative of the large Native population.

These and other Indian protests slowed the Local Council down enough so that it took another look at what was happening in other cities, and then switched their plans from a toilet in East Calgary to a full-fledged Indian centre. This would be complete with meeting rooms, sports facilities, and counselling and referral services. To many Indians, including Pauline, this sounded like a better idea, but there was a fear that this would become a do-gooders' paradise instead of a centre run by Indians. Not so, said Grace Johnson. In a letter to various clubs and organizations she said, "It may interest you to know of the 7 Centres in Western Canada, 3 were formed by the efforts of Local Council of Women in the citys [sic] concerned and in no case, in no case, has the Council of Women in anyway run the centre. They have simply brought the financial and moral support of the women of the city concerned to the aid of the Indians who then manage and run their own Centre."[71]

On the basis of this statement, a Calgary Indian Friendship Society was formed, headed by Grace Johnson as interim president and Ruth Gorman in another official capacity. Pauline became interim treasurer of the group and gave it her full support. She even brought in a cheque for $3,000 from her friend Catherine Whyte of Banff. It was funny – or perhaps not so funny – when Pauline told these white women about the cheque. It was obvious that they were very self-satisfied at what they were doing for the Indians in what was clearly a "master-servant" relationship. The fact that one of the "servants" came up with one of the largest individual cheques of the campaign (other than government money) must have been unsettling. The women showed very little enthusiasm and left me with the impression that they almost resented Pauline for trespassing on "their" turf.

The women worked hard, and some of them, like Joyce Stewart, Pat Waite, and Vera Irving, were truly dedicated. They got money from both levels of government, found a fine old house on 4th Avenue SW, and got it ready for the opening. During all this time, Pauline and others fully expected that when the Indian Centre was ready, it would be turned over to an all-Indian board. However, in the summer of 1964 Mrs. Johnson presented documents regarding the incorporation of the society and the by-laws that would govern the organization. Pauline and I, as well as a number of Native leaders, were shocked. Rather than turning the Centre over to the Indians, the by-laws provided for an Indian staff but a Board of Directors made up of both Indians and non-Indians with no guarantee of an Indian majority nor that the president must be an Indian. When the question arose about making changes to these draft by-laws, those present were informed that they had already been submitted to the Alberta government and were now law. Provision also was made for the interim Board to remain in office for one year before the first election would be held. This meant that Grace Johnson would stay as interim president of the Board, with almost absolute power over the Centre. This was diametrically opposite to the promise she had made when the Centre was first conceived.

The official opening was held in October 1964 and we were all there, with Dad doing the official opening, along with Mayor Grant MacEwan. Pauline still hoped that Johnson's role would be temporary and that as soon as things settled down, she would leave gracefully. But it didn't happen. Lawrence Whitney, from the Sarcee Reserve, was named acting director but it was clear from the outset that he had little or no authority. Grace Johnson was at the Centre daily, completely running things. By the beginning of 1965, some of the others who had helped start the Centre were also having concerns about the way it was being run. The first to leave was Joyce Stewart, who resigned from the Board early in the year. Pauline became disturbed when she learned that Johnson was doing counselling work when she had absolutely no experience and was making decisions without consulting anyone. But the final straw came when, as treasurer, Pauline learned that Grace Johnson was billing the Centre for the cost of her babysitter. Pauline refused to sign the cheque for this expense and, instead, she resigned from the Board.

Matters might have ended right there as far as the Dempsey family was concerned. We now had five children, the twins being only fourteen months old and John still in diapers. Pauline had been planning to leave as soon as the Centre was up and running and in capable Indian hands but obviously this wasn't happening. Once she resigned, she decided that she would just leave it alone and let the Centre work out its own problems.

However, over the next few days Pauline was inundated with phone calls and messages, some from the ruling women wanting her to reconsider, and others from people like Tim Tyler and Pete Many Wounds who were disgusted with what was happening at the Centre. Then she received a visit from a representative of the Citizenship Branch of the federal government, the body that was partially funding the Centre. He urged her to do something to correct the situation and that if she could get enough Indians to support her, he would get the government to make an investigation. I was there when he made his presentation and it was very persuasive. He made it sound like a simple matter to make the request and then the Centre would be placed in the hands of the Indians to run.

A petition was drafted asking the two levels of government to investigate the Centre, particularly "domination by non-Indians, lack of constructive programming for Indian teenagers, and handling of funds," as well as to "examine constitution, methods of counselling, and an inability to cope with alcohol problems."[72] Over the next several days, Pauline and I travelled to all the reserves in southern Alberta while others helped to contact Indians living in the city. Within a matter of days some seventy-five signatures had been gained and Tim Tyler, from the Council of Community Services, advised on the best methods of proceeding. Meanwhile, Mrs. Johnson learned of the petition and launched a counteroffensive. The first we learned of it was when Ed Many Bears asked to have his name taken off the petition; Mrs. Johnson had contacted him and implied that his son's job at the Centre would be in jeopardy if his name was allowed to stand. Then there was a call from Les Tallow, who had been waylaid at the Centre by Mrs. Johnson and persuaded to have his name removed.

The petition was finally submitted to the Alberta minister L.C. Halmrast and federal minister Rene Tremblay, with every effort being made to keep the matter out of the press. However, Bill Wuttunee, a Cree lawyer in Calgary, heard about it and broke the story to *The Albertan* and the *Calgary Herald*, even though he had not been involved. Soon charges and counter-charges were echoing back and forth in the pages of daily newspapers. The first result of this was that the government man who had instigated the whole thing ran for cover like a frightened rabbit and was of no help at all. The second was that the ministers in Edmonton and Ottawa became cautious as the matter became a public football. Had it been kept out of the press, they probably would have proceeded quietly with an investigation but now this was not possible. It was easier for them to sit on the fence. The tower of strength to Pauline during this time was Tim Tyler, as well as people like Gerald Tailfeathers, Pete and Muriel Many Wounds, Leonard Crane, and Rufus Goodstriker.

About this time, the rumour reached me that someone had tried to contact Eric Harvie to get me fired. Harvie was in the Caribbean at the time so I submitted a long memo to John Slatter, Glenbow's president, outlining the whole situation and asking permission to proceed with helping Pauline. I was very gratified to receive word that as long as I didn't take any action in my capacity as an employee of Glenbow, I could do whatever I wanted.

In the end, the Alberta government decided not to act and the federal authorities limited themselves to an examination of the Centre's finances. This was perfect ammunition for Grace Johnson, as Pauline had been interim treasurer during this period. The implication was the Pauline was being investigated, not the Centre. To add to the problem, a few invoices had been mislaid (Pauline found them in her files two years later) and although no money was involved, it was used against her. By this time, the whole situation was becoming unreal. As I mention in my diary for February 19th, "We heard that the meeting called last night by Mrs. Johnson was a real vilification of the Dempseys & followers. We were accused of being jealous, anti-white, etc. and had deceived people into signing. We expected this so it was no surprise...." The only bright spot was that Mrs. Johnson called for a vote of confidence in her work and three Board members actually voted against her.

As time went along, more support came to Pauline. The Council of Community Services, Catholic Family Service, Anglican Diocesan Social Service Board, Calgary Native Friendship Club, and a number of individuals were behind her and as a result they formed the Calgary Indian Services Committee. But it was too late. The two levels of government had already committed themselves to the easy way out and were not about to change. Soon the subject slipped off the pages of the newspapers, and as I mentioned in my year-end summary, "The fight with the Indian centre was a failure and caused Pauline much grief and anguish." In the end Mrs. Johnson remained in complete control.

As for the Calumet Club, it went out with a whimper. As I wrote late in 1965, "In the evening Pauline went to the final function of the Calumet Club before it dissolves.... About 40 teenagers turned up, many of them drunk, and the evening was marked by fights, obnoxious drunks and rowdiness. If it hadn't been for the help of Wilton Goodstriker, Pauline might have had trouble on her hands. This sort of situation has arisen only since the advent of the Friendship (?) Centre."[73]

After Grace Johnson died, Pauline returned to the Board of the Centre as Recording Secretary for the 1970–71 term, and again from 1980 to 1986. By then, it was finally in Indian hands and carried on for another twenty years before folding.

The problems with white do-gooders were based on the fact that both Pauline and I shared the belief that Indians were fully capable of handling their own affairs and did not need to have white people running things. We agreed they were useful in an advisory capacity but only when and as needed by the Indians. I should add that I did not influence Pauline in this line of thinking, neither did I persuade her to take on Grace Johnson and her gang. She had her own strong feelings.

Pauline always had been busy with volunteer work. She had been a board member of the YWCA, vice-president of the Calgary Women's Progressive Conservative Association, member of the University of Calgary Senate, and a member of the Indian Events Committee at the Calgary Stampede. For her various activities she became the first recipient of the Chief David Crowchild Memorial Award, presented by the City of Calgary for the betterment of Indian-white relations. A plaque was placed in the lobby of City Hall, where it still resides today. In the following year she received the Alberta Achievement Award for her services to the province.

Dempsey considered family to be the most important part of his career. Left to right in 1965 are children James, Louise, John, Lois, and Leah, as well as "Duchess," Hugh, and Pauline. (Author's files)

In 1956 Dempsey became the first Archivist of the Glenbow Museum and established the procedures under which it still functions today. (Glenbow photo 265-8)

Eric Harvie, family, and friends visited the Blackfoot Reserve during Glenbow's excavation of the Earth Lodge Village site in 1960. Left to right are Archaeologist Richard G. Forbis, Donald S. Harvie, Mr. & Mrs. H. Gordon Love, Eric Harvie, Mrs. Don Harvie, Glenbow employee George H. Gooderham, and Hugh Dempsey. (Author's files)

As part of the Glenbow Foundation–Alberta Government agreement in 1966, Eric L. Harvie presents a cheque for $5 million to Mr. Justice N. D. McDermid, first chairman of the Glenbow-Alberta Institute's Board of Governors. The cheque was matched by the government. (Glenbow photo NA-4001-1)

When the first Native high school students were sent to Calgary, no plans had been made for their recreation so Pauline and Hugh Dempsey were among those who formed the Calumet Club, which had weekly meetings and dances. Here, in 1961, Nick Breaker is dancing with Pauline Bull Shields while in the back is Delphine Black Horse. (Author's files)

When Dempsey acquired a sacred Beaver Bundle from the Peigans in 1956, he asked his friend John Cotton to perform the ceremonies so that they could be recorded. Cotton is seen here in the Gladstone home with the bundle at his side. (Author photo)

During the Sun Dance on the Blackfoot Reserve in 1961, Dempsey arranged with Dick Brass to go through the ceremony of opening his medicine pipe bundle and to permit Glenbow to film it. Dempsey is seen here at the entrance to the lodge. (Glenbow photo R6-2)

In 1963, Emma Brass approached Dempsey about putting on the Ghost Dance ritual and letting Glenbow take still photographs of it. After an altar was made the ceremony commenced, and at one stage Dempsey was called forward to be painted and blessed. Seen here, ceremonialist Ed Axe performs the ritual while Dick Brass, one of the sponsors, sits nearby. (Glenbow photo 74-13)

One of the greatest honours of Dempsey's career was to be inducted as an honorary chief of the Blood tribe in 1967. Willie Scraping White performed an elaborate ritual which ended with him placing an eagle feather headdress on Dempsey's head. At this ceremony, Dempsey received the Blackfoot name of Potaina, or Flying Chief, the name of his wife's grandfather. In the background are other honorary chiefs, left to right, Hon. Arthur Laing, Minister of Northern Affairs, Dr. J. K. Mulloy, Indian agent Ralph D. Ragan, Chief Stephen Fox, and Albert Swinarton. (Author's files)

A visit to the Gladstone ranch could involve many diverse activities, including this jack-pot rodeo in 1955. Second left is Fred Gladstone while Pauline sits on the rail with her back to the camera. (Author photo)

It was 25 below zero in 1959 when Dempsey photographed cattle on the Gladstone ranch. (Author photo)

In 1971, Hugh Dempsey and his father-in-law, Senator James Gladstone, sign the register at the Old Time Range Men's Dinner at the Palliser Hotel in Calgary. (Author's files)

Duncan F. Cameron was appointed Executive Director of the Glenbow Museum in 1977. He is seen here a year later. (Glenbow photo NA-2864-30568)

Jim Many Bears of the Blackfoot Reserve gave prayers at the opening of *The Spirit Sings* exhibition in 1988. He is seen here with Dempsey, examining one of the displays.

# 8

# *Glenbow–Alberta Institute*

The early 1960s at Glenbow were a lot of fun, but with their own stresses and problems. If Eric Harvie chose – and he sometimes did – he could become involved in even the most minor decisions. When that happened, delays were interminable. This usually didn't affect me too much as far as collecting was concerned because most of the archival items were donated to us. But the poor Art Department sometimes had to wait for months for a decision to buy a painting. To make it worse, the object was often in our hands on approval and the owners were forced to be patient. It got to a point where some dealers refused to send the actual objects, but only photographs.

Also, the swinging doors for directors continued. Claude Humphreys, who had been supervising the collecting departments since 1960, was replaced in 1962 by G.B. Greene, who became Executive Director. I was sorry to see Claude go, as he was a thoughtful and considerate person, always weighing Harvie's demands against the Foundation's needs. Greene, on the other hand, was a retired colonel and everything had to go by the book. We usually got along pretty well as long as I followed the rules, but he wasn't a museum man. Then, in 1963, James Garner was hired as Technical Director, a term I never really understood. Thus we had a dual management situation lasted until early in 1964 when Greene finally resigned and later became a magistrate in Toronto.

Jim Garner was a different matter. He had a degree in anthropology and had reached a high degree of excellence in his knowledge of North American Indian artifacts. In some ways, he was like an avid amateur collector who had become a professional. He could identify objects as to tribe, date, and use, and was usually right. For example, one day a man came into Glenbow with a bone or ivory carving that was obviously bearing a Northwest Coast design. He had found this item half buried in the prairie sod on the Milk River Ridge in southern Alberta. We all wondered how a Northwest Coast item could have wandered so far from home, but when Garner looked at it, he identified it immediately. He said it had been among the items made in Japan in the 1930s and shipped to Canada for the tourist trade. And he was right.

Jim was married to a Sioux woman named Bea Medicine and they had one son, Ted. Our families became friendly and we visited back and forth quite frequently. Bea was a brilliant woman, very outspoken, and deeply immersed both in Sioux culture and in the role of Native women.

Jim was a great storyteller and could keep us enthralled for hours. Personally, I liked him very much. He impressed Harvie with his knowledge and knew how to get his attention. I don't know if it was deliberate or not, but he had a canny way of capitalizing on his boss's personal interests. For example, he became aware of the fact that Harvie liked to think big, so he went to him with ideas for buying entire Indian museums that were for sale in the United States. Harvie loved it. In his three years at Glenbow, Garner arranged to buy the Roe Indian Museum in Pipestone, Minnesota, the Sioux Indian Museum in Sioux Falls, South Dakota, and the Fort Cherokee Indian Museum in Oklahoma. From there, Garner promoted collections from other parts of the world. Some of us disagreed with this shotgun approach. Not only did it add to the workload but it got us far away from our original mandate. Until Garner arrived, the unwritten rule was that the staff collected Western Canadiana and Harvie collected whatever he wanted. As a result of this onslaught, there were rumblings that Harvie was finding the Foundation to be less of a pleasure and this gave rise to the rumour that he might give the whole thing away and we'd be out of our jobs.

I mentioned in my diary, "If this is true, we can thank Jim Garner for driving Glenbow into the ground. He has succeeded in talking ELH into the grandiose schemes of collecting in South America, Polynesia, etc., buying $100,000 collections left and right and in general making a mockery out of what was once a well organized program concentrated on western Canadian history."[74]

Things finally came to a head in 1966 when Garner made some demands on Glenbow and threatened to quit if he didn't get them. He thought he was irreplaceable, but much to his surprise, Harvie accepted his resignation and he was out. Later he joined up with a man named Crawford and they opened a primitive art store in Los Angeles. Apparently it didn't work out, for the next thing I heard he had become a schoolteacher. By then he had split with his wife and Bea went on to become one of the leading ethnologists in the United States.

Meanwhile, some interesting things were happening to me. In 1960, arrangements were made by the Provincial Secretary's Department for me to examine any Alberta government records that were destined for destruction to see if they should be saved. There were plans on the books for a Provincial Archives, so when I looked at material that I thought should be kept, I made a recommendation and the items were supposed to be boxed and stored. Whether they were or not, I don't know, but I did recommend saving a whole range of collections in the early 1960s, including the Social Credit Board papers; some case files under William Aberhart's controversial Debt Reduction Act; early files relating to engineers' licences; and dozens of other departmental records. I also suggested keeping a massive file of questionnaires that had been filled out by people who came to Alberta prior to 1905 and were applying for pioneer scrolls; this was part of an Alberta Golden Jubilee project in 1955.

In 1962, Ray Harrison was commissioned by the Alberta government to design a Provincial Museum and Archives building. He came to see me and we worked together informally for a couple of years. Then, in 1964, the Provincial Secretary, Ambrose Holowach, officially asked Eric Harvie for my "services in a consulting capacity to assist our Museum Consultant."[75] When Harvie agreed, I suggested that I provide guidance along five lines: design of the building, conducting a survey of existing government records, establishing initial cataloguing procedures, recommending archival displays, and procedures for handling the Ernest Brown photo collection.[76] In the end, they opted for only the first suggestion and for job descriptions for various staff positions. We held a series of meetings over the next few months, both with Harrison and me, and sometimes with the architects.

I don't recall too many of the details but I do know that I made three major recommendations. The first was that the archives be in a separate building quite distinct from the museum; I believe that consideration had previously been given to providing the archives only with a floor in the museum itself. Anyway, they got a separate facility. The second was that the building be designed structurally so that it could expand upwards. I don't think I had any success with that one. The third was that the senior position be called the Provincial Archivist. I immediately ran into trouble with the Public Service Commission, which said that the Alberta government was discouraging the use of the word "Provincial" in its title designations, and suggested we find something else. I demonstrated that almost every other province in Canada used "Provincial Archivist" and that Alberta would be out of step if it used anything else. I won that one, too.

One of the results of this collaboration was that in the spring of 1964, Ambrose Holowach offered me the position of Provincial Archivist while the building was still in the construction stage. After careful consideration I turned it down for a number of reasons, including the fact that the pay was far below what I was getting at Glenbow and that the archivist reported to the Director of the Provincial Museum. Ultimately I think Hugh Taylor got the job.

Another flattering incident occurred a couple of years later when I was offered the position of Director of the Montana Historical Society in Helena. I received the request from Merrill Burlingame and felt very complimented. But we had two sons and I had visions of raising them in the United States and then having to send them to one of the wars that the Americans always seemed to be fighting. Besides, I was too much of a Canadian nationalist to seriously consider the offer.

Early in January 1966, Doug Light passed along the rumour that Eric Harvie was going to give Glenbow to the Alberta government. The information wasn't entirely accurate, but it was near enough. Doug was very close to the Harvie people and a great one for picking up information. A month later, Neil Harvie called all the department heads together and made the news official. He informed us that the Harvie family was turning Glenbow over to the people of Alberta. This would be accomplished by the creation of a Glenbow-Alberta Institute Act. The shares of the Glenbow Foundation, plus $5 million, would be given to the Institute by the Harvie family and $5 million from the Alberta government, together with an annual grant of $100,000. The Institute would be run by a Board of Governors, the chairman appointed by the government, three members each by the government and the Harvie family, and three named by the Institute. The Hon. N. Douglas McDermid, justice of the appellate division of the Supreme Court of Alberta, was to be the first Chairman of the Board, appointed for five years. Doug was a former law partner of Eric Harvie, and when he went into business for himself he represented the Harvie interests. He had been appointed to the Supreme Court in 1963.

The Act was passed on April 15, 1966, at which time I noted in my diary that the "Glenbow Foundation no longer exists."[77] I was wrong, for the Foundation remained a legal entity and became the wholly owned subsidiary of the Institute. Its continued existence became a source of real problems. The Act provided that the Board of Governors of the Institute appoint a board of directors of the Foundation. I suspect that in deference to Eric Harvie, the

Board let him choose his own directors, thinking that this was a mere legal formality. In fact, the Foundation still controlled the collections, as well as the Glenbow Art Gallery, and all the employees. Harvie named himself as Chairman of the Foundation's Board, Hod Meech as President, Jim Fish as Comptroller, and Hugh Robinson as Treasurer. These were all on Harvie's staff. In addition, Meech became President of the Institute and Jim Fish the Treasurer.

Generally speaking, Harvie's people were a nice bunch. I liked Hugh Robinson the best; he was always approachable and forthright. Jim Fish was next. He had an excellent mind and was friendly and hospitable. As for Meech, his name was Horace Meech but everyone called him Hod. He was a highly intelligent man from Lethbridge who had been in Harvie's oil business for years. He was president of Managers Limited, the holding company that Harvie had established to run his various oil, mineral, and financial institutions. It was obvious that he was utterly devoted to his boss. At first I got along well with him, probably because as archivist I was in a position of no authority and Harvie was generally pleased with my work. As time went on, however, I crossed swords with Meech quite a few times and found him to be a very tough-minded individual. I also noticed that when Harvie was away for a few months in winter, Meech softened noticeably and became a very reasonable and approachable person. I guess that's because he was out from under the daily unpredictable onslaughts from his boss. But as soon as Harvie returned, Meech reverted to the role of a tough administrator.

He was very astute in giving directives, as one could never be sure if they came from Harvie or if they were his own idea. One time I said aloud, "There is no Hod Meech; he is only a figment of Eric Harvie's imagination." Unfortunately, this comment got back to Meech so it didn't improve our relations.

I should mention that a few noticeable changes were taking place in Eric Harvie by this time. Perhaps it was the first stages of the heart problems that later engulfed him before his death in 1975, but whatever it was, his unpredictable behaviour became much more pronounced as the years passed. It must have been difficult for those taking orders directly from him, for he could go from black to white without any apparent rhyme or reason. And as he was the Honorary President of the new Institute and Chairman of the Foundation, and with Hod Meech on the boards of both the Institute and the Foundation, it turned out that Harvie had just as much power as he had when he owned the place.

Here I must explain my philosophy regarding Eric Harvie. During all the years I worked for him at the Glenbow Foundation, I was always faithful to his trust. If he planned to do something with which I disagreed, I expressed my opinion, but once the decision was made, I carried it out honourably and to the best of my ability. I considered Harvie to be my boss and the man whom I admired and to whom I owned my allegiance. I was also very aware of the fact that he had given me my big chance in my career. However, once the Glenbow-Alberta Institute was formed, its Board of Governors became my new superiors, and I owed my allegiance to them. I still respected Harvie but if it came to a matter of choosing between him and the Board, I had no recourse but to choose the Board. It was sad in a way and sometimes placed me in an awkward position, but it was the only way that I could act in a responsible and honourable manner.

At the time the Institute was created, we still had a divided authority, with Jim Garner as Technical Director and Charlie Masur as Administrator, but with no overall director. In the summer of 1966, I told Meech that I was interested in the position of Executive Director, which would become the senior person at the new Institute. I learned shortly thereafter that Eric Harvie thought I should stay in the Archives while Meech thought I was too young (at thirty-six) for the job. I left it at that, but I learned later that Bill Fleming in our Pioneer & Agricultural Department, Doug Light in Ethnology, and Pat McCloy in the Library all went to Meech to speak in my favour. Dick Forbis also told me that the university people were pressing for my appointment.

It soon became clear that Eric Harvie wanted a "big name" to head the Institute. The first indication of this came in September 1966 when Mitchell A. Wilder, Director of the Amon Carter Museum of Western Art, in Fort Worth, Texas, was invited to evaluate the effectiveness of Glenbow and to make recommendations on its future. After his tour, he was highly critical of the way Glenbow was being organized and run from the top down, but he did tell our Librarian, "If there are any two operations in the entire organization which receive unanimous approval, they are yours and Hugh Dempsey's."[78] When Wilder was offered the position of Executive Director, he was quick to turn it down. He was followed in the new year by George McBeath, Director of the New Brunswick Provincial Museum, who also turned it down.

While this was going on, Glenbow was apparently grooming me for something, for in January 1967 they sent me to the Amon Carter museum to look over their organizational structure, finances, programs, etc., and a month later I was sent to New York to study the Museum of the American Indian and the American Museum of Natural History. From there I went to Washington to study the methods used by the Smithsonian Institution. In all, I was gone for almost four weeks and filled notebooks full of data on just about every aspect of museum management. But there was no job offer waiting for me on my return.

I had pretty well given up on the idea of promotion when on April 20, 1967 I was called to a meeting in Eric Harvie's office. Others there were Hod Meech and Harry Chritchley. Harvie told me that I had been appointed Acting Executive Director of the Institute while Harry became Business Manager. We were both transferred from the authority of the Glenbow Foundation to that of being employees of the Glenbow-Alberta Institute. Maybe it was only in an "acting" capacity and lasted for only a short time, but I still had the honour of being the Institute's first Executive Director. As I mentioned in my diary, "I had expected that the Board of Governors would be in control by this time, but it is obvious that Mr. Harvie is the only boss. As a result, things are going to be a lot tougher than I thought."[79]

Immediately after the meeting, I settled down with Harry to plan a new organizational structure, based in part on what I had learned in my travels, as well from the experience at Glenbow in finding out the hard way what works and what doesn't. A short time later, I moved into the Administration Building and arranged for Sheilagh Jameson to be appointed archivist in my stead. Once we had something to work with, I had a meeting with the Executive Committee of the Institute and it soon became clear there were two entirely different agendas on the table. On one hand, Eric Harvie, as represented by Hod Meech, wanted the Institute and Foundation set up in such a way that he could retain full control. On the other side, some members of the Board of Governors, represented by Doug McDermid and Benton Mackid, wanted a clear chain of command that led straight to the Board.

The situation then became so fluid that it was hard to keep up with it. It appeared that Harvie and the Board were jockeying for position and I was caught in the middle. I think Meech and the others knew by this time that my allegiance was now with the Board. Early in May, I was informed that my title had been changed to Acting Technical Director and that Harry Chritchley had been moved over to Eric Harvie's new organization, the Riveredge Foundation. I was also informed that Dr. Jack Collett, the former principal of Mount Royal College, had been appointed Bursar of the Institute, a title that was changed a few weeks later to Director of Extension. It was apparent that they were still going to look for a "name" for the position of Executive

Director. The next candidates to come to town were Trevor Walden, Director of the Leicester Museums in England, followed by Don Crowdis, President of the Canadian Museums Association. The first was appalled by what he saw and rejected the offer, while Crowdis was not considered appropriate for the position.

Jack Collett proved to be a fine person to work with but he lasted only four months until September, when he resigned in disgust over the ongoing battle between the Board and Eric Harvie. Pat Thomson replaced him as Bursar so I was left in the only senior position at Glenbow. By this time the situation was so unsettled that when the position of Provincial Archivist became vacant again in Edmonton, I actually applied for it. Anything seemed better than the chaos at Glenbow, but when I went for my interview and was offered the job, I turned it down. I just didn't want to leave Glenbow, regardless of its problems.

For the rest of 1967 I did my best to put our house in order. I worked with Thomson in writing job descriptions and specifications, smoothing out organizational charts, working on accessioning and cataloguing procedures, setting up regular staff meetings, and visiting departments whenever possible. I was still firmly under the thumb of Hod Meech but I did as much as I could within these limitations. I managed to hire Lorne Render, fresh out of the museum program at Williamsburg, Virginia, to head up the art program, and Wes Mattie from Edmonton to look after our Cultural History Department. Then, in the topsy-turvy life of Glenbow, I was called into a meeting on December 8th with Doug McDermid, Hod Meech, and Benton Mackid, and told that the Board had approved my permanent appointment as Technical Director. As I mentioned in my diary, "Also, they implied Hod would be pulling out & leaving me to deal directly with the B of G. It took me completely by surprise."[80]

For a while, this appointment seemed to clear the air, and I had hopes that at last we were out of the woods. I launched a little semi-monthly magazine called *Glenbow*, started a lecture series at the museum, and set up a series of weekly meetings at which time department heads explained their operations to the Board of Governors. During the early months of 1968 I was looking after everything from budgets to programs, and working well both with department heads and with the Board of Governors. At Meech's suggestion, I even wrote to Eric Harvie in the West Indies, telling him what was going on and at one point I said, "I'm still not sure just how much authority has been left in my hands, but I just keep sticking my neck out a little more each time and hope nobody cuts it off."[81]

As it turned out, the independence didn't last for long. In February 1968 I was told that in future I had to report to the Executive Committee instead of the Board; Hod Meech was Chairman of the Executive Committee. A short time later I was told to get approval on all financial matters from Jim Fish, Treasurer of the Institute and of Harvie's own organization. This put us right back to where we were months earlier. Then in June, the day before I left for a meeting of the Canadian Museums Association in Quebec, I was introduced to a man named Richard L. Gordon, and was told he was a candidate for Executive Director. By the time I got back to Calgary, he had already accepted the position. Dick Gordon had been a Rhodes Scholar and was headmaster of St. John's-Ravenscourt School for Boys in Winnipeg. Doug McDermid was on their board and he was the one who interviewed Dick and arranged for him to be hired.

When I learned that this was a Board appointment, rather than a Harvie one, I was a little more optimistic. Actually, I was ambivalent about not getting the job myself, as I knew that the war was still on and that the Executive Director would be a visible target. However, Gordon would not be starting until the beginning of 1969 so that left me with the whole can of worms for the next seven months.

At that time I was already committed to attending the six-week Seminar for Historical Administrators in Williamsburg, Virginia. It was an intensive and useful course and I met some very fine people from all across the continent. At one stage, students with any actual experience in museums (about a third of the class) were asked to describe the structure of the organization with which they were currently associated. This was to help determine which was more effective: a weak Board and strong Director, a strong Board and a weak Director, a weak Board and weak Director, or a strong Board and a strong Director. When I outlined the situation at Glenbow, the instructor simply shook his head and said ours was an impossible situation with no solution, and the only answer was for everyone involved to resign. The course was a good one and I came back with quite a few ideas that were later incorporated into Glenbow's programs. One of these was a series of school kits where artifacts were placed in suitcases together with teaching aids and loaned to schools. I designed some of these in 1975 and they became a successful part of our outreach program.

Pauline came to Williamsburg for the last several days of the session and then we spent a short time in New York. There we took in one of the first performances of "Hair," the stage production, and Pauline was more than a little perturbed about the one nude scene. We also had a good chance to see the bright lights and the attractions of the Big Apple.

By the time we got back, Glenbow was well into the 1968 summer holiday season and so I took my holidays as well. It was September before I stepped back into my office, and when I did so, I saw the changes that had taken place. It had been previously agreed that Glenbow would sell its natural history collection to the new Riveredge Foundation for $25,000. This money would be used for paying part of the costs of a new $55,000 Glenbow Art Galley, with the rest coming from the Institute's budget. Harvie decided to personally call the shots for the entire gallery, including its design and installation.

Here is what I say as the project progressed: "We had a meeting with Meech, Render, Debnam [our building supervisor], Bill Robertson [of Managers Limited], and I. It turned out to be a knock down drag out battle with Meech unwilling to make any commitments and demanding that interior partitions, if needed at all, could be built in a 'temporary' manner [even though there was] no money was available for this. He also said that he was not prepared to accept any internal floor plan until the renovations were completed – even when it was explained that we had to know so that exhibits could be selected, catalogues written, and plans made for the opening."[82] Later on, Meech told me that he was designing the art gallery as he went along.

Another idea that came from the Harvie people was to buy three huge trailers that had been used by the federal government during Canada's centennial in 1967 and turn them into travelling museums. I thought it was a good idea, although I favoured getting our own exhibitions in shape before we tackled such a major extension service. But I wasn't asked.

Then there was the problem of the Luxton Museum at Banff. When the Act was passed, this facility had remained with one of Harvie's other companies, Luxton Museum Ltd., and was not included in the deal. In the autumn of 1968 the Harvie people offered to sell the museum to the Institute for $165,000, which was said to be its book value, and to return $65,000 of it as a gift which would be spent under their direction. No one asked my opinion but as I wrote at the time, "Luxton is a simple static tourist attraction which offers nothing in the way of education service or scholarship. I would have suggested we get out of it & loan artifacts to Luxton Museum Ltd. so they can run the museum."[83] But Harvie offered only two alternatives: the Institute buy the building or sell the Luxton Indian collection to Luxton Museum Ltd. In the end he got his way. It wasn't until many years later that Glenbow got rid of this millstone and turned it over to a private agency.

When I spoke frankly to Doug McDermid about the many problems at Glenbow, arising mostly out of Eric Harvie's decisions, he was just as frank with me. He knew what was going on but he pointed out that no one wanted to confront Eric Harvie because, after all, it was his gift that made all this possible. Moreover, Doug had assurances from Meech that this was just temporary and as soon as Dick Gordon arrived on the scene, Meech and the Harvie people would pull out. He said that at the time of the appointment, there was a clear understanding that Gordon would report only to the Board and would be free of interference from the Harvie group. As McDermid later said,

> At this time, the executive management of Glenbow Foundation was performed by Managers Limited, a management company owned by Mr. Harvie, for a fee of $4,000 per month. The chief officer of Managers Limited under Mr. Harvie was Mr. Meech. Mr. Harvie stated he was anxious that Managers Limited be relieved of its managerial responsibilities as soon as possible and that Mr. Meech, who was extremely busy, be relieved of any responsibilities for the conduct of the affairs of the Institute, except those he had as a Governor.[84]

Dick Gordon arrived for work on January 27, 1969, and for a while Glenbow felt like a different place. I liked Dick immediately, both for his candour and forthright manner. For example, he told me he had left St. Johns-Ravenscourt because he had done all he could do and now he wanted to give someone else a chance. He was that kind of person. As soon as he was in office, he informed me that I would continue in my role as Technical Director.

Dick had been assured by Doug McDermid that he had a free hand and he took him at his word. Within days of his arrival, he said he wanted to boost staff morale, so he cancelled the nominal charge being made for coffee and announced that parking in the lot beside the Administration Building would be free, rather than a charge being made as was previously announced. We learned later that this immediately annoyed the Harvie people and started things off on the wrong foot. But Dick was not swayed as he knew he had the support of his Chairman of the Board. As promised, the financial administration was turned over to us, and the reporting structure was changed so that Dick reported directly to the Chairman.

While Dick was receiving support from Doug McDermid, none of us knew that the Chairman of the Board was having his own problems with Eric Harvie. It all started when the Institute was formed and had $10 million from the Harvie family and the government to invest. At one of the Institute's first meetings, Canada Trust was instructed that the funds be invested in short-term securities such as common shares and real estate. While the matter was being considered, McDermid had to go into hospital for an operation and when he returned early in 1967 he learned that the money had been invested in long-term bonds. These brought in a low rate of return at a time when common stocks were performing well. When McDermid looked into it, he found that Harvie had called a meeting of his own people, Meech and Fish, and they approved the investment. McDermid wanted to take legal action against Canada Trust but dropped the matter because of Harvie's involvement.

He then got into a dispute with Harvie over the Glenbow Art Gallery. Instead of using Institute money, McDermid suggested a fundraising campaign, and even found a prominent Calgarian who agreed to head the drive. But, as McDermid wrote, "When I suggested the matter to Mr. Harvie, his reaction was that I was trying to tell him how to spend his money. In view of his reaction, I abandoned the idea and never did raise the question with the Governors."[85]

There undoubtedly were other disputes, all seeming to centre around who was running Glenbow – Eric Harvie or the Board of Governors. However, McDermid was so preoccupied with his own problems that he tended to leave Dick on his own, or at least made no attempt to intercede and further strain his relations with Harvie. By the summer of 1969, a frustrated McDermid told his fellow Board member, Benton Mackid, that he was thinking of resigning. Benton was a good friend of mine, past president of our local Historical Society. While begging McDermid not to leave, Mackid admitted that Harvie "intends to play a more dominant part in the affairs of Glenbow Foundation from here on in."[86] He went on to say that Harvie planned to operate the Glenbow Foundation himself in his role of Chairman and to establish committees in the fields of art, museums, public relations, finance, and education, that would report directly to him.

Rather than backing down, McDermid tried to take some direct action to clarify Dick Gordon's role and to place him back squarely under the Chairman of the Board. McDermid told a meeting of the Executive Committee on October 2nd that he planned to remove all non-corporate responsibilities from the Foundation and to centralize them under the Institute. This would remove

Harvie's people from all aspects of the day-to-day operations. Harvie, in his capacity as Chairman of the Glenbow Foundation, responded four days later with a scathing letter that was hand-delivered to McDermid. In it he complained of his "difficulty getting from the Institute and staff the co-operation and information required to effectively carry out the Foundation's obligations."[87] This was a direct slap at Dick Gordon. He also said that McDermid's proposal was "in direct violation of the Resolutions of the Governors passed in September 1968 and April 1969"[88] and demanded that the Chairman "immediately give the necessary instruction to rectify the situation and advise me that you have done so in such detail that will inform me of the exact situation."[89] Instead of replying, McDermid went to Edmonton a few days later to offer his resignation to the Alberta government.

In pondering the situation some years later, McDermid wrote,

> I considered Mr. Gordon was doing a competent job, although Mr. Harvie had criticized several things he had done, mainly because he thought he was relegating to himself matters which Mr. Harvie thought should have been referred to the Board of Governors. In the fall of 1969, it was apparent to me that I was not successful, but to the contrary, was antagonizing Mr. Harvie.

> In considering my position, it was evident to me that it was necessary that Mr. Harvie be satisfied with the administration of the Institute. The idea for the Glenbow-Alberta Institute had originated with Mr. Harvie; he was the founder and had given half of the seed money and invaluable collections of artifacts; many of these collections were native to Alberta and would have been lost if it had not been for him... However, I was in the position that I would lose the respect of and credibility with the staff and Mr. Gordon if I could not convince Mr. Harvie to discontinue the interference of his organization in the internal administration of the Institute and Foundation."[90]

Neither Dick Gordon nor I knew that all this was going on but Gordon said he himself had "been subjected to almost continuous harassment and interference in the form of meddling in staff affairs, rude memos and criticisms."[91] The whole debacle of 1969 reached its conclusion on November 7th — my fortieth birthday – when Benton Mackid met Dick Gordon on the street and told him that Doug McDermid had been removed as Chairman of the Board and had been replaced by Jim Mahaffy. Dick was absolutely flabbergasted, as he had spoken to Doug only that morning and the subject was never mentioned. Because of the great admiration he had for McDermid, he could only conclude that the Harvie people had gone to the provincial government and got him fired. It was only later that we found out that he had voluntarily resigned. His resignation had sat in Edmonton for quite a while until a successor was chosen and an order-in-council passed. We knew nothing of this.

The great mystery is why McDermid didn't confide in Gordon as soon as he had resigned or why he never mentioned it to him when they met. I know they were great friends and McDermid felt very responsible for bringing Dick to Calgary. At this time I wrote in my diary, "Certainly if Doug goes Dick will not be far behind, for Harvie and Meech ... have said they are out to 'get' him at any cost. His crime is assuming full control of the administrative function, and turning down Harvie on such things as letting him pick what goes into the Art Gallery, letting him work over our art publications before sending them to the printers, etc. Most of the problems are so infantile that Dick still cannot understand why anyone would consider them important."[92]

The next several days were ones of waiting for the next shoe to drop. The place was filled with rumours, some of them untrue or distorted. Dick Gordon "officially" heard about the changeover when Meech phoned our Business Manager, Allan Hammond, and gave him the news. No one ever did inform him directly. I mentioned in my diary for November 12th that by that time "all contact between Dick Gordon and his superiors has ceased entirely," and this was true. It was almost as if he was in isolation, and I spent many hours in his office as he fretted and worried about his future.

At that point I had a telephone call from Jack Herbert, who was now Director of the Manitoba Museum of Man and Nature, saying that his Assistant Director had resigned and wanted to know if I was interested in the job. Under the circumstances it would have been foolish of me not to consider it, so I agreed to travel to Winnipeg for an interview. I spent the entire day going through their museum and was very impressed with what I saw. But in the end I turned down the position because it was too far from the Blackfoot and besides, I remembered the Manitoba winters from my previous visits. But considering the situation at Glenbow, it was a hard decision for me to make.

When I returned after the weekend, I made this notation on the following Monday: "This was a tense and unsettling day as we waited for the Board of Governors meeting tomorrow. Dick Gordon cannot learn what is on the agenda, even though it is usually prepared by us. The whole organization is full of rumours and work is at a standstill as all wait for the next move. There was even a rumour that Dick Gordon, Allan Hammond & I would all be fired tomorrow for opposing Eric Harvie."[93]

Dick attended the meeting on the following day and saw the worst. Resolutions were passed that arranged for Glenbow to provide consultation and technical service to Riveredge, and plans were approved for Ace Caravan Company to take over our travelling museum. These were both major moves that Dick Gordon and Doug McDermid had opposed. Two days later, Gordon submitted his resignation and the whole ugly episode was over. Dick left town after a few weeks and I never saw him again. In his retirement years he turned to writing, producing the novel *The River Gets Wider* in 1974. He died five years later.

Now that is the story as I saw it. Later, Meech and others expressed amazement that Dick had resigned and said the vendetta against him had been only in his imagination. They said he had become paranoid and had seen things that really weren't there. They were so convincing that for a time I believed them, but as time went on, I looked at all the indisputable facts – the almost daily interference in administrative matters, the anger at being denied the Riveredge and Ace deals, the comments by Mackid that Harvie was getting back into running things – and I came to the conclusion that it wasn't anyone's imagination. But I think it's true that Dick's resignation came as a surprise. With McDermid forced out (for that's what it was), I'm sure they believed that Dick would become more pliable and subject to their control. His resignation immediately after McDermid was an embarrassment and made the Harvie people look bad in the eyes of the government.

Strangely enough, Dick accomplished in leaving what he could not do while he was there. He had created a situation that forced the Harvie people to pull back and actually give the Glenbow administration a chance to do its job. It was just a tragedy that it couldn't have happened earlier and without the discord.

About a week after Dick's resignation, our new President, Bert Baker, returned from a holiday in the United States and learned for the first time what was going on. He called a meeting of the staff on December 9th and announced that I had been appointed Acting Executive Director. I also had a private meeting with Baker and Mahaffy and they asked me if I wanted to apply for the permanent position of Executive Director. I thanked them for their consideration but turned it down. I felt that the lifespan of directors at Glenbow was too short. It was strange, but two years earlier I had been actively seeking the appointment, but now after this protracted power struggle I wouldn't have accepted it if it had been offered to me on a platter. I decided that I wanted to get out of full-time administration and devote as much time to public programming and research as possible.

Over the next few weeks I proceeded to carve a niche for myself. Bert Baker brought in Gordon Chandler to help us to reorganize the staff structure and I formed a committee of Chandler, Allan Hammond, and me to study the matter. Then I set up a budget committee consisting of Hammond, Sheilagh Jameson, and me to interview department heads and strike a budget for next year. I also set in motion actions to tackle other work that had remained in suspension during the previous months. In these first few weeks, Meech and others were entirely absent from the scene and we received absolutely no direct communications from them. I didn't know who was responsible for this, but I took full advantage of it in setting up the new structure.

I began attending the Executive and Board meetings, and held regular discussions with Bert Baker, whom I found to be a very pleasant and understanding person. Early in March, our committee came up with a new organizational chart which gave us an Executive Director, and divided Glenbow into three divisions. One was the History Division, of which I would be the Director. This would include the Library, Archives, and Extension departments. Then there was an Art Division, with Lorne Render as Director and consisting of the Art Department, Art Gallery, Display Department, and Glenbow Museum. The third was the Museum Division, with Doug Light in charge of Cultural History, Ethnology, Mineralogy, and Luxton Museum.

Bert Baker and I privately discussed the position of Executive Director. Again he offered it to me, and again I refused. We talked about going outside to find a suitable candidate but we had to face the reality that Glenbow's reputation was so bad in the museum field (everyone knew about the Dick Gordon debacle) that no professional person would apply. We finally concluded that the best candidate was Allan Hammond, our Business Manager.

Hammond had been an accountant at St. John's-Ravenscourt School under some deal that included the tuition of his boys. Dick Gordon had brought him to Calgary and although he was not a museum person he expressed a strong interest in the promotion. I didn't have any feelings about it one way or the other, except that I felt I could easily work with him. So the recommendation was made that he be the new Executive Director.

Bert Baker and I made a presentation to the Board late in April 1970, outlining the new staff reorganization, improved fringe benefits for the staff, new job descriptions, and pay increases. The only change made by the Board was that Hammond was to be appointed Executive Vice-President instead of Executive Director. This became effective on June 9th, at which time I wrote in my diary, "This is something I've been working towards for months. I'll admit it was a bit of a wrench to no longer head the organization but it just isn't my field. Besides, the mortality rate of Directors (or Vice-Presidents) is too high for me to want to fill that uneasy post. That is why I turned it down." So ended my second stint as head of Glenbow, this one having lasted for five months.

Now this is not intended to be a history of Glenbow. I have gone into great detail about the late 1960s because it had such an impact on me, both at the time and in the later directions of my career. Had Eric Harvie actually pulled out and left us to our own resources, I might have stayed in the senior role. But in retrospect I'm glad I didn't, for I had a much more rewarding career doing creative things, rather than simply pushing paper and bossing people around.

───── ∞ ─────

My life in the late 1960s wasn't all Glenbow-oriented. In fact, Pauline used to marvel at the way I could compartmentalize my life. I could have been facing the most horrendous problems at Glenbow during the day, but on the way home these slid off my back and by the time I parked the car I was thinking about family and domestic matters. I seldom, if ever, talked to Pauline about these daily problems unless she asked, for they were simply forgotten once I was in the door. On the other hand, my body was slower to forget. I first began to suffer from stomach cramps in the spring of 1967 while Acting Technical Director and they were soon diagnosed as stress-related. At times it was not unusual for me to come home with a king-sized lump in my stomach, and I would stretch out on the floor for about half an hour before it would disappear.

During the 1960s, we slipped into a nice, comfortable family situation. We now had five children, each with their own personalities and needs. The boys were into Cubs and hockey, while the girls paired up with their best friends and were often down at the playground. Dad and Mom were back and forth all the time, and one or more of our children often accompanied them to the Blood Reserve, especially on holidays. But Pauline wasn't entirely a home body. She was a board member of the YWCA, active in the local Progressive Conservative Association, and worked as an admitting clerk at the Grace Hospital for a couple of years.

Although my only foray into book publishing in the 1950s had been a failure, I was still actively interested in writing. Pauline called it my *grand passion*, and I suppose she was right. I know I was never far away from writing and publishing for very long during my entire career. And if I couldn't write books, at least I could do shorter articles for magazines and newspapers. Besides the *Alberta Historical Review*, I wrote for such publications as *Plains Anthropologist*, *Montana Magazine of History*, and the *Calgary Herald*. I also did a few specialty things, like a chapter for the book *The Lost Lemon Mine*, in 1960; an introduction to the book *The Nose Creek Story*, in 1961; an introduction to a reprint of Jim MacGregor's fine book, *North-West of Sixteen*, in 1968; and a chapter in the book *Masterpieces of Indian and Eskimo Art from Canada*, published by the Musée de l'Homme, Paris, in 1969.

I also launched Glenbow's publishing program in 1965 with the booklet *A Blackfoot Winter Count*, followed a year later with *Jerry Potts, Plainsman*. Then in 1968 I wrote *Blackfoot Ghost Dance* and in 1969, *Indian Names for Alberta Communities*. These were all twenty to thirty pages long and remained in print right through to the end of the century. They were joined by others as time went along, the most notable being the book *Indian Tribes of Alberta*, which was a compilation of articles I had written for *Glenbow* magazine in the 1960s and 1970s. The first edition came out in 1979 and went through at least ten editions and many updates.

Also, a labour of love for me was writing short articles for the *Sun Dance Echo*, a small hand-produced one-man newspaper created by Reggie Black Plume from the Blood Reserve. During its lifespan from 1964 to 1966 I contributed numerous articles, some appearing under my byline, but most of them not. This wasn't because I was shy, but it was just that Reggie kept forgetting to put my name on them. When the paper died, it was replaced in 1968 by the *Kainai News*, a much more professional newspaper that had some decent financing. I contributed to their pages over the years until it finally ceased publication in 1992. By that time, I had been named a gold card member and was given a lifetime membership in their parent group, Indian News Media.

During my involvement with *Kainai News*, I became good friends with Everett Soop, who was a cousin of Pauline's. If I have this right, Everett's grandfather, John Healy, was a brother of Pauline's mother, Janie. In the kind of extended family situation that exists on the Blood Reserve, it means that the two of us were more-or-less relatives. I don't know about him, but I was proud to have Everett as my cousin. I had known him since he was a teenager and from the time he was first diagnosed with muscular dystrophy. His interest was in art and mine was in writing, so we got along very well together as we shared our creative interests.

In his drinking days, Everett and I used to have a friendly insulting relationship, which was part of traditional family practice. He would insult my inaccurate histories of the Bloods and I would insult his rotten writing and miserable disposition. After he stopped drinking, we both seemed to mellow somewhat and he just insulted me for ripping off the Indians by working for a museum while I could only point out that he was still a miserable person who was impossible to get along with. Both of us seem to be refreshed by our friendly dialogue and long discussions on such wide-ranging topics as reserve politics and the state of Indian art.

Everett was educated at St. Paul's Residential School and completed his secondary education at an integrated school in Cardston. During his school years, while his brothers and friends seemed to focus their attention on rodeo and hockey, Everett liked to read poetry, listen to fine music, and become acquainted with classical literature. After he graduated from high school Everett went to the Alberta College of Art in Calgary and a number of other institutions where he studied art and journalism. Coincidentally, he came back to the reserve just as the *Kainai News* was starting and was hired on staff. I remember his first cartoon, entitled "Me and My Shadow," which appeared on July 15, 1968. It showed a puzzled Indian whose shadow was cast in the shape of a Mounted Policeman. This was a not-so-subtle poke at the police for the way that they were dogging the Indians at pow-wows and other gatherings.

Within a short time, Everett was doing four or five cartoons an issue, poking fun at his own people as often as the government and white society. One cartoon showed an Indian in a downpour at the Sun Dance saying, "You t'ink maybe we did somet'ing wrong?" Another showed a hippie saying, "God is dead," and an Indian answering, "Sometimes ah thinks Great Spirit is very ill too."

His writing in the newspaper at first was sporadic, then in 1976 he began to write a regular column entitled "Gitskenip," meaning, "You know." Like his cartoons, these columns presented in the printed word the same kind of message he was offering in his political cartoons. There were no sacred cows; the tribal council, Sun Dance, Native culture, and Indian religion were treated just as irreverently as federal politicians, local bureaucrats, and avaricious businessmen.

So great was Soop's popularity that in 1979, the best of his cartoons were reprinted in a booklet, *Soop Take a Bow*, and I was honoured when asked to write the introduction and to help put it together. Shortly after that, Everett was elected to the tribal council, served two terms, and never went back to writing. By then his muscular dystrophy had sent him from a cane to crutches to a wheelchair and he began devoting his time to the disabled.

I always considered Everett to be a true genius, so in 1990 I convinced him to let me edit a number of articles for publication. Before this, he would never let anyone touch his work but I knew that he trusted me completely. He approved the end result and we published the book at Glenbow as *I See My Tribe Is Still Behind Me*. This title relates to one of his cartoons that shows an Indian chief with arrows sticking out of his back.

In the professional field, I joined the Canadian Historical Association's Archives Section, serving as its vice-chairman in 1961 and 1962, and chairman during the next two years. I resigned from that position to start a magazine called *Canadian Archivist*. It was a one-man effort that lasted until 1967, when I was promoted out of the archives field and no successor to edit the magazine could be found. I also wrote two pamphlets for the Archives Section – *Survey of Archivists' Positions in Canada*, and *Genealogical Services of Canadian Archives*, both published in 1963.

The year 1967 was a big one in my life when I learned I was to be made an honorary chief of the Blood tribe and inducted into the Kainai Chieftainship. I had been interested in that group since 1951, when I wrote an article on them for *The Native Voice*. It was the only group of its kind in North America, an organization of people who had been made honorary chiefs of a tribe. Membership was limited to forty living persons. I found out later that George Gooderham suggested my name to the Blood Tribal Council and they readily agreed. When Dad heard about it he donated the headdress I would receive and the family agreed I should have the name of Pauline's grandfather, *Potaina*, or Flying Chief.

On July 21st Pauline went to the reserve with her sister Nora, husband Ed, and four of our five children. I kept Lloyd with me. The next morning the two of us went to the bus depot where we met my Mother and Dad who had just come from Edmonton for the occasion. As we drove south, Dad was travelling through country he'd never seen before; Mom, on the other hand, had already been to the Gladstone farm with Pauline and me. When we passed Standoff we could see about twenty-two tepees and a bunch of tents at the campgrounds for their Standoff Indian Days.

The next day we drove to the campground and pitched a tent next door to Aunt Suzette. When everything was set up, we went to Fort Macleod, where

Abs Swinarton had a garden party for the nominees. There were five of us: Hon. Arthur Laing, Minister of Indian Affairs; Lieutenant-Governor Grant MacEwan; local farmer Jim Blackmore; Calgary industrialist and millionaire Reg Jennings; and me. After a good supply of food and a plentiful supply of drinks, we went in a cavalcade to the Indian Days. It was an extremely hot and dusty day, but there was a very large turnout, including the press. Afterwards, I was told they did the best job of induction for me of the whole group because the people knew me and I seemed to have been treated as though I belonged.

I was escorted onto the stage where I was introduced by G. Rider Davis, the mayor of Fort Macleod. After that I was ordered to strip to the waist and as I sat cross-legged on a buffalo robe, Willie Scraping White went through a ceremony with me. I was painted, prayed over, and the headdress placed on my head. When I got up, Willie gave me a little push, and announced that I had received the name of Flying Chief. It was all very impressive and I was quite flattered and gratified by this recognition on the part of the Bloods. I had always admired them as a proud and independent people and it had been beyond my wildest dreams to think I would ever be made an honorary chief of their tribe. The ceremony ended after we had smoked a pipe and performed an honouring dance.

When our twins were born, Jim Low Horn had reserved the right to name them and according to custom we could not give that honour to anyone else. After the chieftainship ceremony was over, Jim said he wanted to see us in his tepee. Pauline and I took Leah and Lois over (they were now four years old) and they went through a ceremony of their own. Willie Eagle Plume took Leah, painted her, and gave her the name of *Akai-sumyaki*, or Many Headdress Woman, while Jim named Lois *Natoy-sumyaki*, or Holy Headdress Woman. That evening there was a pow-wow and both Pauline and Lloyd wore their costumes and danced, while I sat with Richard Lancaster, author of the book *Piegan*, and we visited. All in all, it had been a wonderful day.

At the Indian days, Aunt Suzette had mentioned that she was having trouble getting her new tepee painted. It contained the pictographs of many famous Bloods, all the way back to Red Crow and Seen From Afar. After last year's Sun Dance she had asked her son, Ed Spotted Bull, to put it away in the storage shed. Instead of properly folding it, he just tossed it inside so that half of it fell on the earthen floor where it lay frozen all winter. When Suzette found it in the spring, the whole upper portion was rotten but the part with the pictographs was still intact. She arranged to have a new tepee commercially made and Ed promised to paint it. He borrowed some money from her, bought a few tiny bottles of oil paint, and had done only a few inches when he ran out of paint and wanted more money.

At this stage, Suzette didn't know what to do. I looked at the canvas and told her I would paint the new tepee in exchange for the old damaged one. When she agreed, I took both of them to Calgary and used the huge floor in one of our warehouses to lay them out. Then, using charcoal and lead pencils, I transferred the design to the new tepee, bought several cans of canvas paint, and started to work on it. As I was working, just for fun – and to confuse future anthropologists – I put in a few pictographs, such as pointed shoulder figures, that hadn't been seen on Blackfoot pictographs for a century or more. When I finally delivered the final result to Suzette, she was as pleased as I was with the final result.

A few weeks later, I was visiting the Provincial Museum when Bruce McCorquodale asked me if Suzette Eagle Ribs was a relative of mine. When I said she was Pauline's aunt, he gave me a sly smile and told me to follow him. When they got to the storage area, he said, "I guess you don't keep very good track of your aunt. Look what she sold us." And he pointed to the tepee that I had painted only a short time earlier. When I pressed him, he admitted that the tepee hadn't actually been bought from Suzette, but from her son, supposedly acting on her behalf. I knew, of course, that Ed had stolen it but that Suzette would never do anything about it.

With a bit of a grin, I told McCorquodale and his associates that what they had before them was a tepee that had been machine made by white people at a factory, and designs painted by a white man in Calgary! There was nothing "Indian" about the whole tepee. Their glee quickly turned to chagrin. Later, however, I discovered that they made no mention of this in their records. They showed it as a Blood tepee that had belonged to Suzette Eagle Ribs. When I heard about this, I wrote to them and gave the whole story, asking that my letter be placed in their accession file. It never was, and as late as 1999, my son James told me it was on display in the museum as an Indian artifact. To say the least, I was disgusted that they would never admit their mistake and would display the tepee under false pretenses.

A year after painting the tepee I had another adventure, but this had nothing to do with Indians. I had just returned from the museum course at Williamsburg in the summer of 1968 and was cleaning up around the office when I had a call from a Mr. Myers of Heiland Exploration Co. He said that his firm had been working on Melville Island, in the High Arctic, when they found a cache left by the explorer Sir Francis McClintock in 1852. He said that oil crews were starting to loot it and offered to help if we wanted to recover the objects

I did some reading up on the subject and found that McClintock had made several trips into the Arctic, searching for the remains of the Franklin Expedition. In 1852 while his ship was locked in the ice at Melville Bay, he had sent an expedition north to explore St. Patrick's Island. On their way, the men dragged a two-wheeled cart loaded with supplies and left it at the northwest end of the island to use in an emergency on their return. It had remained on the permafrost ever since.

I knew I could never get into the area without the necessary permits, but when I checked with Ottawa, I was told that this would take months. I then spoke to Doug McDermid and he said that the Commissioner of the Northwest Territories, Justice Morrow, was a good friend of his and that he would contact him. He in turn got things moving and within hours of my ·departure I got the necessary clearance. I contacted Panarctic Oils, the main contractor on Melville Island, and they agreed to let me ride on their charter flight that was leaving Edmonton on the night of August 23rd. So I loaded my heavy clothing, cameras, and other items into my duffle bag, and caught an evening flight to Edmonton's municipal airport.

We arrived in Yellowknife at 4 a.m. just as dawn was breaking. After an hour's wait while the pilot tried unsuccessfully to get a weather report from Melville Island, we took off again. When we were barely airborne one of the engines set up a terrible howl and misfired a few times before settling down. It was daylight by this time and I noticed that it seemed to take us ages before we got to a reasonable flying altitude. I learned later that the plane was grossly overloaded and the pilot almost turned back to Yellowknife when he couldn't get any altitude because of bad sparks plugs on the one motor.

As we approached Sherard Bay on Melville Island the clouds closed in and it wasn't until the pilot dropped low over a sea of ice floes that we could see where we were going. A few seconds later, the plane landed on a barren airstrip on a broad beach. As we got off, the cold wind hit us and even though it was August I shivered until I could get my duffle bag and put on my heavy clothes. The area was quite desolate and shrouded in fog. In the distance were some high hills which could be barely seen, and the only signs of civilization were the graded strip, two villages of trailers (one for Panarctic and the other for United Geophysical), piles of gas cans, and a number of helicopters and small aircraft.

I was supposed to have been met by men from Heiland Exploration who were going to fly me inland to the McClintock site, but they were nowhere to be found. After a few enquiries, I learned that the whole crew was up in the hills and completely fogged in. One cheerful soul told me that the area could be fogged in for weeks at a time. So what was I to do? Here I was, a hitchhiker stranded on an Arctic Island about two hundred miles from the magnetic North Pole!

But the fog had also trapped a crew heading for Rae Point, so when they put up two sleeping tents, each containing five double bunks, I quietly picked an upper and no one objected. I also followed them when they went to a cook trailer operated by Panarctic and had no problem in getting a fine meal. Nobody asked who I was or what I was doing there.

The next morning was a Sunday but you wouldn't know it. Business went on as usual. I was awakened by the cook's bell at 6 a.m. and when I looked outside, the camp was still fogged in. Mike McCombe of Roving Exploration Services, who was flying a single-engined Courier to geophysical sites, said he'd be glad to take me to the McClintock site. With navigator Tom Reynolds we flew about sixty-five miles northwest, passing over herds of caribou and muskox until we reached the general area of the site. But as we crossed a small bay filled with ice floes we came to a solid wall of fog that extended right down to the ground. McCombe pointed, shook his head, and turned back to the airstrip. There was no way he could approach the site.

Next morning, the sky around our camp was overcast, and soon it started to drizzle. By late afternoon, there were a few snow flurries and the hills were turning white, which was a dire sign of things to come. It was late August but almost the end of the summer season for the island.

The following day, Tuesday, was my fourth at Sherard Bay, and other than making a bunch of friends, I hadn't done much. Shortly before noon, I saw a long thin line of men walking towards the camp. They proved to be the Heiland crew, who had left everything behind. They had abandoned their camp two days earlier and travelled in two Bombardiers. One vehicle had broken down about twenty-five miles away, so the ten men had all piled into the last machine. It had run out of gas about eight miles away so they ended up making the final trek on foot. They hadn't eaten for two days, had no sleeping bags, and were a pretty tired bunch. Their arrival confirmed that I could expect no support from them.

On Wednesday, August 28th, I was told that Heiland had chartered a Fairchild and it would be arriving at 5 p.m. to pick up the crew. I was booked on that flight and if I missed it there was no guarantee as to when I would get out. Then, at 3 p.m., Mike McCombe told me he was taking a load of dynamite to a seismic rig that was about thirty miles from the cairn, and if I wanted to go with him, he'd see if we could get to the site. I knew it would be cutting it fine, but the whole purpose of the trip had been to salvage the site, so I agreed. I took the place of the co-pilot and the plane taxied to the end of the runway. I discovered that this was where the dynamite was stored, far from the living quarters. Several boxes were loaded in our plane and we took off. It was a fine day and I saw the sun for the first time since my arrival. We had an easy flight to a seismic rig working on the edge of Eldridge Bay, and there Mike landed on the tundra and unloaded his supplies. From there we proceeded on to Sabine Bay, but all we had for guidance was an X marked on my map by one of the Heiland crew. When we could not see any signs of the cache the pilot spent half an hour making sweeps back and forth. At last he said he had only enough gas for one more sweep but, as luck would have it, we finally saw the two-wheeled cart that marked the site.

Here is what I wrote:

> After circling the site, the pilot said the valley was too water logged for a safe landing, so he checked a hill about a mile away. It was strewn with small boulders and rocks but he picked a spot and brought us in for a perfect, although bone-shattering, landing. He taxied to a spot on a hill about ¾ mile from the cart and we walked down the rocky slope to the cache... As we approached the cart, we could see cans and rotten fabrics strewn around. The cart looked to be in perfect condition, with wheels about four feet high... Most of the objects were within 15 feet of the cart, although fragments of canvas were seen 50 to 100 feet away. On the cart itself were a few soggy and rotten fragments of clothing which fell to pieces when touched. A saw, some shot containers and a pemmican cutting board were among the mess. We carried two loads up the hill then found that a third trip was necessary, making 4½ miles of walking for each of us. By this time it was 7:10 p.m. and we had been at the site for exactly two hours and ten minutes... Regretfully, and with a feeling that the job had not been fully completed, I helped the pilot to attach some seismograph ribbons to the cart and poles, to make it easier to see for the person who, hopefully, might pick up the cart for us."[94]

We landed back at Sherard Bay at 8 p.m. and saw that the Fairchild sitting on the strip. I was thankful it was still there, for I had fully expected it would have left and I would have been stranded. At it happened, the Heiland crews had refused to board because two of their men still hadn't been brought out from their base camp. As a result, the departure had been postponed until the following day. That gave me time to scrounge boxes and twine and to pack the McClintock material for shipping. The objects included tin cans, crocks, shoes, coins, lead shot, tools, part of a tent, woollen stockings, sleigh runners, rope, shovel, and a host of other objects. I worked right through until midnight, then had a full meal at the United Geophysical camp before turning in for the night. I was completely exhausted but very satisfied.

Next morning, August 29th, I went to the Fairchild and was surprised to meet a *Calgary Herald* reporter who was in the north and had heard about my little expedition. Also, I met for the first time the field manager of Heiland who was supposed to have made all the arrangements for me at Sherard Bay. He had been told nothing about it.

When everyone was on board, the Fairchild tried to take off but got stuck in the muddy sand. We all got off and watched while the wheels were dug out and the plane moved to a harder surface. At last, at 11 a.m. we took off, made refuelling stops at Lady Franklin and Yellowknife, and got to Calgary at 8 p.m. It had been 29° on Melville Island and 70° in Calgary. I hadn't bathed for a week, had slept in my clothes, and Pauline said I smelled like a dead skunk. But the trip had been successful and we had salvaged some excellent items.

In the following spring, I had a phone call from the Edmonton airport saying that they had a cart there for me, and what should they do with it? I learned that just before Sherard Bay was closed for the winter, one of the helicopter pilots had flown out to the site and brought the cart back in a net. He had unloaded it at the airstrip and attached a tag to it, asking any aircraft deadheading back to Edmonton to take it with them and to call me. I arranged for a transport truck to pick it up and we soon had it safe and sound in our warehouse. All in all, it had been quite a trip. It had been the co-operation of the individual pilots that had made it a huge success. And it had cost Glenbow nothing but a week of my time and an airline ticket to Edmonton.

Perhaps I should end this chapter with a few comments and observations about people I knew during this period.

The first is Bill Marsden, who was one of my closest friends. We had known each other in Edmonton when I was a writer and he was a photographer and we went on many assignments together. Bill was a very talented and exuberant individual. He was a good photographer, had a good business head, and his enthusiasm knew no bounds. He was very unhappy with the government, so when I moved to Calgary I was glad we were able to hire him at Glenbow. He did some good things while he was with us, but he was too much of an entrepreneur to stay around for very long. When the chance arose he went into private business and started Canawest Films. He moved from still photography to movies and did some fine work, both creative and commercial. Finally, he was lured back to the Alberta government and ultimately became the Film Commissioner in Edmonton.

A completely different kind of person was Albert Lightning. He was from Hobbema and a successful farmer. He had become quite interested in the Indian Association of Alberta and was a good spokesman for his people, whether in English or Cree. He was elected President of the Association in 1955, lost to Dad in the following year, and was re-elected in 1957. He served one term and then decided that he would pursue other interests.

I got to know Albert quite well and had a lot of respect for him. He was a quiet person with a low sonorous voice and a fairly strong Cree accent. I don't know the level of his education, but he struck me as one of those people who had educated himself and had done a good job of it. He usually wore a business suit with vest but still looked like a farmer.

During the 1961 Calgary Stampede I met Albert and we had a long talk. I'd heard that he had moved from politics to religion but I didn't know any of the details. After some general chatter, he told me what had happened. About eight years earlier, while foreman of a road crew near Lake Louise, he saw a bright light overhead and a figure floated down to earth. He recognized it as the spirit of Hector Crawler, once a great chief of the Stoneys. He was dressed in Indian attire and had a robe wrapped around him. This spirit told Albert that he had been chosen to lead his people back to their old beliefs. This was the first of several meetings with Crawler, during which time Albert was taught a number of ceremonies. One time, he asked Crawler whether he should continue his work with the Indian Association. The spirit said that if the group ever spoke in favour of liquor, he should leave them. In 1959, when the matter was discussed at the Hobbema conference, Albert gave up his membership and had nothing to do with them from that time onward. Instead, he began learning the curing ceremonies of his people and had a small group of followers at Hobbema, Sunchild, and other Cree reserves.

A year later when I was in Hobbema I dropped by Albert's house. He told me he'd made a lot of progress since the last time we met. He was now travelling around the West, and even into the United States, answering the calls from people who were ill and wanted to be treated. Sometime later he told me, "I've had quite a few blackouts lately. My trouble comes from helping people. You know that people are always coming to me to be cured. The way I help these people is to take their sickness into my own body. If I'm successful in doing that, then they are cured. Then I have to get rid of it. It's pretty hard on me sometimes, I suffer a lot. But that's what I have to do if I'm going to cure them."[95] I kept in touch with Albert over the years and he remained faithful to his calling until his death. He never was involved in politics again but devoted his life to ceremonialism and curing the sick.

Another person who impressed me was George Pocaterra. We invited him to be a speaker at our Historical Society meeting in 1963, and he showed up with his wife, Norma Piper. They had a fascinating history. George came to western Canada from Italy in 1903, was a trapper in the foothills, and then established the Buffalo Head Ranch. In the late 1930s, on a visit back to the Old Country, he met Norma, a Calgary girl, who was studying opera and had sung at a number of opera houses in Italy. They fell in love and were married. At the Historical Society meeting, George told about his early days in the West and his life with the Stoneys. It was a fascinating address and he agreed that we could publish it in *Alberta Historical Review*.[96]

Pauline and I struck up an immediate friendship and we visited them on several occasions in their home just behind Viscount Bennett High School. One thing that impressed us was the fact that the two of them seemed to be as much in love then as when they were first married. They sat beside each other whenever possible, held hands, and were just like a couple of newlyweds. Yet they seemed such a contrast, for Norma was definitely elitist and refined while her husband was rough-hewn. We were usually invited for tea, and it was a formal affair in the old English tradition. George, with his gruff and slightly Italian accent, liked to talk about his experiences with the Indians. I think that's why we got together, for they both admired Pauline.

I met Norma a number of times after George died, and one day I asked her how she had been able to carry on when they had been so close. She replied that there had been so much love between them that it would sustain her for the rest of her life. She missed him but she knew he was still with her in her heart. It was very touching.

Sometime later I had a phone call from Norma's brother. He had come from Montreal to put her in an extended care centre and was arranging to sell the house. Norma had told him to call me and for me to pick up a painting of George that I had admired. When I got to the house, I learned that the contents were going to be sold at auction. As I poked around, I found some wonderful stuff and asked if we could have it for Glenbow. The brother checked with Norma and she agreed. When Ron Getty and I went through the house, we were overwhelmed. In the basement we found a number of wardrobes containing the costumes that Norma had worn for her operatic roles in Italy. We also found some touching love letters in Italian when George was back at his ranch and Norma was singing opera. And there were many other ranching and pioneer objects which were a wonderful addition to Glenbow's collections. But the greatest, in my view, were the costumes that reflected Norma's role in opera and reminded me of her lifelong love affair with George.

I could go on and on, talking about the fine people I knew during this period. But there were others who weren't always so fine. Among them were the Europeans who had a very romantic idea about the Canadian Indians and in their own way were Indian wannabees.

Often these people turned up at the Calgary Stampede, where they wanted to see "real" Indians. Unfortunately, some thought they would be exactly like those painted by George Catlin in the 1830s and still lived in the same fashion. They had a hard job accepting the fact that they now lived in houses, not tepees; rode in cars and trucks, not horses; and wore jeans and jackets, not buckskins. The Germans were the most frequent visitors, having been influenced by the writings of novelist Karl May. One time, a German woman arrived at the village apparently with the idea that she would marry an Indian. And she did. She married Eddie One Spot from the Sarcee Reserve and they had a long life together. She donned a buckskin dress for pow-wows and presumably fulfilled her dream. As for Eddie, some years earlier he had taken my wife as his adopted daughter, so we knew him very well. He credited his German wife for saving his life. He said he probably would have drunk himself to death had she not come along, got him to stop drinking, and really looked after him. His was one of the happier stories.

Then there was Karl Mueller. He was a nice guy and was really taken up with Indian dancing and costumes. When he was dressed for a pow-wow he outshone the real Indians with his outfit and danced with the best of them. When Indians asked him where he got his outfits, he told them that he had made them himself. As a result, several dancers ordered complete outfits from the German hobbyist. I knew Karl and liked him; he was living with Dora Plaited Hair, one of Pauline's old friends.

A slightly different situation evolved with an English woman named Gisela. According to a press report[97] she was an associate of the Royal College of Art who became enamoured with Indians after hearing a Grey Owl lecture in London. From Grey Owl she received the name of a "pen pal," Antoine Commanda from northern Ontario. She came to Canada after the war, married him, and thus legally became a registered Indian. They were together for eight years before splitting up, after which she seemed to have wandered around the Six Nations Reserve, then west to Hobbema. In the spring of 1964 she showed up in Cardston and pitched her tent at the south end of the Blood Reserve. There was a lot of gossip and speculation about her, and then one day one of the Blood chiefs came and took her home. She lived with him for a while, then just as suddenly disappeared, apparently to the West Coast. I met her once but I never did get the rest of the strange story.

A more complex person was a man named Adolf Hungry Wolf. He came to my office one day in the late 1960s and said that he was from California and that his grandmother was a Flathead Indian. I found him to be a very pleasant young man who seemed quite interested in learning about Blackfoot culture. Apparently he had stayed at the Indian Days in Browning and became friends with Jim White Calf, and then went to the Blood Reserve. He had a white wife named Carol and two small children.

A short time later, he moved to Golden, B.C., and I saw him fairly frequently as he came to Glenbow to study documents and books in our collections. Then in 1970 he produced his first local book, *Good Medicine: Life in Harmony with Nature*. He was a very good writer, something in the vein of James Willard Schultz, but more romantic and idealistic in nature, similar to the Good Earth and hippie authors of that time. He wrote of the true meaning of life, of spiritualism found in Nature, and of knowledge that came from the Old Ones. The rest of the book gave hobbyists instructions on how to do beadwork, make sweatlodges, make moccasins, and build cabins. It was obviously written as a guide and inspiration for the hippies and Indian wannabes. Adolf did not look Indian so I thought it was very nice that he was pursuing a study of his Native roots.

From 1970 to 1977 a veritable avalanche of Good Medicine books came off the press, at least fifteen of them. Gradually Hungry Wolf's emphasis shifted, or broadened, to include descriptions of Blackfoot life and religion, taken mostly from published sources and interviews. I was a little disturbed that some of these writings did not give credit to his sources, but I concluded that as he was writing for a popular market, he didn't consider it necessary.

During this time, most people accepted him for what he said he was – a part Native who was interested in Indians. In an interview in 1975, a Calgary newspaper described him as "a native of the Flathead Indian Reserve in Montana."[98] By this time, his white wife had dropped out of the picture and he married a Blood girl, Beverly Little Bear. Her grandfather, Pat Weaselhead, was a senior adviser to the sacred Horn Society and deeply involved in Native religious life.

In the mid-1970s, rumours began to filter back to me from the reserve saying that Hungry Wolf was not an Indian at all but a German whose name was Schmidt, or something like that. Matters came to a head when the radical American Indian Movement put out a "wanted" poster with his picture on it and the inscription "Wanted – Adolph Hungry Wolf Schmidt for the exploitation of Indian People."[99] Accompanying it was a letter from Nelson Small Legs, Jr., southern Alberta director of AIM. It called Hungry Wolf "a dishonest imposter [who is] disguised as an Indian person who is stealing our culture, taking our sacred pipe and setting himself as some kind of Messiah."[100] It also contained the veiled threat that "Hungry Wolf's time is near."

Shortly after it came out, Hungry Wolf came to see me. As I noted in my diary, "He is very concerned about a threat he received ... He has a book coming out on the Bloods in March & is also worried about repercussions, as he says it contains material on the Horns & Old Women's Societies. He is a strange person – sometimes I think he is a sincere & well meaning oddball, and at other times I feel it is a mask for a very shrewd and calculating person who is making a good living for himself under the guise of being a pseudo-Indian 'holy man.' I don't know which is right."[101]

Then the proverbial hit the fan later in 1977 when his book, *The Blood People*, was released by a leading New York publisher, Harper and Row. Probably the most vociferous response to it came from the First Rider family. Some years earlier, George First Rider had made extensive tapes about his life that he sold to the Provincial Museum of Alberta. Hungry Wolf gained access to translations of these and used them extensively in such a manner that one might assume the interviews came from the writer himself. The only problem was that First Rider had some derogatory things to say about people, including his own wife. First Rider's grandson was furious. "Who is this man Adolf Hungry Wolf who calls himself a Blood?" he asked. "He brings disrespect upon my family and above all my grandmother."[102] Hungry Wolf apologized but the damage was done. This book, plus his earlier theft of a medicine bundle from the Provincial Museum while the Horn Society was in the process of trying to get it back legally, made him *persona non grata* on the reserve.

As for me, I was disappointed on two counts. First, Hungry Wolf continued to project the image that he was an Indian, using such terms as "our old people," "our medicine pipe bundles," and "our songs," even though by now it was common knowledge that his birth name was Adolf Gutohrlein. He had been born in Germany, came to California when he was nine, and attended California State University in Long Beach. Before coming to Canada he had published two books on railroads.

My second concern was that I had gone out of my way to help him, permitting him to get scores of photographs from Glenbow for study purposes. The arrangement was that if he published them, Glenbow was to collect its usual permissions fee. When the book came out, I was disturbed to see that he had credited Glenbow for only a few of the photos. Rather, he gave credit to the original photographer or the person who had donated the pictures to us, giving the impression that the Glenbow had not been his primary source. And, if I recall correctly, he never did pay the permission fees, even for the photos that were credited to us. At that point, my disillusionment with this Indian wannabee was complete.

After his sobering experience with the Bloods, Hungry Wolf began writing books in German for overseas sales and went back to his first love, railroads. He returned from time to time to attend medicine pipe ceremonies and pow-wows, and in 2006 produced a four-volume illustrated work entitled *The Blackfoot Papers*. By this time our friendship had come to an end.

Another immigrant from Europe was a Welshman named John Hellson. He arrived in Calgary about 1960, perhaps drawn here because of the Indians. He became an orderly at the Keith Sanatorium, where there were a number of Indian patients, and became friends with them. We met Hellson socially a number of times and found him to be a very pleasant man. Sometime later he married Diane Melting Tallow, whose father Dave worked for the Provincial Museum. Hellson received the Blackfoot name of Yellow Fly and was well known under that name. He described himself as an ethnologist when he worked with botanist Morgan Gadd to produce the book *Ethnobotany of the Blackfoot Indians*.[103]

Hellson gradually slipped into the professional museum business, first as a contractor and then as a dealer. He worked very briefly for the Provincial Museum of Alberta and the Museum of Man and Nature and was fired from Glenbow in 1976 after he got into a fist fight with our ethnology cataloguer. Later he brought in a "rare" pictograph robe containing the exploits of Charcoal, a famous Blood fugitive. As I examined it, I was convinced right away it was a fake, for Charcoal had depicted himself on the robe wearing a fringed jacket that could be seen in the only known photograph of him. However, the jacket had belonged to the photographer who took the picture, so there was no reason it should show up in such a robe. Also, Hellson brought in a collection of Iroquois silver and when we checked with museums in the East, we were told it had been floating around for years and was highly suspect.

In 1981 he was arrested in San Francisco and charged with stealing priceless artifacts from the R.H. Lowie Museum at the University of California. Some 250 artifacts valued at more than $500,000 were stolen supposedly while he was doing research. According to the *Globe & Mail*,

> When Mr. Hellson showed up at the Lowie last December, he said he was a field researcher with the anthropology department at the University of Lethbridge in Alberta. He said he had done extensive research work among more than a dozen Indian tribes in Canada and the United States and wanted access to the Lowie's Plains Indian materials, particularly medicine bundles used by the shamans.[104]

On gaining access to the museum, according to the newspaper report, he took a number of items, mostly netsuke, small Japanese carvings in ivory and wood. He was reportedly caught when a dealer tried to sell Bill Holm a Tlingit "soul catcher" that the anthropologist immediately recognized. The dealer said she had obtained it from Hellson. Shortly thereafter the "grey-bearded, blue-eyed, 49-year-old confidence man" was arrested but only 90 of the missing items were recovered.[105] He was sentenced to two years.

# 9

# *Changes*

When Allan Hammond was appointed Executive Vice-President of Glenbow in 1970, my first goal was to get as far away from administrative work as possible. Besides, I saw this as a good opportunity to get back to working with people and being involved in historical matters. There were no objections, so I carved an office for myself out of the second floor of the Central Park Library, a building that housed our Library and Archives, and settled into place a half-mile away from the executive offices.

Sometime later, I was told that I was "in Coventry," i.e., that I was being given the silent treatment by the Harvie people. I know it is true that I was excluded from many meetings where I might have been expected to be on hand and that as part of the management team I played little or no role in the decision-making process, but I don't really know if I was being deliberately excluded or not. I was told that the best way to destroy an administrator is to cut him out of the loop and leave him hanging. That may be true, but if that's what happened to me, it had the opposite effect. Instead of attending countless meetings, I was seeing researchers, preparing educational lectures for our museum, training docents, writing exhibition catalogues, editing our newsletter, and doing all the things I enjoyed doing. At the same time, the four departments under my care were being efficiently run by Sheilagh Jameson, Len Gottselig, Joe Schmitz, and Trudy Soby. It was an ideal situation, and I enjoyed it thoroughly.

I was particularly glad I was out of the loop when there was some trouble with Eric Harvie. This occurred about four months after Hammond had taken over. Our Art Department had just installed a Gerald Tailfeathers exhibition when Harvie came to see it. Lorne Render told me that Harvie "tore labels off the wall, tore a poster down, and chewed out Lorne and Al Hammond in front of the staff for nailing and sticking things on the wall."[106] I knew that Harvie did not like to mar the walls of offices and fine old buildings, but these were plasterboard panels that would repaired and repainted after every use, and were designed to be nailed, tacked, and stapled.

To me, it was another sign that Harvie's condition was becoming worse as time went on. When I first knew him in 1956 he was a strong, dynamic man with an incisive mind who always seemed to be two steps ahead of anyone else. I admired him for his strength of leadership and his ability to quickly get to the nub of any situation. I was very sad, for here was a man who had done so much for western Canada.

Eric Harvie died on January 11, 1975, but no one knew about it until the family announced it after the funeral. Some weeks later, I was surprised to learn that I was being given a small bequest from the Harvie will. In spite of problems, I guess I never stopped being a part of Harvie's Glenbow family. When I wrote to thank Mrs. Harvie for her accompanying note, I comment-ed, "Over the years, his interest in western Canadian history made it possible for me to do the things I had dreamed of, and at the same time help Mr. Harvie build the kind of Glenbow he wanted."[107]

I may have disagreed with him on some matters but I never lost my respect for him or for what he had accomplished. As long as he paid my salary, I was completely faithful to him, but once I came under the authority of the Institute I owed my allegiance to that institution, which sometimes placed me at odds with the Harvie organization.

The 1969–70 problems involving Doug McDermid and Dick Gordon had succeeded in causing the Harvie people to back off from the day-to-day work-ings of Glenbow, so Hammond had a fairly easy time of it at first. He was able to bring some tranquility to the organization and to improve staff morale. I called meetings in my own division and became involved in discussions rang-ing all the way from audio-visual programs to displays and public relations. Meetings of our Management Committee – Hammond, Render, Light, and me – were held on a regular basis but we never heard much about any problems with the Board so we assumed it was going all right.

My first disagreement with Hammond occurred in the summer of 1971. Glenbow had been approached by the Calgary Convention Centre to see if we would provide exhibitions for a single-level area which was planned for the east end of their facility. At that time, the entire block between 8th and 9th

Avenues, east of Centre Street, was being cleared under an urban renewal program. The Four Seasons Hotel would occupy the west third, the Convention Centre the middle third, and the east third would be for convention displays. During the time it was not required for this purpose, the Centre wanted us to install exhibits.

When Hammond heard about it, he jumped on the idea of making it into a permanent Glenbow exhibition area. From there the idea grew like topsy until he and others envisioned all of Glenbow under one roof at that location. Encouraging noises were being made by civic and provincial government authorities, both of which agreed that Glenbow needed a modern home.

In August 1971, Bert Baker, President of the Institute, asked the three Division heads to respond to this idea, and to pass their responses along to Allan Hammond. I wrote a four-page memorandum in which I was entirely opposed to the relocation. I said that while it would be nice to have Glenbow together in a modern and controlled environment, the Convention Centre was not the place to go. Some of my reasons were a severe lack of parking space, being stuck in the core area of East Calgary, being stuck beside a convention centre rather than in an educational setting, and jumping into something without any advanced planning or study.

I said there were questions that had not been answered: "What are the advantages and disadvantages of locating in the centre core of Calgary? Should we be on or near the university campus? Should we, like the Provincial Museum, be in the suburbs? Should we be in a separate building?"[108] I answered these by saying that "the ideal situation for Glenbow would be to have our own building, with adequate parking, easy public access, and provision for future expansion." And to counter the argument that we had to take advantage of this opportunity, I responded that Glenbow was sufficiently important to Calgary and to Alberta that we would likely find the financing authorities just as ready to assist us in another location as they were in the downtown core.

I conceded that one of our responsibilities should be to respond to the needs of the travel industry, but "our main emphasis should be to educate, inspire and encourage the Alberta public to become aware of its history. We do this through art exhibitions, school programs, providing research facilities, and generally making use of our extensive collections." But the real clincher in my memo came when I made a comment that echoed through the corridors of Glenbow and created considerable anger. I said, "Glenbow should be looked upon as a centre for culture, education and history. To tie us in with a convention centre, complete with beer parlors, hotel, commercial display space, conventioneers, chamber of commerce, etc., is like boarding a nun in a house of ill repute."

When humour is used as a tool for criticism it can be pretty deadly. My "house of ill repute" comment created a lot of attention, laughter, and anger but it didn't change the final decision. Even after all these years, I still believe I was right. At the conclusion of my report I referred to "an alternate site on the Trans-Canada Highway, just west of Foothills Hospital on the north side of the road. This is Provincial Government land which is held, I understand, for long range university expansion. It has the advantages of being immediately accessible from all parts of the city; it is in close proximity to the university campus but not on it; it has ample parking area; there is a sloping hill which can provide for an impressive architectural design; and there is a magnificent view of the Bow River valley. I have no idea if the land is available, but it is the type of site which should be considered."[109] Some years later, I spoke to provincial and university authorities, and both were quite willing to consider Glenbow for that site. I tried to see if there was some way our downtown building could be turned back to the Alberta government and transformed into an office building, but no one at Glenbow was interested so I dropped the matter. In later years, the new Children's Hospital was built near the site.

Once the proposal for a new Glenbow Centre was approved I was up to my ears in work. Not only did I have to work closely with the Library and Archives in designing the sixth floor, but I ended up being responsible for many of the western Canadian exhibits and most of the Indian ones. This meant developing story lines, selecting the artifacts and images, writing captions, and working with the designer on the layout. By the time the museum was getting ready to open in September 1976, I was going flat-out to get all this work finished.

My second disagreement with our Executive Vice-President came in 1972 when he met Jack McClelland, owner of McClelland & Stewart, Toronto publishers. McClelland was a high flier with a stable of writers that included people like Margaret Laurence, Farley Mowat, Pierre Berton, and others who were the cream of Canada's literary society. Somehow, McClelland got the idea that Glenbow was loaded with manuscripts and that with a little effort they were ready to be published so he suggested that his firm form a partnership with Glenbow. Later, Pierre Berton added his weight to the argument and I could see that Hammond was very flattered by all the attention.

Later in the year, the Toronto firm made a proposal to establish McClelland & Stewart West, with headquarters in Calgary. Under the deal, it would publish, promote, and distribute all our books as well as take charge of our publicity and public relations work. I was entirely opposed, mainly because of my belief that "McClelland and Stewart has based its proposal on a series of wild estimates and that the company would not be the profitable venture that they predict."[110] I said that publishing two or three coffee table books a year, prepared by Glenbow, was either unrealistic or would completely consume the time of several members of staff. I thought that their plan to turn our modest eight-page *Glenbow* into a glossy popular quarterly magazine was unrealistic based upon the small size of our market. I added that their idea of increasing our current membership from 2,000 people at $2.00 a year to 7,000 at $10 a year was nothing more than a wild guess. I pointed out that even with its fine magazine, the Royal Ontario Museum had only 4,000 members. I also pointed out that M&S had just received a major loan from the Ontario government to bail them out of their financial predicament and that this was not a favourable indication of their business ability. Finally, I said that mixing public relations with publishing made no sense and that if we wanted this work done by an outside firm, it should be a professional public relations firm.

From the reaction I got, I might as well have included the nun in the house of ill repute statement, as Hammond was angry. He downplayed my objections and in August 1973 the contract was made between Glenbow and McClelland & Stewart West. It gave the company the right of first refusal of any book, pamphlet, or catalogue that Glenbow wanted to publish, and dictated the size, format, and price. Although the contract contained a lot of clauses, the bottom line was that Glenbow would make cash advances for publishing, public relations, and membership promotion, and when the bills came in, we would pay 15 per cent over MSW's supposed actual costs. In addition, we were to get an 11 per cent royalty on any books that were sold.

My philosophy was that if my opinion was sought while a matter was still in the discussion stage, I gave it openly and honestly. However, if the decision was made against my advice, then I was honour-bound to make the project work and my objections evaporated as soon as the matter became policy. I was prepared to do this with MSW but Hammond obviously saw it otherwise. As I commented, "He was evidently piqued & I have been effectively frozen out of all subsequent discussions. The agreement has since been made and all matters are handled directly by Mr. Hammond. I only hear about our future publishing plans indirectly. Strangely enough, I don't really mind, as I have my Historical Society programs to keep my fingers in editing & I always seem to have a lot of writing to do. But I am a bit sad that he doesn't see fit to use my abilities as a writer & editor; instead we are paying sizeable sums to M&S for relatively straightforward work."[111]

As I expected, the program was a disaster. I was obliged to curtail the publication of our little *Glenbow* magazine, but the big shiny quarterly never saw the light of day. Lorne Render was pressed into service to write an art coffee table book, *The Mountains and the Sky,* and it was such a horrendous experience that he would never repeat it. At one stage, Lorne was reading page proofs of the early part of his book while still writing the latter part. The only time he saw a completed manuscript was when he received a copy of the book. It was a great credit to him that it was as good as it was. But that was the only coffee table book we produced. I could go on, but I'll simply say that in 1976 the whole agreement was terminated, by which time Glenbow had lost more than $150,000. As I remarked at the time, if my memo of 1973 was rephrased in the past tense, it could have been used as an explanation of what had gone wrong. It wasn't that I was smart, it was just that everything was so predictable.

Hammond's freedom from the Harvie group appeared to suffer a setback in December 1973 when the announcement was made that Bert Baker had retired as the volunteer President of Glenbow and was being replaced by Geoff Hamilton, recently retired Chief Commissioner for the City of Calgary. We quickly learned that he was no volunteer but would be a full-time administrator, with his salary being paid for by the Devonian Foundation, one of Eric Harvie's organizations. Geoff had not only become the senior administrator at Glenbow, relegating Hammond to second place, but he also had a place on the Board. It was a very unhealthy situation, and had the person been anyone but Hamilton, we might have been in a lot of trouble. We didn't know it at the time, but the Harvie people were dissatisfied with the lack of progress being made in planning for the new museum. They blamed Hammond and Lorne Render and had Hamilton appointed, as I said in my diary, to "break up the ... log jam and get things moving."[112]

But Hamilton was a builder, not a wrecker. It soon became obvious that he was not in the Harvie camp, or in anyone's camp for that matter, and was very sensitive to the pressures that were building up because of the upcoming deadlines for the new museum. He avoided interfering in the day-to-day activities and left these to Hammond, but concentrated on staff-Board relations and discussions with the civic and provincial authorities. Instead of taking anyone to task for the dissension within our ranks, he wisely arranged for all of us to go to a management seminar in Banff with a professional communications consultant. The results were extremely positive and the senior people came back working as a team.

I won't go into detail about the cliques, pressures, and problems that accompanied the construction and installation of the museum, for these happen in any big project. There were blowups, disagreements, and a lot of bitterness, but they were all part of the process of getting the museum open. All I can say is that the Board and Harvie people blamed Hammond for much of the problem when in fact the onus should have fallen on a number of people, including some of those on the Board. At the same time, Hammond was never really a museum person. Rather, he was an administrator and Glenbow needed more than that. Meanwhile, the pressures got to Hamilton and he ended up resigning early in 1976. The museum opened in time on September 22 and Hammond carried on alone.

It was quite an opening, with all the VIPs from Alberta and quite a number from Ottawa on hand for the occasion. One of the interesting little sidelights was that Roy Little Chief, leading a small group from the American Indian Movement, was on hand in the front row and likely to protest something or other. But when he and his friends saw all the big shots and all the security I guess they decided to keep quiet. Anyway, nothing happened. Some days later, Roy met me in the lobby to complain that his photograph was secreted at the admissions desk, presumably to let the authorities know if he turned up. People were really paranoid about AIM at that time. I hadn't heard about the picture so we went to check, and sure enough, there it was. I told our people to remove it immediately, as Roy had done nothing wrong and was not being sought by the police or anybody else.

Roy was a good leader but a real rebel. As a result he was capable of muddling up any good deeds he tried to perform. He was once elected head chief of the Blackfoot tribe, but again he could not settle down to a quiet humdrum life and lasted only one term. Personally, I got along fine with him.

When the Glenbow Museum opened, we were already in the middle of one of our many financial crises, with a shortfall of about $200,000 a year. Late in the year, the Alberta government said it would put $5 million into our endowment fund if Don Harvie would match that amount from the Riveredge Foundation. For some reason, Don refused. Later, the government did give us $600,000 to see us through the opening of the museum and to the end of the year. But that still left us with a $1 million shortfall for 1977 if we kept on the way we were going. In order to break even, we figured we would have to lay off forty-five people, or a third of our staff. Having spent enough time on this merry-go-round, Lorne Render decided to jump off and head for the Royal Ontario Museum. Other senior people were either leaving or being demoted. Finally, help did come from the government, but only after the makeup of the Board of Governors was changed so that Riveredge's representation was reduced from six to four. The two new members would come from Alberta Culture and from Treasury. I didn't mind that part as I hoped it might put a control on some of the unpredictable ideas that were coming forth from Riveredge.

In the autumn of 1977 Duncan F. Cameron was appointed Executive Director and a month later Hammond was gone.

———∞∞∞———

Getting away from Glenbow's situation, there always seemed to be plenty for me to do during the seventies, both in my personal life and professionally. For example, I had been interested in preserving historic sites since 1952, when I produced the booklet *Historic Sites of Alberta*. In 1959, when the Alberta government established the Alberta Historical Advisory Board, I was among those appointed. We held regular meetings that considered such matters as geographical names and preservation of sites. However, there was no real legislation in place for site protection other than the Provincial Parks Act so our powers were very limited. Mostly we talked about plaques, signs, and surveys of trading posts. Then in the late 1960s, pressures were applied by environmentalists to examine many aspects of natural and human history in the province. As a result, in 1971 the government created the Public Advisory Committee on Historical and Archaeological Resources. Dick Forbis was named chairman, to examine the archaeological aspects of the study, while I was appointed vice-chairman to represent the historical community. Others included Jim MacGregor, Bill Farmilo, Alex Johnston, Lou Bayrock, Chief John Snow, Les Usher, and Allan Bryan.

This was a committee that could make recommendations with the whole weight of the government behind it. We started holding regular meetings, but it was clear from the outset that Dick and I were the main players. Accordingly, right after the Board was established I took on the daunting task of finding out what protective legislation existed in other parts of North America. In Alberta we had nothing. I got lists and addresses from the American Association for State & Local History, and wrote to governments all across the United States and Canada. When I had the pile of regulations assembled, I cut and pasted them so that all related topics were on the same page. For example, on the page identified as "Definitions" I had all excerpts defining historic sites, historical property, etc. A fairly clear pattern soon emerged, as it was obvious that many authorities had merely borrowed from each other. A few were virtually identical.

With this information in hand, I wrote draft legislation entitled the "Archaeological and Historic Sites Protection Act." It was back and forth to the Board as it was revised, refined, and fine tuned. When we had something workable, it was submitted to the Chairman of the Public Advisory Committee and he arranged for public hearings. We got some good publicity at the time, all of it favourable. For example, the *Albertan* said, "Let's hope an appreciable number of citizens will respond to the opportunity presented by the forthcoming hearings by showing positive interest. The past is everyone's and everyone is impoverished by its destruction."[113]

By 1973 the work had reached the stage where input was needed from various interest groups. The best way to accomplish this was to introduce the legislation as a bill and let it have first and second readings in the Alberta legislature. Then it would be allowed to die on the order paper, and the draft bill would be used as a basis for discussion before being reintroduced at the next session. In this way, people would have something specific to discuss.

Only it didn't work that way. Our draft was sent to the government lawyers who revised the terminology, and then it was introduced to the legislature. It got first and second readings, but just when the legislature was about to adjourn, a mix-up occurred and the bill was given third and final reading. The Minister of Culture, Horst Schmidt, was away at the time and nobody caught it. As a result, the Act became law, even though there was no budget, no staff, and no machinery to implement it. The people in Culture scurried around for a while, but finally decided that the legislation had to come back to us for amendment, based upon the concerns of various interest groups. Later that year, Dick resigned so I was appointed chairman and continued in that position until 1976 when our work in getting the historic regulations into law was pretty well finished.

Perhaps one of the most exciting projects for me during this time involved the location and preservation of Fort Calgary. This fort had been built by the North-West Mounted Police in 1875 to bring law and order to the region. It was replaced by new buildings in 1882 and in 1914 it was closed, with its large 32-acre grounds being turned over to the Grand Trunk Pacific Railway. By the 1960s, the site was a maze of railway tracks, warehouses, storage yards, and scrap heaps. I had visited the place a number of times.

In 1968 Alderman John Ayer wanted to locate the exact site of the 1875 fort because of a possibility that a freeway might cut right through the area. Once he was satisfied that City officials had given him the proper information, he came to see me for some historical background. During our discussion, Ayer showed me a map on which the location of the fort was marked with an X. I told him it was in the wrong place: it was too far north. He insisted that the City people knew what they were talking about, so I took him out to the site to let him see for himself. Between Allied Farm Equipment and Calgary Metals Limited was a ridge of original soil that had survived because of a fence line on top of it. I showed Ayer the signs of ash, square nails, and other objects that could be seen in the face of the embankment. I explained that I had found enough evidence to indicate that these were the remains of part of the 1882 fort and that photographs showed that the earlier 1875 post had been slightly to the south of it.

Alderman Ayer was convinced and asked if I had located any parts of the original fort. I said no; they had probably been destroyed by all the tracks and soil disturbance. However, once the question was raised, and as there was a danger that the site might be utterly demolished by urban development, I decided to give it a try. There was a bit of extra money in my budget, so with Dick Forbis' guidance, I hired a young archaeology student named Ron Getty to test the site. He and his crew worked for a week in the summer, and while they didn't locate the fort, we were all encouraged by their efforts. Our thinking was that if bits of the 1882 fort could survive the onslaught of urbanization, maybe the original one could too.

I brought Ron back for another try during the summer of 1969. At first, the results were very discouraging, for when they dug a trench across the railway line they found that none of the original topsoil had survived. With only a week left in their summer program, they shifted their attention to a storage yard at the back of MacCosham's warehouse. Here, much to everyone's surprise, the soil was undisturbed and a few inches below the surface they found the palisades of the original fort. I don't know who was more excited, Ron Getty, John Ayer, or me.

The following year, 1970, was the big one. Getty and his crew unearthed the foundations of three buildings and part of the palisade, as well as collecting more than eight thousand artifacts. These included Mounted Police buttons, gold braid, cartridges, clay pipes, bottles, coins, brass parts of uniforms, and a host of other objects. Getty did such a remarkable job that as soon as he left university, we hired him at Glenbow.

When he knew we had found the site, John Ayer launched a campaign to preserve the entire Mounted Police reserve and to turn it into a park. Over the next few years, he was the driving force behind this effort, and with tireless energy he made the whole project a resounding success. He swung the mayor and council to his side, hammered Canadian National to give up the land in exchange for other industrial property, got the Canadian Railway Transportation Commission to let the tracks be torn up and to pay for the cost, and got the Canadian Army to blow up the old railway bridge. He also got the City to declare the site its number one project for Calgary's centennial in 1975, and for the Alberta government to pay a major part of the cost of restoring the site and building an interpretive centre.

In order to accomplish all this, Ayer established the Fort Calgary Steering Committee in 1970, of which I was one of the founding members, along with Sandra LeBlanc and some other enthusiastic supporters. We had informal meetings, often in my office, and from this grew the Fort Calgary Preservation Society. During our discussions, the question of Calgary's centennial arose; it was now four years away and nothing was being done. We called a meeting in my office in January 1971 to consider the matter. Those in attendance were John Ayer, Doug Johnson and Jack Hermann of the Calgary Tourist & Convention Association, Dave Coutts from the Historical Society, Ron Potyak from the Federation of Community Leagues, and me. As a result, we set up the Fort Calgary Centennial Committee which a short time later was changed to Century Calgary. When it got funding and set up committees, we arranged for our Fort Calgary Steering Committee to be placed under its wing. Tom Walsh and Rabbi Ginsberg ran the centennial while we got the site cleared and landscaped and the interpretive centre built.

It was a monumental task. Anyone who had viewed the area in 1969 would have said such a feat would have been impossible. Not only were millions of dollars tied up in the property, but it was on the very outskirts of the downtown area and, in the view of some people, too valuable to be wasted on a park. At times, Ayer was sufficiently discouraged that he even gave encouragement for a junior college or a botanical garden to go on the site (as the only means of saving it), but in the end we got everything we could have possibly wanted. When the fort was well in hand, we next turned our attention to the home of R. Burton Deane, the last commander of the Mounted Police detachment. The three-storey building had been moved off the site to the east side of the Elbow, but we were able to get the City to acquire the property and undertake restoration. In 1976–77, I served a brief term as chairman of the Fort Calgary

Preservation Committee, as well as being on the board of Century Calgary, and when the park officially opened in 1978 I was happily front and centre to see the red-coated horsemen cross the Bow River as part of the opening celebrations.

A third historic sites project that involved me during this time was the preservation of the Cochrane Ranch. In 1969, I had a visit from Harry Tatro, regional officer for Parks Canada, who told me that the federal government had plans to preserve the ranch but these were being dashed by the Alberta Minister of Highways, Gordon Taylor. It's a bit complicated, so let me explain. The federal government program for setting aside National Historic Sites required that provincial governments acquire the core property and donate it to the feds. Years earlier, the federal government had set up a huge park in northern Alberta called the Wood Buffalo National Park. Nobody paid much attention to it until the north began to be developed. When Alberta asked that the land be turned over to them, the feds refused. Now, whenever a potential site was being considered for a National Historic Park, the Alberta government refused to discuss the matter until the Wood Buffalo Park problem was resolved. As a result, there was only one tiny National Historic Park in Alberta; it was located at Rocky Mountain House on land donated by the owners before all the regulations came into being.

In the 1960s, the federal government became interested in the Cochrane Ranch. It was privately owned land just west of the town of Cochrane and had one of the original 1882 ranch houses still standing. Harry Tatro was particularly interested and it was his pet project to see the site preserved as a National Historic Park. At that time even the provincial authorities seemed willing to go along with the idea of donating a core site of 10 acres and letting the federal government buy the remaining 140 acres.

Then, early in 1969, Gordon Taylor threw a monkey wrench into the whole deal when he announced that a new north-south highway to Cremona would be built right through the property and within a few hundred yards of the old building. That's when Harry came to see me to find out if there was anything we could do.

I took the matter to the Historical Society of Alberta and we set up the Cochrane Ranch Preservation Committee, of which I was chairman. Then, as I said in my report, "The Society had some brief unsatisfactory correspondence with the Premier, and then turned to our members for help. As a result, many letters were sent from all over Alberta and beyond, asking the Premier to reconsider. The Society also wrote to all MLA's, outlining our view, while considerable support was gained from the press, radio and television."[114] One of the comments I made to MLAs was that "The tragedy of this situation is that the Federal Government was ready to preserve and develop the historic site, but now they are backing off in the face of Provincial objections. Is history to be destroyed for the sake of convenience?"[115] A short time later, when I was interviewed by the press, I said, "Besides being something worth preserving, it could also be a tremendous tourist attraction. We're not only talking aesthetics; we're talking the cold hard facts of business."[116]

Instead of being influenced by this campaign, Taylor became angry and wrote me a brusque letter in July, accusing our Society of being influenced by political and commercial interests. He also intimated to the press that if the federal government was willing to pay $200,000 to move the planned highway one mile west, he might consider it. This, of course, was impossible. I replied to Taylor on August 6th, "We feel that your Government has a responsibility to future generations. If we are to remain proud of this province, and of Canada, we must preserve those facets of history upon which pride can be based."[117]

Finally, in response to the many letters, the Minister of Highways set up a committee of two to judge the importance of the site. These were William Truch, an engineer, and Juan Corkin, an architect. Meanwhile, I was continuing to gather photographs and other data that indicated the importance of the ranch and the existing ranch house. But the Alberta government was conducting research of its own and in 1970 the committee produced a map that showed the original Cochrane ranch house was at least 150 yards from the one still standing. As a result, they came to the conclusion that this was not the original house and therefore the site was not worth preserving.

I was taken aback by this development, not only because the site was being rejected, but because the government map clearly indicated the house in a different location than the one it currently occupied. Not convinced, I continued my research and spoke to a scholar who had done some writing about the ranch. He produced two surveyors' plans, one for 1884 and another for 1888. When I looked at them, my heart jumped for joy: they showed *two* original Cochrane Ranch buildings, not just one. Further research indicated that both buildings had been erected in 1882 and that one had burned down about 1900.

I immediately contacted Corkin and when the information checked out he promised to add it to their report. About this time, Clarence Copithorne, MLA for Cochrane, had been named Minister of Highways, and I had high hopes that he would support us. I was wrong. Even though he was from an old ranching family he was even more strongly opposed than Taylor. He appeared to favour "progress" for his constituency, and this did not include preserving old ranch sites. Without his backing we could get nowhere, so the highway went ahead and sliced through the middle of the Cochrane Ranch site, the federal government withdrew from the scene, and the effort to preserve the integrity of the site was a failure. Only in later years, when the Alberta government saw the tourist advantage of the ranch, was something done. They set aside the old house and the tiny bit of land not destroyed by the highway, and declared it to be a Provincial Historic Park. They ended up settling for less than half a loaf when Albertans could have had the whole bakery.

There were other campaigns over the years, but none like Fort Calgary and the Cochrane Ranch. There was the successful attempt to save the Burns Block from the wrecker's ball and sometimes less successful attempts to prevent Calgary from turning into a faceless city of glass and concrete.

───── ∞ ─────

In the early 1970s I finally broke into the book publishing field. After my manuscript on Crowfoot had been laying on the shelf for more than a decade, Jack Ewers in Washington suggested in 1971 that I try the University of Oklahoma Press. He had been appointed to their editorial board and was of the opinion it would receive a favourable hearing. I read the manuscript again for the first time in years and saw that it needed some work: it went into far too much detail and one tended to lose sight of the main character. So I did a major rewrite, submitted it, and held my breath. Some weeks later I got some qualified good news. The nice part was that they liked the manuscript and wanted to publish it. The qualifier was that they needed a $2,000 grant to help defray the costs. This had to come from a recognized grant-giving agency. I tried a few local places with no luck, and then someone suggested the Social Sciences & Humanities Research Council in Ottawa. I was somewhat concerned about my lack of academic credentials and was reluctant to try, but at last I bit the bullet and sent in my application. Much to my pleasure and surprise, the Council liked the manuscript and agreed to provide the grant.

In later years, I used this as an example of the problems in trying to create an interest in western Canadian history. Here was me, a Canadian historian, writing about a Canadian hero, and receiving a grant from a Canadian agency, getting my book published in the United States!

Interestingly, when Mel Hurtig heard about it, he took some action of his own. Mel had started the Edmonton firm of Hurtig Publishers and, in fairness to him, it wasn't in existence when I had tried to get my book published in Canada so he had never seen it. Nevertheless, when he learned that it was going to be published in the United States, he made a deal to get a Canadian edition under his own imprint. As a result, the book appeared in both countries and Mel did an excellent job of promoting it in Canada. We became good friends and he went on to publish some of my other books. He also got me involved with the Council of Canadians, a very nationalistic group that was trying to offset the intrusive influences of the United States. I supported it for some time, but then it got too strident and anti-American for my liking.

When my book, *Crowfoot, Chief of the Blackfeet*, came out in 1972, I was as pleased as punch. Looking back at all the other books I published after that date, I still think this was my best. It makes me wonder what would have happened if it had been published in 1958 and I had had another decade of books under my belt. Perhaps I would have tackled some of those that I felt were worthwhile, but by the time I got around to them, I couldn't find enough information to provide a Native viewpoint. These were particularly true of biographies of Piapot and Poundmaker. On the other hand, I was fortunate to find what I did and to get so much of it into print.

But with the one book in hand, I was not about to quit. The other books that I wrote or edited for publication in the 1970s were: *William Parker, Mounted Policeman* (1973); *The Best of Bob Edwards* (1975), and *Wit and Wisdom of Bob Edwards* (1976), all published by Hurtig. One of these, *The Best of Bob* Edwards, won the Alberta Non-Fiction Award for 1975. I also edited *Men in Scarlet* (1974) for the Historical Society of Alberta, and *A Winter at Fort Macleod* (1974) for Glenbow.

---

One of the results of my historic sites campaigns, books, and public speaking, was that I got my name in the paper a lot. Not only was I in the news, but the media found me to be an ideal person to interview. I enjoyed speaking, was usually entertaining, and was knowledgeable on subjects that interested the public. This was particularly true for radio and television, for I was not nervous and talked a good talk. I remember two or three times when I went into a studio to tape a half-hour interview on some general topic and it went so well that the interviewer asked if they could do another one back-to-back, to use at a later date. I said sure, and half an hour later it was done. Columnists also liked to talk to me, so I found myself being featured by people like Eva Reid, Ken Liddell, and Bob Shiels. In 1969, I was named "Personality of the Week" by the *Calgary Herald*, and a full page was devoted to an interview with me.[118]

During this time I tried to limit my public speaking to two or three times a month. That included service clubs, schools, universities, Native groups, academic conferences, and just about any place where a bunch of people came together. My talks included such topics as Indian history, contemporary Indian problems, the importance of teaching history in schools, the Mounted Police, ranching, the role of museums, the science of archival work, etc. There was a standing joke around the office that the preparation of a half-hour speech usually took me about five minutes and was scribbled on the back of an envelope. It was true that I liked to write down topic headings and then to speak extemporaneously.

At no time did I become involved in this for self-gratification. I felt I had a message to give and did it as best I could. I identified myself with Glenbow when I spoke and I know for a fact that this had some very useful spin-offs, both from the standpoint of public recognition and for attracting gifts to the organization. However, not everyone agreed with my frequent appearance before the public, both personally and in print. Word filtered back to me that some of my superiors felt that I was on some sort of ego trip and was doing it at the expense of Glenbow! When I first heard this I couldn't believe it but the rumour was so persistent that I had to accept it as true. But I put this down to jealousy or small-mindedness and gave it the attention it deserved.

Some evidence of this attitude emerged in 1974 when an announcement was made that I was being awarded an honorary doctorate from the University of Calgary. Not only that, but I would be giving the convocation address. This came as a surprise to me, as I had neither lobbied for it nor knew anything about it. I learned later that some of the faculty and students at the university had put my name forward. When the announcement was made, I expected some positive reaction from Glenbow's upper echelon, but there was none. Not even an acknowledgment. So I just shrugged my shoulders and carried on.

The convocation was one of the few times I used a prepared text. My subject was the role of Canadian Indians in modern society, and I was instructed to read my presentation in order to stay within the tight time frame set up for the ceremony. I tried to explain that I could keep within half a minute of any time limit by speaking off the cuff, but they insisted and so I did it. I suppose it was all right, but I always felt a prepared speech was somewhat stilted – at least for me.

There was one amusing incident that occurred at the convocation. Among the people whom I had personally invited were my old friends Ralph and Isobel Steinhauer. I was at rehearsals shortly before the event when the news came out that Ralph was going to be appointed lieutenant-governor. This immediately sent the protocol people into a flap. What could they do? Ralph would not be the vice-regal representative at the time of the convocation so he couldn't be accorded that honour. At the same time, he couldn't be left to sit in the audience. At last they arranged (with his amused approval) that he wear a black gown and pasteboard and join the honoured officials on the platform. We both had quite a laugh over this.

I suppose Glenbow's reaction – or lack of reaction – to my doctorate was on my mind a year later when I was awarded the Order of Canada. This was one of the most flattering compliments of my career and, like the doctorate, I had no idea it was even in the works. I found out later that Sheilagh Jameson and some others in the Glenbow Library and Archives had submitted my name while, quite coincidentally, a group from Lethbridge had also recommended me. It was the kind of recognition I never expected in my wildest dreams to ever receive, so this made it doubly pleasurable.

The news was tempered by the sadness that my father did not live to see me receive this honour. He had been to Calgary when I obtained my honorary doctorate and was alive when the announcement was made about the Order of Canada, but he passed away about three weeks before the big event. I was thankful when he told me that he was proud of me, for he always had difficulty in expressing his emotions to me or to my brothers. He had counselled me to follow a safe and secure path in life, but I had chosen otherwise. I think he realized that I had listened to a different drummer and in the end he was pleased that I had taken a route that was dictated by my heart, rather than by any sense of logic.

The reaction of Glenbow's upper echelon to the Order of Canada was notable for its absence, so rather than going through the embarrassment of asking for time off and perhaps being refused, I decided to use my holidays in order to go to Ottawa. The Governor-General's office was generous in providing first class air fare for Pauline and me, which meant that by changing these to economy tickets and adding a few dollars we were able to take all five children. While in Ottawa, we stayed in Queenie's rumpus room; she was the widow of my brother Harry. So we travelled at a modest expense.

We arrived in Ottawa on October 11, 1975, and for the first couple of days I showed the family the sights of Ottawa and Hull. During this time, we were joined by my mother, who in spite of my father's death wouldn't have missed the event for anything in the world. We all visited the Parliament Buildings, went to the top of the Peace Tower, and saw the House in session. On October

15, we went to Government House, where Mom, Pauline, and the children sat in the spectator area while I was seated with the fifty-nine others who were receiving their awards, including singers Anne Murray and Juliette Cavazzi, philanthropist Martha Cohen, and broadcaster Clyde Gilmour. When my name was called, I stood before Governor-General Jules Leger, received my medal, and made my bow. Later, there was a reception at which Pauline and I attended. For this occasion, Pauline was attired in one of her beautiful Blackfoot beaded velvet dresses and looked magnificent.

Pauline was an avid autograph collector. When my Crowfoot book came out, she transformed her copy into an autograph album and it was filled with names of movie people, politicians, Indian leaders, and many friends. She had it with her at the reception, and when Prime Minister Pierre Trudeau arrived, she knew she already had his autograph but she wanted one from Margaret, his wife. Pauline went to her with book in hand but when she stood in front of her, she saw that Margaret was wearing a dress that was cut so low in front that almost nothing was left to the imagination. This so shocked and unsettled Pauline that she backed off and ended up being too shy or taken aback to ask. Actually, I thought the dress looked pretty good.

Now that we were in the East, we took the opportunity to rent a car and drive to New York. At this time, James was sixteen, Louise fourteen, John twelve, and Leah and Lois eleven. During the two days we were there we saw all the usual sights – Broadway, Greenwich Village, the Statue of Liberty, etc. I had been there several times before so I was in a good position to show them around. At one point, James left us and returned with a pair of snakeskin knee-high boots with six-inch platform soles that had to be seen to be believed. The only downside of the trip was that it was raining when we arrived, raining while we were there, raining when we left, and still raining when we got to Ottawa to catch our flight back home. But it was still a memorable experience, both in receiving Canada's highest order, and in being with the family in the Big Apple. On my return, no one in authority at Glenbow ever mentioned the trip, nor did they comment when I received the Alberta Achievement Award both in 1974 and 1975. But I hadn't expected that they would.

---

The 1970s were a time when I seemed to have become very involved with boards and committees outside of Glenbow. The first of these occurred late in 1969 when I was invited to a meeting of the Tribal Council on the Blackfoot Reserve. The chief, Adam Solway, was looking for ways to commemorate the 100th anniversary of the signing of Treaty Seven, which would occur in 1977. He felt that they would need a lot of lead time if they were going to get organized. The upshot of it was that the chiefs of the Blackfoot, Blood, Peigan, Sarcee, and Stoney agreed to form a Treaty Seven Centennial Committee, and they asked me if I would be the Secretary-Treasurer.

Our first meeting was held early in the New Year, and it was a perfect example of the differences between the two cultures. The meeting was scheduled to take place in my office at 10 a.m. There was no one there at 10 but soon Jim Munro arrived, representing the Blackfoot, and Dick Big Plume, chief of the Sarcees. We sat around and visited until just before noon when Jim Big Throat arrived from the Bloods. At that point, the three of them decided to go for lunch while I took the opportunity to get a little work done. Shortly after one o'clock Munro and Big Throat returned but we never saw Big Plume again. Then, at 3 p.m., Blackfoot chief Adam Solway and Clement Doore joined us and the meeting started.

During this time, one of the people in our office took me aside and said, "Doesn't this drive you crazy? Your meeting was supposed to start at 10:00 but you didn't get going until 3:00." I said it didn't bother me at all. I had scheduled the whole day for the meeting, and while we were waiting we covered a lot of ground – news, business, gossip, and some insights on what was happening on the reserves. Once the meeting started it proceeded in a businesslike way and we covered everything on the agenda. So where was the problem?

At the request of the committee, I wrote to the federal government and eventually we got a cheque for $15,000 – $3,000 for each Treaty Seven reserve. Our committee had no legal status and I knew it might be a while before we used the money, so with the chairman's permission I put it under my own name in a limited chequing account that would draw the most interest. We never heard from the federal government again; they never asked for an accounting of a cent of the money.

Over the next few months we had several meetings and kicked around some ideas, but it soon became clear that Solway had jumped the gun too soon. No one was ready to talk seriously about an event that was still seven years away. Gradually the meetings became fewer and fewer, and when Adam lost out as chief, they stopped altogether. Meanwhile, I was sitting on $15,000 of their money in my own bank account!

Six years later, in 1976, the Treaty Seven chiefs called another meeting and I was invited. None of the original group was there but some of them had heard rumours that the earlier committee had obtained some money. Could

I tell them what had happened to it? When I explained that it was sitting in a bank account in Calgary they were surprised and pleased. I think they had accepted the fact that after all those years the money would have been long gone. Then they were further pleased, or perhaps I should say elated, when I told them that the money had been drawing interest and now totalled $18,000. They asked me to continue as a member of the Committee but I soon found that it would conflict with my appointment as a member of the Alberta Indian Treaties Commemorative Program of the Alberta government. I had already learned that my name was going before the Cabinet as a member of this Committee and, as we would be giving out large grants, I did not want to be in a compromising position.

I was appointed to the provincial Committee in the summer of 1976 and was involved in numerous meetings over the next few months. At this time we had a paid director heading up the project and he had hired a Vancouver public relations firm to carry out much of the work. I know I made myself unpopular with this bunch at our first or second meeting when a proposal was made that we buy some rather poor airbrush paintings of prominent chiefs and use these for promotional purposes. The price per picture was outrageous and I pointed out that all had been copied from well known photographs. Any commercial artist could have turned them out in a day. The Committee agreed and the recommendation was refused. I learned later that these pictures had indeed been turned out overnight, but what I didn't know at the time was that the work had been done by the artist at the public relations firm. They had tried to sell them to the Committee through a dummy company. It had simply been a scam to make a few quick bucks. As it was, they still had these pictures printed and sold commercially and I suspect that the printing costs had been buried in the public relations firm's invoices and paid for by our Committee.

I was involved heavily in the publication side of the program, and later, when we could not find enough people or groups to use the money designated for publications, I suggested that Glenbow get involved. I realized this could be construed as a conflict of interest but the matter was checked out and it was determined that as long as I was not profiting personally from the transaction and that Glenbow could be verified as a non-profit agency, there would be no problem. As a result, we channelled three books through Glenbow – *My People the Bloods*, by Mike Mountain Horse; *My Tribe the Crees*, by Joe Dion; and *Medicine Boy and Other Cree Tales*, by Eleanor Brass. All were by Native authors and with no hope of having them published elsewhere. In each instance, I edited them and prepared them for the printers.

Another committee that took a lot of my time in the seventies was the Alberta RCMP Centennial Committee, also created by the Alberta government to provide grants to municipalities, groups, and individuals. That one lasted for a couple of years and was a lot of fun. If I recall correctly, Jim MacGregor was the chairman and Alex Johnston one of the members, so I was in good company. We started holding meetings in Edmonton in 1972 and these reached their peak in 1973 (the anniversary of the year the Mounted Police were formed) and 1974 (the anniversary of the year they marched West).

As part of the celebrations, the Historical Society of Alberta received a major grant and sponsored a Mounted Police conference in the spring of 1974. I gave a paper on Writing-on-Stone and became general editor in charge of publishing the papers. This turned out to be quite a feat. I was able to get virtually all the presenters to give me their papers before the conference, and while the sessions were underway, everything was being set in type. As a result, the hardcover book, *Men in Scarlet*, was published only a few weeks after the conference.

When the centennial was over, the money spent, and congratulations received for a job well done, our members were very pleased to receive cuckoo clocks with brass presentation plates and fronts carved with the RCMP symbols.

A third appointment during the seventies was a prestigious one. In 1976 I was informed that I had been appointed to the Historic Sites and Monuments Board of Canada as the representative from Alberta. This came as a complete surprise to me, as I understood these were usually political appointments made by the minister involved. A short time later, I was told that the minister, Hon. Judd Buchanan, had selected me and that he had gone to school with me. Then it became clear: the Judd Buchanan who had been one of our bunch at McDougall Commercial in the mid-1940s was the same man who was now the minister. So that's how a card-carrying Conservative was appointed by a Liberal government for a three-year term on one of the most prestigious boards in Canada.

This was my first experience with this type of federal board and it was first class all the way. We had two meetings a year – one in Ottawa in the fall and a second in the field in the spring. Among the places I visited were Dawson City, St. John's, and Stratford. My term with the Board was short, but it was very memorable.

On my first tour in 1977, we had our meeting in Vancouver, at which time I made an impassioned plea to obtain the Bar U Ranch as a National Historic Site. The Board agreed but later the deal fell through when the government took too long to purchase the site. Not until many years later did the opportunity arise again, and the site was finally acquired. At this meeting I was appointed to the Indigenous and Fur Trade Committee. I also became good friends of George MacDonald, of the Canadian Museum of Civilization, and Robert Painchaud, member from Manitoba. Painchaud was particularly interesting, as he studied the French in western Canada and concluded that they had been abandoned by Quebec and had been on their own for many years. He saw the French in the West being closer to their counterparts in the Maritimes than with Quebeckers.

The meeting in the following year, 1978, will always be ingrained in my memory. On June 18, I flew to St. John's, Newfoundland, and got a room in the Hotel Newfoundland with a magnificent view of the harbour. The next day our committee had lunch with the lieutenant-governor, toured the area, and proceeded with our business meeting. The next couple of days saw us in Conception Bay and Torbay, where we were wined, dined, and toured in high style. By this time, our business meeting had ended and we now looked forward to flying to L'Anse Aux Meadows, the Viking site at the north end of the island.

The morning of June 23rd was foggy with a steady drizzle but we were told the north end of the island was expected to be clear. After breakfast we went by bus to the airport, where three Beechcraft planes had been chartered to take us to St. Anthony. From there buses would be waiting to take us to the Viking site. David Smith, Robert Painchaud, and I chatted for a while, and then Robert drifted over to some of the French-speaking members. At 9:00 a.m. we were told to pile our luggage for shipment and to board any of the aircraft that were sitting on the tarmac. There were no reserved seats. The French-speaking group and others boarded the closest one, so David Smith and I got into the second one, along with Margaret Prang, Maurice Careless, Leslie Harris, Frank Bolger, and Mr. and Mrs. Maclean. Although we were second in the row we were the first to be ready and led the way as we taxied to the runway. A small executive jet in front of us took off and we followed. As I looked back, I could see the other two planes taxiing behind us.

We lifted off the ground and into a thick fog but then we got above it to the clear skies and headed north. Almost two hours later we landed on an isolated strip that served St. Anthony, then stood around waiting for the other two planes. When they hadn't arrived after half an hour we thought maybe their flights had been aborted because of the fog. Then, to add to the mystery, a man from the airport came around and asked each of us for our names. He gave no explanation but just returned to the radio tower with his list.

A short time later, we were told the terrible news. The plane after us had crashed into a high hill and everyone on board had been killed. I noted in my diary, "Apparently it had developed engine trouble just after takeoff while still in the fog at 1200 feet. It had tried to return to the field but lost altitude in the fog and crashed into a hill."[119] Because there were no reserved seats the people at the airfield had no idea who was on the plane. The third aircraft had never taken off, so a list was made of those still at St. John's. Then the authorities contacted St. Anthony and got a list of our names. By a process of elimination, they learned the names of those who had been killed. They included my good friend Robert Painchaud, our chairman, Marc LeTerreur, Jules Leger and his wife, Napier Simpson, secretary Brenda Babitts and her husband Alex, and also the pilot, the navigator, and the mayor of Torbay.

We were all in a state of shock. As I wrote, "We had all been so close together during the previous days & now they were gone. We wandered around in a disbelieving daze until the charter aircraft came to take us back to St. John's."[120] On the way back, we still had no details of the tragedy so it was very unsettling to be flying in the same kind of aircraft that had carried our friends to their deaths only hours before. On arrival in St. John's, we were informed that we should stay the night and airline reservations would be made for us for the following day. But I didn't want to hang around. I had a strong urge to get back home and leave this tragic place as quickly as possible. Two or three others felt the same way, so we jumped on the first flight out, which took us to Halifax. I was prepared to go standby all the way but I was lucky and got a seat to Montreal, where I was put on a non-stop flight to Calgary. I had already phoned Pauline to let her know that I was all right and when I reached Calgary shortly after midnight, she was waiting at the airport. As I wrote, "It was like a nightmare but it was real. A quarter of our Board is gone."[121] I couldn't help but recall many years later when my first flight had ended in a crack-up, I said then that the average person would never have more than one crash in their lifetime and I had had mine. Any of us could have boarded that fatal plane, and I could easily have been one of them. But philosophically I thought, "I already had my crash."

I heard nothing more from the Board as the Parks Branch went through the trauma of reorganizing. In the interim I continued to carry out my local duties, which included being master of ceremonies at plaque unveilings, and presiding at the opening of the Rocky Mountain House National Historic Park. The next annual meeting was in May 1979, by which time Leslie Harris had been appointed chairman. We met in Toronto, where a very ironic incident occurred. We were sitting in a hotel room when the results came in of the federal election. I was the only Conservative in the room so there were lots of remarks when Joe Clark and the Conservative party were elected to power. I expressed myself as being quite pleased although, as I stated at the time, "I have many doubts about Clark's ability."[122] We went on to conclude our business and then to tour the historic sites in southern Ontario.

I had now served three years on the Historic Sites and Monuments Board and, according to practice, if a person proved to be capable, they were reappointed for another five years. By this time I was a member of the Executive Committee and chairman of two other committees. Everyone said that my appointment would be automatic. Imagine my surprise and shock a few weeks later when I got a call from Ottawa, informing me that I was off the Board. I had not been reappointed. I later heard that when the Conservatives looked at the reappointment, they automatically assumed that because I had been named by the Liberal government that I must be a member of that party and therefore I had to be replaced. My replacement, Trudy Soby, had formerly worked for me, and I had recommended her for the position of Curator of Fort Calgary Park. The breaking with the traditional practice of reappointments because of political considerations would not surprise me, especially as the approval had to come from the prime ministerial level.

I don't know if I was more angry or hurt. I felt that during my three years I had proven myself, and judging from the phone calls and messages I got from other members of the Board after the announcement, they thought so too. I believed I was now experienced enough to be a real asset to the Board in representing Alberta, but I was denied the chance. But there was nothing I could do.

Meanwhile, I had been elected Secretary-Treasurer of the Kainai Chieftainship in 1969 and I soon discovered that this meant doing most of the work. I had to keep minutes, handle all correspondence, collect donations, and – most important – liaise with the Tribal Council when new chieftainships were being conferred. For example, here are my diary entries for 1976:

> July 14 – "I drove to Fort Macleod for a meeting with Abs Swinarton & Charlie Edgar to let them audit the Kainai Chieftainship books, and then to Standoff for a meeting with several members of the tribal council, plus Marvin Fox, to complete arrangements for next week. I am very impressed with the way it's going together."

July 22 – "Leaving about 3:30 pm, I drove to Fort Macleod & then on to Standoff. The stage for the program was not in place but everything else seemed ok. I had a meeting with Wayne Wells & we ironed out a few more problems."

July 23 – "I was up at 8 am & reached the Tribal Office at 9:30. I made sure everything was in order & was very pleased with Marvin's work. At 11 am we had the annual meeting of the Kainai Chieftainship & I was re-elected Secretary-Treasurer. At noon we had a luncheon for tribal councillors & hon. chiefs & at 1 pm Ralph Steinhauer unveiled a sculpture. After a tour of the building we went to the grounds where Ralph Steinhauer, Tony Anselmo & Colin Low were inducted as honorary chiefs. It all went beautifully. Also the day was sunny & hot & the new Indian Days camp grounds were excellent."

Those diary entries just show the tip of the iceberg, for there were always difficulties and complications, but I had been involved with Indians for enough years to know that we would muddle through and in the end everything would be fine. Sometimes a buffalo robe needed for the ceremony was forgotten; maybe one of the leading participants didn't show up; perhaps the person with the headdresses didn't appear. But I never worried too much, as we adjusted, compromised, and by the time it was over, nobody knew the difference.

That, however, was not acceptable during the visit of the Prince of Wales in 1977. This was the 100th anniversary of the signing of Treaty Seven and big things were planned on various southern Alberta reserves, including the conferral of an honorary chieftainship upon the prince. As I was a member of the Alberta Indian Treaties Commemorative Program as well as Secretary-Treasurer of the Kainai Chieftainship, I became a member of a special committee organized to oversee the prince's visits to the reserves.

Meetings started early in the year. In April, Buck Crump, president of the Chieftainship, and I met with the tribal council, at which time Wayne Wells and Geraldine Many Fingers were designated as our liaison. I then had later meetings with them during which time we set down a minute-by-minute outline of the chieftainship ceremonies. We did it with tongue in cheek to a certain extent, because we knew there was no way we could keep the holy men to a set schedule. If a prayer was supposed to be for three minutes, it might last ten. If a dance was supposed to go one round, it might go four. But we set out the program as demanded by the protocol people, then crossed our fingers and hoped for the best. In mid-May we had a meeting with the Horn Society, as represented by Adam Delaney and Pete Standing Alone, and got their approval before submitting our report to Ottawa.

At the end of the month, a delegation of officials arrived from Ottawa and Buckingham Palace and went over every fine detail, not only of the Kainai Chieftainship, but of the prince's intended visits to the other reserves. On the following day, we all boarded a huge military helicopter – a 42-passenger Boeing Chinook – and flew to Blackfoot Crossing, where we reviewed the site and met with the Native leaders. From there we proceeded to Standoff, then made a bus tour of the places the prince would visit. On each step of the way, the officials seemed to have a dozen questions, and I was stuck with answering a lot of them. I also gave them a long speech about the Sun Dance and its religious significance. From Standoff we flew to Brocket where we met the Peigans, and then it was back to Calgary. It was a bone-shattering and ear-splitting experience on that helicopter and I was glad when we finally touched down at Currie Barracks in Calgary.

Meanwhile, there were lots of other preparations to be made. It was no surprise that we would be having the biggest turnout of the honorary chieftains in history, and these had to be coordinated. In preparation for the arrival of the prince in Calgary, two Stoney chiefs asked me to look over their addresses of welcome and to edit them, but I ended up completely rewriting them. Also, Ralph Steinhauer asked me to write the speech he was expected to make as lieutenant-governor. As I have said, Ralph and I were close friends. A couple of years later, when he was retiring from office, he put my name forward as lieutenant-governor but nothing ever came of it.

The first of the big days for the Royal Visit came on July 5 when our committee members were presented to Prince Charles. He had a brief chat with each of us, and judging by the questions he asked me, he was obviously well briefed. The next day, Pauline and I drove to Blackfoot Crossing where a large camp of tepees had been pitched. After the prince arrived, all the chiefs and councillors were lined up and I was pleasantly surprised when I was asked to join them. After the speeches, Prince Charles presented each of the head chiefs with a replica of the original Treaty Seven medal, and then Ralph Steinhauer made similar presentations to the councillors and to me. I was told that because of the nature of the presentation, we all had the right to wear the medal at any time; I have yet to wear mine but it is a treasured keepsake. Afterwards, everyone was designated to go to a tepee where tea was served. I went to Ben Calf Robe's tepee, where Pauline had volunteered to assist; during the tea a terrible dust storm arose and rocked the entire camp. I learned later that at one point the tepee in which Prince Charles was seated began to rock so dangerously that a number of Mounted Police stood on the edge of the canvas outside to keep it from blowing away.

Just to prove my point that nothing ever goes as planned, during the speeches when the Peigans were supposed to talk, Devlin Small Legs turned the microphone over to Calgary lawyer J. Webster Macdonald, who gave a long and ill-advised speech on Indian land claims.

The next day, July 7th, Pauline and I drove to Fort Macleod, where we met the honorary chieftains, and as a group we proceeded by charter bus to Standoff. A total of twenty-four members turned out, including John Diefenbaker, Davey Fulton, Roland Michener, Jim Cross, George McClellan, Herman Linder, and a host of others. The Royal party arrived at 10 a.m. and the unveiling of a Red Crow monument took place. From there, two buses left to tour the reserve. In the first one was the Royal party and in the second were the Chieftains. The only person who gave us a problem was Diefenbaker, who was clearly past his prime but was still living with the memories of his past glories. Right from the beginning, he did not follow instructions as to where to meet and went straight to Standoff, bringing with him two uninvited guests, Clarence Copithorne and George Cloakey. The latter was very rude when told that they could not join the tour as the bus was completely full.

At the first stop – Kainai Industries Ltd. – Diefenbaker got right off and joined in with the Royal party, striding along beside Prince Charles. This just about drove the protocol people wild and one of the Buckingham Palace officials, not knowing that Diefenbaker had once been our prime minister, came to me in a flap and said, "Can't you do something about that guy?" The next stop was Blood Band Farms and I felt I had no alternative but to instruct the driver to keep the doors closed, and I announced that everyone had to stay on board. There were outbursts of indignation but I felt I really had no choice as clearly Diefenbaker was making himself an unwelcome guest of the Royal party. And that's the way it was for the rest of the tour; at each stop Prince Charles and his party toured while we sat.

When we got to the Sun Dance camp in the afternoon, I decided to stick with Diefenbaker, not only because of his age and possible problems he might create, but because I had always truly admired the man. As we walked across the open field, people stopped him and said things like, "God bless you, Mr.

Diefenbaker," and "We love you, John." As a result, we were the last to get to the platform where the chieftains were seated. All the front row seats had been taken so I directed the former prime minister to a seat in the second row. He gave me a cold look and said, "I do not sit in the second row." So I picked up his chair, tightened up the seating in the front row, and seated him front and centre. It was a small point but I was glad I was able to oblige him. From that point on he was quite happy and gracious, and I did not hear a word from him for the rest of the program.

A small trailer had been set up beside the ceremonial area and after the prince was introduced to the mob of people, he was presented with a buckskin outfit and withdrew to change. After a few minutes, one of the Buckingham Palace people came to me and said they were having some problems. Wayne Wells and I followed him to the trailer, where we found Prince Charles sitting partially dressed and wearing swimming trunks. He said he couldn't figure out how to put on the leggings or the moccasins. I looked at the moccasins and found that when Priscilla Bruised Head had made them, she must have been in a rush, for she had left the laces inside them and had not made holes for the eyelets. Neither Wayne nor I had an awl so we called for Priscilla, who quickly made the holes and laced them. As for the leggings, Priscilla had decided to be "innovative" and had strung them in a most unusual way so that they did not fasten to a belt. She showed us how they supposed to be worn and quickly we got Prince Charles properly dressed. During all this time, the prince was quite animated in his discussion as he made humorous remarks, asked questions, and seemed to be thoroughly enjoying himself.

At last he emerged from trailer and the Bloods went wild. There was cheering, drumming, and even a few war whoops or two as their favourite monarch appeared before them in tribal costume. I don't think I ever saw the Bloods happier or more proud than they were during those chieftainship ceremonies. It was a real pleasure to behold.

During the next half hour or so, Prince Charles went through the whole induction ceremony. He was "captured" by a warrior, Horace Quesnelle, a veteran of World War II, led around the circle, and then seated on a buffalo robe. The holy man went through the purification and painting ceremony, after which he placed a headdress on him and gave him the name of Red Crow. Then followed an honouring dance of the chief and council and the chieftains, with Pauline and I joining in the circle. A surprise followed when Wilton Goodstriker brought out a pinto horse named "Cross Bell" and presented it to

Prince Charles. The prince mounted it and rode out of the circle and over to his helicopter, followed by crowds of cheering Bloods.

The horse had been raised by Wilton's father, Rufus Goodstriker, and when the presentation was made, the protocol people didn't know what to do with it. They didn't want to take it to England, so at last it was placed with a herd of horses used by the Queen's Own Rifles for their parades. We learned later that the horse was a real bully and soon dominated the entire herd.

The next day, Prince Charles visited the Indian Village at the Calgary Stampede, where Pauline was in charge of the bannock booth. She was a member of the Indian Events Committee and the booth had been the brainchild of Pauline and Cheryl Hall. At the same time, I worked with the Bloods on a display they had at the camp and spent the rest of the time visiting with Ralph Steinhauer while the official party made its tour.

The following day, I was up bright and early to get to the unveiling of the Bull Head memorial on the Sarcee Reserve. By this time there were rumours that the American Indian Movement intended to put on a demonstration, and I had to go through three separate RCMP road checks before I was able to get in. While I was waiting for the Royal party to arrive, I noticed a scruffy white man wandering around and I wondered if I should let the Mounties know. But when I got close to him, I saw that he was wearing a tiny gold pin in the shape of a buffalo head, and I knew right away that he was an undercover Mountie. I had been shown one of these pins earlier and was given one after the visit was over. As it turned out, the AIM people never arrived and the undercover cop was the only suspicious-looking character in the whole camp.

When I arrived, Amos Many Wounds took me to the tepee where the ceremony was to take place to show me around, and during the ceremony itself I spent most of my time with Gordon Crowchild and Joe Dion. The rest of the day saw me back at the Stampede where I was taken up with events at the Kinsmen Centre. John Snow presented me with a copy of his new book, and then I went to the bannock booth, where I helped out until exhaustion overtook me. When I got home I slept straight through until the next day, but as I said in my diary, "It was one of the most pleasant times I have ever experienced."[123]

Another board that gave me a lot of fun, as well as a few frustrations, was the Canada Council. In 1978 I was invited to be a member of the Prairie Region of their Explorations Program. It was kind of a catch-all committee that inherited all the grant applications that didn't seem to fit anywhere else. At one meeting, for example, we approved funds for studies of footwear decorations and Easter egg designs, a novel about James Walsh, and a film on the

Chipewyan Indians. There was, however, a strong orientation to history and so I was right in my element. Our first task was to select about one out of every seven applications and then do the fine tuning from there. We met at various places – Ottawa, Winnipeg, Prince Albert, Yellowknife, etc. – often seeing the craftsmen and writers who were applying for grants. After two years, I became chairman of the committee and also was appointed to the national board in Ottawa. That was a little different, because grants often became political and territorial. But it was a good experience and the secretary, Kate Wilkinson, was a tower of strength.

A little closer to home was my involvement in trying to get more Canadian history into the Alberta school system. Author Jim Gray had lobbied long and hard in this direction and when his efforts paid off, I was invited, along with Grant MacEwan, Doug Francis, and a number of others, to join him in 1987 on the Advisory Committee of the Alberta Heritage Learning Resources Program. There was $8 million to spend and our mandate was to look at reprinting books, either out of print or still in print, that should be placed in Alberta school libraries. We were to include history, general non-fiction, fiction, an atlas, and school kits.

However, we had not anticipated the attitude of a few influential members of the Alberta Education bureaucracy. After only two meetings, Jim Gray sounded off in his usual forthright way. He said, "my suspicion is aroused that the department of education is now embarked on a vast boondoggle to spend its $8,000,000 filling more vast warehouses with 'learning materials.' We have already two such warehouses in Calgary ... surrounded by pyramids of this junk."[124] He believed, instead, that ten basic books on western Canadian history should become required reading for anyone teaching Social Studies.

I had concerns as well. These were based on the bureaucratic philosophy that history was a subject that should be taught only if it had relevance to the present and to the lives of the students. Teaching history simply for gaining an insight and knowledge of the past was anathema to them. In a report to the Advisory Committee I stated, "I do not believe that history should simply be a vehicle to enable the student to better understand himself and his contemporary society. I realize that I am trying to swim against the surging tides of educators with that philosophy and can be cast upon dangerous shoals. Yet just as we teach the sciences without trying to relate everything to the daily life of the student, so should history be a distinctive course of study."[125]

At the beginning, it was a head-to-head struggle, with Gray being so outspoken and vociferous at times that it was almost embarrassing. However, once he had had his say, everything settled down and some really positive results were achieved. Whole sets of books were reprinted, including one or two of mine, and sent out to schools, as were the atlas and school kits. Unfortunately, I was off and running on other matters so I never really had a chance to measure the success of the program. I do know it was very unsettling to see the books appear in second-hand stores not long after the program was finished. I do hope, however, that all the efforts of the Advisory Committee and some of the really dedicated members of Alberta Education such as Al Michener did manage to touch some of our Alberta students.

My life when not at Glenbow work or on committees was still involved primarily with Indians and our own nuclear family. Dad's activities still took a lot of time, particularly as I wrote most of his speeches and both Pauline and I did his record keeping and scheduled his appointments. But in the spring of 1971, at the age of eighty-four, he retired and spent most of his time in Alberta. Then, on September 4th, we learned that some friends among the Kootenay tribe, the Ambrose Gravelles, had some tanned hides to sell, so we decided to take a weekend jaunt. Mom, Dad, Pauline, our nine-year-old son John, and I set out for British Columbia amid beautiful fall weather. When we got to Fernie, Dad collapsed from a heart attack and was rushed to the local hospital, where he died. To say that we were devastated is an understatement. Our whole lives had circulated around him and his work for the previous twenty years, first in the Indian Association and later in the Senate. He was the head of our clan, the leader of our extended family, and the person who seemed to give us a direction in life. We were guided by his humility, his honesty, his intelligence, and his dedication to the Indian people. As we began to drive back home to Cardston without him, the world suddenly seemed to be a more barren place.

As one could imagine, the funeral at St. Paul's church was huge. Hon. Jean Chrétien, Hon. Bud Olson, Len Marchand, Harold Cardinal, and many other dignitaries were there, together with the Gladstones, the Healys, the Tailfeathers, and many others from the reserve.

But the tragedies in our family were not over. Just a month later, blood was found in the urine of our eight-year-old daughter Lois. The doctors said that nephritis had attacked both kidneys and at the time of their tests, 50 per cent of their effectiveness had been destroyed. Dialysis was barely in its infancy and not considered effective for a young child, and the doctors said that if the deterioration continued there would be little chance of saving her life.

Then a miracle happened. There was a new experimental drug on the market called Immuran so the doctors decided to try it to see if it could control the nephritis. To our joy, the drug was immediately effective and by the end of the year Lois was able to go home. She had to go on a salt-free diet and take drugs but she came through the whole ordeal remarkably well. The miracle of this eleventh-hour discovery made me recall something that had happened a year earlier. The best way to describe it is to quote from my diary, telling about a trip to the Blood Reserve.

I went to see Willie Scraping White who went through a prayer ceremony with me. I had had a bad dream about Lois and as Willie is known for his proficiency in these matters, I decided to see him. After I explained my need, he called Mike Yellow Bull to put some wood in the stove to get charcoal. Then Mike got a canvas bag from a trunk, from which Willie extracted a necklace and paint bags. He put on the necklace, which bore a decorated iniskim and small decorated bag.

Mike put a live coal on the altar and crumpled some sweetgrass on it. Willie began to pray and rubbed the paint on his hands. I then sat in front of him and he painted a round solid circle on my right forehead, a wavy line across my front forehead and another solid circle on my left temple. He then drew lines down the sides of my face. He put a solid circle on my right wrist, top, & left wrist, then gave me a paint-covered [buffalo] stone which he pressed to my right hand and pressed my right hand to my heart. He took the stone and encircled my body with it four times, praying all the time.

It was a most solemn occasion and one which I took very seriously. He then instructed me to leave the paint on until next morning. When I got home, I was to take some of the paint from the circle on my right temple and rub it on Lois' forehead (which I did). I left him with a blanket and money for his prayers.[126]

Such ceremonies were offered to help the sick. The *iniskim*, or buffalo stone, was an important part of the rite, and such an amulet became very important to Lois in later years when she again needed another miracle.

Then, on April 3, 1975, my close friend Gerald Tailfeathers died of a heart attack. He was only fifty years old. He had had a bad heart since contracting undulant fever as a teenager, and his doctor had been urging him to have a bypass. However, Gerald kept putting it off, with this fatal result. I was one of the pallbearers at his funeral, and on the day in question I awoke in Calgary to a raging spring blizzard. Not knowing how far the storm extended, I decided to set out; nothing was going to keep me from paying my last respects to Gerald. As I proceeded south, I plowed through snowdrifts and fought the savage conditions of high winds and blowing snow. For most of the trip, I was the only vehicle on the highway and there was no letup in the storm as I continued south. At last I got to the Blood Reserve, where I was not surprised to discover that the funeral had been postponed. The storm soon blew itself out, and a few days later, I was back for the final farewells. As with Dad, I missed Gerald tremendously. We never lacked things to talk about, and as Pauline and Irene were old school chums, we always made a convivial foursome.

About this time, our family had a real family outing when I was asked to give a week of lectures to Cree researchers on the Rocky Boy Reservation in Montana. They were undertaking a major interviewing project, funded by the J.F. Kennedy Foundation, and wanted direction as to how to go about it. When we arrived at Rocky in scorching 104-degree heat our cabin was not ready so we had to spend the first night in a tent. Next day we attended the Indian Days, and on August 6th I finally started teaching at the Rocky Boy school. The whole idea was to enable the researchers to tape record the experiences of their elders. One of the requirements of the grant was that they had to get instructions from a professional as to how to proceed. That's where I came in: I was to give them a one-week course in collecting oral history. There were a dozen or more in the group, including Joe Small, Art Raining Bird, and Walter Denney. Over the next few days, I covered everything from Cree history to conducting interviews, to documenting their material afterwards. While I was teaching, Pauline and the children travelled around the countryside and we all gathered each night at our cabin for supper.

On the second evening there was a reception, and while we were chatting, a man came up to Pauline and asked if she was a Gladstone. When she said she was, he stuck out his hand and introduced himself as her relative. His name was Four Souls. But more important to me, he was a son of Imasees and grandson of Big Bear, the famous Cree chief. The way we figured the relation-ship with Pauline was as follows: Four Souls' aunt (Big Bear's daughter) married Lone Man Johnson, and their daughter married George Gladstone, Dad's half-brother. That made them relatives from the Indian point of view, and from that time on the Four Souls family referred to my wife as Aunt Pauline. And she loved it, as the people there were very friendly to us.

I asked Four Souls if he knew anything about Big Bear, and in reply he invited me to visit him and he would tell me some stories. All next evening, I listened and wrote and he told me story after story about Big Bear and his family, most of it never recorded before. He gave me the names of Big Bear's parents, previously unrecorded, and established the fact that rather than having risen from obscurity to become a chief, Big Bear was actually the son of a prominent leader. Four Souls told me of his grandfather's experiences in Montana and of his spiritual powers. By the time I left, I knew I had to write a book on this great Cree chief. It didn't happen right away, as I had other projects in the fire, but I did make further trips to the Rocky Boy Reservation and Four Souls and I became good friends. Pauline and I were present at his funeral and both of us were honoured by being treated as part of his extended family.

Speaking of Pauline, she wasn't sitting idly at home during the 1970s. She served a term on the Senate of the University of Calgary, was vice-president of the Women's Canadian Club, and of the Calgary Women's P.C. Association. At the beginning of the decade she became a coordinator/counsellor for the first Indian students entering Mount Royal College. She found them housing, which sometimes was a problem considering the level of discrimination from people who were not used to well-educated, well-motivated young Indians coming to the city. And she acted as a go-between with Indian Affairs. She was very popular with the students and accomplished a lot in her three years there. One particular act was memorable. Normally cheques for the students arrived a day or two before the end of each month, when Pauline distributed them and made sure the rents were paid. In one month, however, the cheques failed to appear and when she checked she found there was a typical Indian Affairs screw-up and the money wouldn't arrive until after the first of the month. She knew that some of the landladies, who already were leery about having Indian tenants, would never put up with this, and the students would be out on the street.

To solve the situation, Pauline went to a local bank, showed them the Indian Affairs papers, and then borrowed $1,800 under her own signature. When the government cheques did arrive, each student signed them over to her and she repaid the loan. When government officials heard about it they were appalled. They said if they students had kept their cheques there would have been nothing she could do about it. But she trusted them, and they trusted her.

In 1972, Pauline moved over to the University of Calgary, where she continued her work as counsellor. In this instance, she not only working with Indian Affairs, but with teachers and other faculty members. This included a lot of new challenges, particularly in the university bureaucracy. But it paid off, for quite a number of graduates went on to have successful careers. Then at the end of the decade, Pauline took her counselling work a step further when she became a crisis counsellor at the Calgary Women's Emergency Shelter. All this was in addition to looking after five children, two or three dogs, and one husband.

I must mention something amusing that happened to Pauline about this time. There had been a number of protests taking place across Canada as Indians expressed their anger by temporarily taking over Indian Department and other government offices. When a young group chose to have a sit-in at the Calgary offices, Pauline decided after a day or two to see how they were doing. So she bought a bag of oranges and boldly walked past the police lines to deliver them. When she got upstairs to the offices she found them in a mess. The copying machine was jammed, and the kids were trying to two-finger type a press release.

Pauline took over. She rounded up some girls and put them to work tidying the office. She fixed the copier and then did all the typing, including the press releases. It was a busy afternoon.

Two days later, the Hon. Judd Buchanan, Minister of Indian Affairs, was in town for an official function at Glenbow, to which Pauline and I were invited. During the afternoon, he presented our Chairman of the Board, Douglas Harkness, with a medal that had been given to Chief Crowfoot by the Marquis of Lorne in 1881. During the visit, Buchanan and I recalled our days as fellow Grade Ten students at McDougall High in Edmonton. After the presentation, the minister, Pauline and I and others went about half a block to one of our other buildings to view our ethnological collection. As we walked under heavy guard (the sit-in was still in effect) I told Buchanan about Pauline's involvement with the dissidents. He called her a naughty girl and we all had a big laugh about it. The guards were outside and the "enemy" was within.

All in all, the seventies had their highs and lows. I was in my forties and was probably experiencing the most active time of my career. Pauline and I were always busy but we both enjoyed it, particularly when we were involved with family or relatives.

# 10

## The Cameron Years

The appointment of Duncan Cameron as Executive Director of Glenbow in the fall of 1977 was like a breath of fresh air. Our whole world suddenly changed. As soon as he assumed complete control, he proved to be the finest CEO we ever had, before or since. He had been the director of the Brooklyn Museum and brought with him a level of professionalism previously unknown to the organization. The only person who might have come even close to him was Jack Herbert, but even he wasn't in the same league. I know some would disagree with my comments, as Duncan was a very controversial figure, but that's the way I saw it.

Duncan was appalled at what he found at Glenbow. Not only were we in financial turmoil, but the administrative structure was a mess. Although we had some fine collections and a few good staff, we had none of the systems in place that he felt were essential for the running of an efficient and success-ful museum. When he came, he had a mandate to change this. As he later said, the Board of Governors "wanted to turn Glenbow around and wanted to build a strong professional staff, raise the profile of Glenbow, and become a professional institution that was taken seriously not just in Canada, but else-where."[127] In the first few months, he did much to accomplish these goals. He had written policies developed for ethics, acquisitions, exhibitions, loans, staff development, etc. He also prepared the first list of goals which reinforced the principle of a western Canadian focus, but adding that it would be told in "an international context of human history, art and culture."[128]

Then he took the Ethnology Department out of mothballs, where it had languished for a year, and established Central Registration and Conservation departments. He also initiated a computerized cataloguing program which became part of a national registration system.

In addition, a considerable amount of reorganizing and new staffing took place. I was appointed Assistant Director (Collections) with the responsibility for the Library, Archives, Ethnology, Art, Cultural History, Military History, Conservation, and Education departments. I was also put in charge of several committees of the Board, including a new Acquisitions Committee which had monthly meetings to approve both accessions and de-accessions. The latter is an oxymoronic term for "getting rid of things." My other favourite oxymoron was "permanent loan."

When the new museum building was designed, I had carved out an office for myself on the sixth floor, beside the Library and Archives. I was part of the management team, but away from the rarefied atmosphere of the executive suite on the eighth floor. This way, I could spend less than half my time on administration and the rest working with historians and, admittedly, doing some of my own research. However, after my new appointment, Duncan moved me up to the executive suite. For years I had been able to avoid full administrative duties, leaving time for things that were important to me, but Duncan must have seen that, and located me next to his office where he could keep an eye on me. I guess it was a good idea, and although I managed to sneak in some research time, it was quite a change. Mind you, I didn't mind administration, as I had been doing it ever since I joined Glenbow, but I wanted to balance it with something more creative.

As Cameron brought in such professional people as Program Director Barbara Tyler and Registrar Annik-Louise Bawden, and encouraged existing staff, the face of the museum began to change. A year after his arrival, Glenbow had its first real international show, the art of Pablo Picasso. Admission was charged for the first time and the response was excellent. This was followed by the "Treasures of Ancient Nigeria," with Calgary being the only Canadian venue after showings in New York, Detroit, San Francisco, and Washington. At the same time, Duncan got the staff busy organizing its own travelling exhibitions, beginning with photographic presentations such as the Hutterites, Plains Indians, and Western Alienation. By 1981 we had twenty-two exhibitions "on the road."

This had a great impact on all of us. Departments that were accustomed to looking inwards to their own collections now were busily engaged in planning and fielding shows. As I mentioned in one report, "almost every curatorial department was heavily involved with exhibitions. Even the Library and Archives, which are normally considered to be concerned with reference services to the public, devoted an extensive amount of time to the exhibitions aspect of Glenbow's operations."

⌘

During these years, I had a steady stream of visitors. Many were visiting professionals, local journalists, businessmen, etc., but many were Indians. Eleanor Brass, Louis Soop, Willie Big Bull, Rick Tailfeathers, and Russell Wright were just a few.

There were two particularly interesting visitors, or at least the outcome of their visits was interesting. The first was Adolphus Weasel Child, who had worked with me on the Sun Dance film. He was my wife's sister-in-law's brother-in-law. He came in one day just for a visit, and while he was there I showed him around our Ethnology storage area. As we passed by some new accessions he pointed to a roach dancing headdress and said, "Where in the hell did you get that?" I said we bought it the day before from a Blackfoot Indian. Adolphus' surprise was understandable when he explained that the headdress was his and that he had loaned it on Friday to a friend. The man was supposed to have worn it to a dance on Saturday and returned it to Adolphus. On Monday we bought it. I asked Adolphus if he wanted the headdress back. He said, "No, just tell me how much you paid him for it, and I'll get the money out of the other guy."

The other visitor was Peter Many Wounds, from the Sarcee Reserve. Pete and I had been great friends ever since Pauline and I moved to Calgary and we always had something to talk about. His wife, Muriel, was the daughter of Ralph and Isobel Steinhauer, and Pauline had gone to Alberta College with her.

Pete and Muriel were an odd couple. Pete was a big, gruff Sarcee with a limited education, while Muriel was a schoolteacher, and quite refined. Both were highly intelligent people in their own ways and Pete showed the potential of being a great leader if he could control his battle with liquor. Gradually, however, booze got the better of him, and he slipped out of his family situation and onto the streets of Calgary. Glenbow was located at the edge of a slum area and more than once when I came to work in the early morning I saw Pete among the homeless and unfortunates who had probably slept in neighbouring alleys. Pete sometimes saw me but deliberately never acknowledged my presence.

Then, one morning I had just entered my office when I had a call from the security person at the front desk. When he heard my voice, he asked me if Mr. Dempsey was there. This was a well-used code to indicate that there was a drunk or other undesirable asking for me, probably to borrow money. I would ask the name, recognize one of the usual east Calgary crowd, and say I wasn't in. In this instance, the security person said the visitor was Pete Many Wounds. I said to send him up. The security person asked me if I was sure, and was obviously worried. Even if someone was a friend or relative coming to borrow money, I would usually go down to the front desk, not invite them upstairs to the executive suite. I insisted it was okay, and a short time later, Pete was delivered to my office under an escort, not left to come up on his own. I told the security person everything was okay and to leave us, and he did, the worry lines still in his brow.

Pete looked like death warmed over. His clothes were dirty and unkempt, and his face showed the ravages of alcohol and street life. While we had coffee, Pete told me that he had awakened in an alley a short time earlier, and as he lay there, he said to himself, "Pete, what are you trying to do? Kill yourself?" For the first time in almost ten years, he really looked at himself and his wasted life. As I said, he was highly intelligent, and when he faced up to his life, he didn't like what he saw. I was very flattered that the first person he wanted to see was his old friend – or perhaps it was just that I was the closest.

Pete and I spent a long time just talking. He didn't say much about his life on the streets, but rather, what he would like to do with his life. He knew he had to quit drinking, but now that he saw it as the pivotal point between life and death, he appeared ready to face it head-on. I gave Pete some money (which he returned within the month) and he headed for his reserve. He was not able to return to his family situation but lived nearby. Over the next few months, he had one more short binge and that was it. He stopped drinking. His old friends supported him and a position was found for him in the tribal administration. Most fittingly, it related to alcohol counselling work.

It could have been a story with a happy ending, but it wasn't. The ravages of liquor and street life were so disastrous that Pete died about a year later. I am saddened when I think of him; he was the perfect example of the fact that education and wisdom are not necessarily the same. Pete was wise but he never really had much of a chance to use his wisdom. But, as they say, blood will tell. His sons, Dean and Peter, have done very well for themselves. Peter is playing a prominent role in Sarcee economic development and in the delicate and sometimes thorny dealings with the adjacent City of Calgary.

Unfortunately, Pete wasn't the only tragedy I encountered. When speaking to a gathering of provincial judges in Lethbridge, I recall saying to them that many of my friends from my twenties were now dead, almost all due to alcohol. Even in our own family, the bottle became a disruptive force but there was a strength of will among the Gladstones that enabled them to fight it and ultimately to overcome it.

—∞∞—

When Duncan joined Glenbow, the initial relationship between him and the Board was quite positive. Some years earlier, when I had attended a seminar for historical administrators in Virginia, we were told that the best balance for a museum was to have a strong Board and a strong Director. I am sure this is true, but if both parties are too strong, it can lead to trouble. Duncan's approach to the Board was to be forthright. At times when he was instructed to do something he did not feel was right, he had no hesitation in saying no. Unfortunately, such occasions usually involved Don Harvie or Hod Meech, who were both powerful figures unto themselves. Neither side was afraid of a fight, nor of expressing their candid opinions.

My wife Pauline was quite active at this time. In 1975 she had helped organize an Anglican conference in Yellowknife, entitled "Women of Three Cultures." This referred to white, Native, and Inuit women. She took her fashion show of Blackfoot women's costumes with her where it was very well received. However, on the way home, Western Airlines forgot to take her stuff off the plane and it ended up in the United States. When the dresses were returned to Calgary, the Customs people at first refused to allow entry because of the existence of eagle feathers and other forbidden objects. Finally, they said they would allow the shipment in if was approved by someone from the National Appraisal Board in Calgary. One of the members' names they had on their list was Hugh Dempsey! Naturally, it was approved and logic prevailed over bureaucracy.

Three years later, the collection was southbound again when Pauline was invited to the first Plains Indian Seminar organized by the Buffalo Bill Museum in Cody, Wyoming. Here she met collectors and Indian enthusiasts from all across the United States and felt very much at home when she saw Jack Ewers and his wife Marge. The seminar went on to become an important annual event and Pauline was lauded in later years for being on the initial program.

—∞∞—

In 1977, our whole family world was turned upside down when our youngest daughter, twelve-year-old Lois, lost her fight with renal disease and had to be put on dialysis. Three times a week we had to take her to the hospital and watched with aching hearts while she was hooked up to all the tubes and wires needed for the three-hour cleaning of her blood. In those times, she was of more help to us than we to her, as she was cheerful and upbeat to a point that made us both ashamed and proud.

The doctors said she was a good candidate for a transplant but we had to wait six months for the first attempt. Then, after two agonizing weeks, the kidney was rejected and she was back on dialysis. In the months that followed, Lois got on with her life, but in a different way than one might have expected. She began to devote her attention to other patients, assisting the nurses, and even helping new patients in getting started and allaying their fears about the process. As a result of her efforts she was named Renal Patient of the Year.

She had a second unsuccessful transplant in November 1982, a third in May 1983, and a fourth in October 1983. This was tragic enough, but it was worse to know that most, if not all, had been due to something euphemistically called surgical error. It meant simply that the doctor had screwed up. I know in one instance he attached the kidney to the wrong vein. In 1985, now twenty, she was thoroughly disillusioned with the surgeon in Calgary, particularly as there were some rumours circulating about his alcohol problem. So she contacted the renal people in Toronto but was told they had no room to dialyse her there, that she would have to stay in Calgary. However, she decided to go anyway, saying she would die on their doorstep if they turned her down. Of course, they had to accept her so she got on their transplant list and worked as a chef in that city.

At one point she returned to Calgary, and while here, she got word that they had a kidney for her in Toronto. We had her on an Air Canada flight within three hours. As soon as Duncan Cameron heard about it, he told me to go to Toronto as well, that Glenbow would pick up the tab for travel and expenses. I was never so grateful to anyone in my life. When I got there, I learned that the transplant itself had been successful, in spite of massive scar tissue from her previous failures, but the kidney itself had not yet started to function.

Then started the waiting game. After the kidney stabilized it began to work a little but not enough to be sure. Early signs of rejection followed so she was given a new drug to counteract it. However, she soon got into an argument with the doctors, saying she could feel that the drug was causing rejection, not stopping it. She insisted that they reduce the drug and increase her regular drug or she would refuse her medication. When the doctors reluctantly agreed, the rejection miraculously disappeared and the kidney began functioning. Sometime later, tests elsewhere did show that in some cases that drug in question did cause rejection. Lois always said she knew her body better than the doctors did.

Shortly after my arrival, I loaned her my *iniskim* necklace that had been given to us by Bobtail Chief several years earlier. It had been owned by Red Crow's wife, Coming Singing, and was credited with providing spiritual protection to the user. This was the same *iniskim* that I had credited with saving Lois' life when her kidney first started to fail several years earlier. In Toronto, Lois was convinced that this played a major part in her kidney starting to function and when she told others about it, some patients even wanted to borrow it from her. I had stayed with Lois for the first couple of weeks and was relieved by Pauline, who came later. Finally, five months after her admission to hospital she was released with a fully functioning kidney.

<hr />

Going back to publishing, I was pleased when my second major book, *Charcoal's World*, was published in 1978. This was the story of a Blood Indian who killed his wife's lover in 1896 and then became a fugitive, taking the persona of a rabid wolf. During the manhunt he killed a Mounted Policeman and finally was turned in by his own brothers. It was a well-known story on the reserve. I actually started my research in the early 1970s and picked away at it whenever I had the time. I interviewed a number of elders such as Willie Scraping White, George Calling Last, Jack Low Horn, John Yellow Horn, and Laurie Plume. I also learned that my wife's aunt had been with some girls who had discovered the lover's body and that others remembered seeing Charcoal's widow in later years when she visited the residential school.

The story of Charcoal was such a fascinating one that I felt it needed a dramatic treatment – but factual – rather than just a mere recitation of events. It was apparent to me that there were three major players in the drama – Charcoal, Indian agent James Wilson, and Mounted Police officer Samuel B. Steele. To me, Steele was such an Imperialist blowhard that he would make an ideal foil to the diminutive Charcoal. Agent Wilson was included in the story, but I placed the emphasis on the Mountie and contrasted him with Charcoal whenever possible. Also, I dealt with all the mystical elements in a straightforward way, treating them as facts in the way that the Bloods believed them.

When I included conversations in the book, I ran into critics who said I was fictionalizing the story. I explained that the conversations weren't mine; these were part of the story as told to me by the elders. The Bloods have no written language, so when an elder related an event, he was passing it down word-for-word the way it had been told to him. Conversations were an integral part of the story, and so I included them.

When I was ready to start writing the book in the late 1970s I had a bit of trouble getting into the spirit of it. About that time I went on a business trip to New York, so I took along my little portable typewriter and notes with me and hoped I might have some spare time to work on it. That first night in New York, I was in my room when a huge thunderstorm rattled over Manhattan. Lightning was flashing through the skies and the thunder roared in sheets, seemingly echoing along the tops of the skyscrapers. It was such an awesome spectacle of nature that I suddenly felt akin with the natural world. I pulled out my typewriter and spent most of the night swinging into the rhythm of the book. From there I never looked back and a few weeks later the first draft of the manuscript was finished. I thought afterwards: what a strange place to feel close to nature, amid the steel and concrete of a faceless city.

My book was accepted for publication by Western Producer Prairie Books of Saskatoon, and its manager, Rob Sanders, became a good friend. Most publishers' contracts are pretty straightforward but in this instance I felt that the story was so good that I reserved all movie and television rights for myself, rather than turning them over to the publisher. It's a good thing I did, for I made far more money off movie options than I ever did on royalties. It's been optioned five times since it was published but a movie has never been made. I have read two movie scripts and a few story lines for the films that ranged from the sublime to the ridiculous and I collected annual option payments as long as the film makers thought there was a chance of getting it produced. But in all instances they just couldn't find the money. The big payout for me would have come if the movie had actually been made. But I didn't worry: my outlook from the beginning was that it would never come to fruition, and if it did, that would be an unexpected bonus.

As with most of my other Native books, I submitted *Charcoal's World* to the Blood tribal council before it was published to see if they had any objections. They didn't. Actually, the chief, Jim Shot Both Sides, had been most interested in the fact that I had been working on the story. Generally speaking, I really can't recall any major criticism coming to me from Native people about any of the books I have written. I was told a couple of times by white "do-gooders" that I should not write about Indians but leave that to the Indians themselves, but I never heard this from an Indian.

There was a full-page review of my book in the Blood newspaper, *Kainai News*. One comment was, "It is the author's sincere attempt to give the Indians' point of view that humanizes the story, instead of projecting the usual stark raving mad, half-naked savage which some writers would have capitalized on for the sensationalism. Mr. Dempsey was careful not to offend the natives by using the word 'savage', unlike Pierre Berton who still uses the phrase freely."[129]

By the time this book came out, I was already working on another – the biography of Red Crow, head chief of the Bloods. Because of his position, there was quite a bit on him in the official records, but again it was the interviews with elders that gave me real insight into the career of the great chief. I had a chance to interview his son, Frank, and great grandson, Jim Shot Both Sides. I also spoke to a woman who hated him: she was descended from a part of the family that had feuded with the chief a hundred years earlier. After all those years, the resentment was still there.

If I had known Red Crow, I don't know whether I would have liked him or not. He was proud, independent, and with a lot of political savvy. But he also lacked vision and was very deep within himself. I don't know if any white man really got to know him. For quite some time I could not get started on the book because I really didn't understand him. On one hand, Red Crow had been a tough, merciless warrior, and a hard drinker who had killed his own brother in a quarrel. But he also was a respected leader who enabled the Bloods to maintain their pride and identity in the face of government bureaucracy and repression.

I always said to myself that I had to get into a person's head if I was to understand them. I think I was able to do it with others, but Red Crow was a real challenge. Finally, after speaking to a lot of people and analyzing my material, I came to the understanding that there had been massive changes in Red Crow's life. About 1870 his uncle and father had died of smallpox and he was thrust into the responsible position of head chief. This was followed immediately by the onset of the whisky trade, wherein Red Crow was powerless to halt the tragic destruction of his people. With the murder of his brother and the death of friends and relatives he became chastened and turned to a new pathway in life to guide and protect his people. When I gained this knowledge, I could see of the many parts of the story that seemed incompatible suddenly made sense. With this in mind, I launched into my book and saw it into print in 1980.

Shortly after it came out, I was approached by Don Peacock, Manager of Public Affairs for the Bank of Montreal, and Ruth Fraser, a freelance editor and a good friend of mine. I was told that the bank had acquired a number of works of art by Nicholas de Grandmaison, and they asked me if I would help to prepare a coffee table book on the artist and his Indian portraits. I got the okay from Glenbow and started to work right away. I had two assignments. One was to write a biography of de Grandmaison, and the other was to help select the images and to write a short biography of each person. The latter was harder than it sounds, for many of the portraits were unidentified.

I knew Nick fairly well. He was a crazy old coot but a tremendous artist. I remember in the 1950s he had come to the Gladstone farm in a house trailer converted into a studio. His son was driving – I think it was Rick. I guess Nick had met my mother-in-law, Janie Gladstone, sometime before and now he wanted to paint her. "You've got a good squaw's face," he told her, apparently unaware that nobody used that term anymore. He jollied her into stopping whatever she was doing and to sit on a chair in the front yard while he did her portrait in pastels. He would not let any of us stand behind him to see what he was doing, and when it was finished he covered it with another piece of pastel paper and took it to his mobile studio.

In later years I asked him about the portrait to see if we could buy it. He said it hadn't worked out and he had destroyed it. However, in the 1990s we were at an art show in Lethbridge and there, big as life, was his portrait of my mother-in-law. It was beautiful.

When he finished the painting, Nick got into an argument with his son over something and refused to get into the trailer. Instead, he set off on foot towards Cardston, five miles away. I suppose this had happened before, as his son just followed a few dozen yards behind him in the trailer and when they were about half a mile away, Nick finally relented and got on board.

Another time, Nick contacted my father-in-law and invited him to his studio in the Palliser to sit for his portrait. I wasn't there so I don't know the details. But when my father-in-law was appointed to the Senate in 1958, Nick called me at my office and asked me when "Jim" was going to be in town. As it happened, he was coming from Ottawa in a day or so, so Nick told me he wanted to see him, that he had something for him. When Dad arrived, we went to the Palliser Hotel and upstairs to Nick's studio. What a mess! It was littered with paintings, paper, easels, paint supplies, and everything else one could imagine. I don't think the cleaning ladies ever had a chance to step inside the door.

Nick congratulated Dad on his appointment to the Senate and repeated what he told me, that he had something for him. He fished around and came up with a roll of pastel paper. When he unrolled it, there was a wonderful portrait of the Senator. Others had tried to paint him, but with his funny nose and twinkle in his eye, no one had really succeeded. But Nick did: it was perfect. When Nick said that he wanted Dad to have it, the Senator was very flattered and accepted it. Nick then rolled it up, gave it to Dad and said, "That will be fifteen hundred dollars."

I just about dropped through the floor, but Dad was amused and gave him a cheque for the amount. He remarked later that it was one of the most expensive gifts he'd ever received.

When I started to work on the book, Nick's daughter, Sonia Szabados, kindly let me have access to her father's letters, files, and reminiscences. I was able to trace Nick from military college in Russia to the 1914 battle of Tannenberg, where he became one of the first officers captured by Germans. During his four years in prison camp he developed his art, painting portraits of German officers. Transferred to Britain after the war, he carried on with his work but was finally "encouraged" to go to Canada in 1923 after his undue attention to officers' wives, and other women, particularly Lady Dundas. He worked as a graphic artist in Winnipeg, then "discovered" the western Canadian Indians in 1930. From then on, he devoted the rest of his career to them. Over the years he produced fine portraits of Blackfoot, Blood, Stoney, Cree, and other Indians, and when he was short of money, he painted children's portraits for wealthy clients in Calgary and elsewhere.

The writing part of the book was fairly easy. My only problem was to keep it short, as the story was so fascinating that it could have filled the book without the use of the portraits.

Once the pictures had been selected, it was my task to get their biographies. Quite a number Pauline and I had known personally while in other instances I knew the family or had something in my research files about them. The problem was with those who were unidentified. Armed with colour prints, I toured the reserves and was surprised at how many names I got. Among those assisting me were Jim Small Legs, Vickie McHugh, Dave and Daisy Crowchild, John Samson, Jim Shot Both Sides, Eleanor Brass, John Yellowhorn, Eddie Bad Eagle, and others. But perhaps the most help came from my wife, who could look past the "prettiness" of Nick's portraits to see the real likenesses. Nick always made his subjects look handsome, sometimes sacrificing accuracy for art. One of the best examples of this is Shot Both Sides, a Blood chief, who was not the handsomest of men, but Nick made him look pretty good. Of the sixty-four portraits in the book, I was able to identify fifty-four and get their stories.

The book, *History in their Blood: The Indian Portraits of Nicholas de Grandmaison*, was published in 1982. It was a beautiful work, the bank sparing no expense in reproducing portraits in full colour, first class all the way.

During this same period, I saw an American coffee table book about Christmas produced by the *Saturday Evening Post*. I thought it would be great to do something on western Canada so I brought together a potpourri of data – historical events, stories, recipes, photographs, and poetry – all from the western prairies. It was published as *Christmas in the West* in 1982 but I was quite disappointed in the outcome. The first problem was that my publisher, Prairie Books, had made a good deal in buying a quality of matte finish book paper and decided to use it for all their books that year. Mine had a large number of photographs that should have been printed on semi-gloss paper where they would have looked good, but on the matte paper they were flat and unimpressive. The second problem was that I had planned the book so that it would be timeless, to be put in the book stores every September to take advantage of the Christmas trade, then stored away until next year. That is what the *Saturday Evening Post* was doing. Instead, the publisher carried it year round for a year or two and then dropped it. I still think it was a good book.

After the success of getting my various manuscripts into print through Hurtig and Prairie Books, my so-called leisure hours were spent in researching new books. I never did write my books on Glenbow time, and did very little on evenings or weekends. Rather, I waited for my holidays and tried to find a secluded place to work. I could not settle down to writing at home: there were just too many distractions and disruptions.

One year, I decided to use an abandoned house on the Gladstone farm. This was in the middle of summer, so I didn't need any heat. I went there with just my electric typewriter, research notes, sleeping bag, hot plate, and food. All the doors and windows were intact but there was nothing in the house except an old chair and table. When I checked for electricity, I found there was only one line into the house and no fuses in the box. However, with the use of a penny instead of a fuse I got one outlet working. That meant if I wanted to type, I couldn't have a lamp, so that confined me to the long daylight hours. And if I wanted to cook, everything else was shut off. Actually, this worked fine as most of my time was spent on the typewriter.

I noted my routine in my diary. What I said here was true of most of my writing:

I always work in fits and starts which is why I have to be completely alone. I will stare at the typewriter for a while, shuffle my papers, and then perhaps type for 20 minutes. Then I'll get up, look out the window and wander back to the typewriter. Sometimes I'll stretch out on the bed for 10 minutes or at other times I might sleep for an hour. But always I gravitate back to the typewriter and work for another 20 minutes to half an hour – seldom any longer than that without a break.[130]

As I sat in the rickety chair in that old house, I could look through a window to see Chief Mountain, and I could hear meadowlarks, crows, bees, and other sounds of nature. I quite liked it. All I had for company was a huge spider in a corner near the ceiling. He was there when I came and there when I left. I figured he lived there and I was a guest, so I left him alone. Including his furry legs, he was about half the size of a saucer, but there was no red hourglass design on his body denoting a black widow, so I decided he was harmless.

When I was ready to do a book on Big Bear in the summer of 1982, I used my notes from his grandson Four Souls as a beginning point, supplemented with scads of material in the National Archives, old newspapers, diaries, trial documents, and other sources. Then I hit the trail to the Cree reserves to see what I could find. My first stop was Hobbema, where my old friend Johnny Samson explained the difference between the words for hanging, and for having a rope around one's neck, which was essential to the book. The first implies criminal behaviour and the latter the loss of freedom. In his 1876 speech, Big Bear was referring to the latter, but was accused of the former – a misunderstanding that dogged him for the rest of his life. Interestingly, when I was lecturing to Native inmates in Calgary, I was asked if it was true that under the treaty no Indian could be hanged for murder. I was puzzled by the question until I realized that it probably came from the misunderstanding with Big Bear. The mistranslation of Big Bear's words was published and the word must have spread about his request that he was asking never to be hanged. I was surprised that this story in a somewhat garbled form had filtered its way down to a young inmate a century later.

The next day I drove to the Poundmaker and Little Pine reserves. I knew John Tootoosis but when I stopped at the Poundmaker band office for directions I was given a very unfriendly reception. I then drove to Tootoosis' house and after I knocked on the door, it was opened an inch or two by a very suspicious woman who told me that Johnny was away. All this time the sky was grey and moody, but when I crossed over onto the Little Pine reserve it suddenly became bright and sunny. I could feel the friendliness in the air. I went to the band office and there I met a bunch of young men. They were very interested in what I was doing and when I asked about an interpreter, one of the men, Gavin Baptiste, suggested his uncle, Joe Kennedy. The differences between the two reserves was as absolute as night and day.

Kennedy agreed to be my interpreter and so we toured the reserve. We saw Napachit, Allen Sapp, Alex Bonaise, and Lucy Favel, all of whom had good information. But the best interview of the day came from John Sokwapance. I made the following notation about our meeting: "Sokwapance is 97 years old and when we found him, it was a hot day. He had left his house and had gone down into the trees. He was sitting in the shade of his turkey house and we had the interview while turkeys gobbled and gobbled around."[131] John had a number of wonderful stories to tell about Big Bear, including his youth and his spiritual powers.

The following day I went to the Sweetgrass Reserve, where I met Alphonse Little Poplar and his wife. Alphonse not only had a lot of information for me, but it was the beginning of a good friendship. He had an avid interest in the past and was considered to be the historian of the band. He later wrote me a number of long letters about the history of the area and went out of his way to interview Mrs. Annie White Calf about Big Bear, after which he sent me a six-page letter of his findings.

Sometime later I was able to return his kindness when he told me he had been separated from his sister fifty years earlier and wanted to find her. They had been in Battleford Indian Residential School together and when she left he never heard from her again. All he knew was that her name was Marie Louise and that she had married someone named Ward. I made a number of calls to friends and when that produced no results I contacted the Indian Affairs Branch in Edmonton. They came up blank but passed my letter along to Hobbema, Battleford, and Lesser Slave Lake. I then wrote letters to the editor to *The Windspeaker* and other Native newspapers, asking if anyone knew the whereabouts of Marie Louise.

In April 1985 I got the following letter from Alphonse, "To day I am the happiest man around. It would take some doing to find a happier man. I have located Mary Louise. This morning I received in the mail a letter from her... Hugh, thank you again the part you played in making this happen. In fact if it wasn't for you it would not have happened."[132] He then attached the letter from Mary Louise, which said, in part, "My dear brother, It is so hard for me and I don't know what to say. I am so happy to hear from you through the Native paper. I would be happy to see you. Yes, I am married to James Ward and we have been married 39 years now... Could you phone me. We live in Edmonton."[133] After that, Alphonse and I kept up our chatty correspondence until he passed away a few years later.

Returning to my research trip, I drove to Saskatoon, where I had a nice session with 93-year-old Joe Buller, grandson of Four Sky Thunder, who had played a prominent role in Big Bear's band. Joe met his grandfather for the first time in 1907. "He spoke Cree to me," he said, "and gave me a lot of information."[134] I also spoke briefly to Mary Pimee, Big Bear's daughter-in-law, but mentally she was pretty well out of it.

A couple of days later I was in Onion Lake where I looked up an old friend Wilfred Chocan. He had acted as interpreter some time earlier when I was on a Glenbow field trip. He suggested that we see ninety-four-year-old Jimmy Chief, both of whose grandfathers had died during the rebellion. One, a chief named Sakaskootch, was killed at the Battle of Loon Lake, and the other, Little Bear, was hanged for his part in the Frog Lake massacre.

When we arrived, Chief's granddaughter was just serving him lunch and asked us to come back in fifteen minutes. We learned later that she wanted the time to tidy up the house and set up chairs for her guests. Before the interview began, I learned that Chief was very deaf, and Wilfred suggested that we let him tell his whole story without interruption. He spoke for the better part of an hour, starting with the days before the Frog Lake massacre and following all the way through to the trials at Battleford. I considered myself a good interviewer but on this occasion Chief ran the show and told his story better than I could ever have obtained through questions. Along the way, I made side notes, and after the interview was over, I wrote questions on a piece of paper and passed them to him. It worked very well. I ended up with an interview that was a manuscript unto itself.

The only downside of the whole trip occurred when I stopped at a bar in Delmas for a couple of beers on my way home. I hadn't been there long before the chief of the Poundmaker band came in. He was a big gruff man and obviously had been drinking. He found out that I was the person who had been at the band office a few days earlier so he reeled over to my table and began shouting at me, saying that I had been trespassing on his reserve. I tried to argue with him but that only made him madder. At one point he threatened to take me outside and beat me up, or worse. He became so belligerent that the bartender finally said, "Henry, shut up or get out!" The man quieted down a bit but still made loud derogatory remarks, so after my second beer I took off for more friendly domains.

When I was ready to write the book, I knew it would be a challenge because of all the one-sided government sources, the misinformation about Big Bear, the starvation years, and the Riel Rebellion. There was a need for a completely new interpretation of his life, based on both oral interviews and the documents. But to put it into some cohesive order would take more than just a three-week holiday. As a result, I spoke to Duncan Cameron and he very kindly gave me a sabbatical – not a new practice for some other museums but a complete innovation for Glenbow. It was part of his effort to encourage more research and academic activities among his staff.

The first two months were spent entirely on research, photocopying data, reading books in my own library, and organizing data. I knew I could not do the writing at home, so I searched for an alternative. Finally, I went out on the Trans-Canada Highway to a nest of motels on the edge of the city. It was off-season so I succeeded in renting a room in the Roman Anthony Motel for $80 a week. The first thing I asked them to do was to take the television set out of my room. They could hardly believe it: no one ever did that. I then gave myself a quota of fifteen typewritten pages a day, but what with rewriting, interruptions, etc. I wasn't always able to keep up that pace. With a bare room, there was nothing else to do. I went home a couple of times a week and Pauline brought me food once in a while, but mostly I was on my own.

My usual routine was to get up at 8 a.m., have breakfast, and work sporadically until noon. I then broke for lunch and could not really get going again until about 4 p.m. Then I typed steadily until 9 or 10 p.m., had supper and went to bed. Sometimes at night I went to a nearby strip bar for a couple of beers and watched the strippers at work. I was singularly unimpressed at their tired, tedious routines, but it was the closest thing I had to television.

By the middle of April I had the first draft done but I needed more information. As I was writing, I realized that I had missed something or needed to confirm a conclusion I was reaching. Instead of stopping work, I "wrote around" the subject, leaving a bunch of dotted lines as a reminder, and then carried on with the writing. When I was finished, I went to Glenbow to catch up on some business and then was on the road again. I drove to Montana to visit with Four Souls and then did research in the Indian Department microfilms at the University of Calgary. By the time I was finished, the manuscript was ready. It was published in 1984 by Douglas & McIntyre under the title *Big Bear:The End of Freedom.*

My next book to get into print was a biography of my father-in-law, James Gladstone. Even before his appointment to the Senate in 1958, I knew he had an important place in the history of Native people in Canada. As a result, I started to interview him any time there was an opportunity. His memory for details was phenomenal and he told stories the old way, complete with conversations that had taken place. Supplementing these extensive notes were records in the Blood Agency files and in recollections of other persons. All this material was important, not only for Dad's life but in placing it in context with the events taking place on the Blood Reserve.

Actually, I started writing this book in the summer of 1980 — two years before Big Bear — but it wasn't finished at that time. Back then, I had looked for another quiet secluded place to write, and found it in Water Valley, a remote area in the foothills. Our friends Harvey and Marg Buckmaster owned a cabin a few miles into the bush from the town and were willing to let me use it. In appreciation, I said I would cut down all the young saplings on the slope in front of the cabin that were obstructing the view of the foothills and mountains. Harvey was a physicist at the University of Calgary and still has an active interest in history and the environment.

When I got there, I noted, "It is a large log cabin on an 80-acre plot that has never been logged over. It is on the slope of a hill and from its picture window there is a superb view of the mountains."[135] I loved the isolation and right away I began turning out fifteen and twenty pages a day. I had to go into the city a couple of times for a birthday and more research but I stuck close to the cabin. I cut saplings as a break from writing, cut down dead trees for firewood, and constantly admired the view. Two weeks later, when I left the cabin, I had 222 pages done. But then it was back to work at Glenbow and the manuscript went on the shelf.

I still had some holidays coming, so I took these in late November 1980 and headed back to the cabin. The autumn had been lovely and there was practically no snow on the ground so I was optimistic about getting my work done in the next week or so.

A couple of days after my arrival it started to snow, and snow, and snow some more. In two days there was more than six inches on the ground with no letup in sight. However, I kept writing and hoping the good weather would return. No such luck. On the fourth day I noted in my diary:

> It turned very cold last night. I kept the stove going until about 6 am but gave up. It was warm under the blankets. The Franklin

stove uses lots of wood – particularly poplar. The cabin is an open plan so I blocked off the stairwell to the second floor and strung blankets around the stove to form a partition. I also brought a bed down from upstairs as it is too cold to sleep on the floor. Now my rigged up room is nice and warm beside the fire.[136]

I managed to put in another two days of writing while wearing a coat and constantly feeding the fire. But the temperature continued to drop and the stove just couldn't keep up. On December 3rd I heard a radio report that another blizzard was on the way so I decided to leave. However, when I tried to drive out to the cutline road I immediately became stuck in the deep snow. Obviously I needed help, so I walked about a mile to the nearest neighbours, the Oldfields. The men were out with the cattle so I left a message about my plight and walked back. A little while later, Mr. Oldfield and his two big sons arrived with their truck and spent the next hour shovelling snow and pushing my unwilling car through the drifts. At last we got to the cutline and then it was downhill for the next half-mile. Once we reached the secondary highway, the Oldfields insisted on following me until we got to the village of Water Valley. I was very grateful.

It was now late afternoon and the town was virtually closed down. So I decided to head out to the main highway and get home as fast as I could. However, I had gone only a mile past the town when the motor started to act up. I nursed it along for another mile and then it died completely. When I raised the hood to check the problem, I found the motor well entirely clogged with snow and the fuel line frozen. As I looked around, I saw a small farmhouse and barn about two hundred yards away. I was poorly dressed, not expecting the storm, so I trudged over, but when I knocked at the back door there was no answer. I could see the lights were on so I tried the door and found it unlocked. It was so bitterly cold that I thought I would freeze to death on the doorstep so I went inside and called out hello. No one answered. The house was warm and comfortable but not a soul was in sight.

I thought it would be a good idea to phone Water Valley for a tow truck, but when I looked at the phone, I saw it was one of the old hand-cranked types. I fiddled around for a few minutes until something from my childhood memories reminded me that there was a little button under the unit that one had to push to make the connection. When I got it going, I phoned Water Valley but they had no truck and suggested I try Cremona. When I got them on the line, they at first refused but when I explained my plight they sent a truck. About fifteen minutes later it arrived so I left a note of thanks and money and rushed back to the car. I never did find out who owned the house but I was thankful that it was warm and open. It was the only farm in sight and I don't know if I could have survived the two-mile walk to Water Valley. In retrospect it seemed almost like a spiritual occurrence, that the warm farmhouse had been put there just to protect or save me.

Once in Cremona, I asked them if they could thaw out the fuel line but they were just closing. I asked if the car could be put in their warm garage overnight but they said it was full with regular customers. With no options left, I phoned my wife and she came to pick me up. During the two-hour wait I went to the local beer parlour and – of all the coincidences – I met a son-in-law of Malcolm Norris, a leading Metis leader who had played a major role in the formation of the Indian Association of Alberta. I had just finished dealing with that subject in my manuscript.

I had to wait three days for the garage people to thaw out my car. All my papers were in the trunk, so my writing came to an abrupt halt. Months passed before I could get back to it and with other projects intervening, six years went by before it was published as *The Gentle Persuader*.

⸙

As the months passed at Glenbow, the combined efforts of Duncan and the Board became evident and started a positive momentum that carried on through the 1980s. Soon there was weekend music, art tours and lectures, and other activities for the public. We restarted the old *Glenbow* magazine, but this time it was a glossy full-colour production that was reaching eight thousand people on a semi-monthly basis. I began to write regular articles on such subjects as Indian games, early aviation, and Calgary-Edmonton rivalry. In 1981 the museum brought in a world class art exhibition, *Four Modern Masters: De Chirico, Ernest, Magrette, and Miró*, sponsored by the Royal Bank and Norcen Energy. The same year, we produced our first really big exhibition, *Pipes that Won't Smoke; Coal that Won't Burn*, dealing with West Coast argillite. A year later, my work on de Grandmaison resulted in the Bank of Montreal's exhibit *History in their Blood: Nicholas de Grandmaison*. The practice of finding major sponsors in the business community was quickly elevating Glenbow to international stature. In 1983, when we put on *The Dinner Party*, featuring the work of Judy Chicago, no fewer than 62,000 people showed up. Now here was a museum performing a function for which it was intended!

In the next three or four years there were exhibitions of gold and jade from Costa Rica, the life of the American cowboy, post-Impressionism, Carl Rungius, Japanese print making, and many more. Among the sponsors were TransCanada Pipelines, Esso, United Technologies, Texaco, and IBM.

Meanwhile, one of the problems that Duncan and the Board couldn't solve at Glenbow was its funding. In 1977, the museum had negotiated a five-year deal with the Alberta government to address its serious shortfall. Unfortunately, when it came up for renewal for 1983, the province had just experienced the collapse of oil prices so Glenbow's funding was frozen at $3.51 million. Also, the 10 per cent annual increase previously in effect – which had already been built into our 1983 balanced budget – was eliminated. In addition, the recession caused a dramatic drop in private sector donations. Just to maintain the status quo the museum would need to cut some $400,000 from our budget.

Word was received that the government's decision was firm and that it affected all groups in Alberta receiving cultural grants. To make an exception of Glenbow would have every cultural group on the government's back. There were several ways that Glenbow could have gone. It could have quietly trimmed the budget and downsized departments that did not have a public face. The matter could have been left to the Board to use its political influence to get more government money. Or it could have launched a last-minute public and corporate appeal for funds to carry it over for another year.

Duncan Cameron decided to do none of these. Instead, he launched a major power play against the government by holding the Library and Archives for ransom, so to speak. On July 22nd, he called an all-staff meeting and announced that effective August 22nd the Library and Archives would be shut down, the fourth floor exhibition area closed, Sunday programs and touring displays cancelled, school programs reduced, the museum closed on Mondays and Tuesdays, and twenty-seven people laid off. This news hit the staff like a bombshell; people were crying and others were in a state of shock.

The news made the headlines all across Canada. "Cameron denied the cutbacks were designed to put pressure on the provincial government," reported the Calgary Herald, "but he said some of the belt-tightening measures could be reversed or postponed if additional sources of income could be found."[137] There were cries of outrage from the public, angry editorials in the press, and expressions of disbelief from the academic community. Mary LeMessurier, the Minister of Culture, made a public statement that the matter would be reviewed, but we learned that she was furious at the Glenbow ploy. Apparently she had asked Glenbow for detailed information to take to the cabinet but instead of an answer, she was hit with the public announcement.

In order to fight this closure a number of academics formed a "Save the Glenbow" committee, with my close friend Don Smith as head of the Calgary group and Rod Macleod for the Edmonton group. A petition with over a thousand names was sent to the government, letters were written to newspapers, and private meetings held with Ed Lewis, Chairman of the Board. Initially, everyone blamed the government for the upcoming closure of the Library and Archives. Then some doubts began to be expressed. The *Red Deer Advocate* commented that "The Glenbow ... cannot be absolved of guilt; museum management cut its most visible and most used sectors, likely in an attempt to spur public outcry directed at the government."[138] They were so right. Don Smith, in a letter to the editor, said that the decision of Glenbow's Board "reminds one of the old public school joke, 'Do you want to lose 25 pounds? We'll cut off your head.'"[139]

I had missed much of the prelude to the crisis because I had been on sabbatical, and did not return until a month before the drastic decision. Privately, I was shocked at the action that had been taken, even more so when I learned that the Minister of Culture had been stonewalled and embarrassed by our actions. Such a situation would not auger well for the future. On August 5, I wrote in my diary, "Meeting with Save the Glenbow Committee. Their attack is directed at us, not the government – with good reason. The historians feel that they are being held for ransom by Glenbow to force the government to give us more money."[140]

Shortly before the deadline, the Alberta government did come to Glenbow's rescue, but not in the way expected. On August 8th, acting deputy minister of culture, Frits Pannekoek, phoned me and asked a lot of questions about the budget for use by the cabinet. He called again the next day for more information but none of it did us much good. Instead of $500,000 to balance its budget, the government gave $150,000 specifically for the purpose of keeping the Library and Archives open. As I commented, "We are in a state of shock for we are now worse off than before."[141] The government had put in just enough money to placate the public and left us no further grounds to negotiate. The pressure play had backfired and we had made some pretty formidable enemies in the Alberta government.

At the same time, the Board members were busy during the crisis contacting corporations and individuals to seek contributions to meet our new shortfall. The Fund Raising Committee under John Porter raised an impressive

$500,000 by the end of the year. In the end, ten positions were lost, not the projected twenty-six. Duncan called it a "success story," but I wondered at the time, and still wonder today.

In spite of this crisis, and others to come, Glenbow was a very fine place to work. As I mentioned in my diary in 1981, "I am enjoying my work, even though it is becoming more and more administrative day by day. I am more relaxed and less concerned about minor problems."[142] There were a few internal discords as is common in any business, but the general atmosphere was convivial. My division, in particular, fared very well and my supervisory role was quite limited because of the quality of the department heads. I did not believe in a "hands on" approach. If a department was being well run, was kept within budget, and was meeting my expectations, I pretty well left it to its own resources. I did have meetings whenever required, but usually these were on a one-on-one basis where a department had a problem that needed solving.

---

Quite a bit of my time was taken up with committees and organizations outside of Glenbow. The latter was encouraged, as it helped identify Glenbow with public service and academic activities. The list is too long to recite but in the 1980s they included being chairman of the Alberta Geographical Names Committee, member of the Head-Smashed-In Buffalo Jump Scientific Advisory Committee, the federal Postage Stamp Advisory Committee of Canada Post, Alberta 75th Anniversary Advisory Committee, the National Archival Appraisal Board, and the Accreditation Committee, American Association of Museums. Also I was still very much involved with the Historical Society of Alberta and the Kainai Chieftainship.

In 1979 I had a call from Interdisciplinary Studies at the University of Calgary, saying they wanted my help in designing a half-year course on the Indians of western Canada. Two or three of us had a meeting and put together something that was primarily historical but with aspects of anthropology and sociology added. The course went through all the university red tape and was listed in the catalogue for the 1980 fall semester. Then I had a call from Marsha Hanen saying they couldn't find anyone to teach the course. Would I do it? I got the approval from Duncan and agreed to teach three hours a week in the late afternoon. That way, I missed only an hour or two of work.

It was really very funny. Twenty-five years earlier I had contemplated trying to go to university as a student. But when I attempted to enrol at the

University of Alberta I was told that did not have the necessary qualifications. Now, here I was being accepted as a teacher!

I had fifteen students that year, two being from the Sarcee tribe. In addition Don Smith and Tony Harrison, both professors, audited the course. I had a ball. My initial course notes were on scraps of paper and covered such subjects as prehistory, social organization, treaties, religion, mythology, reservation life, political movements, and contemporary problems. I had one guest speaker, Russell Wright from the Blackfoot tribe. The session went off without a hitch. The class was responsive and I kept the lectures as informal as possible. By the time it was over, only two students had failed.

That set the pace. For the next fourteen years I taught the course using my basic outline but changing and updating it as needed. For most of my classes, I simply sat on the edge of a table and chatted, using my summary notes as a guide. But very early on, I learned that I had to be careful when telling jokes – which was quite often. The first time I tried it, I noticed that most of the students had their heads lowered. They were writing down the joke! I quickly discovered that they had a Pavlovian response to their teacher. He spoke: they wrote. As a result, I got into the practice of saying, "Don't write this down," before telling a joke or story. As I had no reference texts for the students to use, everything they learned was from their notes, so these stories gave them relief from writer's cramp.

I was pleased at the number of Native students who took the course and the interest they showed in their history and culture. At first there was a cap of thirty students on my class but this was later removed. By 1990 it had grown to the point where I could no longer handle it on an informal basis and it became less and less fun. Finally in 1994, when the class size surpassed a hundred, I said forget it and resigned. As a result, they dropped the course.

Because of my teaching, I was asked in 1983 if I would take on a half-year course for the Department of History. It was entitled "Writing Local and Regional History" and its purpose was to examine books to use as models for writing regional histories. This was right down my alley, and although it was a bit onerous, I thought I could handle it for the fall session in addition to my own history class. I prepared outlines for a series of lectures, designating two or three published regional histories for making comparisons and researching archival, library, and newspaper sources to substantiate or refute the findings of these books.

When I went to the first class, I saw expressions of confusion and doubt in the eyes of the students. We can compare two books, but how can we research their backgrounds? How can we find such information? How can we tell what's reliable? After a few searching questions, I realized that these third- and fourth-year students knew nothing about research. If they couldn't find something in the university's computer bank, then to them it didn't exist.

Right there and then I decided to throw out the whole course and concentrate on writing skills generally and on researching history. The volume of unpublished materials at the university library was limited so I divided the course between the classroom and Glenbow. My new topics were on gathering oral history, how to do research, the use of folklore data, how to structure a history book or paper, how to improve writing skills, and in general how to do many of the things they should have learned in high school or their first years in university. When they came to Glenbow they were given practical assignments that required them to use finding aids, search newspaper files, and report on their findings. It went over very well and I think the students really learned something about research and effective writing.

A further teaching assignment came to me in 1984 when Mount Royal College asked if I would teach a course on Indians at Spy Hill Jail on the outskirts of town. I agreed provided that it could be taught jointly with my son James, a historian and graduate of the University of Calgary. I had been in the formidable Stony Mountain penitentiary in Manitoba when doing research on Big Bear so I was not too intimidated by the jail, but I think James was suitably impressed by the surroundings. Doors were unlocked in front of us and locked behind us as we made our way to the lecture room. The course was being offered to Indian inmates and about a dozen showed up. I knew the parents or grandparents of quite a few of them.

The lectures included some of the topics from my university course but James also had a responsibility for such subjects as pan-Indianism, treaties, etc. I included some subjects that were of special interest to the inmates – use of the pipe, incense, and the sweatlodge. Together we made a good team.

In addition to teaching, I was called upon to do a lot of public speaking and to act as chairman or master of ceremonies. As I never did have enough common sense to get nervous, I thoroughly enjoyed the tasks. I spoke to everything from service clubs and school groups to academic conferences and university classes. Because I knew my subject, these involved practically no preparation time. Then in 1980 I was flattered when the Smithsonian Institution invited me to give a paper at a symposium in Washington, D.C., in honour of Jack Ewers and Waldo Wedel. A year later I was chairman of a Plains Indian Seminar in Cody, Wyoming, again in honour of Ewers.

In some cases, my involvement in public speaking was much more personal. In 1980, for example, the Blood tribe asked me to be master of ceremonies at a program honouring Jim Shot Both Sides, who was retiring as head chief after twenty-four years in office. At that time I took the opportunity to present Jim with a first copy of my book on his great-grandfather Red Crow. Similarly, in 1985 I chaired a session in honour of my brother-in-law Fred, a national calf roping champion, and later another for Everett Soop, the gifted Blood artist. I wasn't bad as an MC but I could never hope to equal the excellence of such people as Rufus Goodstriker, his son Wilton, and Marvin Fox. Their mix of humour and eloquence could not be equalled. I recall one time when Rufus was master of ceremonies at a banquet for the Indian Rodeo Cowboys Association. He just about brought down the house when he started his speech, "Welcome cowboys and Indians..." Of course, they were one and the same.

Another time, Percy Creighton was chairing a session of the Indian Association of Alberta, being held on the Blood Reserve. Many of the delegates were hunters and trappers from the far north. Percy explained to them that the Bloods knew nothing about trapping, and said there was a little beaver on Bullhorn Coulee that kept damming up the creek. He wanted to know if the Crees could trap that little beaver for him. This started a running joke that continued through the entire three-day conference. Speaker after speaker brought the little beaver into discussions in ingenious ways, always causing gales of laughter. It was Indian humour at its best.

At another Indian Association meeting a chief from Saddle Lake arrived and, talking in Cree, he said he could not speak English and would have to use an interpreter. The next time he arose he would speak a sentence or two in Cree and the interpreter would translate into English. Then, so skilfully that at first it wasn't noticed, the chief began to speak in English and the interpreter in Cree. It took a few seconds before people were aware of the switch. The pair had successfully played a joke on the whole meeting and everyone roared when they realized that they had been taken.

Other matters were keeping me busy. In 1978 Glenbow got some outside funding to do a film on the Blackfoot treaty. Using still photos and maps I laid everything out, wrote a script, and got Canawest Films to do the production. We arranged for Marvin Fox, from the Blood Reserve, to do the narration, and all in all I thought it was a good educational film. Then, sometime later, the Department of Indian Affairs asked me to write a research paper on the 1877 treaty. The 107-page report was divided into five sections – historical background, preparation for the treaty, Indian perception of the treaty, government perception of the treaty, and later events. Once it was done, it took two years to get it published, as government lawyers claimed it was too favourably inclined towards the Indians. I sure hope so.

About this same time, Glenbow Ethnologist Julia Harrison and I discussed what might be done to commemorate the anniversary of the Riel Rebellion of 1885. We thought of putting together an exhibition showing the events of the rebellion, but when we delved more into it, we changed course. As I said to a reporter, "As we continued our investigations, we determined there was a more important story – the historical development and culture of the Metis people themselves."[143] We asked ourselves, is there a distinct Metis culture? And if so, what is it?

"The problem has been identifying what is distinctive about the culture," I told the reporter. "And the distinctive thing is what you find when you bring a body of artifacts together – Indian, French, Scottish and certain manufactured items." One of the things we wanted to find out was, were the Metis a third culture? The problem was that virtually every object we examined could be traced back to Indian or European cultures.

It took two years of research and travel, but the results were worth it. Julia and I made three field trips, one to St. Albert, another to Batoche, and a third to Manitoba, and we turned up a veritable gold mine of Metis-related artifacts. It seems that no one, not even the Metis themselves, had ever thought about preserving their material culture. Even Glenbow had only thirty Metis items in its collection before this project; when it finished it had three hundred. One particularly good source was the Rowland brothers who lived on the original family river lot in St. Albert. Their old house yielded such objects as an accordion, beadwork, and early photos. At the bottom of their river lot was an old shop that contained original tools for building log houses, as well as for logging and farming.

On our trip to Manitoba, we located a wooden travelling chest belonging to Ambroise Lepine, beaded clothing, a flintlock gun, l'Assomption sash, handmade rolling pin, and some fine early furniture. One item we looked at was the chain that was supposed to be the one that Louis Riel stepped on to prevent government surveyors from surveying Metis river lots into quarter sections. This was one of the actions that precipitated the Manitoba Rebellion of 1869–70. However, the owner, a member of the Lagimodarie family, refused to part with it, as he hoped it was going to be incorporated into a statue of Riel that was being made.

Julia was the curator for the show *Metis: People Between Two Worlds*, and she did a fine job. It was the first time any museum person had really looked at the subject and so the 1985 exhibition was a fitting tribute to a group she called "a forgotten people."[144]

Meanwhile, as we toddled on towards the 1988 Olympics, Glenbow seemed to be firmly in the "big league" as long as we had the money and the leadership we so desperately needed. With both in hand, we could do wonderful things.

When the University of Calgary was conferring an
honorary doctorate upon Hugh Dempsey in 1974, he
invited his friend Ralph Steinhauer as his guest. When
the announcement was made that Steinhauer was to
be appointed Lieutenant Governor of Alberta, the
university insisted that he join him on the platform.
(Author's files)

In 1972, Dempsey was given the Alberta Non-Fiction Award for his book *Wit and Wisdom of Bob Edwards*. The award is presented here by the Hon. Horst Schmid, Alberta Minister of Culture. (Author's files)

John Diefenbaker, former prime minister, was escorted by Dempsey while attending the conferral of an honorary chieftainship by the Blood tribe upon Prince Charles in 1977. Both Dempsey and Diefenbaker had previously been made honorary chiefs. (Author's files)

As a historian, Dempsey gave many talks to academic organizations, clubs, and Native groups in the West. Seen here in 1979, he stands before the grave of Crowfoot and is giving a talk on this great man's life. (Author's files)

Dempsey was master of ceremonies at a tribal retirement ceremony for Blood head chief Jim Shot Both Sides in 1980. During the occasion, Dempsey presented the chief with the book *Red Crow*, the chief's great grandfather. (Author's files)

Four enthusiasts about history and Native peoples met at the Calgary Stampede in 1985. Left to right are: Donald B. Smith, University of Calgary historian; Colin Taylor, English authority on Plains Indians; Hugh Dempsey; and Fraser Pakes, school teacher and hobbyist. (Author's files)

In 2001, Hugh and Pauline Dempsey were invited to join a parade on the Blackfeet Reservation in Montana celebrating the preservation of the Blackfoot language. Standing left to right are Pete Standing Alone, Hugh, and Pauline. (Author's files)

When Dempsey and his senior staff returned to Glenbow after a business trip to Edmonton in 1989, this photo was on his desk. It is inscribed, "Nothing terribly exciting happened while you guys were gone on Friday." Left to right are Julia Harrison, Anthony Cooney, secretary Deb Green, Pete Eisenmenger, Fred Greene, and Barry Agnew. (Author's files)

Hugh and Pauline on the Blood Reserve, 2001. (Author's files)

In order to soak up some of the atmosphere, Dempsey positioned himself on the Montana plains while writing a book. (Pauline Dempsey photo)

These authors contributed to the book, *Centennial City: Calgary, 1894–1944*. Left to right, front row: Lynette Walton, Donald B. Smith, Grant MacEwan, Hugh Dempsey; middle row: Kathleen Snow, Maria Murray, Marianne Fedori, Catherine Mayhood; back: Max Foran, Roger Gibbins, Harry Sanders, Jennifer Bobrovitz, and Harry Hiller. (Author's files)

The American Indian Seminar, held annually at Cody, Wyoming, was a good time to meet old friends. Here, left to right in 1994 are Lloyd James Dempsey, John C. Ewers of the Smithsonian Institution, and Hugh Dempsey. (Pauline Dempsey photo)

In 1960, Dempsey arranged for the Weasel Moccasin family of the Blood tribe to re-patriate a medicine pipe bundle for their use. Here, left to right, are Percy Old Shoes, Daniel Weasel Moccasin, his father Dan Weasel Moccasin, Hugh Dempsey, and Florence Weasel Moccasin. (Glenbow photo P-4150-5)

One of Dempsey's last acts before retiring from Glenbow was to write and design the coffee table book *Treasures of the Glenbow Museum*. He is seen here autographing the book at the museum. (Author's files)

# 11

# *The Spirit Sang*

When the announcement was made in 1983 that Calgary had been selected as the site for the 1988 Winter Olympics, Glenbow got busy to see what it could do and who it could find to pay for it. Julia Harrison suggested bringing together some of Canada's finest Native objects then in museums in Europe and the United States. The federal government gave us $4,000 to study the feasibility of the project and when Julia returned from Europe she deemed it both desirable and possible. She estimated that some 300 to 500 pieces would need to be borrowed, two-thirds from Europe and one-third from the United States. The tentative name of the exhibition was "Forget Not My World," later changed to "The Spirit Sings." I was not directly involved in the day-to-day activities, as this was an exhibition program, but as a member of the Glenbow executive team I could not help but take part in the decision making. I also had my finger directly in the pie on a number of occasions.

The planning was going well until 1986. It was a massive task, involving negotiations with European and American museums, with External Affairs, and with possible sponsors. Julia took all these in hand, and soon Glenbow was engaged in planning, designing, and laying out the show. But hiding in the weeds was an unexpected factor, the Lubicon Indians. Let me say at the outset that I had no sympathy for the Lubicons or, more particularly, for their claims and methods. Here is the background to their problem as I saw it.

In 1899 the federal government made a treaty with the Indians of northern Alberta. The official party travelled along the Peace and Athabasca Rivers, expecting the Indians to come out from the hinterlands to accept the deal. Some of them, including those from the Lubicon Lake area, did, and were registered with the Whitefish Lake band. As time went along, more of them took treaty, and in 1908 a reserve was set aside at Whitefish Lake. In later years this reserve was expanded to take into consideration additional people not included in the original land allocation.

In 1933, fourteen treaty Indians who were on the paysheets of the Whitefish Lake Reserve asked for a reserve at Lubicon Lake. In 1940 the government indicated that of those being paid at Lubicon Lake and Little Buffalo Lake, all but 8 of the 127 persons were members of the Whitefish Lake band. So, contrary to all later hoopla, these were not, as the Lubicons claimed, people who "never signed a treaty or ceded their rightful historic jurisdiction over their traditional territory"[145] Rather, they were Indians who had accepted treaty and were seeking a separate reserve.

At this point, the Department of Indian Affairs managed to mess everything up. Officials had no problem in allocating land to the group and in 1940 sent surveyors to lay out the reserve. However, they were unable to land because of a forest fire and they just didn't come back. In 1949 the Alberta government did set aside some land for the federal government to use as a reserve, but the feds failed to respond and in 1954 the offer was withdrawn. It is too bad the way the Lubicons were mishandled by Indian Affairs, but it does not change the fact that they were treaty Indians, mostly registered at Whitefish Lake, who wanted their own reserve.

In 1979, Bernard Ominayak, chief of the Lubicons, hired Fred Lennarson to assist him in his efforts to get a reserve. The Chicago-trained political activist had previously worked for Harold Cardinal and there is no doubt he was a dynamic and aggressive fighter. Shortly afterwards the oil boom struck northern Alberta and the wilderness was filled with seismic crews and drilling rigs. The provincial government considered that Aboriginal rights had already been extinguished in the region and had no hesitation in issuing exploration and drilling permits. The Lubicons applied for an injunction to stop the work, but this was rejected by the Court of Queen's Bench in 1983 and by the Alberta Court of Appeal. The Lubicons then appealed twice to the Supreme Court of Canada to review the case but in both instances it refused to hear their application.

There is no question that the band had run headlong into the gross inefficiency and mismanagement of the Department of Indian Affairs, which was a common situation for Indians all across Canada. Now the Alberta government was failing to provide land for a reserve and threw the area wide open for development. An appeal by the Lubicons to Alberta's independent ombudsman found no evidence of cultural genocide, harassment, or trickery by either the Alberta government or oil companies. Stupidity perhaps, callousness, most likely, and hardheartedness, most certainly.

The Lubicons shifted into high gear to pressure the government into making a settlement. Appeals were sent to church groups and others for support and the real issues became submerged in a flood of verbiage about exploitation, violation of human rights, implied starvation, destruction of culture, and many other claims that would tug at the heartstrings of impressionable people. The aim seemed to be to halt oil exploration and to gain recognition that the Lubicons still had Aboriginal rights for their whole hunting ground. The fact that they were simply treaty Indians seeking a new reserve seemed to be lost in the shuffle.

In 1984, the Alberta government confirmed that the majority of members of the Lubicon band could be traced to the Whitefish Lake and Wabasca reserves or had accepted half-breed scrip. There were less than a dozen who, although treaty Indians, were not attached to any other reserve. In spite of this, the Alberta government a year later offered to provide 25.4 square miles of provincial land to the Department of Indian Affairs for a Lubicon Reserve. This was based upon the band's population in 1940, when the reserve was first offered to them. The Lubicons refused the offer, demanding 80.2 square miles based on their current population. The government then upped its offer to 40 square miles and Ominayak came back with a demand for 91.4 square miles. Thus started a long and acrimonious dispute, involving not whether a reserve should be allocated, but how big it should be.

This was when Glenbow was unsuspectingly and innocently swept into the maelstrom of political infighting, bickering, and high-pressure publicity that marked the Lubicon issue. Early in 1986 the band announced plans for an international boycott of the Olympics, claiming it was sponsored by two of their adversaries – the Alberta government and the oil companies. A month later, when Shell Oil Canada gave Glenbow a grant of $1.1 million to become the main sponsor of our show, the Lubicons shifted their focus. The combination of an oil company sponsor, a museum created through oil money, and an exhibition that dealt with Indians, was just too good to ignore.

Soon the Lubicons were turning out press releases calling for museums in Europe and North America to refuse to loan artifacts to the exhibition. They freely tossed around such expressions as "genocide" and accused those who organized the Olympics of being "actively seeking to destroy the Indian people."[146] To accuse oil companies and governments of such deliberate actions was both irresponsible and unconscionable. Just three months earlier, the federal government had given the Lubicons $1.5 million as a show of goodwill to help them with their legal costs.

I don't know what the Lubicons expected would happen. Did they think Glenbow would intercede on their behalf with federal officials? Certainly one white Lubicon supporter said that the museum had to use its influence in Ottawa to resolve the band's claims. Influence in Ottawa? We didn't even have enough influence to get half the grants we were seeking. Obviously what the Lubicons really wanted was to bring worldwide attention to their plight, and they planned to use the boycott as a vehicle for international recognition. The fact that their actions could possibly ruin a Native-based exhibition seemed to be of no importance to them as they launched into their greater cause. This show was not only about Indians but also for Indians. As one official said, "the native peoples will benefit and our visitors from around the world will benefit from a greatly enhanced understanding of native people and their deeply rooted cultural traditions."[147]

However, the Lubicons in their campaign overlooked one factor – Duncan Cameron, our director. He had no intention of rolling over and playing dead for Fred Lennarson, Bernard Ominayak, or anyone else. As he said, "We think we're doing something that is very much in the interests of our native peoples, creating a heightened awareness of their rich cultural tradition."[148]

Duncan and Julia had a meeting with the Lubicons early on but they could not find any area for compromise. Besides letters being sent to major museums around the world, the Lubicons sought and received support from a number of Native political groups, such as the Assembly of First Nations, Indian Association of Alberta, and the Joint Council of Chiefs of Quebec. It has been a truism that when a situation occurs that pits Indian against non-Indian, other Native groups will support the Indians, right or wrong. Therefore, it was with some trepidation that I heard the Lubicons were seeking support from the Blood, Blackfoot, and other southern Alberta tribes. I must say I was pleasantly surprised when initially the Sarcees, Stoneys, and Blackfoot refused to join the boycott while the Bloods sat on the fence, taking the side of neither. As one chief said, "Calgary has always treated its Indian people fairly, and almost always included us in things that were happening, and so we want to help Calgary and Canada make the Olympics a success."[149]

To combat the European letter-writing campaign against the exhibition, Canadian embassies contacted museums and provided them with details about the dispute that had not been mentioned in the welter of press releases and "informational" letters from the Lubicons. However, in the first onslaught of publicity, some museums did withdraw from the exhibition. One claimed it was afraid that the exhibition would be bombed or the artifacts damaged by Lubicon supporters. Others felt sympathy for the Lubicons and either did not want to become involved or wanted to show their support.

As matters progressed, or regressed, the Lubicon attacks became personal and vicious. At one stage Lubicon leaders wrote to a European museum that "The people ... at Glenbow are our mortal enemies, the murders [sic] of our children."[150] He also said that Duncan was "a hypocrite more concerned with saving artifacts than human lives."[151] I remember wondering: where does Duncan have a choice between saving artifacts and saving lives? Also, the fact that the Lubicon population was increasing (according to their compensation demands) instead of decreasing, gave the lie to the whole statement. Other releases attacked Glenbow because it had been started with oil money and the show was being funded by Shell, seemingly implying it was in league with the oil companies to destroy the Lubicons. Such comments really bothered me, as they defied all sense of logic.

By the summer of 1987 we were seeing the results of the boycott. A number of museums had originally agreed to lend objects to us, but with the Lubicon tirade a few had withdrawn and others were considering it. One of the major losses occurred when James Smith, curator of the Museum of the American Indian in New York, managed to get his board to change its mind and withdraw. Others that bailed out were the Peabody Museum, National Museum of Denmark, Ethnographic Museum of Norway, and the Musée d'Histoire in Switzerland. But Duncan fought back. When Bruce Trigger, the honorary curator at McCord Museum in Montreal, tried to get the institution to back out of its loan, Duncan went directly to the governing Board, who honoured their previous commitment. The curator resigned. Similarly, when Bill Sturtevant, a friend of mine at the Smithsonian Institution, tried to pull his institution out, Duncan went to their Secretary and got the loan confirmed. But there is no doubt we were worried. If other museums followed the half dozen or so that supported the boycott, our exhibition could become seriously compromised. Duncan worked very hard to see that this did not happen.

About this time, I wrote to my friend Jack Ewers, in Washington, "Our native exhibition is still running up against a well engineered boycott by a group of Indians and their advisers who are trying to wrest a $1 billion land settlement deal from the Canadian government. We are the innocents caught in the middle. It has certainly added to Glenbow's work load."[152]

I added my own contribution to the fray when I prepared a three-page "Selected Chronology of Events Relating to Lubicon Land Claims and Boycott." The account began in 1899 with the signing of Treaty Eight, then followed with the promise of a reserve to the treaty Indians, the government screw-ups, and then the court-related incidents after the discovery of oil in the area. Finally, it explained Glenbow's role in the 1988 Olympics, quoting a Native newspaper that complained the exhibition was "being used as a pawn in the game of selfish politics." This chronology was sent to all the museums that had been approached by Glenbow make the loans. A Lubicon supporter reacted by saying it was "wildly inaccurate and deliberately misleading."[153] The only specific point he challenged was the failure to mention the Fulton report which, in fact, actually was in my chronology.

By autumn of 1987 the tide had changed in favour of Glenbow. Duncan's tireless efforts to keep European museums on side was succeeding as boards decided to keep out of the Lubicon political dispute. At the end of the year I wrote to Ewers that "A number of people worked very hard to try to get museums not to loan to us." These included leading figures from the Heye Foundation of New York and Bill Sturtevant at the Smithsonian of Washington. The Lubicon group started off by writing to museums all over the world and to pressure them not to loan. "Fortunately," I added, "they had no idea who we were borrowing from and, in the end, their effort failed. I think there were eleven museums which would not loan, but more than sixty did. As a result, we have had a minor inconvenience but no major setback."

───── ∞ ─────

When opening day arrived, *The Spirit Sings* was a joy to behold. Of the 665 artifacts, many were world famous and had appeared in coffee table books and art publications. To actually see these items was quite a thrill. I had arranged for my old friend Jim Many Bears to give the opening prayer and showed him around the exhibition before it opened. He was very impressed, and was even more impressed when I presented him with a l'Assomption sash that I had picked up in an antique shop during my travels.

The boycott was a total failure. Within a short time we had more than 85,000 visitors and the remarks were very flattering. In the end, the attempted boycott had only increased public interest in the show. Someone commented that the dispute involving Glenbow and the Lubicons could have only one result – one would be a complete winner and the other a complete loser. That's what happened. And now, these many years later, the Lubicons still have not settled their case.

One thing that the boycott did achieve was to raise the awareness that Native people should be involved in the preparation of such shows, even if they dealt with a time period far earlier than any local experience. There were enough questions raised about The Spirit Sings to bring about a change and to have Native participation for any such future exhibits. Julia Harrison was particularly adamant on that point.

As part of the celebrations, Glenbow designed an Olympic pin that used The Spirit Sings logo as its main feature. These were given out to special guests. Also, just about every business or group involved in the Olympics had its own pin. In the mall just outside Glenbow the Coca-Cola company erected a large tent to promote its own pins and to have what it called a pin trading centre.

As the Olympics progressed, we were bombarded by people who wanted our pins, many wanting to trade those from their own companies. That's when I got the idea that Glenbow should collect as many pins as possible as an historical record of the event. One of our staff, David Spindel, was an inveterate collector, so he jumped at the chance when we offered to give him a supply of pins and send him out to the mall to start trading. Glenbow's pins were rare and special, so Dave didn't just trade one for one. He wheeled and dealed, sometimes getting three or four pins for one of ours. At the same time, I sent letters to just about every firm that had a pin, and even to the company that manufactured them, seeking pins for our collection. As an added feature, I wrote to the Olympic committees of participating countries.

As the collection piled up, Ron Getty and I decided to put them on display in the lobby. We rounded up some old cases, and Ron organized the pins in a way that would appeal to collectors. In no time flat, hundreds of pin collectors were storming our lobby, finding out what they were missing and looking for people to trade with. Many of the Olympic countries were generous in donating their pins, and in some cases copies of their medals, so people came to look at items that could be seen nowhere else in Calgary. By the time it was over, some 46,000 people had come to Glenbow just to see the pins. After it was over, the cases were dismantled and the pins placed in our collections.

# 12

## The Aftermath

The year 1988 had started off in grand style for Glenbow, but it was too good to last. And it didn't. After the Olympics and the transfer of our exhibition to Ottawa, a sort of malaise set in. We had been working non-stop for months; now it was over and it was time to face some ugly truths. One was that regardless of the millions in grant money we had spent for the Olympics, our basic financial situation was still perilous and we were coming to the end of a long-term funding agreement we had with the Alberta government. Past experience showed that the government reluctantly endured us, rather than giving us its wholehearted support. It financially supported its own Provincial Museum but we were treated like poor cousins.

Another problem was that the pressures of the exhibition had placed a strain on just about everyone. Duncan stated that "nerves were frayed in the latter months [and] tales of the physical and nervous exhaustion [were] rampant in the ranks."[154] One sign of this occurred with Duncan, who, under pressure from the Board of Governors, drafted a five-year plan that called for new and expanded programs with existing staff. This did not go over well with some of our people. As I commented in my diary, "Our staff is already doing so much that the stress level is high & dissatisfaction among the rank & file is great. We have a very unhappy place at present. Duncan is an excellent director but he has been under so much pressure from the Board that it is telling on him. I just hope we won't lose him in the process."[155]

The response of the Board to our unhappy post-Olympic situation was to engage a management consulting firm to make a study of management and Board activities. They came around and interviewed each of us on the management team and left us all feeling somewhat insecure. Our Assistant Director of Administration, Joe Konrad, was convinced he would be fired because he did not support Duncan's expanded program. Others felt equally uneasy. Then in August, Duncan called me into his office and told me that the report had been made to the Board. Among other things, it called him a tyrant and dictator, another of our team incompetent, another an over-promoted secretary, and said that I spent half my time in the library. Of those, mine was the most accurate description and, although it was meant as a criticism, it had never been a secret where my primary interests lay.

In September, I left Glenbow's problems behind as Pauline and I travelled by air on our first trip to Europe. We first went to Hastings, where we spent some enjoyable time with Colin and Betty Taylor. Colin had written a number of books on the Plains Indians and was a real enthusiast. Pauline was absolutely enchanted by the view of the English Channel from our window. We then went to Folkestone and found the church where my Mom and Dad had been married in 1916 and also looked up Mom's grand-nephew, Clifford Sharp. We found him in a pub on the waterfront and he couldn't have cared less if we were alive or dead. Next was a double-decker bus trip to Canterbury Cathedral, where Pauline stood on the stone in the church that marked the burial place of Becket. We then prowled around London for a week, visiting all the tourist spots, and got back to Calgary three weeks later, exhausted but happy.

But what a homecoming! Duncan told me as soon as I arrived that he had had an unpleasant meeting with the Board and it ended up in him tendering his resignation. I don't know if he had a choice. Certainly matters had come to a head by this time and the gulf between the Director and the Board was as wide as the Pacific. Summing up the situation, I made the following comments about Duncan:

> He had an uncanny knack for knowing what kind of shows would do well in Calgary & had the organizing genius to make them happen. There was no question that "The Spirit Sings" would never have opened without his leadership. He had the ability to stick his (and Glenbow's) neck out a mile in financial matters and always came out on top. When he had confidence in people, he had no trouble in delegating authority to them. For the most part, he operated a good team process, with excellent relations among staff. He has the sensitivity, nerve, intelligence, experience, and ability that cannot be matched by another museum director in Canada.[156]

On the negative side, I said, "He loved an argument and seemed to relish stonewalling the Board. You can do that only for so long." Other problems included his aggressiveness, his drinking, and his tendency to involve himself in Glenbow matters even after he had delegated them to someone else. He was a great person to have on your side, but not so nice if he lost faith in you or your performance.

In early October, Duncan and I went to the Chairman's office to wind up the legal matters and I was asked if I would take over as Acting Director. I said yes. I was also asked if I wished to apply for the position of Director. I said no. Afterwards, Duncan told me he was sure I'd change my mind, but it was not to be. In my diary I noted, "I have already decided that I do not want the job permanently. I do not want to spend the rest of my time fighting with the Board or worse, knuckling under to them while they interfere with our administration. Also, I think we are going to be in for hard financial times and I do not want the worry."[157]

The following day, the Board announced Duncan's retirement, effective November 1st, stating that he would become Director Emeritus and be given an office and a secretary until March 31, 1989. I was to take over until a new Director had been named.

When I assumed the position there were a thousand things to do, including a lot of fence mending. Our management committee and some of the senior staff had been torn apart by the events of the previous few weeks and my first task was to get them back working as a team, just as they had during the Olympics. I appointed Ron Getty as acting chief curator to relieve myself of departmental responsibilities and made Joe Konrad chairman of our budget committee. The departments that were doing well, such as the Library, Archives, and Cultural History, I left alone while frequent meetings were held with curators of the others.

Because of the consultants' poor representation of our management committee, the Board decided to have one of its members attend our weekly meetings. Some of our people were up in arms, one almost hysterical, saying that our daily operations were being taken over by the Board. I had a different reaction. I said the Board seldom had a chance to see us in action on a day-to-day basis. Here was an opportunity to show them what we really could do, and how unfair some of the consultants' assessments had been. Bob Erickson, vice-chairman of the Board, was chosen to be their representative. I knew Bob when I liaised with the Collections Management Committee of the Board, of which he was chairman, and I knew he was a considerate and gracious man.

The others in the management group had no choice but to go along, some reluctantly. But it turned out I was absolutely right. Bob reported back to the Board, but after a couple of months he said that it was a waste of his time, that we were doing a good job. In the meantime, I attended meetings of the various committees of the Board and tried to keep our staff informed. One time I wrote, "Met most of the morning with all Department heads to bring them up to date on Glenbow's fast-moving crap game" and on another occasion, "At this particular time, relations between Board & Management are very convivial. I wonder how long this will last?"[158]

Once I had taken over as Acting Director, I decided to enjoy myself. There always had been a lot of little things I had wanted to do but never had the chance. One of my first foolish actions was to round up a bunch of toys. As a reporter wrote, "In a corner of the director's office is an elegant antique museum display case. Dempsey has filled it with a dozen beautiful old toys, including a fire engine, a tractor, and a couple of dolls."

He quoted me as saying, "I'm only going to be in this acting capacity for a few weeks, so I'm going to have fun. And if you're going to have fun, what better way is there than to have a few toys about you?"[159]

Actually, I held the office for the better part of a year, and it wasn't always fun. I had to attend innumerable meetings, keep peace between departments, work on the budget, and generally keep the place running shipshape. At the same time, I continued to teach a half-year course at the University of Calgary where attendance numbers were increasing so fast that it had become quite a workload. When I had twenty students, I could sit on the edge of my desk and chat with them. When it trebled, the formality seemed to fade under the weight of sheer numbers. Exams, marking essays, etc., also became much more onerous. My other activities during these months included acting as general editor of the Alberta Records Publications Board, editor of the quarterly *Alberta History*, member of the federal Postage Stamp Advisory Committee, and a bunch of other things.

After I was well into the new job, I told Jack Ewers, "In all honesty, I must say I've enjoyed myself – mainly because I've been able to accomplish something I always felt needed to be done."[160] It was demanding work but I think we got a lot accomplished. There were some things, however, like long-range financial planning, that had to be left to the incoming Director.

Much to my surprise, I was appointed to the Board's Search Committee, headed by our new chairman, Catherine Evamy. This placed me in the odd position of helping to choose the person who would become my boss. The

same thing had happened in 1970 when I was in an acting capacity and recommended Allan Hammond for the top job. I guess history does repeat itself.

After the advertisements were sent out, we sat back and waited for the
results. I had hoped that some top people, or those second in command of
some of the big eastern or West Coast museums might apply, but they were
noticeable by their absence. I concluded that Glenbow's bad reputation in the
museum world, compounded by the unfavourable publicity surrounding *The
Spirit Sings* exhibition, had a lot to do with it. I must say I was disappointed by
the results. Most of the applications were from prairie people, some at smaller
museums or with no museum experience at all.

I did the initial sorting and ruled out those who obviously had neither
the experience nor the skill to handle the job. Catherine and I then made
day trips to places like Saskatoon, Regina, Edmonton, etc., to interview our
short list. We also went to Yellowknife, where we interviewed Bob Janes, who
was Executive Director of the Science Centre of the Northwest Territories
and previously had been Director of the Prince of Wales Northern Heritage
Centre there. He had known Duncan quite well and had been to Glenbow a
number of times. He seemed to be the best of the bunch. Catherine described
him as "a dynamic individual, a natural leader who will be able to guide
Glenbow into the 1990s."[161] My initial impressions of Bob were good. He
struck me as an intelligent, kindly person who was well motivated and – to my
liking – was quite interested in Indians.

When the appointment was made, I wrote to Ewers, who had been in
a similar situation to mine. He had been the Ethnologist at the Smithsonian
Institution in Washington, D.C., when he was asked to oversee the construction of their new Museum of History and Technology. He was appointed director but made it clear he would remain only until the building was opened. I
don't think anyone believed him. After all, he had a corner office, a secretary, a
parking place next to the door, and was invited to all sorts of official functions.
It was a civil servant's dream. Therefore there was shock and disbelief when the
museum opened that he actually did step down and resumed his old position
in a small office, with no secretary, and parking space in the boondocks. All he
had to do now was his research and writing.

In my letter to Jack I said:

> I can understand now why you were so happy to step out of the
> Museum of History and Technology and back to your job as
> Ethnologist. When Duncan Cameron left our organization last

October, I agreed to be Acting Director until the new person was appointed. Well here I am, at the beginning of July, still holding down the same post. The new director, Bob Janes, will not be taking over until September 1st. That means it will have been almost a year that I've done nothing but administration. I'm so worn out at the end of each day that I've done only two major writing assignments since October. And I've done practically no research.[162]

When Bob took over, I thought I would return to my previous ways but I was wrong. Bob turned out to a real bureaucrat. Meetings quadrupled, accountability became paramount, and management meetings changed from being relaxed to ones that were tightly controlled. This ran counter to my philosophy of team management, open discussions, and open doors. I also believed "if it ain't broke, don't fix it." The Library, for example, operated so efficiently and smoothly that I just left it alone. No more. Now I was expected to hold regular meetings with them, scrutinize their performance, and look for ways of improving their operations. As it turned out, even after all the extra work nothing really changed in an already efficient operation.

But I must balance these comments with the fact that Bob was under a great deal of pressure about our financial problems right from the time he entered the organization. The budget was, and had to be, the big feature in his life. And he had the misfortune to enter Glenbow just at the time when it was in danger of going down the slippery slope. I am sure there must have been many times when he wished he was back in Yellowknife.

Over the years, our funding from the Alberta government had been taking a beating, and in spite of all restraint measures, we were looking at major layoffs of staff. Board members had been discussing the problem in Edmonton but this didn't seem to produce any results.

I must say here and now that in my opinion, Glenbow's greatest enemies were some of the senior bureaucrats in the Alberta government. Time after time, agreements appeared to be ignored during periods of financial restraints, promises were broken, and benefits never seemed to come our way when times were good. When Eric Harvie made his deal in 1966, it resulted in the Glenbow-Alberta Institute being formed, and our first museum was called the Glenbow Foundation–Alberta Government Museum, all indicating our special relationship to the government. Yet I was told that there was just one culture budget from which funds came for government institutions while all the non-government arts institutions were lumped together. In bad times, the government agencies got their money but the others, including us, were cut back. There was no recognition of the fact that we were not like all the other arts groups. Time after time, the government's own Provincial Museum, the Remington Museum, and Tyrrell Museum at Drumheller got money for capital expenses and adequate funds to operate. One didn't hear about big layoffs and financial crises at these places. Glenbow seemed to be the victim of bureaucratic manoeuvring. I don't know what the various ministers were told, but they seemed to go along with the bloodletting at Glenbow, and Eric Harvie's gift to the people of Alberta in 1966 became their poor relative in the Alberta museum world.

When Bob Janes came on the scene, government support was continuing its decline. We held numerous meetings to try to come up with some solutions but the bottom line was always not enough money. Government grants covered only 65 per cent of the budget, with the balance coming from donations and admissions. Bob thought that a Strategic Plan might cause the government to get a better idea of what we hoped to accomplish. But it all came to naught and by spring of 1990 we were looking at a layoff of twenty people, or 15 per cent of our staff. As I told Jack Ewers, "As a result, the stress level is unbelievably high and the sickness rate and absenteeism is unbelievable. I had two department heads crying in my office last week and have had to deal with three departmental confrontations. If it keeps up, I think I'll seriously look at early retirement and devote myself to writing."[163]

Looking at all these factors, I finally concluded that I could not live with Glenbow's malaise and decided to resign.

But just as I was contemplating my move, I was handed two assignments that caused me to delay my decision. First, a $150,000 grant had been given to Glenbow for it to prepare a book featuring its treasures. The second was the task of preparing an exhibition based upon Eric Harvie's favourite acquisitions. These were in recognition of Glenbow's silver anniversary in 1991. I was seconded from my regular duties in September 1990 in order to carry out these two pleasurable tasks. This also gave me the chance to finish a couple of projects that had been held in abeyance. One was a book of essays by Everett Soop and the other was the publication of the reminiscences of William M. Graham, onetime Indian Commissioner. I was proud of the fact that my son James was writing the introduction to this latter book.

An incident occurred about this time that ultimately had a great impact on Glenbow and its relations with the Blackfoot. In June 1990 I got a call from Phil Stepney, the Director of the Provincial Museum, asking me if I could attend a meeting with some Bloods. When I got to the reserve, I learned that the Bloods wanted me to be a witness and an honest broker in any dealings between them and the government. The meeting was held in Dan Weasel Moccasin's rumpus room, in the shadow of the Belly Buttes. As usual, it started with long prayers and the passing of the pipe, after which the Bloods explained their problem. Dan wanted his son, Daniel, to become a medicine pipe holder but there was nothing available on the reserve. He wanted the government to loan one of its pipes for four months of each year, starting in the spring just before the first thunderstorm.

Stepney turned the request down flat and later I heard he told his staff that he had had a confrontation with the Bloods. It wasn't like that at all. The Bloods believed that because he had smoked with them, he would accede to their wishes.

After everything broke up, a number of us were visiting when I remembered that Glenbow had a Blood medicine pipe bundle in its collection. I was always opposed to us getting active bundles, but in this case the pipe had been transferred without proper ceremony and the owner could not use it. I took it from the man, Steve Oka, on the condition that if he changed his mind within a year he could get it back but he never did.

Our Board was just as hard-headed as the Provincial Museum when it came to giving back bundles, but I had managed to get a loans policy approved that could, in a stretch, be applied to medicine bundles. So I told Dan about the bundle and said if he made a formal application I would try to get permission from the Board for him to borrow the Oka bundle. You never saw a happier bunch at the prospect. The application was made, and when I took it to the Board, I made it sound so routine that they just rubber-stamped it. A few days later, Dan took the bundle to the Blood Reserve and two days later I commented in my diary, "Medicine pipe ceremony at Dan Weasel Moccasins. Pauline & I went. There were about 20 men & women participating, including Pauline & me, and another 15 looking on."[164] A formal transfer was conducted after the first thunderstorm, when four pipe holders acted as surrogate owners and transferred the pipe to Daniel. The family erected a large open-sided tepee and more than 2,500 happy people turned out to witness the historic event.

My expectation (or perhaps my hope) was that once the pipe was loaned, we'd probably never see it again. But I was wrong. The Weasel Moccasin family faithfully returned it each year to be re-issued to them, and when Daniel died and the pipe passed to someone on the Peigan Reserve, he too honoured its terms. That became the thin edge of the wedge. As time went along, and after I had retired, this incident could be used as a model for making other loans in the future. I was very happy about it.

I also agreed at that meeting to loan a Natoas Sun Dance bundle to the Old Shoes family, but there was a death in the family and they never followed through with it.

Jack Ewers strongly disapproved of my decision. In a hard-hitting three-page letter he asked, "Is not the idea of loaning items from museum collections for Indian temporary use a denial of the museum's responsibility for preservation of items in its collections?" He added, "I think I am sensitive to Indian concerns, but I am also a dyed in the wool museum man."[165]

This opened up a whole dialogue between us on Indians, religion, and revisionist history. Jack commented, "I cannot understand the current Indian attitude (I hope it does not extend to all or a majority of them) that only Indians can know the real history."[166]

He told me that he had been approached for advice by the National Parks Service where their display people were removing all the stems from the pipes and laying them side by side. This was because a young Indian had protested, saying that the only time that the stem and bowl should be together was during a ceremony. Jack and I talked about this and figured out what had happened. The young Indian had gone to a ceremony, probably for the first time, and saw a holy man take his pipe and bowl out of the pipe bag, fit them together, and begin the ritual. After it was over, he separated them and put them back in the bag. "Ah!" thought the young Indian, "the pipe and stem are only together during a ceremony." He didn't ask, or he would have been told that to keep them together in the pipe bag would probably have resulted in the bowl being broken. Besides, together they would be too long to fit into the bag. So with this "discovery" the young man went to the National Parks people and they, without checking with anyone, acceded to his wishes. Jack was disgusted.

I followed with a story of my own. A group of Native students on a computer upgrading course were on a tour of our exhibition floors with one of our Ethnology people. During the tour, a student remarked that no Midewiwin material should ever be placed on public display. Immediately, this staff member recommended that we pull everything. I pointed out to her that we had

had actual Midewiwin practitioners in looking at the exhibition and not only did they give it their blessing but they offered us information about some of the artifacts. When I asked the ethnologist about the qualifications of the student who made his statement, she couldn't tell me. The fact that he said he was an Ojibwa was enough. The exhibition stayed where it was.

When this situation occurred, I told Jack, "I think this current attitude in many museums is simply a form of racial discrimination; the staff is not prepared to give equal treatment to Indians but somehow must exhibit their superiority and collective guilt complexes by overreacting to many situations."[167]

Over the years, my thinking about medicine bundles had undergone considerable change. Of course, I never wanted Glenbow to have them in the first place, but once we had them, I thought it was our duty as a museum to keep and protect them. But by the 1980s, a revival was taking place at a time when there was still knowledge of the proper use of bundles. The more aggressive young people started to demand these bundles back, and even the more conservative people were saying that bundles were still important to the well-being of the tribes and that some accord should be reached with museums. I told myself that if they could be a source of identity and strength on the reserves, maybe they should be returned.

Jack Ewers disagreed but in the end we agreed to disagree.

Mind you, I am not talking about all religious items being given back holus-bolus. I believe that if a museum has objects from an active and ongoing religious body, and their possession of those objects restricts the practice of those rituals, they should give them back. As far as I am concerned, there are only a few religious groups where this situation applied. These are the Horn Society and Motokix Society on the Blood Reserve; the Blackfoot Sun Dance; the Cree Wetigo dance; and the Ojibwa Midewiwin. Also, I had no problem in refusing a loan when Indians said they wanted to "revive" a ceremony that had died out. I had no doubt that in the end any such ceremony would bear little resemblance to the original and be pan-Indian in nature.

As I told Jack, I didn't think it was a question of legal right, but of moral right. If a museum by holding religious objects was contributing to the demise of that ritual, then I didn't think it was proper.

Another problem for both of us was religious and historical revisionism. As I told Jack, "Some of the stuff that Indians are coming out with today regarding their history and culture is so fanciful that it's hard to comment on it. It is a classic case of Indians perceiving their history as they would like it to have been, rather than as it was."[168] I added, "I see our role as presenting an accurate portrayal of native life, based upon solid anthropological research. Now, however, the young people (Indians and white) are saying that the early records can't be trusted because they were written by white anthropologists and contain too many biases. They say that the only way one can get the real story is through consultation with native elders."[169]

I have heard it said by elders that the Blackfoot never scalped their enemies, that women were treated equally with men, that at Treaty Seven their chiefs surrendered only the top six inches of soil, that Indians still had the mineral rights, and that the Indians had lived in harmony with Nature. All, in my opinion, were wrong. On the last point, Stan Cuthand was right when he said that Indians were in a constant battle with Nature in order to survive.

But what really bothered me was the willingness of museum people and university staff in their effort to be politically correct, to take all this stuff seriously. Many Indians have an idealistic and unrealistic view of their history, but some of the curators seem prepared to incorporate their ideas into exhibits because this is what Indians today accept as correct. There seems to be an apparent willingness to "listen to the Indians" to the extent that I felt it compromised their (and Glenbow's) integrity. Personally, I think their history is impressive and remarkable enough without having to resort to revisionism.

⸎

Getting back to my secondment, I spent the better part of a year on the book, called *Treasures of Glenbow*, and on the Harvie exhibition, *The Eclectic Collector*. Both were a lot of fun, as I had a completely free hand.

In preparing the book, I wrote all the chapters, selected most of the images, and did all the design work. I also had a chance to include a chapter on the history of Glenbow, which never had been done before. Ron Marsh, our photographer, did a masterful job and when it was completed we had a beautiful book. Also, it was finished a month early and $10,000 under budget. And to put a little icing on the cake, it won the 1991 Alberta Book Sellers' Award for the best book published in Alberta.

The exhibition enabled me to draw on my memory for the things that Eric Harvie had liked. There was a pair of porcelain swans that graced his desk, several paintings that I knew were his favourites, some carved military figures, and a bunch of other impressive objects. Again, the final results were spectacular, thanks to some good work by our exhibition staff.

While I was working on these projects, I decided that I wanted my tenure at Glenbow to reach thirty-five years, so I asked to retire on February 1, 1991.

This was approved and I was sent off in grand style. The staff made a "throne" for me in the auditorium and I was given all sorts of weird and wonderful gifts. After it was over, I went back to the book project and the exhibition, but now I was on contract so, in theory, I was as free as a bird.

Before sailing off into the sunset, I must bring the sad financial story of Glenbow up to the time of this writing – at least in my prejudiced view.

When facing a serious shortfall for 1993, Bob's strategy at first was to sell the government on a multi-year funding commitment – which was a good idea – but this was rejected out of hand. This was not surprising, considering the way the government had been band-aiding our operations for years. The next strategy, in my opinion, was ill-advised. Instead of trimming just enough to barely meet the year's shortfall and fighting for a better deal, the plan was to cut deep and come up with a type of budget that could be maintained for the next few years. As a result, Glenbow trimmed a massive $1.1 million, or 20 per cent of its budget, and laid off about a third of its staff. This consisted of thirty-one employees with another eleven reduced to part-time status. In my view, this played right into government hands. Glenbow simply proved it could survive such a cut, and was ripe for further cuts in the future.

Also, the various departments were transformed into five "work units" and a business plan formulated. One of the ideas was to sell off parts of its collection. This, to me, was desperation in the extreme. But there was worse to come. Instead of launching an all-out battle for a better deal through the MLAs, the press, and anyone else who would listen, the decision was to roll over and play dead. I honestly couldn't believe it in 1997 when I learned that the Board of Governors had turned its entire collections over to the Alberta government and became an independent non-profit institution! In return, the government was supposed to provide enough funds for the care and mainte-nance of the collection. This meant that the government no longer had any responsibility for Glenbow itself, as indicated by the original 1966 Glenbow Act, just the collections, which it now owned.

These collections had been Glenbow's only bargaining chip. As long as it had them it could threaten to sell off popular parts of the collection, show the public its sad state of affairs because of a lack of government funds, and even hold the collections for ransom as Duncan had tried to do with the Library and Archives. Glenbow should have fought the government, publicly if necessary, tooth and nail, before surrendering its collections.

According to press reports in that year, "the museum receives only $2.5 million of its $9-million budget from the province."[170] This was only 22.5 per cent of its total budget. Meanwhile other museums were receiving from 50 to 90 per cent their funding from their governments.[171] The rest of Glenbow's money had to be obtained through fund raising, interest from its endowment, opening a cafeteria, and expanding a craft shop. The results were predictable. By 2000 the situation had become so desperate that the Library staff was chopped from five to one person.

To add to the misery, a decision was made to sell the Edward S. Curtis volumes and portfolios on the North American Indians. These went for a cool $1 million for Glenbow's acquisition fund. When a museum starts selling off parts of its collection to raise money, it is abdicating its responsibility both to the public and future. Then in 2001 half the Military staff was laid off, and fifteen more general staff were cut in 2002. As a Glenbow employee wrote in 2002, "The Museum is at the point now where further cuts to staff will seriously endanger the care of the collections and limit attempts to increase public interest in the museum as exhibit preparation and community outreach are compromised. The heritage collections and staff knowledge base at Glenbow are a provincial resource. We think it is time the provincial government recognized it."[172]

By this time, Bob Janes had resigned and was replaced by Michael Robinson. It is a real tribute to his remaining staff that they were able to continue with its programs, albeit in abbreviated form. At the Board and senior level, the focus now had to be on fundraising, to the detriment of social and business activities. Exhibitions continued to be fielded, many home grown, while a major international show was *Mysteries of Egypt* in 2001. Donations also enabled the museum to refurbish its Native galleries with the show *Nitsitapiisinni, The Story of a Blackfoot People*, while major productions were *Mavericks* costing some $8.5 million and exhibition of the art of Charles M. Russell and Frederic Remington.

But with its limited staff and financial woes, Glenbow was in no position to provide full service to the public and to its collection. By 2009 it faced a deficit of $1.6 million and revenue was down 14.5 per cent. Much of this shortfall came from donations which virtually dried up during the recession and from a decline in value of its endowment. The ripple effect was devastating. Late in 2009 eleven positions disappeared from Glenbow, the most disastrous being the reduction of three Archives positions, leaving a skeleton staff of two.

The stringencies will remain and the staff numbers will continue to decline unless the Alberta government steps up and shoulders the responsibilities which are theirs. The intent of the agreement made by Eric Harvie in 1966 is clear, and to renege on this and cast one of Canada's major museums to the wolves is unspeakable. I loved Glenbow when I worked for it; I love Glenbow today, but I am saddened by what it has become due – as I have said – entirely to the actions of the Alberta government and some of its mandarins.

That's my editorial for today.

# 13

## *Retirement?*

When I retired, I was hardly aware of it. I had been working on *The Treasures of Glenbow* for months and from there I slipped effortlessly into my own research and writing. One of my first projects was to gather together a bunch of Native stories I had obtained through interviews and research. None was long enough for a book in itself but I thought they might make a nice collection of Blackfoot tales. I finished the manuscript before the end of the year, but it was 1994 before it was published by Prairie Books and University of Oklahoma Press under the title *The Amazing Death of Calf Shirt and Other Blackfoot Stories*. The only problem was that in the interim I had written another book, *Calgary: Spirit of the West*, that was published by Fifth House in the same year. That placed me in the odd position of having to go on promotional tours for two books at the same time.

I guess inside every non-fiction writer is a novel crying to be written. In 1992 I decided to try my hand. And to make a holiday of it, I moved into a little tree-shrouded cabin just off the main square in Sonoma, California. In the six weeks it took me to write the novel (an Indian detective story) my wife stayed with her sister about a mile away. It was a productive time but to this point the manuscript has never seen the light of day. Actually, I never really tried to market it after a couple of rejections.

Then it was back to Calgary and reality as I started research on a number of writing projects. I was also contracted by Ted Byfield to be a consultant and writer in the first of a series of thirteen volumes he was preparing on the history of the province entitled *Alberta in the Twentieth Century*. This carried on for two or three years. Meanwhile I was churning out articles for publications such as *The Beaver*, *Natural History* (New York), *Alberta History*, *Montana Magazine*,

*Russell's West* (Great Falls), and others. I also wrote introductions to a number of other books, and even had a short article on the Blackfoot published in Russia. In fact, I was doing all those things I never had time for during the last few years at Glenbow.

In 1991 I was appointed to the Stephen Avenue Area Development Society, a City-run program to improve the appearance of downtown Calgary. In an earlier study in which I was involved, we said that 1914 had been the time when Calgary's city centre had the most attractive appearance, and recommended that 8th Avenue (now reverted to its original name of Stephen Avenue) be the main area for attention. We suggested grants be given to property owners to renovate their facades, going back to the original designs which often were hidden behind chrome and plastic store fronts. In particular, we wanted to restore the old sandstone buildings that gave a definite atmosphere to the street. All of this was approved.

Over a period of ten years our group was given about $1.5 million from the City and from the Alberta Historical Resources Foundation which we gave out in grants. Almost every building along Stephen Avenue from 1st Street East to 1st Street West was affected. Grants of $150,000 and $175,000 were quite common, and we had experts on our committee that could oversee the work. My input was historical but I also had a lot of opinions to offer, good or bad. I think it was a very successful committee. Janice Dickin from the University of Calgary as president, and City employee Rob Graham as secretary did masterful jobs in guiding the projects through to completion.

Our oldest restored building was the T.C. Power Block, built in 1885 by an American firm of ex-whisky traders. The most impressive restoration, in my opinion, was the beautiful sandstone Bank of Montreal on the northeast corner of Stephen Avenue and 1st Street West. Probably the most interesting was a sandstone building at 123 - 8th Avenue West, which we dubbed the "red, white and blue" building – and for good reason. It seems that some time ago, the owner who lived in Germany became angry with the City over some tax matter and got his revenge by painting the whole sandstone front red, white, and blue. It was ghastly. To add to the problem, the owner's lawyer was in Edmonton and he seemed even more antagonistic than his boss. The result was that the letters and phone calls went nowhere, or worse, seemed to feed the fires of discontent. Finally, after getting the owner to visit Calgary, the offer of $150,000 to remove the garish paint was accepted. A good thing, too, for we were just in the process of winding down the whole program. It would have been a shame to leave the monstrosity untouched.

But in the end it turned out to be a very worthwhile program. We totally revamped the face of the area and the streetscape was declared a National Historic Site. Now, all that was needed was to bring the people back to the centre of town. When the program ended, this still wasn't happening and most of the time, except during the lunch hour, the street looked like a deserted wasteland.

A big change in my retirement career occurred in 1994 when I became involved in Indian legal matters and ultimately was considered to be an expert witness. The first call came from lawyers representing the White Bear Reserve in Saskatchewan. Two years earlier, they had studied gambling casinos that were springing up on reservations all over the United States and decided to build one of their own, the first in Canada. This step was taken in spite of the fact that the Saskatchewan government was opposed to casinos on reserves. White Bear believed that the Province had no jurisdiction on their reserve. However, twenty-one days after the casino was opened it was closed by the RCMP, citing provincial regulations, and the band was charged with unlawfully conducting a casino operation.

As part of its defence, White Bear asked me to provide evidence of the historic hunting area of the band, tribal society, intertribal relations, how its economy functioned, and the existence of gambling by Crees with non-Cree people prior to treaty. As a result, I prepared a twenty-six-page document, "Gambling, Political Organization & Trade among Canadian Plains Indians, with Special Reference on the Cree, Assiniboine & Ojibwa." After this, I went to Carlisle, Saskatchewan, where I gave my testimony as an expert witness. Except for a murder trial some years earlier, this was my first time to testify and it all went very well. The Crown tried to use some of my books against me but there was nothing serious.

Well, we lost the case but it turned out to be a win in the long run. As a result of the publicity the Saskatchewan government was forced to negotiate with the Federation of Saskatchewan Indians, and ultimately a deal was made for casinos to be operated on a number of reserves. One of these was the Bear Claw Casino, which reopened on the White Bear Reserve.

My next foray into legal matters occurred in 1995 when the Blood tribe asked me to do some research on their "Big Claim." In 1882, a total of 3,542 Bloods were given their annual treaty money. A year later, when the reserve was being surveyed, the number receiving money was reduced to 2,589 – almost a thousand people. The reserve was then surveyed on the basis of five people per square mile using the 1883 figures. The Bloods claimed that they had been victimized and laid a claim against the federal government – a "big claim" – for the missing land. If approved, the reserve would extend far south beyond the present town of Cardston.

Initially I was given a two-month contract to find out how and why the reduction of population occurred, to determine the actual population at treaty time in 1877, and to examine the mortality rate between then and 1883. I did nothing else during that time but go through old annuity and census records. I found a lot of inconsistencies, church records that did not match government records, and doubt as to whether the big cut was made to reduce the size of the reserve, or because of the economic depression taking place at that time, or for other reasons.

I completed my two-month stint on phase one, providing population figures and other data that they requested. It then became part of a larger report that was submitted to the Specific Claims Branch of Indian Affairs. I didn't hear much more about it until 1997, when I was again asked to do research. This time my part of phase two was much broader, including locating and researching the records of early surveyors, missionaries, policemen, Indian agents, and any newspapers that might be useful for the Big Claim. I was also told to examine particular events, such as Red Crow's selection of the reserve in 1880, traditional voting procedures, and a host of other requirements.

I did a major report on decision-making methods and in the fall I reported on my travels and extensive research. I did not say this specifically in the report, for it had no legal grounds, but I was of the opinion that some political skulduggery had resulted in the loss of the southern section of the reserve. A Conservative named John Parks, head of the North-West Land & Grazing Co., had taken out a grazing lease on the piece of land south of the reserve before the 1883 treaty. His son-in-law was William Pugsley, onetime federal Minister of Public Works and from what I read, a not-too-honest individual. Pugsley was the driving force behind the North-West Land & Grazing Company, and when he learned that the 1882 survey of the Blood Reserve included his lease, he travelled to Regina, the Territorial capital. Coincidentally he arrived in the city three days before the Lieutenant-Governor, Edgar Dewdney, left the city for a trip to the Blood Reserve. This trip resulted in a land survey, a new treaty, and the southern boundary being moved to its present location.

As interesting and compelling as this information was, I never found a smoking gun to prove that Pugsley had influenced fellow Conservative Dewdney to take the action that would save his lease. I realized that the lawyers really couldn't do anything with this information but I still have my suspicions that something unsavoury was going on.

I also found that Blood oral tradition was right regarding Standoff bottom lands. They always said this prime piece of land was supposed to be part of the reserve, but the surveys and 1883 treaty said otherwise. In the William Pearce papers at the University of Alberta Archives there is an indication that Lief Crozier, superintendent of the NWMP at Fort Macleod, bought a log building on Standoff bottom in 1882 and then leased the building to the police for a detachment. It was bringing him money and he probably didn't want to give it up. Pearce wrote, "It is stated that through the persons interested in this claim and their influence with the Blood Indians, this Reserve is considerably changed from that which the Indians asked for and where it would have been in the public interest to locate it."[173]

Over the next few years I did a few more projects, such as evaluating the worth of Fort Whoop-Up. For the loss of that bit of land they got over $1 million, but I think the Big Claim was rejected in 1999. An appeal was equally unsuccessful.

My next legal project was a claim regarding water rights. In 1995 I explained to John Ewers, "I've just agreed to undertake a study for the North Peigans in relationship to a land claim case. They are claiming that part of the water that runs through the reserve is theirs for irrigation purposes. The government says no. I think they have a strong case relating to water use in the valley of the Oldman River, to their selection of the location at Treaty Seven, and the fact that at the reserve, the river is not considered to be a navigable stream. Anyway, the research and reporting is supposed to be done by February, and court testimony following about a year later."[174]

In the time available to me, I wrote a general history of the Peigans prior to treaty and then concentrated on their relations with the government, farming practices, and use of water. I proved that the way the reserve had been surveyed on the basis of five people per square mile, the entire river had to be included in the land allocation. That meant that if everybody took their exact share, some of them would have been living at the bottom of the river!

During the time of my research, the irrigation matter became a hot political issue and the matter was resolved by negotiation so I never had to testify. When I finished, I suggested the report could be revised and published as a history, but I never got a response.

At that time I commented to Colin Taylor, "The interesting thing is that I can earn more in consulting fees in a month with this kind of work than I can from the royalties of one or two books – each of which takes me several months to research and write. Something's wrong here."[175]

My next consulting tasks were started in 2001 for the Ermineskin and Samson bands at Hobbema. Ever since my book on Big Bear I had been approached by a number of individuals and groups seeking information about the Crees and I realized that I knew a lot more about them than just the Big Bear biography. Actually, I had been interested ever since 1952 when John Rabbit and his wife at the Louis Bull Reserve had shared some of their knowledge with me.

The first to contact me was the Samson band, through its lawyer, Priscilla Kennedy, and a short time later the Ermineskin band, through its lawyer, Barbara Fisher (now a B.C. judge), also contacted me. Here is the problem as I understood it. When the treaty was signed, Bobtail was given a reserve just south of Ermineskin and Samson. In 1885, Bobtail was angry about the treatment of his family and people during the Riel Rebellion, so he and his followers abandoned the reserve and took half-breed scrip. In 1896, the Montana authorities rounded up scores of Crees who had fled to the United States after the rebellion and forced them back into Canada. The Canadian government decided that the almost vacant Bobtail Reserve would make a good home for these refugees, so they settled there and its name was changed to the Montana Reserve.

That's the view of the bands. The government, on the other hand, said the Bobtail Reserve had been surrendered in 1909 and thus ceased to exist. It also said the reserve had been completely vacant when the Crees arrived from Montana.

In the 1940s, when oil was discovered on the three reserves and at their fishing station at Pigeon Lake, Montana was given its share of royalties. However, Samson and Ermineskin claimed that the Bobtail Reserve had never been properly surrendered and claimed that their royalties should have gone to Bobtail's descendants, now living on the Ermineskin and Samson Reserves.

My projects for Samson and Ermineskin were quite different. For Samson, they wanted a biography of Big Bear, not unlike my book, but more fully documented and in greater detail in certain areas. The Ermineskins, on the other hand, were looking for evidence regarding Bobtail, Ermineskin, and Samson prior to the so-called surrender in 1909. My specific tasks were to determine the relationship between Bobtail and Ermineskin, relationships between members of the three bands, Cree customs relating to band membership, and the collective use of lands.

I was always under the impression that the bands at the Hobbema Agency – Bobtail, Ermineskin, Samson, and later Louis Bull – were all one people divided into separate bands through the happenstance of the treaty-signing process. Now it was my task to try and prove it.

But I was almost stopped in my tracks when the lawyers sent me documents they had already gathered in the case. They filled about a third of my garage, box after box piled three high. I could never get that much into the house, so I had to drag in one box at a time, use the finding aids they provided to see if there was any wheat among all that chaff. There wasn't much, but what they did have was very useful, particularly the half-breed scrip records that provided data on the Bobtails who had left the reserve in 1885.

Pretty soon I was on the road to Ottawa, Edmonton, and other places, as well as to Glenbow and into my own files. I found plenty to support the belief that Bobtail and Ermineskin were brothers and were sons of Louis Piché, a Metis who could be found in fur trade records back to 1811 and missionary journals in the 1840s. After Piché was murdered in the 1840s, missionary influence became so strong that both the Methodists and Catholics promoted their own adherents as the new leader. For the Catholics it was Bobtail and for the Methodists Maskepetoon. The separation became much more apparent when they settled on reserves, with most of the Methodists being with Samson and the Catholics with Ermineskin and Bobtail.

My report, "A History of Bobtail and the Bear Hills Crees to 1885," was completed early in 2002, and this time I did have to appear as an expert witness. After it was over, here is what I wrote to Colin Taylor: "I drove to Edmonton to be prepped by my lawyers. That took a day and a half. Then I was in the witness box for another 2½ days. I was warned that the cross examination would be tough, but I actually enjoyed it. They caught me up on a couple of things but hey! nobody's perfect."[176]

In the following year I testified for the Samson band, and while I didn't get a rough ride, my testimony did. First, I was not allowed to testify about the unity of the three bands as that had not been included in my range of expertise when presented to the court. Then there was a fight about admissibility of some of my evidence but our lawyers got it in. After 2½ days I was turned over for cross-examination for another 2½ days of answering questions. As I commented in my diary, "There were a few rough moments but all in all I enjoyed the whole procedure. It was fun."[177]

Over the next several years, a few honours drifted my way. I was given the Eric L. Harvie Award by the Glenbow Museum, the Contributor of the Century Award by the Historical Society, lifetime membership by the Alberta Society of Archivists, and the Lieutenant-Governor's Award by the Alberta Museums Association.

In between all the lawyer work I was still editing the quarterly *Alberta History*, and writing books. For a few years there was a virtual deluge of books after the Calf Shirt and Calgary volumes in 1994. Following them were *The Golden Age of the Canadian Cowboy* in 1995; *Tom Three Persons: Legend of an Indian Cowboy*, and *Tribal Honors: A History of the Kainai Chieftainship*, both in 1997; Indians *of the Rocky Mountain Parks* in 1998; *Firewater: Impact of the Whisky Trade on the Blackfoot Nation* in 2002; and *The Vengeful Wife and Other Blackfoot Stories* in 2003. Also, in 1999, Colin Taylor and I collaborated to produce *With Eagle Tail: Arnold Lupson and 30 Years Among the Sarcee, Blackfoot and Stoney Indians on the North American Plains*, published in London, and co-edited the two-volume *The People of the Buffalo: Essays in Honor of John C. Ewers*, published in Germany in 2003–4.

In 2007 I decided to do a book on Maskepetoon, based partly on what I had learned during my legal research. I received a grant to cover my travelling expenses and went to Hobbema, Winnipeg, Victoria, Edmonton, and Seattle to gather material. A lot of new information came to hand and, considering that the chief had been killed by the Blackfoot way back in 1869, there was quite a bit on him. Early on, I was told that Maskepetoon had no descendants, and some even questioned if his band had settled at Hobbema. Yet I soon found that he actually had plenty of descendants and that Samson, head of the Samson band, was his younger brother. It's funny, but years ago I asked Johnny Samson if he knew anything about Maskepetoon and he said he'd never heard of him. Yet he was Maskepetoon's grand-nephew. I think my mistake was in the pronunciation of Maskepetoon. At first I pronounced it the way it looked: "mass-key-petoon," but learned I should have said "mass-kep-a-ton." So Johnny probably never understood what I was asking.

The general belief was that Maskepetoon had gone to Washington, D.C., in 1832 and had met Andrew Jackson, the president of the United States. I even included this in a biography I wrote on Maskepetoon for the *Dictionary of Canadian Biography*. Then, much to my surprise, I learned that there had been another chief named Maskepetoon. He was leader of the Turtle Mountain Crees in northern North Dakota, and it was he, not our Canadian friend, who made the journey. When I told this to some of the people at Hobbema, they refused to believe me. I don't blame them, as this story had always been a source of pride to them.

Yet there was much to be proud of in the career of Maskepetoon. His travels, his wisdom, and his leadership made him an outstanding figure in western history. My book, *Maskepetoon: Leader, Warrior, Peacemaker*, was published in 2010.

---

In retirement, there are many memories that remain with me. Here are some of them.

In 1986, while Lois was still in hospital recovering from her kidney transplant, Wilton Good Striker suggested that we get painted on her behalf. Wilton was a co-leader of the Horn Society. So Pauline, Leah, and I went to the Blood Sun Dance on the appointed day to receive their blessings. In all my years with the Bloods I had never had the courage to enter the sacred Horn Society lodge. Like others, I looked upon the society with reverence and respect.

The Horn Society lodge was in the centre of the camp and consisted of two tepee canvases joined together to provide a large enclosure. When I stepped inside I was filled with awe and wonderment. The lodge was fairly dark, with smoke and incense hanging heavily in the air. Inside we walked along a passageway created by folded tepee covers, poles, and crooks on one side, most of them holding headdresses and other parts of society regalia. On the other side was the wall of the tepee, with medicine bundles lining the route. It was like walking into the past and the atmosphere was so sacred to me that I almost faltered. In the centre of the double tepee was a fire burning in a circular rock fireplace, while next to it was an alter for burning sweetgrass. As we were led along the path we could hear the low buzzing murmurs of prayers being recited by the holy men and women. We passed places where others were being painted until we came to Wallace Mountain Horse, where I was told to kneel.

I said to Wallace that the prayers were for our daughter, and I told him her Blackfoot name, *Natoy'simyaki*, Holy Headdress Woman. He then proceeded to mix red ochre and fat in his palms and using his fingers as a paint brush, he painted my face, two horizontal lines at my eyes and mouth, and then painted both my wrists, all the time praying in Blackfoot for Lois and our family. The prayers I accepted by crossing my arms in front of my chest. When I moved aside, Pauline and Leah went through the same ceremony. Once done, I left four gifts for Wallace, as was the custom; we then continued to follow the circular path until we reached the entrance. Never, never have I felt such solemn emotion. It was unforgettable.

Another impression, or several impressions, that stayed with me were meetings with elders as they told their stories. Bobtail Chief, Sinew Feet, Shot Both Sides, John Cotton, Jack Low Horn, and a host of others were readily willing to share their stories to me. Speaking in Blackfoot with my father-in-law interpreting, they told of buffalo hunts, wars, the supernatural, the achievements of great chiefs. Commonly the elder sat on his bed, a tin can nearby for a spittoon, and a cane not too far away. His hair in thin braids, his face lined with years of exposure to the prairies, his clothes plain and unadorned, and often with moccasins on his feet, he was a reflection of the past, a reminder of a better life when the buffalo coursed the plains. As he spoke he became quite animated, waving his hands in meaningful gestures, or laughing at some long-ago event. As I sat nearby, dutifully taking notes, I was completely captivated by the scene.

On another occasion I was driving across the Big Lease one night when I stopped the car and turned off the lights. The prairie was in utter darkness. I stepped outside, then lay on my back, and looked up into the cloudless night sky. There above me like a huge canopy were millions of stars, the great constellations, and the moon. I could understand at once why the Blackfoot considered this to be another world inhabited by Sky People. The Pleiades and Ursa Major reminded me of the stories of people who had gone to the sky to live and how the Morning Star sent his wife to earth to carry the ceremonies of the Sun Dance. Looking at the sky that night, I said, how can it not be?

Then there was the excitement of discovery while archivist at Glenbow. There was the unforgettable thrill of going into the basement of a soon-to-be-demolished house in east Calgary and finding a cardboard box containing files of correspondence of Richard Hardisty while he had been chief factor of Fort Edmonton during the 1860s through to the 1880s. Or going to another soon-to-be-demolished building and finding the glass plate negatives of a long-forgotten photographer piled on the rafters in the attic. Or seeing a collection of negatives from another pioneer photographer sitting under a man's bed, and buying them when the wife demanded that her husband get them out of the house. Or finding a William Aberhart campaign poster in the attic of a Fort Macleod building, or an 1883 CPR bill of sale for the Calgary townsite in a Winnipeg vault.

And I will always remember listening with pride while Pauline stood on the stage at the Smithsonian Institution in Washington and gave a solemn prayer in Blackfoot to the memory of John Ewers. Or seeing our children grow and blossom over the years. These were all memorable experiences.

I've always said that during my life I had the luck to be in the right place at the right time. I got into the newspaper business because of a friend I met on the street; I met my future wife and found my future career because I was sent to cover a meeting of the Indian Association of Alberta; I joined Glenbow because earlier I had met an anthropologist who became that institution's first Director; and I retired from Glenbow just before it entered its most dismal downslide. That plus a wonderful wife and family – who could ask for a better life?

# NOTES

1. Interview with Lily Dempsey, 8 July 1978.

2. Ibid.

3. Ibid.

4. Ibid.

5. My nickname came as the result of some imaginative and convoluted gyrations with the English language. Somehow, my friends made the quantum leaps from Hugh, to Hughie, to Hugh-kie, to Kewkie, to Cucumber – and then shortened it to Cuke.

6. Letter, McKinnon to Dempsey, 25 June 1948. In author's possession.

7. *Edmonton Bulletin*, 31 May 1950.

8. Ibid., 6 February 1950.

9. Ibid., 13 June 1950.

10. Postcard, Laurie to author, 14 June 1950. In author's possession.

11. Letter, Joseph William Hyde to author, 22 January 1951. In author's possession.

12. Letter, Jennie Wright to author, 16 January 1951.

13. Letter, Mrs. Alicia C. Humphries to author, 15 December 1950.

14. *Edmonton Bulletin*, 19 September 1950. In author's possession.

15. Postcard, Laurie to author, 14 June 1950. In author's possession.

16. *Edmonton Bulletin*, 16 September 1950.

17. *Edmonton Bulletin*, 20 January 1951.

18. Letter, C.M. Elliott to author, 14 February 1951. In author's possession.

19. Letter, Mildred Tennant to author, 23 January 1951.

20. Undated letter, Jim Sherbaniuk to author.

21. Letter, 19 September 1952. In author's possession.

22. "Alberta Government Acts to Fight Rabies Epidemic," *Within Our Borders*, 1 November 1952.

23. Letter, 21 September 1952. In author's possession.

24. Letter to Pauline, 9 March 1952.

25. "Percy Two Gun Paints from his Bed," *The Native Voice*, 5:7 (July 1951): 16.

26    Interview with Iron, 24 December 1951. In author's possession.

27    Letter, MacGregor to G. Rider Davis and others, 10 October 1952. Historical Society of Alberta Papers, M2059, file 10, Glenbow Archives, Calgary.

28    Idem., MacGregor to Edmonds, 4 June 1953.

29    Winter 1953: 65–72.

30    "Whiskey Forts of the Old West," vol. 34 (1952): 29–32, and "Red Crow, White Man's Friend," vol. 35 (1953): 65–73.

31    "Star Child," 7:2 (1953): 6–16.

32    "The Scarlet Trail," vol. 34 (1951): 13–21.

33    "Social Dances of the Blood Indians of Alberta, Canada," *Journal of American Folklore*, 69:271 (January–March 1956): 47–52.

34    Interview with Mrs. John Rabbit, 20 April 1952. In author's possession.

35    Letter to Pauline, 9 July 1951.

36    Minutes of general meeting, IAA, 12–13 June 1952, p.1. Gladstone Papers, Glenbow Archives.

37    *Calgary Herald*, 13 June 1952

38    Letter to James Gladstone, 25 June 1952, Gladstone Papers.

39    Interview with Jack Black Horse, 22 October 1953. In author's possession.

40    Letter from Jack Black Horse, 7 June. Year not indicated but likely 1955. In author's possession.

41    Letter from Percy Plain Woman, 26 October 1955. In author's possession.

42    Interview with Mrs. Jennie Duck Chief, 14 March 1957. In author's possession.

43    Interview with Bobtail Chief, 28 March 1959. In author's possession.

44    Interview with Charlie Pantherbone, 24 July 1954. In author's possession.

45    Letter, 27 August 1954. In author's possession.

46    Letter to Douglas Leechman, 4 January 1956.

47    Letter, 11 July 1955.

48    Memo, Dempsey to Herbert, 31 December 1956. Glenbow Archives Files.

49    Letter, Lamb to Herbert, 7 March 1957. Glenbow Archives Files.

50    Diary entry, 30 June 1960. All diary entries are from the author's files.

51    Talk, "Archives in Review," Staff Conference file, 1958. Glenbow Departmental Records.

52    *Calgary Herald*, 15 February 1988.

53    *Journal of the Washington Academy of Sciences* 46:6 (1956): 177–82.

54    Diary entry, 12 April 1960.

55    Diary entry, 23 August 1960.

56    Diary entry, 14 October 1960.

57    Letter, Nat Owl Child to author, 16 November 1961. In author's possession.

58    Ben Calf Robe, *Siksika': A Blackfoot Legacy* (Invermere, B.C.: Good Medicine Books, 1979), 46.

59    Ibid.

60    Letter, 9 July 1956.

61    University of Oklahoma Press, 1969.

62    *Alberta Historical Review*, 4:3 (Summer 1956): 31.

63    *Alberta Historical Review*, 7:2 (Spring 1959): 31.

64    Interview with Clarence McHugh by Hugh Dempsey, 5 March 1961. In author's possession.

65    Diary entry for 25 June 1961.

66    Diary entry for 24 June 1961.

67    Diary entry for 22 June 1963.

68    Letter, Ralph Steinhauer to Hugh Dempsey, 23 May 1965. Indian Association of Alberta Papers, Glenbow Archives, M7811.

69    Cited in a report in Pauline Dempsey Papers, Glenbow Archives, M6854.

70    Diary entry for 4 March 1963.

71    Letter, Grace Johnson to "President and Members of our Society," 4 November 1963. Copy in Pauline Dempsey Papers, Glenbow Archives, M6854.

72    Original petition in Pauline Dempsey Papers, Glenbow Archives, M6854.

73    Diary entry, 17 December 1965.

74    Diary entry for 10 January 1966.

75    Letter, Holowach to Harvie, 15 June 1964. Copy in "Glenbow Foundation" file, Dempsey Papers.

76    Memo to E.J. Slatter, 22 July 1964, Glenbow Archives.

77    Diary entry for 19 April 1966.

78    Letter, Wilder to McCloy, 19 September 1966. Copy in "Glenbow Foundation" file, Dempsey Papers.

79    Diary entry for 20 April 1967.

80    Diary entry for 8 December 1967.

81    Letter, Dempsey to Harvie, 25 February 1968. Copy in "Glenbow Foundation" file, Dempsey Papers.

82    Diary entry for 18 November 18, 1968.

83    Ibid.

84    "Memorandum re Glenbow–Alberta Institute," undated document by N.C. McDermid, transmitted to Hugh Dempsey by his son, David McDermid, on 28 January 2000. Copy in "Glenbow Foundation" file, Dempsey Papers.

85    Ibid.

86    Letter, Mackid to McDermid, 30 July 1969. Original transmitted to Hugh Dempsey by his son, David McDermid, on 28 January 2000. Copy in "Glenbow Foundation" file, Dempsey Papers.

87    Letter, Harvie to McDermid, 6 October 1969. Original transmitted to Hugh Dempsey by his son, David McDermid, on 28 January 2000. Copy in "Glenbow Foundation" file, Dempsey Papers.

88    Ibid.

89    Ibid.

90    "Memorandum re Glenbow-
      Alberta Institute," undated
      document by N.C. McDermid,
      transmitted to Hugh Dempsey by
      his son, David McDermid, on 28
      January 2000. Copy in "Glenbow
      Foundation" file, Dempsey
      Papers.

91    Letter, Dick Gordon to James
      Mahaffy, 27 November 1969.
      Copy transmitted to Hugh
      Dempsey by N.D. McDermid's
      son, David McDermid, on 28
      January 2000. Copy in "Glenbow
      Foundation" file, Dempsey
      Papers.

92    Diary entry for 7 November
      1969.

93    Diary entry for 25 November
      1969.

94    Notebook, "Trip to the Arctic,
      1968," In author's possession.

95    Interview with Albert Lightning
      at Hobbema, 23 August 1981. In
      author's possession.

96    George W. Pocaterra, "Among
      the Nomadic Stoneys," *Alberta
      Historical Review* 11:3 (Summer
      1963): 12–19.

97    *Sun Dance Echo*, October 1964.

98    *Calgary Albertan*, 25 March 1975.

99    Photocopy in author's possession.

100   "Notice," 1 January 1976.
      Photocopy in author's possession.

101   Diary entry, 31 January 1977.

102   Letter to the editor, Sheldon First
      Rider, *Kainai News*, January #2,
      1978.

103   John C. Hellson and Morgan
      Gadd, *Ethnobotany of the Blackfoot

      Indians*. Ottawa: Canadian
      Ethnology Service, 1974.

104   *Toronto Globe & Mail*, 28
      September 1981.

105   Ibid.

106   Diary entry for 26 October 1970.

107   Letter, Dempsey to Mrs. Harvie,
      7 March 1975. Copy in author's
      possession.

108   Memorandum, Dempsey to
      Hammond, 23 August 1971.
      Copy in author's possession.

109   Ibid.

110   Memo, Dempsey to Hammond,
      24 January 1973. Copy in author's
      possession.

111   Diary entry, 31 December 1973.

112   Diary entry for 18 December
      1975.

113   *Calgary Albertan*, 10 April 1972.

114   *Alberta Historical Review*, 17:4
      (Autumn 1969): 29.

115   Letter, Dempsey to MLAs, 17
      July 1969. Historical Society
      Files, Glenbow Archives.

116   *Calgary Herald*, 5 September 1969.

117   Cited in *Alberta Historical Review*,
      17:4 (Autumn 1969): 29.

118   *Calgary Herald*, 5 September 1969.

119   Diary entry for 27 June 1978.

120   Ibid.

121   Ibid.

122   Diary entry for 22 May 1979.

123   Diary entry for 10 July 1977.

124   Letter, James H. Gray to
      Chairman and members of the
      Advisory Committee on the
      Heritage Learning Project, 27

January 1978. Copy in Dempsey files, Glenbow Archives.

125 Letter, Hugh Dempsey to the Advisory Committee, 16 July 1978. Dempsey files, Glenbow Archives.

126 Diary entry for 18 January 1970.

127 "Interview, Duncan Cameron," *Glenbow*, Winter 1989, 12.

128 "Goals of the Glenbow," approved 6 March 1980. Minutes, Board of Governors, Glenbow Administration files.

129 *Kainai News*, November #2, 1987.

130 Diary entry, 16 May 1978.

131 Interview with John Sokwapance, 17 August 1982. In author's possession.

132 Letter, Alphonse Little Poplar to Hugh Dempsey, 18 April 1985. In author's possession.

133 Letter, Mrs. Mary L. Ward to Alphonse Little Poplar, n.d. In author's possession.

134 Interview with Joe Buller, 18 August 1982. In author's possession.

135 Diary entry, 27 July 1980.

136 Diary entry, 1 December 1980.

137 *Calgary Herald*, 23 July 1983.

138 *Red Deer Advocate*, 3 August 1983.

139 *Calgary Herald*, 2 August 1985.

140 Diary entry, 5 August 1985.

141 Diary entry, 9 August 1985.

142 Diary entry, 4 January 1981. Dempsey papers.

143 *Calgary Herald*, 21 October 1981.

144 Catalogue, *Metis: A Glenbow Museum Exhibition*, 1985, 3

145 Press release, "Austrian Ambassador Misled by Alberta Officials," 14 August 1944. http://www.nisto.com/cree/lubicon/1944/19940816.html.

146 *Calgary Herald*, 17 May 1986.

147 Ibid.

148 *Calgary Herald*, 15 September 1986.

149 Bruce Starlight in *Kainai News*, 4 March 1987.

150 Cited in Frances W. Kaye, *Hiding the Audience* (Edmonton: University of Alberta Press, 2003), 162.

151 *Calgary Herald*, 15 September15, 1986.

152 Letter to John C. Ewers, 6 September 1987. In author's possession.

153 *Red Deer Advocate*, 26 December 1986.

154 Duncan Cameron, "Message from the Director Emeritus," *Glenbow Museum Annual Report 1989*, 9.

155 Diary entry, 11 August 1988.

156 Diary entry, 22 September 1988.

157 Diary entry, 1 November 1988.

158 Diary entries, 8 and 13 December 1988.

159 Patrick Tivy, *Calgary Herald*, 30 January 1898.

160 Letter to John C. Ewers, 6 July 1989. In author's possession.

161 *Glenbow Magazine*, Summer 1989, 22.

162  Letter to John C. Ewers, 6 July 1989. Copy in author's possession.

163  Letter to John Ewers, 17 April 1990. Copy in author's possession.

164  Diary entry, 17 November 1990.

165  Letter from John C. Ewers, 19 September 1990. In author's possession.

166  Letter from John C. Ewers, 28 October 1989. In author's possession.

167  Letter to John C. Ewers, 5 January 1990. In author's possession.

168  Letter to John C. Ewers, 24 February 1991. In author's possession.

169  Letter to John Ewers, 15 October 1989. In author's possession.

170  *Calgary Herald*, 21 March 1997.

171  *Glenbow Museum Annual Report* for 2004–2005.

172  Letter to the Editor from the executive of CUPE Local 1645, employees of the Glenbow Museum, *History Now*, April 2002, 9.

173  Memo, William Pearce, November 13, 1885. William Pearce Papers, University of Alberta Archives, MG 74-169, file 9/2/4-1.

174  Letter to John Ewers, 16 October 1995. In author's possession.

175  Letter to Colin Taylor, 17 February 1996. In author's possession.

176  Letter to Colin Taylor, 6 December 2002. In author's possession.

177  Diary entry, 25 February 2003.

# INDEX

259, 283, 294, 303, 305, 309–11,
317, 347, 381
Dempsey, Otto, 1, 6–12, 14–15, 17–18,
20, 22, 24, 39, 45–46, 48, 58, 84,
98, 139, 293, 319
Dempsey, William Samuel, 2, 11, 31
Denney, Walter, 309
Depression, 2–5, 12, 15
Devine, Mike, 219
Devique, Father, 83
Dewdney, Edgar, 376
DeWolf, Rev. J.E., 88
Dickin, Janice, 374
Dickson, Sam, 82
Diefenbaker, John, 211, 303–4, 343
Dion, Joseph, 152, 296, 305
Dixon, Bud, 45
Doore, Clement, 295
Doucette, Dr., 201
Dover, Mary, 219
Down, Mrs. H.E., 213
Drinking. *See* Liquor
Duck Chief, Jenny, 98–99
Duck Chief, Rosary, 192
Duhaime, Father Antonio, 82, 88
Dusenberry, Verne, 208

**E**

Eagle Child, Phyllis, 223
Eagle Plume, Willie, 164, 263
Eagle Ribs, Suzette, 78, 98, 262–64
Earth Lodge Village site, 155
Economic relief payments, 3–4, 6
Edenshaw, Charlie, 62
Edgar, Charlie, 300
Edgerton, AB, 1–2, 9, 84
Ediger, Eleanor, 126, 138–39
Edmonds, Rev. W. Everard, 80–81,
208–9
Edmonton, AB, 3–119
*Edmonton Bulletin*, 19–20, 37
description, 38, 52, 54, 59, 142
Edmonton City Dairy, 11

Edmonton Exhibition, 7–8
Edmonton Fire Department, 63–64
Edmonton Indian Agency, 48, 58, 84
Edmonton Indian Agency records,
131–32
*Edmonton Journal*, 44, 60
Edworthy, George, 79
Eisenmenger, Pete, 346
Eklund, Ivor, 90
Elliott, Peter, 66, 89, 91
Eric L. Harvie Award, 380
Erickson, Bob, 361
Ermineskin land claim, 378
Etter, Art, 44
Evamy, Catherine, 362
Ewers, John C., 74, 94–95, 107, 123,
155, 189, 191, 207, 290, 317, 349,
362–63, 367–68, 382
Ewers, Marge, 75, 207, 317

**F**

Farmilo, Bill, 284
Favel, Lucy, 326
Fawn's Cafe, Edmonton, 39, 44–45, 52,
61
Fedori, Marianne, 348
Fedoruk, Ernie, 44
Ferris, Nels, 22–23
Fiddler, Fred, 197
Fidler, Peter, 155
Finn, Theo, 201
First Rider, George, 273–74
Fish, Jim, 140, 159–60, 247, 251, 254
Fisher, Barbara, 378
Flach, Don, 44
Fleming, Bill, 160, 248
Fleming, Iris, 158
Foran, Max, 348
Forbis, Dick, 128, 138–39, 155, 157, 248,
284–85
Formby, George, 58
Fort Calgary, site of, 285–87

Woodsworth, Harold, 131
Wormington, Marie, 126
Wounded Horse, John, 199
Wright, Jennie, 54
Wright, Russell, 315, 335
Wuttunee, Bill, 226

# Y

Yellow Bull, Mike, 308
Yellow Fly, Ken, 184, 193
Yellow Fly, Mrs. Teddy, 193
Yellowhorn, John, 98, 218, 319, 323
Yellow Old Woman, Gordon, 193
Yellow Sun, Tom, 185
Yellowknife, NWT, 54, 71–72
Yuzicapi, Doris, 198

# Z

Zubick, J.J., 154